W0017108

PUBLIC SECTOR REFORM IN HONG KONG

Public Sector Reform in Hong Kong

Into the 21st Century

EDITED BY
Anthony B. L. Cheung
AND
Jane C. Y. Lee

The Chinese University Press

Public Sector Reform in Hong Kong: Into the 21st Century
Edited by Anthony B. L. Cheung and Jane C. Y. Lee

© **The Chinese University of Hong Kong** 1995, 2001

All rights reserved. No part of this publication may
be reproduced or transmitted in any form or by any
means, electronic or mechanical, including photocopying,
recording, or any information storage and retrieval
system, without permission in writing from
The Chinese University of Hong Kong.

ISBN 962–996–011–7

First edition 1995
Second edition 2001

THE CHINESE UNIVERSITY PRESS
The Chinese University of Hong Kong
SHA TIN, N.T., HONG KONG
Fax: +852 2603 6692
     +852 2603 7355
E-mail: cup@cuhk.edu.hk
Web-site: www.chineseupress.com

Printed in Hong Kong

Contents

Foreword

Woon-kwong Lam

Secretary for Home Affairs and Former Secretary for the Civil Service

Hong Kong has been a big success by any standard of measurement. We have built up this great city through the diligence and resilience of our people; through the adaptability and entrepreneurship of our investors; through the rule of law; and through pragmatic public policies implemented by a clean and efficient civil service.

But past achievements are no guarantee to future success. Our public sector excels by being institutionalized and impartial. Cronyism has no place in this civil service. But the other side of this coin is that we are prone to be rigid and bureaucratic. The Administration is therefore conscious of the need for regular systemic reforms to keep the public sector alert and responsive. Various initiatives have been taken to reinvigorate the civil service over time. The latest effort is the Civil Service Reform, launched in March 1999, which aims to make the civil service more open, more accountable, more able to attract talents and remove poor performers, and more cost efficient.

We have entered the 21st century with an unprecedented sense of optimism. For the first time in centuries, we do seem to have secured relative peace on earth. Nations and corporations now agree that competition should be through trade and markets, not through exploitation backed by weapons. Information technology, globalization of trade and finance, and intense competition are changing the landscape of our economy in more fundamental ways than we could imagine.

At the same time, the fundamentals of governance have also been shifting irreversibly: from providing for subsistence to providing for quality; from subservience of the public to respect for the public's rights; and from "big brother in the government knows best" to public participation in policymaking.

The way that public services should be delivered will have to undergo major changes. But it is much easier said than done. Reform needs more than just leadership from the top. To succeed, it needs to communicate its vision, to master supporting coalitions, to initiate and anchor cultural changes, to plan for short to long term strategies, and to make adjustments along the way to suit real life circumstances.

This book is therefore timely. At the time when the Administration is undertaking one of the most fundamental management reforms to the civil service, we welcome serious and in-depth analysis on this important subject. We also welcome the wide range of perspectives presented by the authors. It will no doubt be a useful reference book to theorists and practitioners alike in the field of public administration.

April 2000
Hong Kong

List of Contributors

Brian Brewer is an Associate Professor in the Department of Public and Social Administration at the City University of Hong Kong.

Ho-mun Chan is an Associate Professor in the Department of Public and Social Administration at the City University of Hong Kong.

Anthony B. L. Cheung is a Professor and former Head of the Department of Public and Social Administration at the City University of Hong Kong. He is also Associate Director in charge of the "comparative public management" research programme at the University's Centre for Comparative Public Management and Social Policy.

Richard Common is a Senior Lecturer in the Department of Sociology and Applied Social Studies at London Guildhall University. He is a former Research Assistant Professor of the City University of Hong Kong.

Ki-on Hui is the former Commissioner of Police of the Hong Kong Special Administrative Region Government. He retired from the service in February 2001.

Jane C. Y. Lee is the Chief Executive of the Hong Kong Policy Research Institute, a non-governmental policy think-tank. She was also a former Senior Lecturer and is now an Honorary Research Fellow of the City University of Hong Kong.

Joan Y. H. Leung is an Associate Professor in the Department of Public and Social Administration at the City University of Hong Kong.

P. C. Luk is the Postmaster General of the Hong Kong Special Administrative Region Government, heading The Hongkong Post.

Tony Miller is the Director of Housing of the Hong Kong Special Administrative Region Government.

Colin Sankey is Head of the Efficiency Unit of the Hong Kong Special Administrative Region Government, charged with promoting and integrating various public sector reform initiatives.

Introduction

Anthony B. L. Cheung and Jane C. Y. Lee

When we edited the last volume of *Public Sector Reform in Hong Kong*, the notion of public sector reform in Hong Kong was still a rather novel one. The 1989 *Public Sector Reform* document, published by the Finance Branch (now Finance Bureau) to unleash the reform programme, had then surprisingly received only scant public attention, not to mention a full policy debate, whether inside or outside the government. This was quite in contrast to the heated political and ideological discussions which accompanied public sector reform in Organization for Economic Cooperation and Development (OECD) countries, together with an ever-expanding practitioner and academic literature on reform throughout the 1980s and 1990s. Unlike in overseas countries, there was not the same kind of urgency for change locally at that time, as Hong Kong by and large still enjoyed economic prosperity and fiscal stability, and the overall efficiency of its civil service had not been really questioned. Quite in the opposite, the civil service as a meritocratic institution was held in high esteem as part of the pre-1997 legacy.

By the beginning of the new decade and new century, however, public sector reform has become very much part of a wider reform agenda of the new Special Administrative Region (SAR) government. In March 1999, the Civil Service Bureau published a *Civil Service Reform* consultation document[1] which has subsequently created much controversy inside and outside the civil service. In his 1999 and 2000 Budget Speeches,[2] Financial Secretary Donald Tsang made EPP (enhanced productivity programme), contracting-out, privatization and reduction of the civil service establishment the more immediate targets of the government's reform efforts. Public sector reform is no longer a distant plan as in 1989, but is now very much into specific measures and initiatives.

The reaction to public sector reform so far from affected stakeholders has been rather mixed. For the first time in two decades, civil servants went to the streets in May and June 1999 to protest against some civil service reform proposals. Social workers held protest rallies in March 2000 in opposition to the introduction of "lump-sum" funding allocations to subvented welfare organizations, as part of the government's broader attempt to transform the existing system of subvention to the social welfare sector, the aided schools sector, the Vocation Training Council and the Hospital Authority (para. 125 of the 2000 Budget Speech). Housing Department staff resorted to high-profile actions to oppose the phased transfer of public housing estate management and maintenance services to private operators. Water Supplies Department staff also demonstrated against the rumoured privatization of water supply services. All in all, there are much anxiety, hostility and scepticism from civil servants and public sector employees towards reform proposals which are crouched in the virtue of efficiency and value for money.

On the other hand, there is substantial public support for revamping the civil service structure and service delivery systems, partly because of the general perception that civil servants cost much more than their private sector counterparts. The repeated discovery of civil service waste and sleaziness cases by the Director of Audit in his "value for money" audit reports after the 1997 handover has drawn out further public dismay with the performance of the civil service and thus greater pressure for reform. Against such a background, one can say that there is now clearly a domestic agenda for change in Hong Kong.

Globally, the "new public management" (NPM) has gained greater momentum across governments, nations and cultures, fast becoming a new global paradigm seen by many to replace the traditional bureaucratic model of public administration (see discussion in Chapter 2). Whether the new patterns of changes in governance in various countries have already led to convergence as Patricia Ingraham (1996)[3] put it, that "the commonalities are more important than the differences" so that eventually there is isomorphism because of similar national reform efforts in coping with and responding to similar challenges and needs within an increasingly globalized environment, is still a bone of great contention. But as Larry Lynn Jr. rightly pointed out in his recent plenary paper to the Fourth International Research Symposium on Public Management held in Rotterdam in April 2000,

To argue for convergence, one must argue that we are witnessing a fundamental transformation in the historic role of the nation state and of the force of nationalism, in the generative forces of public administration, socio-political and economic transformation of a character that "predicts" the new paradigm as a resultant.[4]

He further argued that if the bureaucratic paradigm is rational/legal in the Weberian sense, then a post-bureaucratic paradigm featuring quasi-markets must be founded on a different basis of legitimacy — perhaps different forms of rationality, different jurisprudential principles, a different allocation of property rights, a different ideal towards the role of the state in protecting individual rights and creating collective goods.[5] So, ultimately, it is about the nature and functions of governance, as well as the relations between state and society (and market). There is also the question of whether NPM as a new administrative paradigm has achieved what it is claimed and intended to bring about in terms of a better and more efficient government. To answer this question involves debates on how to define and measure performance and efficiency. Empirical studies of reform implementation are still much in want to provide analytical tools and perspectives to facilitate such debates.

Recent developments seem to indicate that further to the privatization boom of the 1980s and early 1990s, the NPM trend is now geared towards transforming rather than downplaying and downsizing government *per se*. Indeed the Clintonian rhetoric of "reinventing government" in the USA and the British New Labour government's "modernizing the government" project have carried a new sense of re-affirming and revitalizing the role of the state and public sector, though in a new institutional context and with a new face and new *modus operandi* (that of a steering state). This evolving international NPM agenda will bring new lessons and inspirations to public sector reform in Hong Kong. If we take up Lynn's argument, then what will be the new basis of rationality and legitimacy in Hong Kong's reformed public administration? Furthermore, how will the Hong Kong reform experience contribute to answering the substantive questions raised above about NPM in practice?

With Hong Kong entering the new SAR era and confronting the challenges of a new political and economic environment in the 21st century, there is clearly an urgency to reflect on the progress of public sector reform so far and to map out the next steps that should be taken in light of past experience and future expectations. This new volume, though published as a revised edition of the first volume, is in fact an entirely new edition, as a sequel to the 1995 volume. All the chapters are new ones. The only repeated material is the 1989 *Public Sector Reform* document which continues to appear as an important appendix of the book, so as to provide readers with a picture of the original thinking of the reformers.

The present book is organized into three parts. **Part 1** gives the overview and international context of public sector reform. Colin Sankey, who heads the government's Efficiency Unit and was one of the original initiators of the 1989 programme, outlines the latest reform thinking of the government under the overarching theme of "Serving the Community" and elaborates the various aspects of the current reform — namely customer service, managing for results, and improving productivity (*Chapter 1*). He explains the government's ultimate goal of securing a culture whereby public sector managers continuously challenge their use of resources to ensure the maximum benefit to the community — in terms of better service to their customers and greater accountability for delivering results. He sees past reforms as being for the most part driven by internal rather than external pressures. The process of change has been evolutionary rather than revolutionary which in his view was the right strategy for the period of uncertainty prior to the handover in 1997. But then he also observes that "what we are now seeing is an escalation of public sector reform onto the political agenda, raising challenges to both the pace and content of the government's reform programme." Such politicization brings both problems and opportunities to the reform process.

Anthony Cheung in *Chapter 2* searches for the rationale and agenda of public sector reform worldwide, to enable a better understanding of Hong Kong's position within the global NPM reform phenomenon. He argues that even among OECD countries, while all seem to be playing up similar NPM reform rhetoric and goals, the focus, locus and style of reforms vary according to their administrative tradition and culture, as well as their national politics and institutional features. The global NPM boom greatly intermingles with the domestic agenda of bureaucratic politics and governance, and is not as anti-bureaucratic as the reform rhetoric suggests; in fact, there is a new re-empowerment of the "transformed" bureaucrats now dressed in new managerial clothing. Richard Common (*Chapter 4*) addresses a similar question: Are Hong Kong's public sector reforms converging with the international trends? Drawing upon the policy convergence and policy transfer literature, he argues against a "one size fits all" approach to understanding the impact of NPM. According to his analysis, Hong Kong, like many other NPM-adoptors, has resorted to the use of NPM policies and programmes because of very pragmatic considerations — namely a pick-and-choose strategy towards some internationally popular approaches which have received recognition and even policy legitimacy in other advanced states.

Jane Lee's chapter (*Chapter 3*) complements well the other three chapters in this Part by focusing on the changing domestic scene of policymaking in Hong Kong after the 1997 handover, and comparing and contrasting it with the pre-1997 setting so as to unveil the opportunities and constraints for public sector reform in the new era. She argues for the importance of bottom-up commitment to the reform in addition to top-down management preferences, as well as the need for the government to develop alliances with various sectors of society in the process of reform so as to ensure that its initiatives gain credibility and legitimacy. Following her line of analysis, a crucial factor of reform is a democratic leadership that is visionary, open-minded and able to secure the community's trust and support.

Part 2 contains three chapters each giving the reform story of a unique government department, namely a commercial operation (Post Office), a social service (Housing Department) and a core service (Police Force). Each of these three agencies moves along a different route of institutional reform. In the case of the Post Office which has become a self-financing and self-accounting "trading fund," the merits of greater managerial autonomy and commercialization of service provision have to be weighed against the new commercial risks of the market. As the Postmaster General P. C. Luk writes in *Chapter 5*, "the Post Office will face ever increasing demands and pressure ... to adapt its operation to take account of new processes, new technology, movements and shifts in traffic patterns affected by economic cycles, and to act in a competitive way — returning a reasonable dividend to its owner (the government)." He sees complete freedom to act commercially and to trade competitively as critical to the success of the reform. However this is where the constraints lie as the Post Office is still required to comply with some government rules and regulations and its flexibility in cost structure is still hampered by the fact that trading fund staff are in the main civil servants, thus subject to the control mechanisms and practices of a unified civil service regime and bound by civil service-wide pay scales and conditions of service.

The Housing Department is arguably the most controversial department over the past year or so in terms of public sector reform. There has been great tension, if not outright confrontation, between management and staff unions over the so-called phased transfer of estate management and maintenance services, in effect a contracting-out strategy but with the condition that the private operators securing the service contracts have to absorb a prescribed level of Housing Department staff as a solution to solve the expected redundancy problem. Director of Housing Tony Miller in *Chapter 6* chronicles the evolutionary journey of his Department's broader reform programme, known as the "management enhancement programme" (MEP) dating back a few years earlier. In addition to describing the objectives and features of various reform measures, he also discusses the policy-reform interface as well as the reform-people interplay. Speaking from experience, he makes the following observation which no doubt will be shared by many other reformers:

> Getting people started on a journey is not easy; keeping them going when it gets rough is harder. It is sometimes necessary to force the pace, but equally it is necessary to stop periodically, to rest, to let the stragglers catch up and to take fresh bearings. It is also necessary to accept that wrong turnings can be taken on a path, that steps may need to be re-traced, and that, when someone suggests that the party is headed in the wrong direction, he is given a fair hearing. At the same time, a sense of direction must be agreed on by those responsible for leading the way and they in turn must convey it to those following.

One would have imagined a major law and order agency like the police would be the last to be reformed because of its quasi-military organizational tradition and the disciplined nature of its staff and operations. But the interesting reality is that in Hong Kong the Police Force is among the pioneers of public sector reform. It is one of the five government departments chosen to pilot-experiment the "one-line vote" budgeting innovation two years ago. Its reform agenda, as the former Commissioner of Police Ki-on Hui writes in *Chapter 7* (while still Commissioner), aims at developing a police force that is accountable, lives within its means, manages for performance, and is service-oriented. A dual approach of reform has been adopted, to promote service quality and performance management, through organizational restructuring, programme restructuring, operational and skills innovation, as well as value reorientation. The theme running through this entire approach, in Hui's words, is "a desire ... to move away from an autocratic command and control style of management, to a more modern managerial style of leadership." The outcome of the Police management reform should be much worthy of attention because if the theoretically most command-oriented and rules-bound hierarchy in the government can manage to transform its organization, management and culture, then surely other less bureaucratic institutions should have no good excuse for not changing.

Part 3 consists of 3 case study chapters contributed by academics. Anthony Cheung's study of trading fund performance (up to 1998) (*Chapter 8*) suggests that all is not as rosy as the reform rhetoric puts it in terms of how those services now run as trading funds have enhanced productive efficiency and consumer gain. What have been witnessed so far from the trading fund reform are mainly benefits to the public service managers concerned. In his judgement, "[t]he original objectives of creating a customer-led rather than producer-driven system and of promoting cost-consciousness and efficiency through competition or quasi-commercial pressures do not seem to have been borne out in operation." The case of efficiency can only be tested if these trading funds are fully exposed to a competitive market. Cheung's chapter complements well the earlier "departmental" chapter on the Post Office Trading Fund (*Chapter 5*).

Joan Leung and Ho-mun Chan in their joint chapter (*Chapter 9*) revis-its the implementation of the School Management Initiative (SMI) (now re-styled School-Based Management — SBM) which as a reform dates back to 1991 and aims at encouraging human initiative, teacher participa-tion and self-management in school decisions. The reform is also intended to change the longstanding hierarchical relationship between the Educa-tion Department and aided schools so as to decentralize managerial author-ity and to empower individual schools. Based on their empirical findings obtained in 1997, the authors argue that there has been actually no "para-digm shift" in the school management system. They see no real decentrali-zation of power to the school level; the discretion granted to schools under the new funding arrangements is still very limited. Their findings further indicate that there is no major difference in the management style between SMI and non-SMI schools in terms of participatory decision-making or the empowerment of frontline teachers. More critically, contrary to the general assumption that a liberal and open management is conducive to better school performance, their findings show that better student academic results are correlated to tighter control and closer supervision by the principal and the board of directors or school council instead.

Brian Brewer's final chapter (*Chapter 10*) critically evaluates the recent Civil Service Reform proposals as a package of human resource management reforms. It examines the reform philosophy and principles, as well as the specific reform measures proposed in civil service employment, pay and conditions, discipline and conduct, and performance management, training and development. Emphasizing the distinction between the public sector and private sector in human resource management in that the former seeks to achieve public as opposed to private goals, which makes an outright borrowing of the latter's philosophy and practices by the former problematic, Brewer also points to some inherent contradictions in philosophy in the civil service reform proposals. While the intention to achieve much greater flexibility in civil service staffing, with increased opportunities for mobility between the public and private sectors, seems to move in the direction of Theory Y, he sees the restrictive alignment between pay and performance more in the philosophical mold of Theory X; the same holds true for disciplinary matters.

Like all edited volumes, this book does not present any unified views on the merits and implications of public sector reform. Instead, the ten chapters are so arranged as to make a wide and multi-dimensional reform discourse possible. If not for the constraints of space and time, we would have liked to include more "government department" chapters to portray the variety of reforms in progress, though securing senior public sector managers to write for academic books has not always proved to be easy. As expected, individual chapter contributors all hold their own strong professional, academic, practitioner or even ideological stance on the issues of reform, which is reflected in their chapters. Contributors do not necessarily agree with one another, but this is exactly what this book aims to achieve — that is to bring together a diversity of views, outlook and experience so that readers can benefit from such diversity and the scope of debate which it underpins.

Most of the chapters were completed in early 2000, and so have not fully covered subsequent developments. However we believe their main lines of argument remain valid and relevant. Like the previous edition, we as editors in putting together the present volume, hope very much that this book can both be of interest to the general readers and be a useful reference to students of public administration as well as practitioners who are either engaged in or affected by public sector reform one way or the other. We also hope that the discussion in this book can stimulate further debate and insight within government institutions and among scholars and researchers on the future direction and prospect of reform.

Before concluding, we would like to thank all chapter authors for their contributions. Without their arduous support, the editors' somewhat ambitious attempt to put together an informative and analytical text on the latest public sector reform in Hong Kong would not have materialized. Such support from those heads of government departments and agencies who took out precious time from their very busy schedule to research for and write the "departmental" chapters is particularly appreciated. The former Secretary for the Civil Service, Lam Woon-kwong, has all along been very supportive of this book project. He has also kindly written the Foreword (while still in his previous capacity). His support and his government colleagues' chapter contributions together mark a good example of collaboration between academics and practitioners on a subject in which they share the same fervour though not always the same view.

Finally we would like to record here our great gratitude to Kitty Poon, the senior research assistant, and her student helpers, who put in much hard work and patience to the preparation of the final computer typescript, the bibliography and index. The permission of the publishers of *The International Review of Administrative Sciences* and *Public Administration and Policy* for Anthony Cheung's two published articles to be included as Chapters 2 and 8 of this book after modification is gratefully acknowledged. We also thank the Centre for Comparative Public Management and Social Policy of the City University of Hong Kong for providing a publication grant to support the production of this book.

January 2001
Hong Kong

Notes

1. Civil Service Bureau, *Civil Service into the 21st Century: Civil Service Reform Consultation Document* (Hong Kong: Printing Department, March 1999).
2. D. Tsang, *The 1999–2000 Budget: Onward with New Strengths*, Speech by the Financial Secretary moving the Second Reading of the Appropriation Bill 1999 at the Legislative Council (Hong Kong: Printing Department, 3 March 1999); D. Tsang, *The 2000–01 Budget: Scaling New Heights*, Speech by the

Financial Secretary moving the Second Reading of the Appropriation Bill 2000 at the Legislative Council (Hong Kong: Printing Department, 8 March 2000).

3. P. W. Ingraham, "Play It Again, Sam, It's Still Not Right: Searching for the Right Notes in Administrative Reform," paper presented at the Waldo Symposium, The Maxwell School, Syracuse University, USA, 27–29 June 1996.

4. L. E. Lynn, Jr., "Globalization and Administrative Reform: What Is Happening in Theory?" paper presented at the closing plenary session of the Fourth International Research Symposium on Public Management, Erasmus University, Rotterdam, The Netherlands, 10–11 April 2000, p. 13.

5. Ibid.

PART ONE

Overview

1

An Overview of Public Sector Reform Initiatives in the Hong Kong Government Since 1989

Colin Sankey

Head, Efficiency Unit

1. Introduction

Although by international standards we have "small government" in Hong Kong, government's functions are nonetheless many and varied. It regulates, facilitates, purchases and provides services on behalf of the community. It acts as a safety net — dealing with the needs in the community to which no one else responds.

Such needs continue to grow and expectations continue to rise. Gone are the days when the public was grateful to be the recipient of standardized "one size fits all" services. The community now rightly expects to be treated as a paying customer for quality services.

Unfortunately the resources available to meet these increased demands is finite, limited within the confines of economic growth. Thus, in a period of slower economic growth as we are experiencing at present, it is not difficult to see why government's performance in managing these resources efficiently and effectively is very much the flavour of the day.

The civil service is currently attracting critical commentaries from politicians, the media and the public generally about its efficiency. The gist of this criticism suggests that a major overhaul of the civil service is long overdue and that a "colonial style government" staffed by permanent employees needs to be given a dramatic shake up if it is to meet today's needs.

Some of this criticism can be attributed to the fact that people are simply unhappy in these difficult times and looking for someone to blame; some of it overlooks the significant improvements that have and are already taking place, particularly in service delivery; but equally some of it is fair.

For the most part, past reforms have been driven by internal, rather than external, pressures for the civil service to develop a more customer and performance orientated culture. The process of change has been evolutionary rather than revolutionary which was probably the right strategy for the period of uncertainty leading up to the transition. But what we are now seeing is an escalation of public sector reform onto the political agenda, raising challenges to both the pace and content of the government's reform programme.

This brings both problems and opportunities: Problems in managing expectations given the scope and magnitude of the change required; Opportunities to harness this new political will and take some bold initiatives en route to becoming a truly world-class civil service.

This chapter describes where government lies on this journey and some of the fundamental issues that still have to be tackled. It also examines the success or otherwise of past initiatives and shows how they are being pulled together through an innovative reform structure.

The chapter focuses primarily on developments during the 1990s under the "Serving the Community" banner and only briefly discusses earlier stages of reform as these have been well documented in previous papers.[1] It should be noted that the views expressed in this chapter are the personal views of the author, although he has drawn considerably on his practical experience with the Hong Kong Special Administrative Region (SAR) government and on insights gained from discussions with colleagues whose assistance is acknowledged.

1.1 *"Serving the Community"*

In 1992 the Efficiency Unit was set up, reporting directly to the Chief Secretary for Administration, to develop and implement a programme of public sector reform (titled "Serving the Community" to better reflect the real objectives from this work). An early task for the Unit was to set aims and values to reflect the vision and the basic ethics of public service that it wished to inculcate into the civil service. These were set for the longer term as a basis for developing future plans, assessing the effectiveness of new initiatives and programmes, and raising awareness of the need for change.

These aims and values were translated into the following four core principles to be applied consistently throughout the government's management process.

- **Living within Our Means**, because the government must determine how best to meet the community's needs within the resources available.
- **Managing for Performance**, because the government must deliver the best possible services for public money.
- **Developing Our Culture of Service**, because the government must be a responsive organization, committed to quality service.
- **Being Accountable**, because the government has an obligation to answer to the community which it exists to serve.

Because the community rightly expects effective and efficient services to be delivered in a proper and ethical way, generic values were promoted to support these principles including Openness; Integrity; Responsiveness; Efficiency; Effectiveness; Commitment and Courtesy.

Then, to raise awareness and understanding of these ideals and the cultural change being sought, various initiatives were packaged around the theme of "Serving the Community." The best examples included:

- A **"Serving the Community" Booklet,**[2] which described the aims, principles and values of the public sector; where responsibilities lay to put these ideals into practice; and the key management tasks that needed to be addressed.
- **Management Seminars**, which covered the following topics — vision, mission and values; continuous improvement and the service imperative.
- A **Conference,** to which international speakers were invited to address civil servants on the latest thinking in public sector management.
- **"Serving the Community" Week,** which provided a platform for departments to promote their services to the community; and raise awareness among staff of the importance of their contributions. Some 170 different activities were organized by 50 departments

throughout the week and over 16,000 people attended a special one-day carnival.

Other initiatives included receptions for front-line staff; training videos and a whole range of "Serving the Community" promotional material.

Through these efforts, civil servants and members of the community gradually became more aware of the "Serving the Community" programme and the importance government attached to providing customer friendly public services.

But defining and raising awareness of these principles was one thing, putting them into practice another. It was decided that the best way forward was first to overlay the basic management process onto our core principles. Then to use the forces driving change to introduce a range of programmes with supporting initiatives to improve the key areas of the management process and reinforce the basic principles (see Annex 1.1).

These improvements have evolved over a period of time and it can be seen from Annex 1.1 that in addition to the early reforms which addressed some ethical concerns and economic problems in the 1970s and 1980s, there have been three other key programmes under "Serving the Community."

- **Customer Service,** which has focused on improving the quality, timeliness and culture of service across the civil service;
- **Managing for Results,** which aims to establish a clear top-down, policy-driven hierarchy of outputs and targets for government to use in managing delivery (supported by the development of an Internet-based executive information system); and
- **Improving Productivity,** which is being developed as an essential response to the current economic downturn and is being used to drive the longer term agenda (even with the current economic downturn, the government sees itself more in the business of searching for improved value rather than cuts).

2. Customer Service Programme

In 1992 it became clear that the then Governor, Chris Patten, with his political background, wished to focus on openness, accountability and customer service.

The Efficiency Unit's early initiatives were therefore quite deliberately customer facing with a view to securing visible improvements in service. This was seen as the best way of gaining credibility for the change programme and at the same time actively involving both the public and civil servants. Some of the best examples are:

- **Performance Pledges,** which set out in plain terms the standards of services which the public have a right to expect. These pledges inform individual members of the public of the promised level of service for their particular transaction, be it the issue of a licence or attending a clinic.
- **Trading Funds,** for certain departments which offer more commercial services. This accounting arrangement allows departments to retain revenue and operate with more financial autonomy in order to improve services. These departments must maintain the commercial viability of their operations.
- **Customer Liaison Groups,** comprising departmental representatives and identified customers who meet regularly to discuss the views of customers and potential service improvements.
- **Code on Access to Information,** developed as part of the government's commitment to a more open and accountable government. The Code authorizes and requires civil servants, on request, to provide information within specified time frames unless there are good reasons for not doing so. The Code also sets out procedures for review, or for complaint to the Ombudsman, if a member of the public considers that the Code has not been properly followed.
- **Customer Service Improvements,** introduced by a number of departments over recent years. For instance, the Department of Health piloted a successful exercise to improve service in clinics which is now being cascaded through all government out-patient clinics with the full involvement and commitment of staff. More recently we have seen the Hong Kong Police pay particular attention to service aspects and they have recently launched an improvement programme focusing on a pilot study at North Point Police Station. The aim is to create a benchmark for service delivery and culture within the Police.
- **Helping Business Programme,** designed as an integral part of overall efforts to better serve the community. It aimed to make the government more business friendly, founded on the belief that more should be done to help the business community generate the economic growth on which Hong Kong's future prosperity depends.

It is worthwhile reflecting in more detail on three of these initiatives, Performance Pledges, Trading Funds and Helping Business, with a view to assessing their success or otherwise.

2.1 Performance Pledges

The Performance Pledges Programme sought to help departments better manage their relationships with customers; impart a customer focus and provide performance standards for staff; act as a management tool for daily operations; and provide a mechanism for reporting performance to customers and the community at large.

Wide publicity was given to performance pledges when they were first launched to ensure that both the public and civil servants fully understood their rights and obligations. Press briefings were conducted to enable the public to know more about the subject. Letters and pamphlets were issued to staff councils, staff unions and departments setting out the details.

The government adopted a phased approach to the extension of this initiative. The first batch of seven departments representing a fair cross-section of government services issued their pledges in 1992. By 1995, all 50 departments providing direct services to the public had published their performance pledges. Since then 12 internal services departments have followed suit along with 12 non-government public bodies which have an important interface with the public.

A recent review (August 1998) (Annex 1.2) of the performance pledges initiative was particularly encouraging. Feedback from departments and customers indicated that in general, the Performance Pledges Programme has achieved its objectives and the pledges are considered to be very useful. Key findings were published and departments were invited to examine how the lessons emerged from the review would apply to them.

The review identified a few areas for improvement — greater customer and staff involvement; greater publicity of its objectives and the results; regular review and improvement of targets; extension of its coverage; and support and assistance available from the centre.

2.2 Trading Funds

In the "Public Sector Reform" booklet published in 1989,[3] the trading fund concept was identified as one of the options available for improving the delivery of government services.

Trading funds differ from traditional government departments primarily in their ability to respond more readily to changing market conditions and customer demand. The general manager of a trading fund has a greater degree of autonomy than a controlling officer of a traditional vote-funded government department, subject to being able to finance expenditure and liabilities out of trading income.

As emphasized by the government during Legislative Council debates, although trading funds are required to meet a quantified target rate of return on capital invested, their primary role is not financial but rather to improve services and their delivery.

Enabling legislation — the Trading Fund Ordinance (TFO) — was enacted in 1993. Under this Ordinance trading funds have been established in the Companies Registry (August 1993), Land Registry (August 1993), Office of the Telecommunications Authority (OFTA) (June 1995), Post Office (August 1995), and Electrical and Mechanical Services Department (EMSD) (August 1996). The Sewage Services Trading Fund was established in 1994 but closed in 1998 because the fund was not allowed to raise fees to a level sufficient to meet the costs of its operations.

No trading funds were established in 1997 and in 1998.

All the Trading Funds have maintained financial viability whilst keeping price increases well within inflation levels. There are noticeable improvements in customer service and business processes. Annex 1.3 illustrates some of the improvements.

But perhaps of more importance is that they have begun to release the entrepreneurial energy within departments resulting in wider benefits being passed on to customers. (Annex 1.4)

In general terms, it is clear that the trading fund environment has definitely focused management's attention much more on customers' needs and they are increasingly using productivity gains to drive improvements.

Looking forward, over the next few years, there are plans for:

- The Post Office Trading Fund to introduce a Public Certification Authority service in 1999–2000 for e-commerce service providers;
- The Companies Registry Trading Fund to provide on-line search facilities for the public;
- The Electrical and Mechanical Services Trading Fund to provide

support for the development of energy saving programmes in government departments to reduce electricity charges;
- The Office of the Telecommunications Authority to provide licence application service on the Internet for a number of telecommunication licences.

There may well be criticisms about specific aspects of performance of trading funds, but there is no doubt that overall performance of these areas compared to pre-trading fund days has moved up a gear. There are no longer continuous complaints about quality and timeliness of service and generally very positive feedback is received. It is also worth noting that these improvements have been brought about without being a major drain on government resources.

2.3 Helping Business

Whilst Performance Pledges and Trading Funds represent the highest profile initiatives, the Helping Business Programme that the Efficiency Unit launched had some very important objectives including cutting red tape; eliminating over-regulation; reducing the cost of compliance with government regulations and transferring services out of the public sector to the business sector where appropriate market conditions prevailed.

The Efficiency Unit commenced with phase one of this programme in May 1996 and conducted seven pilot studies over the next few months with a view to assessing the potential for further work. The studies included:

- looking at methods of payments and collection for business transactions;
- providing public forms through the Internet;
- business studies of Marine and Trade Departments to look at deregulation opportunities;
- a review of the process for land exchanges and lease modifications;
- the introduction of "one stop shop" Business Licence Information Centre; and
- providing an improved Hong Kong Background Information service.

Some of these pilot studies were carried on through to implementation and others provided the basis for further work.[4] Annex 1.5 shows some current statistics on some of the early initiatives. Eventually because of the long-term and service-wide implications of the Helping Business Programme, it was decided that a dedicated and permanent office was needed to steer, co-ordinate and secure implementation. A new office, the Business and Services Promotion Unit, was therefore set up in May 1997 in the Financial Secretary's Office and one of its key remits is to take forward this programme.

2.4 Need for Wider Reform

There was, however, always a limit to the improvement that could be achieved solely through the Customer Service Programme. It was clear that core management processes also needed to be improved. But this had always proved to be difficult. Management processes and programmes were often unique to departments and policy bureaux, yet it was clear that real improvements could only be secured by bringing together efforts across traditional organizational boundaries.

3. Managing for Results

The return of Hong Kong to China in July 1997 provided the impetus to tackle the core management processes when it became clear that the Chief Executive, Tung Chee-hwa, intended to focus more on managing for results. In his first Policy Address, he made a range of promises to the community on education, care for the elderly, economic development and housing that cut right across a range of policy areas and departments.

The government had been examining the need to change the management processes, learning from overseas experience, especially in New Zealand. It seized the opportunity of the Chief Executive's challenging agenda to propose a Target-based Management Process (TMP). The then Secretary for the Treasury, K. C. Kwong, supported by the Efficiency Unit, was charged with implementing the process as a means of focusing government on managing for results by results. Implementation is well under way and the government now has policy objectives covering the whole of government reflecting the outcomes it is seeking to achieve for the community.

Designed to focus on results, the process helps direct resources to priorities, clarify responsibilities and relationships and manage delivery across government.

3.1 Focus on Results

When resource allocation and performance was debated in government, the questions frequently asked included:

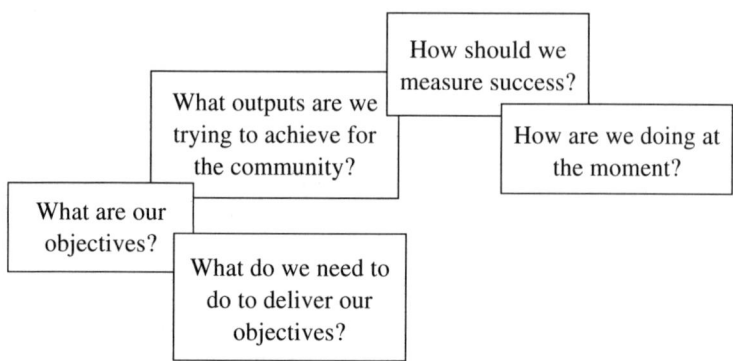

All too often the existing management process did not provide the answers to such questions because objectives and outcomes were not sufficiently explicit, performance measures often focused on inputs rather than outputs and outcomes, and there was little linkage between measures at government-wide, policy and operational levels.

TMP is overcoming this by establishing a top-down hierarchy from explicit policy objectives to the operational level:

- **Policy Objectives (POs),** represent the strategic, high level statements of the outcomes the government will deliver to respond to the needs and concerns of the community. Policy Objectives must be concrete enough for success to be judged in the longer term. Typically delivery of a PO will involve more than one Bureau and several Departments. There are currently nearly 40 POs covering the whole of government.
- **Key Result Areas (KRAs),** which support each PO. They are the areas where the government must do well to achieve the overall PO. Perhaps more importantly, they are also the elements or components of the process for delivering the PO. KRAs will typically be easier to measure than the PO, and results should be quicker to come at this level.
- **Initiatives,** which are the practical steps, at the next level down, that government is taking to improve performance in order to

deliver the KRAs and thus the overall PO. Initiatives are easier to measure in terms of delivery to timetable and often in terms of results, such as increasing the capacity of a service.
- **Activities,** which are at the same level as initiatives, and represent the on-going day-to-day activities which deliver services to the community and occupy the majority of resources. Delivery of the POs is equally dependent on these baseline activities. Measures are typically more concrete at this level.

A full set of policy objectives covering the whole of government activities was published with the 1998 Policy Address. The above structure flows through each and they provide a very open and accountable position of what government is seeking to achieve and lead responsibility in each case. In 1999, these booklets were further enhanced to show progress to-date against the various indicators and targets.

TMP also includes a hierarchy of targets and measures at each level. The PO level is the most important to measure and set targets for, but it is also often the most difficult. In some cases where measurement is particularly difficult, or there has been no measurement in the past, we are currently using more general indicators. The government is therefore developing measures of success that will form the basis of targets in future years.

Also, to improve performance measures at departmental level, a steering group, chaired by the Secretary for the Civil Service, W. K. Lam, has overseen the development of a "Best Practice Guide on Performance Measurement."[5] The old adage of what gets measured, gets done is as true for the public as it is for the private sector. Research in both the public and private sectors shows that good systems of performance measurement can facilitate dramatic increases in the quality of services provided and brings increased job satisfaction to employees. For managers in the public sector, comparative performance information is essential in assessing whether the best services are being provided or purchased at the lowest cost, and whether those services are meeting the needs of the community, i.e. they achieve the desired outcomes.

Over time it is hoped that these developments will lead to significant changes in the indicators and targets currently reported in the Controlling Officer's Report (COR) which supports Departmental Estimates of Expenditure. Ultimately we might expect departmental measures and reporting to develop so that COR contains clear statements of:

- **Outputs a department will deliver** — Reflecting the outputs commissioned by Policy Secretaries in support of the delivery of policy objectives.
- **Resources to be consumed in delivering these outputs** — Showing the resources to be consumed by activities carried out by a department and contributing to the overall delivery of key result areas and policy objectives.
- **Actual performance against plan** — Covering both the delivery of the outputs commissioned and the resources consumed to deliver them.

3.2 Direct Resources to Priorities

All too often in the past managers felt swamped by the volume of data being produced about current operations, but starved of real information or knowledge about how well government was doing in achieving objectives. TMP provides a structure for performance information by layering it at PO, KRA and initiative level. Managers can focus attention on the information appropriate to their role.

This top-down hierarchy has been supported by the development and implementation of an Internet-based Performance Review System.

By introducing this system the government has radically reduced the requirement for long paper performance reports to be produced, circulated and copied. Instead the system allows on-line access to whatever level of detail is required. This promotes the sharing of information and working together across traditional boundaries.

Besides providing easy access to the right information TMP also provides a mechanism to communicate government's overall priorities very clearly. The selection of the high level POs sends a clear message about what government is seeking to deliver for the community. At the next level down, the KRAs identify the areas most important to the delivery of the POs, whilst the initiatives turn these into operational priorities for departments.

As well as influencing managers in their day-to-day priority setting, the TMP hierarchy also provides a robust basis for judgements on relative priorities during the government's annual Resource Allocation Exercise (RAE). The POs send a message on priorities to Bureaux and Departments considering making bids and provide criteria for deciding between competing bids.

3.3 Clarifying Responsibilities and Relationships

Successful delivery of the POs will require clarity about what is to be delivered together with explicit accountability for delivery. TMP provides a new focus for relationships and accountability, ensuring debates about performance are focused on the right issues and carried out at the right level. The roles and responsibilities within the improved management process can be summarized as:

- The Chief Executive, Star Chamber, and Policy Groups set the overall vision, total expenditure and priorities, and review performance.
- Policy Secretaries take the lead on delivery of individual POs and co-ordinate efforts across government. They identify community concerns, develop and agree POs with the Chief Executive, Star Chamber and Policy Groups, develop options and define results.
- Policy Secretaries then define the outputs needed, commission these from Departments, and define how success will be judged.
- Departments manage their activities and resources to produce the commissioned outputs, and report results to Policy Secretaries, accounting for shortfalls and how they are being tackled.
- Policy Secretaries focus at policy level on outputs and outcomes, adjusting commissioning agreements as necessary and reporting progress to the Chief Executive, Star Chamber and Policy Groups.

3.4 Manages Delivery across Government

Delivery of the POs requires co-operation across traditional organizational, functional and financial boundaries. Historically the management and delivery of work has concentrated within these boundaries. The POs cut through this structure, concentrating on external delivery, not internal organization.

Delivery of the POs requires the government to take a different perspective on how it operates. It needs to:

- Understand the delivery process for the POs including the links, roles and responsibilities, both internally and externally.
- Be clear about priorities and define the required results so as to provide a focus for working together.

- Ensure there are clear responsibilities and targets at each level, together with effective monitoring of progress and results.
- Establish mechanisms for people to work together across structures irrespective of levels and hierarchy — for example one Policy Secretary commissioning another.
- Emphasize the shift in culture — delivery of the results is more important than protecting departmental turf.

It is early days yet to measure success or otherwise. Bedding in such a management system takes time because of the need to influence the way people have always worked. But there are some early signs of success and that the system is being used proactively to manage delivery of baseline activities and new initiatives. Managers are also looking for the system to be enhanced further to provide more information, particularly in respect of costs. It is envisaged therefore that over time, the system will become an integral part of a wider executive information system.

4. Improving Productivity

The current economic downturn serves as a driving force to improve "Managing for Performance." The Chief Executive launched an Enhanced Productivity Programme (EPP) in his 1998 Policy Address. The Chief Secretary for Administration is providing overall leadership of the programme through her Public Services Policy Group. The programme is designed to achieve both short-term quantified productivity gains and a lasting improvement in public sector productivity. It will do this by a combination of reduced growth in baseline expenditure, reviews of major spending areas, and changes in the management framework intended to secure a more proactive resource management culture. EPP is being delivered as two phases:

- **Phase One**, which will deliver short-term quantified productivity gains. This phase is led by the Secretary for the Treasury and coordinated by the Finance Bureau.
- **Phase Two**, which is addressing more fundamental issues to help secure a sustained improvement in public sector productivity. This phase is being co-ordinated by the Efficiency Unit on behalf of Public Services Policy Group.

In taking forward EPP, the policy objectives are serving as a vital management tool in good and bad times alike. When additional resources were available, the objectives served to prioritize bids. Now, less new resources are available, value for money from existing spending is even more essential and the explicit policy objectives ensure that resources and efforts are directed to real priorities.

4.1 Phase One

The immediate task for the short-term phase is to require government departments and government subvented organizations to provide new or improved services using existing resources or to deliver real dollar savings in the 1999–2000 financial year through productivity gains. In addition, between 2000–01 and 2002–03, they are required to deliver a further 5% improvement in productivity.

A variety of measures will be taken to deliver these improvements including simplifying procedures and removing duplication in work processes; using human resources more flexibly; contracting out work where it is more cost-effective; and cutting down on overtime payments.

4.2 Phase Two

One of the government's key messages in launching EPP is that it should not be seen in isolation or as a knee-jerk reaction to the economic slowdown. Economic growth will, after all, return in the mid-term and Hong Kong's fundamental economic advantages remain. Though it is vital to respond effectively to the current situation, it is also important to use EPP to further the longer-term agenda.

The aspiration at the heart of EPP is to shift the resource management culture so that managers continually review and challenge their use of resources in order to maximize their contribution to delivering the government's overall objectives. This is very much in line with the broad direction of the public sector reform and "Serving the Community" agenda in Hong Kong. It takes the public sector closer to the vision set out by the Chief Secretary for Administration in her speech to the Hong Kong Institute of Directors in April 1999. The Chief Secretary for Administration described a government which is recognized as:

- Accountable and responsive to the community's needs
- Focused on delivering clear outputs and outcomes.

– More concerned with ensuring needs are met, but less concerned with meeting all needs through in-house services.
– A provider of efficient and effective public services.
– Economic in the use of resources.
– Customer friendly.

Some key elements of this phase of EPP are described below.

4.2.1 The Programme

The programme is project driven to speed up delivery of results from major areas of expenditure; targeted to complement Phase One; forward looking to ensure sustainability of efficiency identified; and cross departmental to eliminate duplication. It is also exploiting technology solutions to provide seamless service delivery and drive productivity improvements.

The programme includes four work streams, each consisting of a series of projects. The four work streams are:

– Fundamental Expenditure Reviews
– Service Delivery
– Support Services
– Institutional Change

The first three work streams relate to identifying specific savings/redeployment opportunities. Work stream four will establish the institutional arrangements and management processes we need to promote ongoing improvements in productivity. Ultimately improved productivity will be driven by accountable managers with resource flexibility engaged in a continuing search for improved results from available resources.

(a) Fundamental Expenditure Reviews (FERs)

There will be a phased programme of FERs to examine major areas of government activity. The FERs will be top-down, policy-driven and will consider fundamental issues. This will include whether policy objectives could be achieved more efficiently and effectively by alternative means, and whether activities still need to be carried out by the government. The FERs will start from the government's published POs. The outcome of each FER will be a comprehensive picture of the policies, activities and resources devoted to the PO, together with agreed proposals to maximize the impact achieved from those resources.

(b) Service Delivery

The use of technology and streamlined operational processes can improve productivity significantly by allowing services to be delivered in new ways. For example, significant effort goes into handling telephone and other enquiries from the public and following them up. It can be difficult for the public to know which department to call, and the process of dealing with enquiries is much less efficient if calls are passed from department to department.

A different model is to set up call centres to deal with particular issues. Such call centres would provide one-number convenience for the public and improve efficiency by dealing with most queries at the first point of contact. Call centres could use technology not just to make sure that staff have the right information at their fingertips, but also to deploy resources to respond to a problem.

At present, the government has over 900 hotline numbers which create difficulties for the public in knowing where to enquire, complain or generally to provide feedback. By comparison, the Brisbane City Council, which operates a very impressive one-number call centre, has eliminated some 600 numbers in the space of a few years.

It is therefore hoped that through a similar project, the Hong Kong SAR government can make serious in-roads into the number of hotlines it has. This will both improve customer service and deliver productivity gains through the re-engineering of processes that support this service.

Another key initiative for improving front-line service is electronic service delivery. The Information Technology and Broadcasting Bureau is currently focusing on establishing a world-class infrastructure for electronic transactions between the public and government. This is being delivered quickly by outsourcing the service and when completed should also drive re-engineering of processes to exploit the radically lower transaction cost of e-commerce.

(c) Support Services

Support services inevitably represent a significant part of total government expenditure. Whilst effective support services are essential to front-line delivery, we must ensure that they are delivered in the most cost-effective way. Often support services are managed as an add-on to other duties, and represent a distraction for already stretched managers. In the private sector and other governments there are moves to manage support services differently, for example by bringing together support processes in one location, using specialist managers and staff. Sometimes this is linked to outsourcing the work.

Often it is necessary to take a cross-government or at least cross-departmental view of support services to realize the potential of such improvements. Recent work in the government on records management has given a good indication of the potential benefits from this approach. We see similar opportunities in many other areas, including accommodation, procurement, personnel records, financial processes and despatch services. Annex 1.6 illustrates a typical pattern that emerges from this type of work.

(d) Institutional Change

There is also a need to pursue institutional change as a mechanism to sharpen accountability in exchange for resource management flexibility. Progress is being made on a number of fronts.

Human Resources Flexibility

The Civil Service Bureau is leading developments on increased human resources flexibility for managers. As staff are the largest and most important resource for delivering services to the community, increased financial management flexibility will mean little unless matched by flexibility in managing staff.

In this respect, the Civil Service Bureau has just published a consultation document outlining the overall framework and initial thinking on their planned reforms for the civil service. The objectives of these reforms are to create:

- **An open, flexible, equitable and structured civil service framework,** with means of entry and exit to allow for the intake of talent and removal of non-performers at all levels;
- **An enabling and motivating environment,** using a more competitive remuneration package and performance-based reward system to attract, retain and motivate civil servants; and
- **A proactive, accountable and responsible culture,** by increasing the sense of responsibility and motivation of civil servants at all levels, enhance efficiency and quality of service, and nurture a performance-based and service-oriented management culture.

The scope of the reform will involve reviewing entry and exit mechanisms; pay and fringe benefits; disciplinary procedures; and performance management, professional training and personal development.

Further details are available in the consultation document.[6]

New Trading Funds and Increased Flexibility for the Trading Funds

The challenge at the heart of EPP is to shift the resource management culture so that managers continually review and challenge their use of resources in order to maximize their contribution to delivering the government's overall objectives. The introduction of trading funds has already been successful in engendering a more proactive and entrepreneurial management culture in the funds created to date. The funds have been given additional flexibility in managing resources in exchange for sharper accountability for delivering results, and this has led to increased productivity.

As part of EPP the government will be examining the benefits of giving additional flexibility to the trading funds (for example on staffing and procurement), and the creation of additional funds. One group of candidates is the internal service departments, following the precedent of Electrical and Mechanical Services Department where trading fund status has led to significant improvements.

New Managerial Frameworks

Government is also looking at the potential for new managerial frameworks for selected departments combining increased flexibility in resource management (both financial and staff), with sharper accountability for delivery. Such tailored management frameworks draw on overseas developments, where many governments, including those in New Zealand, Australia, the US, Singapore and the UK, have introduced new management frameworks to reflect the different operational and managerial requirements within the executive arms of government. The one-line votes introduced in 1999–2000 for the Hong Kong Police, the Treasury and the Civil Service Training and Development Institute is a move in this direction. Building on this, further financial flexibility might include proposals such as end of year budget flexibility, multi-year budgets and budgets net of revenue. Staffing flexibility might include making greater use of contracts as proposed in the Civil Service Bureau's "Civil Service Reform" consultation document referred to earlier. Clearer accountability would be achieved through a requirement for outputs statements linked explicitly to policy objectives and targets for measuring success. These outputs statements and targets should be the centrepiece of business plans linking resources to outputs.

This approach could operate in selected, volunteer departments that meet the criteria for improved accountability, rather than being applied across the board. The aim would be to pilot such changes on an administrative basis rather than go for legislative change.

Visibility of Cost

At present the government does not have a system of interdepartmental charging other than for trading funds. There is no doubt that introducing charging for a wider range of internal services, e.g. accommodation, will drive improved productivity. Such changes would be the first step in a broader trend to make costs more transparent and open up services for competition.

5. Way Forward

Enhanced Productivity Programme, as the latest stage in our Public Sector Reform programme, is seeking to answer such fundamental questions as: Are resources allocated to the real priorities? Do current activities deliver the maximum results? Are there new and better service models and what is government's most effective role? These questions are at the heart of the search for improved productivity and go far beyond incremental efficiency improvements. They are also posed on a government-wide basis, because the problems faced by the community are no respecters of government's traditional organizational boundaries, or indeed of the divide between public and private sectors. Overcoming these boundaries has huge potential to improve the management and delivery of public services.

New technology often is part of the answer. It has the potential to transform service models — from one stop shops and enquiry call centres that deal with all services and transactions, to self service on the Internet or over dedicated electronic networks. Yet technology alone is not the answer.

There is much to learn from world-class best practice in the private sector. The government needs to be willing to unravel and transform outdated working practices and tear down traditional professional and organizational boundaries. Nor is increased central control the answer. We have all seen the effects of an overly powerful central resource function that believes it knows best. The government needs to unleash the entrepreneurial spirit of its managers, which have been dulled by the embrace of bureaucratic control.

The ultimate aim of the reforms is to secure a culture where managers continuously challenge their use of resources to ensure the maximum benefit to the community[7] — where improved productivity becomes their focus because they can better serve their customers, and because they are in no doubt about their accountability for delivering results. A lot of progress has been made but this is a journey not a destination. There are also many lessons to learn from and share with commentators in Hong Kong and fellow travellers in other public sectors.

Notes

1. C. Sankey, "Public Sector Reform: Past Developments and Recent Trends," *Hong Kong Public Administration,* Vol. 2, No. 1 (1993), pp. 71–93.
2. Hong Kong Government, *Serving the Community* (Hong Kong: Government Printer, 1995).
3. Hong Kong Government, *Public Sector — A Sharpen Focus* (Hong Kong: Government Printer, 1989).
4. More information on these studies and others is available on the Public Sector Reform Forum website (http://www.info.gov.hk/eu) under "Helping Business."
5. This Guide is available on the Efficiency Unit's web-site — Public Sector Reform Forum (http://www.info.gov.hk/eu).
6. Civil Service Bureau of Government Secretariat, *Civil Service Reform Consultation Document* (Hong Kong: Government Printer of the Special Administrative Region, 1999).
7. The discussion paper on "Setting World Class Standards in the Public Sector" (August 1996) is available on the Efficiency Unit's web-site (http://www.info. gov.hk/eu) under "Useful Materials."

Annex 1.1 Sequence of Public Sector Reform Initiatives

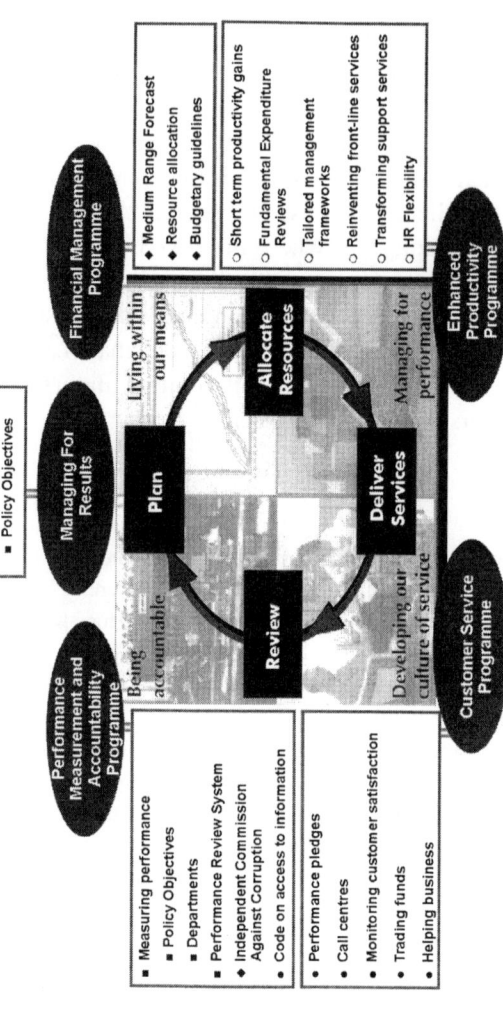

- Policy Objectives

Financial Management Programme

- ◆ Medium Range Forecast
- ◆ Resource allocation
- ◆ Budgetary guidelines

- ○ Short term productivity gains
- ○ Fundamental Expenditure Reviews
- ○ Tailored management frameworks
- ○ Reinventing front-line services
- ○ Transforming support services
- ○ HR Flexibility

Managing For Results

Living within our means

Plan

Allocate Resources

Managing for performance

Enhanced Productivity Programme

Performance Measurement and Accountability Programme

Being accountable

Review

Deliver Services

Developing our culture of service

Customer Service Programme

- ■ Measuring performance
  - ■ Policy Objectives
  - ■ Departments
- ■ Performance Review System
- ◆ Independent Commission Against Corruption
- ■ Code on access to information

- ● Performance pledges
- ● Call centres
- ● Monitoring customer satisfaction
- ● Trading funds
- ● Helping business

◆ Early Reform (1980s)　● Serving the Community (early 1990s)　■ Managing for Results (late 1990s)　○ Improving Productivity (late 1990s)

Annex 1.2 Performance Pledges — Key Survey Findings

	Rating ★★★★★
Customers' View	
85% satisfied with performance against pledged standards	★★★★
84% found the pledges useful	★★★★
81% satisfied with departments' response to their views	★★★★
62% thought pledges contributed greatly to improving services	★★★
Departments' Performance	
95% have a monitoring/review system in place	★★★★★
75% reviewed pledges annually and many made service improvements	★★★★
62% included all services they provide in their pledges	★★★
51% put up notices stating their pledged targets at service points	★★★
Departments' View	
87% thought the Programme provided effective management standards for staff	★★★★
79% considered it effective in managing departments' daily operations	★★★★
77% considered it effective in imparting a customer focus to staff	★★★★
72% considered it effective in managing the relationship with customers	★★★

Annex 1.3 Trading Funds — Process Improvements

Trading Fund	Activity	Year		Service improve-ment
		1993–94	**1997–98**	
Companies Registry	Registration of an overseas company	38 days	27 days	29%
	Register general documentation for a local company	33 days	14 days	56%
Land Registry	Document registration	28 days	20 days	29%
	Copying of land record	60 minutes	25 minutes	58%
		1996–97	**1997–98**	
EMSD	Response time to faults with electrical and mechanical equipment	3 hours	1hours	67%
	Response time to repairs	2 days	1 day	50%
OFTA	Licence applications for the establishment of a new mobile radio system within 2 months	94%	98%	4%
	Licence applications for the ship station within 10 days	92%	95%	3%
		1994–95	**1997–98**	
Hongkong Post	Delivery of locally posted letters to addressees by the following day whilst absorbing increased traffic (items) from 1,138 million to 1,280 million over some period.	97%	98%	1%

Annex 1.4 Trading Funds — Other Benefits to Customers

Trading Fund	Initiative	Benefits to Customers
Land Registry	– Launching of Direct Access Services and the computerization of the New Territories land registers.	– Remote access to the "one-stop" search service, imaged copies by fax and remote orders for copies of land documents.
Companies Registry	– Review and redesign forms.	– Standardized and user-friendly forms are now used and conveniently available.
	– Use of electronic signatures to sign certificates of incorporation.	– Enabling certificates delivered 1 day earlier and company names index updated 2 days earlier.
	– Introduction of an on-line search service for company names and document indices via Internet.	– Daily updated data available to customers on-line.
OFTA	– Introduction of Calling Number Display service.	– All land and mobile users can now take up this service.
	– Licensing for Virtual Private Network service.	– More effective and economical communication within corporate groups and organizations.
	– Early termination of the exclusive Hong Kong Telecom international licence.	– Encourage competitiveness and hence bring down the cost to the customers.
EMSD	– Regionalization and re-organization. – Technology and process improvement.	– Reduce price changes from 1999–2000 to inflation minus 5%.
Hongkong Post	– Resumption of Sunday collection. – Longer opening hours. – More frequent collections. – Better parcel delivery in Central.	– Improved services without any increase of the postal rates.

Annex 1.5 Progress of Early Initiatives

Initiative	Progress to-date
Public Forms on Internet	– About 700 most popular forms were available on the Internet as at March 1999 – Around 60,000 copies were downloaded in 1998
One-stop Business Licence Information Centre	– About 45,000 enquiries have been received (including 35,000 through Internet)
Hong Kong Background Information service	– About 47,000 hits between July 1997 and March 1999 via internet

Annex 1.6 Transforming Support Services

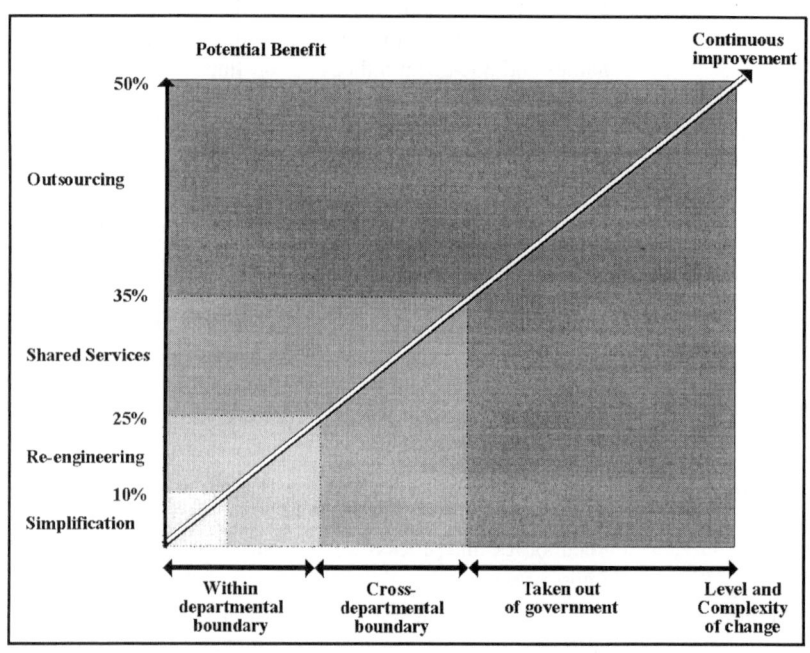

2

Understanding Public Sector Reforms: Global Trends and Diverse Agendas*

Anthony B. L. Cheung

Professor, Department of Public and Social Administration,
City University of Hong Kong

1. Introduction: Emergence of a Global Movement

In a recent issue of the *Public Administration Review*, H. George Frederickson observed that "no movement associated with the administrative aspects of modern American government has had the visibility of reinventing government."[1] The idea of "reinventing government" was made popular by the high-profile National Performance Review of the US Federal Government and the 1992 best-seller by Osborne and Gaebler which claimed that the rise of a new "entrepreneurial government" was an inevitable shift rather than a temporary fad: "In government after government and public system after public system, reinvention is the only option left."[2]

The shift towards "entrepreneurialism" is not only evident in the US. In Europe Metcalfe and Richards had earlier described the new market approaches to public management as the "modernization" of public organizations, asserting that "[g]overnments in most advanced countries are in the process of reconsidering or revising basic assumptions about the boundaries between public and private sectors, the scope of regulation and the opportunities for deregulation."[3] Aucoin went further by suggesting

* This chapter is a revised version of an article published in *International Review of Administrative Sciences*, Vol. 63, No. 4 (1997), pp. 435–57.

that: "What has been taking place in almost every government in developed political systems and highly institutionalized administrative states is a new emphasis on the organizational designs for public management ... This *internationalization* of public management parallels the internationalization of public and private sector economies"[4] (my emphasis). In a similar vein Yeatman claimed new public management as nothing short of "a cultural revolution."[5] Such lines of discourse in public management sound somewhat akin to Francis Fukuyama's "the end of history" thesis about the inevitability of liberal democracy.[6]

The questions posed in this chapter are: whether the changes observed in the public sector across countries constitute an inevitable convergence of public management principles and practices on a global level; and if so, how should such *global* developments be understood and interpreted. In other words, is there going to be a universalist agenda in public management reforms? A concomitant question is how new is the "new" public management approach which is claimed as representing a paradigmic or cultural transformation of public governance, in terms of its efficiency and post-bureaucratic exhortations.

2. Discovery of a New "Paradigm"

The newly discovered "paradigm" has many names. Both Aucoin and Pollitt described it as "managerialism" which they distinguished from traditional bureaucratic "administration."[7] Hood grouped the set of newly emerging administrative doctrines as "New Public Management" (NPM)[8] which has subsequently become a common terminology in the debate. In the US, Lan and Rosenbloom detected the rise of a new "market-based public administration,"[9] which is of course closely associated with the "entrepreneurial government"[10] advocated by Osborne and Gaebler. Outside the Anglo-American literature, French scholars Belloubet-Frier and Timsit attested to what they depicted as the change from an old administrative apparatus characterized by instrumentality, unity and rationality (the "monocratic administration") to a "transfigured administration" through "market-type mechanisms."[11]

Different commentators and advocates of the new public management approaches have emphasized different aspects of the emerging administrative doctrines and there exists a degree of variation in the way and scope in which these new doctrines are applied by various governments.[12]

Nevertheless, some key components of the new trend can still be identified: (a) a letting managers "free to manage" ethos; (b) setting explicit standards and measures of performance; (c) greater emphasis on output controls; (d) breaking up public sector entities and systems into "corporatized units around products"; (e) greater competition through term contracts and public tendering procedures; (f) adoption of private sector management styles; and (g) greater discipline and parsimony in resource use.[13]

In practice the new paradigm for public management is reported to have fostered a more performance-oriented culture in a less centralized public sector among OECD countries, characterized by:

- a closer focus on results in terms of efficiency, effectiveness and quality of service;
- the replacement of highly centralized, hierarchical organizational structures by decentralized management environments where decisions on resource allocation and service delivery are made closer to the point of delivery, and which provide scope for feedback from clients and other interest groups;
- the flexibility to explore alternatives to direct public provision and regulation that might yield more cost-effective policy outcomes;
- a greater focus on efficiency in the services provided directly by the public sector, involving the establishment of productivity targets and the creation of competitive environments within and among public sector organizations; and
- the strengthening of strategic capacities at the centre to guide the evolution of the state and allow it to respond to external changes and diverse interests automatically, flexibly, and at least cost.[14]

The OECD Public Management Service (PUMA) considers the so-called globalization of public management principles and practices to be part of a broader globalization process, caused economically by "a shift from a world of distinct national economies to a global economy in which production is internationalized and financial capital flows freely and instantly between countries" and driven by the information revolution that has helped overcome national barriers so that "even the framework of social policies affecting individual citizens is becoming more sensitive to international influences, including the global news media."[15] Structural and institutional reforms have therefore become unavoidable. The globalized economic and informational contexts have also facilitated an international exchange of ideas and policy options, so that "governments can draw on experimentation in other countries in the process of defining their own policy responses."[16] However, as the quoted OECD-PUMA report admits, the actual extent to which such policy convergence is occurring has yet to be ascertained — whether the convergence is to the lowest common denominator (i.e. national governments trying to cope with international practice in order to remain competitive) or the highest common denominator (in terms of importing "best practice" from international counterparts).

3. The Degree of International Convergence — No Single Source, No Single Way

Care has to be exercised in interpreting the new public management developments as reported by national governments. Flynn and Strehl, for example, have argued that while OECD-PUMA reports the results of its survey of OECD member countries, it may have favoured the direction in which change is progressing which it identifies as a convergence of views and actions towards a "managerial" approach, to the extent that the survey consists mainly of a search for elements of managerialism, ignoring changes which are outside the "managerial" paradigm. The two authors also suggested that there might be a gap between the official reports and rhetoric and the degree to which reforms are really implemented. Even taking these reasons for scepticism aside, the paths of reform in OECD countries are not necessarily identical upon closer scrutiny.[17]

Despite some common stories on the emergence of new public management measures in some developed countries, some critics have pointed out that not all OECD countries had moved to adopt NPM principles to the same extent during the 1980s, and that marked differences existed even within the same "family groups" of countries.[18] For example, while New Zealand and UK concentrated on "agencification" and "managerializing" their core public services, Germany left the style of its public service largely intact and instead focused its attention on the creation of private-law companies outside the boundary of core government and the readjustment of administrative functions and financial responsibilities between the federal and *Lander* governments. This different emphasis drove Derlien to comment that there was no bureaucrat-bashing or desire to remould the civil service in Germany in the same way as in the UK[19] and that "[o]ther European countries with their specific administrative problems might as well escape international scientific attention unless they somehow relate to the mainstream Anglo-Saxon discussion."[20]

Variations in reforms among OECD countries do not occur only along allegedly mainstream Anglo-Saxon and non-mainstream lines. The Swedish-style state, for example, is a typical embodiment of the new "holding state" characteristic of the NPM approach to governance.[21] March and Olsen described how the Nordic countries had early on in their post-War administrative reforms moved away from the centralist, corporatist welfare state, to emphasize consumer sovereignty and market competition.[22] There does not therefore appear to be a clearly mainstream source of NPM initiatives which were then spread to other non-mainstream countries. Thus Halligan questioned the US parentage of the new reforms: "There are even indicators of 'reinventing' history in order to identify the US initiative of [reinventing government] with international change. When we are informed that governments everywhere are reinventing, it suggests acceptance of the US concept, and by implication that what has already occurred elsewhere is in fact concurrent with the US which only recently arrived on the scene."[23] Cross-fertilization there may be in administrative practice, but the urge for change and the form of change have emerged from more pluralistic contexts and considerations which are shaped by national political and bureaucratic factors and other needs of governance.

3.1 Variations in Locus and Focus of Reforms

A glimpse from the brief profiles of OECD countries in their recent reforms and trends at the beginning of the 1990s (see Annex 2.1), developed from information derived from the official OECD survey,[24] shows a rich diversity in emphases as well as in the main approaches to reform their public sectors.[25]

No uniform reform pattern can be established from the broad comparisons in Annex 2.1, except that the following are the most commonly-pursued measures in OECD countries: *financial and management reforms, devolution, delegation and deconcentration within core government.* The four Anglo-Saxon countries (UK, Australia, New Zealand and Canada) and Ireland (historically and geographically close to the UK) had all made important efforts in reforming their civil service, including opening up the senior structure, pay reform and contractual management, with New Zealand being probably the "forerunner" by introducing chief executives with limited tenure and (also in the case of UK) business-like executive agencies. Australia, New Zealand and the UK had all gone for *commercialization* measures, but only New Zealand was prominent in the *corporatization* of state-owned enterprises, a characteristic shared by Finland and Germany (the latter particularly in its efforts to turn former East German state enterprises into public-law corporations). The Nordic countries (Sweden, Norway and Denmark) had not featured in civil service restructuring in the OECD reports, not because they had clung to the classical bureaucratic types, but because the ministry-agency form of government had long been part of their system since the post-War period.

Unlike the UK, which was also active in *privatization*, Germany, France and even Australia or New Zealand did not treat privatization as an important element of their current public sector reform programme. Both France and New Zealand opted for granting more autonomy to state-owned enterprises through means such as performance contracts. *Decentralization* to lower-level bodies such as regions and communities was a prominent feature of reform among countries like Belgium, France, Germany, the Netherlands, Spain, Canada, Denmark and Turkey, some of which were facing more serious centre-locality power distribution problems (as in France and Germany). However, such territorial decentralization was virtually absent from either the UK (a unitary state) or the US and Australia (both federalist). *Deregulation* of private sector activities was only sparingly adopted, principally in the US, and also Portugal and the Netherlands. The UK on the other hand has recently moved into "re-regulation" of the utilities following their privatization.[26]

Such comparison can continue into greater depth, but the point in the present discussion is that there is no "one best practice" to public sector reform as implied by some literature. The variations in approach to reform are understandable if diversities in historical, institutional and policy endowments, as well as differences in national politics and economies are recognized. Japan was easily the least enthusiastic reformer among OECD nations in the early 1990s, with reform targeted mainly at *efficiency measures* (control over the size of the government workforce and reorganizing and abolishing some government bureaux) and the *privatization* of three major public corporations (railways, telephones, and the tobacco and salt industries),[27] though administrative reform was given considerable political publicity during the 1980s.[28] This "exception" was probably partly because of its more consensual style of national politics which made drastic and rapid changes more difficult to get through the political process.

The diversity in reform emphasis is further corroborated by a comparative survey of new public sector management initiatives adopted by OECD countries during 1994.[29] While the rough ratings provided by national correspondents of OECD do not permit simplistic comparison of those initiatives, it would be fair to say that different countries have rated the relative salience of reform initiatives differently (from "major initiative" to "no significant steps taken") within their national context (see adapted profiles in Annex 2.2a and 2.2b).

3.2 Variations in Logic, Style and Motives of Reform

In terms of logic and style of the reform process, the Nordic countries have differed from the UK and US. In the latter, public sector reform was seen very much as extending the logic of privatization which had broadly gained acceptance within the political community in the 1980s, particularly during the New Right governments of Thatcher and Reagan. In the Nordic countries, according to March and Olsen, "privatization" provoked strong negative reactions even when the term was used to refer to ordinary processes of adjustment between the public and private sectors. Hence in contrast to the stronger political and ideological rhetoric used by the British and US governments, Nordic reforms were couched substantially in an apolitical language, namely "modernization."[30]

In the UK administrative reform took place mostly as a top-down process directed by the centre ("a policy tool for the prime minister," in the words of March and Olsen[31]), whereas US administrative reform was enmeshed in the political competition between the Congress and the Presidency. Though both the British and US experiences during the 1980s were one in which reform was actively defined as a political project, the structure and traditions of US politics "drove the issue from the mainstream political agenda."[32]

Comparing the Next Steps reforms in the UK with public service reforms in Canada and New Zealand, Greer discovered some important differences in the approaches and substance of these national reform programmes. Unlike the UK, the Canadian emphasis was more on creating a unified public service and was more about restricting appointments from "outside" than encouraging greater movement. Canada had not gone so far down the Next Steps route of "management by contract" though, similar to the UK, there had been moves to strengthen existing reporting and accountability frameworks.[33] The New Zealand reforms were similar to Next Steps in principle but were considered faster and more radical. In contrast to the British reform experience which was politicians-led, the main advocates of the New Zealand reform were the Treasury officials who drew up the main policy proposals which were subsequently given force by special legislation. Whereas the UK and New Zealand both went down the path of structural change, Canada attempted only to reform existing structures.[34]

3.3 Divergences within Universality

In summarizing the latest situation, OECD, while of the view that member countries' reform strategies have many points in common, has to admit that "there is no single model of reform, there are no off-the-shelf solutions."[35] Differences among countries are seen in emphasis and take-up of particular reform initiatives. There are even several important divergences in reform objectives, with some countries setting a reduction in the size of the public sector as a specific objective while others opting for more stress on improving its performance and strengthening its role.[36]

Exploring the national variations in public management reforms during the 1980s, Hood came to the conclusion that some generalized explanations of NPM could not stand.[37] Rather contrary to conventional belief, the degree of emphasis laid on NPM did not seem to be always related vigorously to fiscal stress and government overload, to New Right political ascendency, or to the degree of economic internationalization. For example, public sector reform in Hong Kong, where there is a relatively small public sector and where the civil service enjoys high esteem and has not suffered particular economic or fiscal crises, stands out as a significant "exception" to the familiar NPM story attributed to economic and social crises.[38] Based on variations in "motive" and "opportunity" for change, Hood has identified four distinct NPM-reform types within OECD countries: namely the "Japanese way" (low in motive though high in opportunity); the "German way" (high in motive but low in opportunity); the "American way" (low in both motive and opportunity); and the "Swedish way" (high in both motive and opportunity).[39]

Following Hood,[40] it can be suggested that if policy outcomes are a result of *external* pressures (like new ideas, interests and changes in social habitat) as well as *internal* institutional dynamics, then national variations in such factors would have led to rather different reform styles and strategies to cope with the specific pressures or problems encountered by the reformers. Different combinations of various internal and external factors would yield diverse configurations of public sector reforms.

4. International Trends, Different Domestic Circumstances

Public sector reforms could have covered some similar policy and instrumental tools being adopted in different political circumstances for vastly different reasons and with different impacts. Such a possibility is not without precedent in administrative history.

Mueller's study of the civil service examination system in England and Prussia during the 19th century found that whereas the Prussian system aimed at bringing the emerging middle class into the administrative elite, in England the opposite was the case, which was to keep the public bureaucracy intact as an exclusive territory for the upper landed gentry class that continued to dominate Oxbridge.[41] Contemporary examples are also found with privatization policies. Vickers and Wright, in reviewing industrial privatization programmes in several Western European countries, identified a rather diversified picture of: motives and ambitions of the privatizers, different starting points from which privatization proceeded, political and institutional structures in which the privatizers operated, and different financial regimes through which the transfer of ownership to private investors was implemented.[42] Liou also observed that Taiwan, experiencing strong and sustained economic growth for the past several decades and facing none of the major economic problems or pressures which propelled Western countries onto the road of privatization, had nonetheless pursued an active policy of privatizing state-owned enterprises only in the early 1990s partly as a result of political democratization and partly because of taking up economic "liberalization and internationalization" policy goals.[43] Similarly this author's study of public sector reform in Hong Kong has found that the reform was induced more by an attempt to "re-manage" the changing political realities of both the external and internal environments in order to restore legitimacy for the public service institutions, than by an economic paradigm of efficiency.[44]

Sometimes opposing means may be contemplated for apparently the same objective. For example, as Holmes discovered, "many middle-income countries see standardization in the wage and salary area ... as a prerequisite to improving performance [while in] most developed countries the argument is that deregulation in the wage and salary area is a prerequisite to improvements in public performance!"[45] China is a good case in point. Recent civil service reform, despite the obstacles imposed by the ideological rhetoric of maintaining a system with Chinese socialist characteristics, aims to improve efficiency and effectiveness of government administration through building up a legal-rational Weberian-type bureaucracy,[46] a system which ironically is already being discredited and challenged by NPM-type reforms of the West within a post-bureaucratic perspective.[47]

Whereas the fundamental impetus for public sector reform in developed nations (such as OECD countries) was the need to achieve governance within a contracting economy — i.e. the management of decline — the reason for reform in newly industrialized countries like Taiwan and Korea or fast-growing developing countries such as China and Malaysia may be of an entirely different order. In the latter cases the problems of governance are essentially those of managing state building and economic growth, albeit growth which demands closer coordination and cooperation between the public and private sectors. In the transitional economies of Central and Eastern Europe the administrative reforms were "primarily defined in terms of a process of getting away from the previous situation instead of arriving at a desired state of affairs."[48] While Western efforts to "privatize" were usually intended to increase the efficiency of the economy, privatization efforts in Central and Eastern Europe were largely aimed at constructing a market system which was absent in the first place.

Paraphrasing Wallace Sayre, public sector reforms among governments can be said to be "fundamentally alike in all unimportant aspects."[49] There is not sufficient evidence to support an *international administrative convergence thesis*. Rather, it would be more meaningful to explore how different governments and their bureaucracies face the challenge of political management in their respective changing socio-political circumstances and proceed with public sector reform amidst an increasingly world-wide urge to try new methods and organizational designs, rather than to lump all such national efforts into a tidy-looking global paradigm which may point only to superficial similarities and hide more salient diversities. The OECD reform agenda seems to have contrasted significantly with the administrative reform experience of non-OECD countries. Even among OECD countries, there is considerable variation in reform focus and approach as discussed above.

5. New Public Management: Revolution or Reinvention

Public sector reform under NPM is very often credited with a fundamental value change. Cost effectiveness, efficiency and value for money represent the core values against which the forms of public service provision are increasingly measured. Such values also underline the attempt to debureaucratize the civil service through decentralization and marketization, and ultimately to transform the culture of the civil servants which would entail new regimes of motivation, incentives, work conditions, rewards and sanctions. The core values can finally be summed up by the efficiency value which Hood described as *sigma*-type value.[50] Indeed, both the promoters and doubters of reform have shared one common ground — they both advance their arguments within an efficiency discourse, with the former advocating reform as the only means to achieve greater efficiency and the latter expressing worries that the reform would emphasize efficiency at the expense of other values (such as equity) and considerations. Neither side has disputed the presumption that public sector reform is about efficiency and can bring about efficiency. The new reform is further seen as a negation of the traditional model of public administration characterized by the twin-principles of politics-administration dichotomy and bureaucratic organization[51], or what Moe described as the administrative management paradigm in the US constitutional context,[52] to the extent that it denotes the advent of a "post-bureaucratic" paradigm.[53]

5.1 A Paradigm of Efficiency?

As this author argues at length elsewhere, the traditional civil service bureaucratic regime which NPM-type public sector reform aims to get away from is not one short of "efficiency." On the contrary the Weberian bureaucratic model assumes the paramount importance of efficiency and rationality.[54] Weber argued in the beginning of this century that the purely bureaucratic type of administrative organization was "capable of *attaining the highest degree of efficiency* and is in this sense formally the most rational known means of exercising authority over human beings" (my emphasis).[55] Historically, the traditional model of public administration was a result of the amalgamation of several institutional elements which came from different contexts and at different times, not necessarily out of the same institutional logic. The European concern for public administration had grown out of principles inherited from the imperial, monocratic past and focused very much on the perfection of the governing class. The civil services of Napoleon's France and Frederick the Great's Prussia were modelled on military organization and followed the same principles of centralization, discipline and the solidarity of an "officer class."[56] These classic features of the European bureaucracies were subsequently rationalized by Weber.

The American quest for administrative improvement started from a different reality in which rivalry and conflict resulting from the spoils system of political patronage were seen to have crippled public administration. The then new "Progressive" public administration was concerned about eliminating corruption, waste and incompetence associated with the spoils system. The Wilsonian call for separation of administration and politics in the 1880s[57] represented an attempt to depoliticize public administration through professionalization and vocationalization. Thus it can be seen that efficiency in public administration at the turn of the century was defined, both organizationally and politically, within the context of the specific problems of governance that were confronted at that time.

By the 1980s, the context of public administration had changed. "Big Government" was being scorned upon, fuelled by the intellectual challenge from the public-choice school of economics which characterized bureaucratic behaviour as essentially budget-maximizing and inefficient.[58] As Frederickson remarked, "[t]hroughout the reinventing government literature is the argument that the 'bureaucratic paradigm' is the problem" and "the antibureaucratic thesis of reinventing government certainly fits the mood of contemporary times."[59] The traditional model of bureaucratic rationality and efficiency was no longer sustainable in both the political and intellectual arenas.

There is therefore nothing *new* about the overriding concern for "efficiency" in new public management. Indeed, what had transpired throughout the decades were ever-changing views and theories about the causes and sources of inefficiency in government, what efficiency meant and how it was to be achieved. If so, the claimed paradigm shift in the values of public administration was less *fundamental* than assumed in the "new paradigm" literature surrounding the NPM phenomenon. As a set of doctrines prescribed for good administration (or management), NPM and previous movements of administrative thought (such as the Northcote-Trevelyan proposals of the 1850s in Britain, the Progressive movement in the US in the late 19th century, and the scientific management movement of the 1930s) all appeal to a broadly similar range of core values. Hood and Jackson even found that NPM had much in common with Late Cameralism which had once prospered in 18th-century Europe.[60] So nothing is particularly new in the world of administrative philosophy; administrative thoughts, like fashion, are very often products of a recycling of ideas. What are *new* in contemporary public sector reform may not be its central themes of efficiency and managerial competence, but rather the "new" political and ideological contexts in which such themes are to be re-articulated (or "reinvented") and given acceptance on the reform agenda.

5.2 An Anti-bureaucratic Paradigm?

The public-choice underpinning of new public management gives the impression that public sector reform is anti-producerist and anti-bureaucratic.[61] As Lynn put it, it is the suspicion of bureaucratic power and the aggrandizing tendencies of bureaucratic elites which began to intensify in the 1980s, producing the changes documented by the discoveries of "new paradigms."[62] Despite the apparent anti-bureaucratic origin of public sector reforms, there is no logical conclusion that these reforms will produce a global post-bureaucratic paradigm. Hood argued, for example, that the future of public management will be more "plural" than what Osborne and Gaebler had anticipated because of two reasons. First, there is a diversity of agendas which lie behind the apparently consensual criticism of the earlier progressive public administration. Second, there are various intermediate possibilities between "state" and "market" solutions within public management reforms so that transforming the Public Bureaucracy State does not lead simply to a Minimum Purchasing State.[63]

There is no question that NPM rides on similar prescriptive private-business doctrines as privatization in challenging the performance of the public bureaucratic state, or what the Australians would call the wave of economic rationalism.[64] However, upon closer examination, NPM as a reform strategy can be viewed as rather more pro-public sector than it was commonly believed to be because it seeks to reform the bureaucracy instead of dispensing with bureaucracy altogether (as in outright privatization).

Reviewing the state of public administration in the US, Kettl has identified two kinds of attack on bureaucracies.[65] From the right, advocates of privatization were pushing for the replacement of governmental power with market competition through privatization.[66] From the left, people like Osborne and Gaebler called for beefing up government by making it more entrepreneurial. There is a clear distinction between the privatizationist agenda and the reinventionist agenda of reform. NPM falls into the latter, and can be argued to be a strategy to "save" the government and to repackage it through reinvention — a kind of managerial solution to deal with a political question. Such a strategy would understandably be more acceptable to both political leaders and bureaucrats inside the government. And as public service workers and recipients are becoming more worried about the negative impact of outright privatization on their interest and welfare, an NPM-oriented reform would present a more palatable alternative. Public sector reform can be used to withstand further attacks from the privatizers who cannot now challenge reforms which are carried out in the name of a look-alike logic as that of privatization.

Instead of breaking up the power of the public bureaucracy as some NPM rhetoric seems to suggest, NPM in action is capable of helping preserve the bureaucracy though in different wrappings. The fundamental shift in debureaucratization may turn out to be more cosmetic than real.

5.3 Politics of Empowerment

To appreciate public sector reform as a defensive strategy requires an understanding of the politics of reforms. In this case, politics occur among three main groups of actors — the political executives, central agency mandarins and line department managers. The political executives try to exert political management on the bureaucracy, the central agencies try to exert political management on line departments, and the line departments try to assert autonomy in operational and resource management in face of central control. The new public management paradigm concurrently offers each of them a plausible empowerment agenda.

As Campbell and Halligan observed in Australian reforms, "[m]anagerialism offered both a new approach for directing the public service and a rationalization of exerting greater ministerial control." It provided the political executive (namely the ministers and politicians) with a more comprehensive and strategic approach to achieve more effective control over bureaucratic performance, quite contrary to the rhetoric of managerial freedom[67] — a paradox also noted by Aucoin who remarked that the managerialist paradigm saw the bureaucracy as both the cause of the problem and the solution to it![68]

Peters and Savoie have similar observations. Examining recent Anglo-American civil service reforms, they argued that the 1980s constituted a "hostile environment" to the civil service bureaucracy. However, pushing civil servants towards managerialism has not meant the dilution of political control. While civil servants were placed in a position of increased accountability down to the clients and to the market, they were also required to increase accountability up to politicians. Because of the primary concern for political control, Peters and Savoie found that "the fear of strengthening the policy role of officials prevented the political leadership of [the US and Canada] from reforming the policy formulation, coordination, and evaluation machinery in government." [69] In the UK, Pollitt argued that the Conservative Government turned to managerialism in part to implement a political agenda — using private-sector disciplines to strengthen political control, reduce professional autonomy and weaken public service unions.[70] Using administrative and management reforms as a means towards a political end has abundant examples in administrative history, for example, the Fulton reform (1968) and the CPRS (Central Policy Review Staff) initiative (early 1970s) in the UK. These reforms were abandoned when the political atmosphere changed after the ascendency of a new government espousing a different set of political agenda and strategy.

The other dimension of political management is the adjustment of relationship between central agencies and line departments, involving new capacities of central control while managerial responsibilities are claimed to have been devolved to line departments.[71] The impact of Hong Kong's public sector reform during the 1990s on "re-ordering" institutional relationships between policy branch mandarins and executive department bureaucrats, and between administrators and professionals within the civil service, serves to illustrate this point.[72] Inasmuch as central policy branches attempted to impose effective policy control, departments as an agency sought to enhance their operating autonomy, and emerging professional power in some departments also demanded a better power-sharing regime with the administrative officers who used to dominate the government centre. Two sets of bureau-shaping strategies[73] were in action, and public sector reform provided the ground for the two sides to interact and reach a more settled basis of institutional relationships. Policy branches had their policy and resource-control functions fully recognized, in exchange for granting managerial autonomy and micro-budgetary powers to departmental managers.

There have of course been multiple motives and rationales for reform in Hong Kong, with cost-cutting concerns becoming more prominent most lately following the impact of the 1997 Asian financial crisis. Civil service failure in a sense was played up because of the public dismay with the government's performance in managing major crises and the economy. Sleaze cases reported also served to trigger the larger tide against the civil service as a whole, fuelled by media criticisms and attacks by politicians. On the surface, the post-1997 crisis of the civil service is simultaneously one of efficiency, efficacy and probity among civil servants. Both the global NPM trend and the domestic political and economic fluctuations have served to focus public attention increasingly on how costly it is for the civil service to deliver public services. This opened a political window for the government to put forward drastic proposals on civil service reform.[74] Given the objective to deal with political problems faced by the new Special Administrative Region government after the 1997 handover of sovereignty, civil service reform can also be understood as part of a political agenda pursued by the bureaucratic elite to strengthen its crisis-weathering capacity. Such a perception is to some extent corroborated by accusations in some quarters, particularly the staff unions, that the current civil service reform is an exercise targeted at the bottom rather than the top. There is strong rank-and-file suspicion that the administrative mandarinate is sacrificing their subordinates in order to contain the damage of its political crisis.

If institutions are perceived as "locales of politics" where contestation, negotiation and struggle between different groups and rationalities occur as a matter of routine,[75] then the process of organizational change serves to sharpen the focus as well as intensity of such "political" struggles. Organizational change is brought about by conflict as well as itself bringing about a negotiated order to conflict. An existing institutional arrangement represents a settled order and pattern of interest/value distribution among different stakeholders. It is therefore a fact of organizational life to expect divergence and conflicts to evolve around new issues of contention generated by any reform process — ranging from issues of power, autonomy, culture to job conditions, security and survival.

The public choice or budget-maximization models of bureaucracy are based on a causal link between bureaucratic behaviour and government expansion, and are therefore unable to explain dynamically the mega-trends of privatization and public sector reform which had met with such low-level resistance from senior public service bureaucrats.[76] An alternative bureau-shaping model suggested by Dunleavy seeks to advance a more robust interpretation of privatization by arguing how senior bureaucrats' interest could be safeguarded or even enhanced in the change process, displacing whatever cost there was onto rank-and-file workers, clients and the wider community.[77] A bureau-shaping explanation applied to NPM can suggest that senior bureaucrats now acting as "managers" would see public sector reform as providing a new horizon for the expansion of *managerial power*. Those managerialist means imposed by political leaders to monitor and exact performance and results from bureaucrats can be manipulated to the advantage of the mangers, so that instead of being an instrument for more effective control over bureaucratic performance, NPM can equally become a useful platform for asserting the bureaucrats' managerial autonomy and values within the segments of the fragmentized public sector.

In this perspective, public sector reform can be seen to be an interactive process involving various institutional (and bureaucratic) actors each of whom is active, inventive, assertive and goal-seeking, trying to find an appropriate strategy to enhance its self-interest in the midst of ambiguities and contingencies within choice-laden contexts. The new consumer focus in NPM[78] can serve to justify the view that the new public managers who consider themselves analogous to their private sector counterparts are more capable of getting closer to their "customers" than traditional politicians whose job had been to represent and articulate the needs of the pre-customerized public. This *consumerist paradigm* in public sector reform is easily susceptible to manipulation by the public managers and would be used by them to strengthen and legitimate their institutional power *versus* that of politicians, producers and consumers. Given that managers define managerially consumer needs, help politicians set performance expectations and evaluative criteria, and negotiate with producers to determine a set of "acceptable" performance standards, the new paradigm is as capable of *empowering* the managers as empowering the citizens, if not more so.[79]

6. Conclusion

This chapter questions the "globalist" interpretation of contemporary public sector reforms. While there may appear to be some kind of convergence in terms of reform rhetoric and the generalized ends of reform (which is to put in place a framework of structures and programmes that can enable governments to achieve better performance and more effective governance within changing socio-economic circumstances), the means employed to pursue the ends are of considerable variety in both locus and focus depending on the history, politics and institutional features of the countries involved. The national motives and styles of reform also vary.

Despite the anti-bureaucratic or post-bureaucratic claim of public sector reform, the outcome of the reform process is less certain as it entails institutional negotiation in which public bureaucratic or professional power tries to reconstitute itself and its autonomy and domination within newly fashionable "managerial" culture and context. What has actually changed in terms of values and power relationships under public sector reform should thus be re-examined. The much-celebrated efficiency value of public sector reform is only new in terms of its new rhetorical articulation. There is no automatic assumption that marketization, consumerization and decentralization will necessarily bring about the demise of the bureaucracy and the ascendency of the citizens as consumers or customers of public services. Public sector reform may have in effect achieved to empower public managers more than the consumers.

Notes

1. H. G. Frederickson, "Comparing the Reinventing Government Movement with the New Public Administration," *Public Administration Review*, Vol. 56, No. 3 (1996), pp. 263–70.
2. A. Gore, *From Red Tape to Results: Creating a Government That Works Better and Costs Less — Report of the National Performance Review* (New York: Plume, 1993); D. Osborne and T. Gaebler, *Reinventing Government: How the Entrepreneurial Spirit Is Transforming the Public Sector* (New York: Penguin, 1992; London: Plume, 1993), p. 331.
3. L. Metcalfe and S. Richards, *Improving Public Management*, 2nd ed. (London: Sage Publications Ltd., 1990), p. 156
4. P. Aucoin, "Administrative Reform in Public Management: Paradigms, Principles, Paradoxes and Pendulums," *Governance*, Vol. 3, No. 2 (1990), pp. 115–37.
5. A. Yeatman, *Bureaucrats, Technocrats, Femocrats: Essays on the Contemporary Australian State* (Sydney: Allen & Unwin, 1990), p. 13.
6. F. Fukuyama, *The End of History and the Last Man* (London: Hamish Hamilton, 1992).

7. P. Aucoin, "Contraction, Managerialism and Decentralization in Canadian Government," *Governance*, Vol. 1, No. 2 (1988), pp. 144–61; C. Pollitt, *Managerialism and the Public Services: Cuts or Cultural Change in the 1990s?* 2nd ed. (Oxford: Blackwell, 1993).

8. C. Hood, "Beyond the Public Bureaucracy State? Public Administration in the l990s," inaugural lecture (London School of Economics, 16 January 1990); C. Hood, "De-Sir-Humphrey-fying the Westminster Model of Governance," *Governance*, Vol. 3, No. 2 (April 1990), pp. 205–14.

9. Z. Y. Lan and D. H. Rosenbloom, "Public Administration in Transition?" (Editorial), *Public Administration Review*, Vol. 52, No. 6 (November/December 1992), pp. 535–37.

10. Osborne and Gaebler (Note 2).

11. N. Belloubet-Frier and G. Timsit, "Administration Transfigured: A New Administrative Paradigm?" *International Review of Administrative Sciences*, Vol. 59, No. 4 (December 1993), pp. 531–68.

12. C. Hood, "A Public Management for All Seasons?" *Public Administration*, Vol. 69, No. 1 (Spring 1991), pp. 3–19.

13. Ibid.

14. OECD, *Governance in Transition: Public Management Reforms in OECD Countries* (Paris: OECD, 1995), p. 8.

15. OECD, "Globalization: What Challenges and Opportunities for Governments?" (Paris: Public Management Service, OECD, July 1996).

16. Ibid.

17. N. Flynn and F. Strehl (eds), *Public Sector Management in Europe* (London: Prentice Hall & Harvester Wheatsheaf, 1996), p. 5.

18. F. G. Castles, "The Dynamics of Policy Change: What Happened to the English-speaking Nations in the 1980s?" *European Journal of Political Research*, Vol. 18 (1990), pp. 491–513; Hood, "De-Sir-Humphrey-fying …," (Note 8).

19. H. U. Derlien "Historical Legacy and Recent Developments of the German Higher Civil Service," *International Review of Administrative Sciences*, Vol. 57, No. 3 (September 1991), pp. 385–401.

20. H. U. Derlien, "Administration Research in Europe — Rather Comparable Than Comparative," *Governance*, Vol. 5, No. 3 (July 1992), pp. 279–311.

21. See Note 11.

22. J. G. March and J. P. Olsen, *Rediscovering Institutions: The Organizational Basis of Politics* (New York: Free Press, 1989), pp. 99–101.

23. J. Halligan, "The Art of Reinvention: The United States National Performance Review," *Australian Journal of Public Administration*, Vol. 53, No. 2 (June 1994), pp. 135–43.

24. OECD, *Public Management: OECD Country Profiles* (Paris: Public Management Service [PUMA], OECD, 1993).

25. The profiles produced in Annex 2.1 are meant to be indicative rather than defini-tive in nature because the country reports from which the information is generated are prepared by different national authorities which may have "observer bias" in the reporting process and may also have engaged in descriptions and interpreted reform measures in ways not entirely coherent in semantic usage or evaluative standards. There is also the potential problem of generalization when different national reform measures are categorized and grouped under major "focus" head-ings by this author in producing the Annex. However, while precise comparison of national performance on the basis of these profiles can be problematic, they can still provide a reasonably useful basis of broad understanding about national reform trends.

26. C. Price, "Economic Regulation of Privatized Monopolies," in *Privatization and Regulation: A Review of the Issues*, edited by P. M. Jackson and C. M. Price (London: Longman, 1994), ch. 3.

27. OECD (Note 24), p. 175.

28. A Provisional Council for Promotion of Administrative Reform was set up under the Cabinet in 1987 to oversee administrative reforms.

29. OECD, *Public Management Developments Update 1995* (Paris: Public Manage-ment Service [PUMA], OECD, 1995), Tables 1.A and 1.B.

30. March and Olsen (Note 22), pp. 102–3.

31. Ibid., p. 105

32. Ibid.

33. P. Greer, *Transforming Central Government: The Next Steps Initiative* (Buckingham: Open University Press, 1994), ch. 8.

34. Ibid., p. 114.

35. OECD (Note 14), p. 25.

36. Ibid.

37. C. Hood, "Exploring Variations in 1980s Public Management Reform," in *Civil Service Systems in Comparative Perspective*, edited by H. Bekke, J. L. Perry and T.A.J. Toonen (Bloomington: Indiana University Press, 1996).

38. A.B.L. Cheung, "Efficiency as the Rhetoric: Public-sector Reform in Hong Kong Explained," *International Review of Administrative Sciences,* Vol. 62, No. 1 (March 1996), pp. 31–47.

39. Hood (Note 37).

40. C. Hood, *Explaining Economic Policy Reversals* (Buckingham: Open University Press, 1994), ch. 1.

41. H. E. Mueller, *Bureaucracy, Education and Monopoly: Civil Service Reforms in England and Prussia* (Berkeley: University of California Press, 1984).

42. J. Vickers and V. Wright, "The Politics of Industrial Privatization in Western Europe: An Overview," *West European Politics*, Vol. 11, No 4 (1988), pp. 1–30.

43. K. T. Liou, "Privatizing State-owned Enterprises: The Taiwan Experience,"

International Review of Administrative Sciences, Vol. 58, No. 3 (September 1992), pp. 403–19.

44. A.B.L. Cheung, "The Politics of Administrative Reforms in Hong Kong: Corporatization of Public Services during the 1980s," unpublished PhD Thesis, London School of Economics (1995); Cheung (Note 38).

45. M. Holmes, "Public Sector Management Reform: Convergence or Divergence?" *Governance*, Vol. 5, No. 4 (October 1992), pp. 472–83.

46. L. S. Dong, "The Establishment of the Chinese Civil Service System: A Delayed Political Reform Programme," in International Institute for Asian Studies, *Administrative Reform in the People's Republic of China Since 1978*, Working Papers Series 1 (The Netherlands: Leiden, 1994), pp. 43–61; A.B.L. Cheung, "Civil Service Reform in Shenzhen: Expectations and Problems," in *Economic and Social Development in the Pearl River Delta*, edited by S. MacPherson and J.Y.S. Cheng (Aldershot: Edward Elgar, 1996), pp. 76–106.

47. O. E. Hughes, *Public Management and Administration: An Introduction* (London: St Martin's Press, 1994); M. Barzelay, *Breaking Through Bureaucracy: A New Vision for Managing in Government* (Berkeley & Los Angeles: University of California Press, 1992).

48. T.A.J. Toonen, "Analysing Institutional Change and Administrative Transformation: A Comparative View," *Public Administration*, Vol. 71 (Spring/Summer 1993), pp. 151–68.

49. Quoted in G. T. Allison, Jr., "Public and Private Management: Are They Fundamentally Alike in All Unimportant Respects?" in *Current Issues in Public Administration*, edited by F. S. Lane, 3rd ed. (New York: St Martin's Press, 1986), pp. 184–200.

50. Hood (Note 12).

51. Hughes (Note 47), chs. 2–3.

52. R. C. Moe, "The 'Reinventing Government' Exercise: Misinterpreting the Problem, Misjudging the Consequences," *Public Administration Review*, Vol. 54, No. 2 (March/April 1994), pp. 111–22.

53. Barzelay (Note 47), ch. 8.

54. Cheung (Note 38).

55. M. Weber, *Economy and Society*, Vols. I–II (Berkeley: University of California Press, 1978), p. 223.

56. A. Dunsire, *Administration: The Word and the Science* (London: Martin Robertson, 1973), p. 78.

57. W. Wilson, "The Study of Administration," reprinted in *Political Science Quarterly* 56 (December 1887/1941), pp. 481–506.

58. P. Dunleavy, *Democracy, Bureaucracy and Public Choice — Economic Explanations in Political Science* (Harvester: Wheatsheaf, 1991), ch. 6.

59. Frederickson (Note 1).

60. C. Hood and M. Jackson, *Administrative Argument* (Aldershot: Dartmouth, 1991), ch. 8.

61. P. Self, *Government By the Market? The Politics of Public Choice* (London: Macmillan, 1993).

62. L. E. Lynn, Jr., "The New Public Management as an International Phenomenon: A Skeptical View," paper presented at the Conference on The New Public Management in International Perspective, St Gallen, Switzerland, 11–13 July 1996.

63. C. Hood, "Beyond 'Progressivism': A New 'Global Paradigm' in Public Management?" *International Journal of Public Administration*, Vol. 19, No. 2 (February 1996), p. 172.

64. A. Yeatman, "The Reform of Public Management: An Overview," *Australian Journal of Public Administration*, Vol. 53, No. 3 (September 1994), pp. 287–95.

65. D. F. Kettl, "Public Administration: The State of the Field," in *Political Science: The State of the Discipline*, edited by A. W. Finifter (Washington, DC: American Political Science Association, 1993), pp. 407–28.

66. E. S. Savas, *Privatization: The Key to Better Government* (NJ: Chatham House, 1987); S. H. Hanke, "The Theory of Privatization," in *The Privatization Option: A Strategy to Shrink the Size of Government*, edited by S. M. Butler (Washington, DC: The Heritage Foundation, 1985).

67. C. Campbell and J. Halligan, *Political Leadership in an Age of Constraint: Bureaucratic Politics Under Hawke and Keating* (Sydney: Allen & Unwin, 1992), p. 41.

68. Aucoin (Note 4), p. 126.

69. B. G. Peters and D. J. Savoie, "Civil Service Reform: Misdiagnosing the Patient," *Public Administration Review*, Vol. 54, No. 5 (September/October 1994), pp. 418–25.

70. Pollitt (Note 7), p. 49.

71. Campbell and Halligan (Note 67), ch. 2.

72. Cheung (Note 38).

73. Dunleavy (Note 58).

74. Civil Service Bureau (Hong Kong Special Administrative Region Government), *Civil Service into the 21st Century: Civil Service Reform Consultation Document* (March 1999).

75. S. W. Clegg, "Radical Revisions: Power, Discipline and Organizations," *Organizational Studies*, Vol. 10, No. 1 (1989), pp. 97–115.

76. P. Dunleavy, "Explaining the Privatization Boom: Public Choice versus Radical Approaches," *Public Administration*, Vol. 64, No. 1 (Spring 1986), pp. 13–34.

77. Dunleavy (Note 58), ch. 7.

78. See S. Richards, "Changing Patterns of Legitimation in Public Management," *Public Policy and Administration*, Vol. 7, No. 3 (Winter 1992), pp. 15–28.

79. Refer to detailed discussion by this author in Cheung (Note 38).

Annex 2.1 Focus and Locus of Public Sector Reforms in OECD Countries, 1993

	Within core government						Beyond core government					Remarks
	Efficiency measures (1)	Financial & management reform and devolution (2)	Decentralization within government (to lower level bodies)	Reforming and restructuring civil service (3)	New management methods & culture	User participation	Commercialization and market mechanisms (4)	More autonomy for SOEs (5)	Corporatization	Privatization of SOEs	De-regulation of private business	
Australia												
Austria												
Belgium												
Canada												
Denmark												
Finland									*			* Public enterprise model
France						*						* Public services charter
Germany									*			* Public law corporations
Greece												
Ireland				*								* Open up top posts, performance pay
Italy												
Japan												
Netherlands												
New Zealand				*								* Chief executives on term contract
Norway												
Portugal				*								* Human resource management reform
Spain												
Sweden												
Switzerland												
Turkey												
United Kingdom				*		#						* "Next Steps" agencies # Citizen's Charter
United States of America				*								* Pay reform

Source: OECD, *Public Managemen.: OECD Country Profiles*, Paris: Public Management Service (PUMA), OECD, 1993, information rearranged.

Notes: (1) Including costs reductior schemes, downsizing of government organization and cutbacks

(2) Including administrative deconcentration, delegation of authorities and results-oriented reforms

(3) Including contractual management and business-like executive agencies

(4) Including contracting out and user charging

(5) Including use of performance contracts

SOE = State-owned enterprises

▓ = Reform emphasis

Annex 2.2a New Public Sector Management Initiatives: OECD Countries, 1994 Size and Structure of the Public Sector

	Limits to the size of the public sector	Privatization	Commercialization/ corporatization of public bodies	Decentralization to sub-national government	Deconcentration within central government	Use of market-type mechanisms	New roles for central management bodies	Other restructuring/ Nationalization
Australia								
Austria								
Belgium								
Canada								
Denmark								
Finland								
France								
Germany								
Greece								
Iceland								
Ireland								
Italy								
Japan								
Luxembourg								
Mexico								
Netherlands								
New Zealand								
Norway								
Portugal								
Spain								
Sweden								
Switzerland								
Turkey								
United Kingdom								
United States								

□ = No significant steps taken
▨ = Less important measure
▩ = Major initiative

Source: OECD, *Public Management Developments Update 1993*. Paris: Public Management Service (PUMA), OECD, 1995.

Annex 2.2b New Public Sector Management Initiatives: OECD Countries, 1994
Other Main Fields of Public Management Reform

	Management of policy-making	Performance management	Financial resources management	Personnel management	Regulatory management and reform	Improving relations with citizens/enterprises	Management of information technology	Other
Australia								
Austria								
Belgium								
Canada								
Denmark								
Finland								
France								
Germany								
Greece								
Iceland								
Ireland								
Italy								
Japan								
Luxembourg								
Mexico								
Netherlands								
New Zealand								
Norway								
Portugal								
Spain								
Sweden								
Switzerland								
Turkey								
United Kingdom								
United States								

= No significant steps taken
= Less important measure
= Major initiative

Source Ibid., Table 1.B.

3

The Changing Context of Public Sector Reform and Its Implications in Hong Kong

Jane C. Y. Lee

Chief Executive, Hong Kong Policy Research Institute

1. Introduction

Since the publication of an internal document on public sector reform in 1989 by the then colonial government, Hong Kong has undergone dramatic political changes and economic turbulence. By 1999, Hong Kong had experienced ten years of reform. Since the 1997 handover, the momentum for reform has not slowed down. Both continuity and change are evident. The newly established Hong Kong Special Administrative Region (HKSAR) government has pushed forward with further reforms, and initiated a number of new policy innovations. This chapter first analyzes the changing context of public sector reform in the HKSAR. It compares and contrasts the economic and political environments within which public sector reform developed before the handover and in the first two years after the transfer of sovereignty. It then discusses challenges in the post-1997 period, analyzing government strategies, and highlighting the importance of changing management strategies to further develop public sector reform. Common issues and experiences of other countries will be drawn upon to throw light on the implications of Hong Kong's ongoing reforms.

2. Public Sector Reform in Hong Kong: Continuity and Change

2.1 The Context During the Political Transition 1989–97

Public sector reform was initiated in Hong Kong in 1989 and was implemented quietly. It generated little discussion in the media, legislature or academia. Even within the civil service itself, interest in public sector reform was limited to senior level officials responsible for implementing the reform programme. The whole initiative was undertaken in a low profile manner.

Reforms were first initiated as part of an internal exercise in financial management reform, and focused on enhancing the responsibilities of managers in resource allocation. The establishment of trading funds, for example, was a major initiative, which allowed pilot departments greater flexibility in resource allocation.[1] The reform process began in the late 1980s at a time when economic growth in Hong Kong showed signs of slowing down. In 1989 the real economic growth rate had slowed to 2.7%. Other countries had resorted to privatization and government downsizing to cope with budgetary and resource constraints. Hong Kong was relatively fortunate compared with other countries in that by 1989 it had never experienced a serious economic recession. However, the increasing complexity of public affairs and the projected increases in public expectations had prompted the government to undertake a self-awareness exercise. Top-level officers were required to allocate resources more efficiently and effectively, which had implications for human resource management and structural change. In fact, there had been no real public pressure for administrative reform in Hong Kong, only weak demands for democratic reform.

Two months after the document on public sector reform was released, the Tiananmen Square incident took place in Beijing, and Sino-British relations entered a period of low ebb. In October the same year, Governor David Wilson announced in his annual Policy Address to construct a new airport and expand tertiary education without the consent of the Chinese government. Senior Chinese officials reacted with concern that these new initiatives might cause financial burden for Hong Kong and the future HKSAR government. However, despite the political, financial and economic pressures facing Hong Kong in the five years before the handover, the economy grew stronger, with an average growth rate of about 5% per annum. The government's financial reserves were strong, and the unemployment rate remained below 3%, one of the lowest in the world (See Annex 3.1). The pressure for administrative reform remained weak, even though political controversies continued to rage.

By the early 1990s, Britain had initiated a series of civil service reforms, including Prime Minister John Major's "Citizen's Charter." In 1992, Chris

Patten was appointed Governor of Hong Kong, replacing David Wilson. Soon after taking office, Patten adapted the Citizen's Charter concept in Hong Kong, though he renamed it the "Performance Pledges Programme." In the same year, an Efficiency Unit was set up within the government to implement the reforms.

The colonial government promoted the Performance Pledges Programme in a high profile manner. The programme enhanced the customer-oriented image of the public services, and was also considered a useful management tool, providing performance standards for departments and staff. Both customers and departments considered the pledges as useful and effective benchmarks. As a result of the programme, the level of public satisfaction with the government improved.[2]

As part of the process of providing more information to the public on the accomplishments of the government, the Chief Secretary, Anson Chan, compiled a progress report every year and released it together with the Governor's annual policy address in October. In the two years after 1997, the Chief Executive, Tung Chee-hwa has continued this practice. For example, according to the 1997 Progress Report, 830 pledges were made in 1996–97, of which 94% were accomplished.[3] In 1998, it was reported that 922 commitments had been made in 1997–98, of which 96% had been completed.[4] The whole exercise had become an important means of projecting an image of a more transparent and open administration.

However, there was no evidence to suggest that public sector reform in Hong Kong had been successful. By 1997, the scale of the reforms remained quite limited. For example, before 1997 the reforms focused on enhancing the customer-oriented culture of departments by making them more business friendly. In addition to performance pledges, the government set up customer liaison groups, developed a code on access of information, and also set up various other customer service improvement programmes in individual departments.[5] Within the civil service, public sector reform was mainly confined to financial management reform at the top, with limited structural change. The government had been careful not to tackle human resources reform drastically because of restrictions contained in Hong Kong's mini-constitution, the Basic Law. The Basic Law guaranteed that the terms and conditions of civil servants should remain unchanged after 1997.[6] At a time when Hong Kong was experiencing a legitimacy crisis, maintaining the confidence of the civil service became a top priority for the government administration. The continuity and stability of public services was regarded as an important means of securing the confidence of the international community. Nevertheless, the traditional civil service terms and conditions increasingly became an obstacle to further reform. The permanent and pensionable terms of employment, for example, became an obstacle to redeploying redundant staff in case a plan for corporatization or privatization was considered necessary. It therefore imposed significant constraints on any major plans for downsizing. Major changes, if any, could only be considered after 1997 by the new SAR government.

2.2 The Context after the Return of Hong Kong to Chinese Sovereignty

Public sector reform continued without interruption under the administration of the newly established HKSAR government. It was, however, conducted within a new political and economic context. First of all, the implementation of the "one country, two systems" framework was successful.[7] Yet the degree of societal politicization was much greater in 1997 than in 1989. By 1998, the legislature had become fully elected, through both direct and indirect elections, but mainly played a monitoring role rather than engaging in policymaking. Freedom of speech remained undamaged. Yet the media exercised a much stronger monitoring role in public policy than in the pre-1997 period. Moreover, the labour unions and human rights groups were quite active as a result of more strained labour relations at a time of economic recession.[8]

Second, the post-1997 administration no longer aimed at merely managing issues relating to the smooth handover, but developing long-term plans for Hong Kong. On 1 July 1997, immediately after the handover, Chief Executive Tung Chee-hwa announced three major goals for his government: policy reform in education, housing, and care of the elderly. The whole administration was obviously required to re-prioritize itself to meet the Chief Executive's goals. In his first Policy Address in October 1997, Tung incorporated public sector reform in the context of the three major policy goals by asking "the Secretary for the Treasury to lead a special group to develop and implement a Target-based Management Process (TMP) for continuous improvements in public services."[9] This was a process by which resources would be directed more specifically to priorities, responsibilities and relationships clarified, and co-operation across departments, financial and functional boundaries improved.

Third, a major difference after 1997 was seen in Hong Kong's economic environment. The three policy goals announced in the Policy Address were quickly interrupted by the Asian financial crisis, which triggered off a period of economic recession in Hong Kong beginning in late October 1997. Within a year of the handover, real economic growth had fallen from +5.3% to –5.3%. The unemployment rate rose dramatically, from 2.4% in July 1997 to 6.1% in May 1999. By mid-1998, the government was forced to readjust its budget from a balanced one to a deficit one.

In October 1998, Tung Chee-hwa initiated an Enhancement Productivity Programme (EPP) in his second Policy Address. Under the terms of the programme, departments and subvented agencies were required to improve productivity and ensure the realization of the government's main priorities. They were also required to "deliver productivity gains of the operating expenditure between now and 2002."[10] In the short term, this would be achieved either through the provision of new or improved services, or the delivery of real dollar savings in the 1999–2000 financial year.[11] The Financial Secretary, Donald Tsang, also pursued this line in his Budget Speech of March 1999, saying: "the reduced growth rate has significant implications for the growth in government expenditure over the medium term" and that:

> We may need to maintain a similar degree of restraint over the growth in expenditure in the medium term for a further two years after 2002–2003. This underscores the need for us to achieve the savings targeted under the EPP and to re-prioritize the different areas of government spending.[12]

Under the EPP, all government departments and subvented agencies were required to cut 5% of their budget between 2000–2001 and 2002–2003. In actual practice, a Fundamental Expenditure Review (FER) was implemented to force departments to re-examine the priorities of existing programmes and re-deploy resources, whenever necessary.

Hong Kong's financial crisis did not stop the Chief Executive from trying to implement his policy goals. However, Tung had to readjust his housing policy plan; that is, to abandon the target of producing 85,000 housing units per annum. Although he no longer emphasized the quantity issue, he continued to insist on suppressing property prices to ensure buyers could afford to buy flats. It was also part of his plan to readjust the bubble economy and resume the long-term competitiveness of Hong Kong. The most immediate effect of his policy was that the Hong Kong government could no longer rely on land sales and stamp duties from property transactions as a substantial source of revenue. The economic crisis gave impetus to public sector reform, especially in the aspects of financial management reform. Although it aroused some resentment among government departments and subvented agencies, on the whole, the civil service and related agencies felt that they had no choice but to reform.

2.3 The Strategy of the HKSAR Government: Policy Innovations and Reforms

The Chief Executive's strategy was to advocate new policy innovations while moving forward a number of reforms simultaneously during the economic recession. In his 1998 Policy Address, Tung announced a list of ten policy strategies, which included plans for several new policies. These strategies were: (1) repositioning Hong Kong as the capital of Asia in the areas of finance, tourism, investment, information and transport; (2) developing Hong Kong as a regional hi-tech centre; (3) enhancing the development of Hong Kong's information technology industry, telecommunications, broadcasting and film industry; (4) establishing Hong Kong as an international centre for Chinese medicine; (5) maintaining Hong Kong's position as one of Asia's leading financial centres; (6) cultivating Hong Kong as an important tourist destination by establishing an image of Hong Kong as the Asian centre of arts, culture, entertainment and sport; (7) setting up an Small and Medium Enterprises (SME) office to enhance government assistance to such enterprises; (8) investing in basic infrastructure; (9) stabilizing the housing market, and (10) anchoring the fundamentals of "one country, two systems," i.e. guaranteeing the rule of law, judicial independence, freedom of speech, the press, information and the free market. In the following 12 months, steps were taken to realize these goals. In March 1999 the government announced plans to develop a "Cyberport," in July 1999 a "Silicon Harbour" and an international centre for Chinese medicine and biotechnology. All of these projects involved the active participation of the business sector.

These policy innovations did not, however, receive much public support. One reason was that the public was sceptical about whether the newly launched directives for science and technology industries would be viable in Hong Kong. Another reason was that the public wanted the government to provide immediate solutions to alleviate economic problems and financial hardships caused by rising unemployment and salary cuts. The government, however, insisted on dealing with long-term development issues, rather than short-term remedies. Meanwhile, the government also targeted areas that would be obstacles to Hong Kong's long-term development, and therefore pushed forward a series of policy reforms and reviews.

In 1998–99, several major reform programmes were publicly announced (for a list of key policy reforms in this period see Annex 3.2). These reform initiatives, however, came in for a good deal of public criticism. A few examples are discussed below.

First, the government published a consultative document called *Review of the District Organizations*. After three months' consultation, a policy report was published which suggested discontinuing the two municipal councils. In his Policy Address of October 1998, the Chief Executive clearly stated that he did not see the need to retain the two municipal councils after the terms of office of the existing members had expired at the end of 1999.[13] The functions of the two councils in food hygiene, sports and recreation, and in culture and arts would be replaced respectively by a newly formed Bureau on Environment and Food and its subordinate, a Department of Food and Environmental Hygiene, and a Leisure and Cultural Services Department under the Home Affairs Bureau. The reform was proposed after a series of crises relating to food hygiene, especially the mishandling of the "bird flu" epidemic by the urban services departments. Public opinion was divided and thus did not have a strong preference in favour of dissolving or retaining the two municipal councils. The elected representatives to the two councils, however, promised a hard fight. The staff of the two urban services departments also felt uncertain about their future terms of employment after the restructuring, but their livelihood was unlikely to be affected by the reshuffle. In any case, morale was low and management was seen as weak and ineffective.

A second reform was related to education. In July 1998, a consultation report on the *Review of the Education Department* was published, which called for a re-organization of the structures and functions of various units within the Education Department. Following this, the Education Commission initiated a high-profile public discussion on the Aims of Education. Parents, teachers and educational professionals had longed for reform, and so the initiative to review the structure of the Education Department was welcomed. However, the contents and direction of reform aroused heated debate. Moreover, the government enforced the application of mother tongue teaching as the medium of instruction immediately after the transfer of sovereignty, and rigidly classified schools into those which were qualified to use English and those which had to use Chinese as the medium of instruction. Other policies (such as enforcing school principals to retire at the age of 60[14]) were also implemented without much consultation or flexibility. These policies aroused much local and international concern regarding the management style of the HKSAR government. An authoritarian image of the Chief Executive was quickly established in the minds of the general public.

Other reforms were related to social security policies, such as a review of the level of Comprehensive Social Security Assistance (CSSA) payments, and reform of the healthcare system. In his Budget Speech of March 1999, the Financial Secretary claimed that for 1999–2000, education, health and social welfare would account for half of the total recurrent public spending, at 21.3%, 14.6% and 14.1% respectively. In the five-year period between 1994–95 and 1998–99, recurrent spending in these three areas increased in real terms by 28% for education, 45% for health and 103% for social welfare. The government was concerned that in view of rising unemployment and an ageing population, government spending on social security and healthcare would be bound to increase substantially.[15] The reviews of CSSA payments and healthcare, announced in December 1998 and April 1999 respectively, aroused much public debate. The discussions on healthcare reform, in particular, generated much criticism. One reason was that the consultation document, presented by a team from Harvard University, called for a drastic restructuring of the healthcare delivery system and mode of financing. The Harvard consultants proposed that Hong Kong should adopt mandatory health insurance and savings schemes amounting to contributions of 3% from individuals' salaries.[16] The review made the public aware of the limits of healthcare expenditure, yet generated an equal amount of concern about substantial increases in individual medical expenses. Most media commentaries rejected the proposals on the grounds that the 3% contribution would be equivalent to a taxation increase. The public responded by giving a clear signal that the existing system should be reformed, but mandatory insurance was unacceptable.[17]

Another controversial reform was related to the civil service. This was the most important reform, but also the most difficult one. Against this background was the publication of a consultant report on private sector involvement in the management and maintenance services for public housing estates in March 1999. The report reviewed the services of the Housing Authority and considered that its current role was too complicated, involving policy formulation, planning, development, construction, maintenance, management, marketing and sales, financial assistance and social services. The report proposed, therefore, that the Housing Authority should not be a service deliverer, and should confine its role in future to that of a facilitator involved in policy formulation, planning and development, financial incentives and subsidies, and service procurement.[18] Accordingly, the government announced its intention to privatize the services relating to estate management and maintenance. If the proposals were implemented, the government would transfer the services to the private sector within 5–7 years. During the process, the livelihood of 9,000 staff might be affected. The document caused an uproar among Housing Authority staff. In April 1999, the staff unions of the Housing Department organized several strikes and demonstrations which attracted the participation of about 10,000 people each time. The protests also gained the support of other civil service unions.[19] Civil servants in other departments were concerned that the government would extend the reforms to other departments, such as Water Supplies Department. All these proposed changes would have an effect on the conditions of service and the security of tenure in the public sector.

In March 1999 the government published the consultative document entitled *Civil Service Reform*.[20] The most controversial aspect of the document was a proposal to apply fixed-term agreement (or contract) terms to "basic ranks" throughout the civil service. The proposal did not violate the stipulations of the Basic Law as it would not affect existing employees, but was intended to apply to new recruits. It was envisaged that in 20 years' time, fixed-term agreements would cover about two-thirds of civil service employees. Although the government argued that the new policy would not affect existing staff and later on dropped the idea altogether during public discussion, its proposal triggered a strong sense of uncertainty within the civil service workforce. In fact, while the consultation was still ongoing, the government had already started to make some contract-term appointments at market rates.[21] The salaries of the new recruits were substantially lower than usual in the civil service. In the same period, the Audit Commission published its Value-for-Money reports and revealed problems (e.g. laziness) among junior civil servants.[22] Civil service staff believed that the government had intentionally highlighted a few bad examples to seek public support for reform. Staff unions argued that the government did not appreciate the hard work and contribution of its employees. They were upset by the management's strategy of openly criticizing junior staff, while never publicly admitting policy flaws at the top level, or rebuking mis-management by heads of departments.

3. Implications of Environmental Change for Public Sector Reform

3.1 Changing Environmental Context

In addition to the adjustments which had to be made following the transfer of sovereignty, the above-mentioned controversies occurred against a background of unprecedented economic recession in 1998. These issues had significant implications for the implementation of public sector reform in the post-1997 context. First, to what extent were the few policy reform initiatives related to public sector reform? Did there exist a coherent and integrated strategy? Second, what had been the focus of public sector reform in view of the crises which had occurred? Did the crises represent the success or failure (or inadequacy) of the public sector reform programme? Third, in comparison with 1989, to what extent should the post-1997 public sector reform operate differently in order to cope with drastically different socio-economic and political conditions?

The post-1997 external environmental context was obviously in stark contrast to the initial situation when the programme was first implemented in 1989. First of all, the reforms after 1997 were no longer confined to a self-awareness exercise within the civil service to make public managers more resource-oriented. The public sector was confronted with real external pressures in 1998–99, as well as genuine budgetary constraints. Second, there has been much greater public pressure for more effective managerial and financial reforms to enable the government to cope with crises more efficiently and in a more co-ordinated manner. This obviously became an important part of Target-based Management Process (TMP) — that is, to clarify responsibilities and relationships, as well as to enhance co-operation across departments, financial and functional boundaries. Third, there was a much greater demand for reforms. Nevertheless, the implementation of any reforms in 1998 and 1999 was confronted with much stronger resistance than in 1989 both internally (from civil servants) as well as externally (from politicians, the media, the general public and the business sectors, especially property developers). By 1998 the legislature was fully elected, but elected politicians had become a kind of opposition, playing a much more critical role without political responsibility. At the same time, economic recession had engendered a strong sense of social frustration. Compared with 1989, the HKSAR government was confronted with much stronger political opposition than it had been experienced ten years earlier.

Public sector reform was related to, and in fact becoming an important part of, crisis management initiated by the HKSAR government at the same time as policy innovations and reforms were undertaken. By focusing on the three major policy goals of housing, education, and the elderly in 1997, for example, the government's overall priorities became very clear. Public sector reform became an important tool to ensure that resource allocation met policy priorities. In view of the economic crisis, the objectives of public sector reform would be to complement the government's policy decisions, and ensure that internal management integrated with policy priorities. Having reviewed the events of 1998 and 1999, an integrated set of strategies of the Hong Kong government could be observed and summarized as follows:

- Overall policy priorities and political commitments be identified at the top level (principally by the Chief Executive);
- A few major areas of innovation, such as to develop Hong Kong as a centre of information technology and Chinese medicine, be announced publicly;
- Fundamental expenditure reviews be enforced in all government departments and subvented agencies to ensure internal priorities be reviewed within limited resources;
- A few areas of reform, such as social welfare, education and health, be targeted to ensure that social expenditure items were managed within a tight budget in the medium term;
- Reform of human resources management and civil service structures be initiated so that policy priorities and reforms would be implemented within a reasonably flexible structure. Civil service reforms would involve sensitive issues like pay and conditions of public

services. Structural changes would take place in the form of the corporatization of government services (such as public housing estate management and water services), privatization of government enterprises (such as the Mass Transit Railway),[23] and outsourcing or contracting out (as in the case of home meal services for the elderly).[24]

Having identified the strategies for public sector reform, it was clear that the HKSAR government had the political will to introduce new policy directives as well as to deal with old problems inherited from the colonial period. However, the question remains as to whether the strategies have been implemented with the right tactics in times of economic recession and social frustration.

In what ways should the post-1997 public sector reform be operated differently under new social, economic and political conditions, drastically different from those of 1989? What should be the strategy of "change management" in an unfavourable environment?

3.2 Problems of Managing Change

The few controversial cases discussed above clearly reveal that the government lacked the appropriate tactics and skills in managing change. First, although the government had strong political will, it lacked political support to carry out the reform process. In 1997, the HKSAR government had quickly obtained legitimacy from the central government in Beijing, but did not establish any local mass base from the bottom. In the first two years following the transfer of sovereignty, the general public remained sceptical about the newly formed government, perceiving it to be directly controlled by Beijing. The provisional legislature was replaced by a fully elected one in 1998, but it did not enjoy political power. The media played an important monitoring role outside the institutional channel, and became increasingly effective. The executive government was much weaker than that of 1989. What the government needed was a political alliance with either politicians elected to the legislature, the media, the civil service, or the business sectors, or ideally all of them. The government should first communicate adequately, persuade and convince the public, and the opposition in particular, the importance of reform and change before it publicizes any major proposals and makes final decisions. Without adequate dialogue with all sectors of society, the government not only failed to gain solid support before any proposal was announced, but incited criticism. Frustrations were felt in different sectors of society. It was much more difficult for the government to push forward any reforms without clearly identifying sources of alliance and support.

Second, the government had the difficult task of relying on the civil service to implement major cuts in social expenditure (primarily heath care and CSSA), but at the same time requiring civil servants to achieve structural and human resource reforms. Meanwhile, FER exercises were conducted, which further tightened the resources in departments. As a result, the government was confronted with resistance from both the general public as well as grievances from within the civil service.

In fact civil service reform received public support when it was first introduced in March 1999 at a time of economic recession.[25] Both the public and the private sectors felt frustrated with the civil service system. For example, the salary levels in the public sector had been lagging behind the market throughout the 1990s. The government had little choice in civil service employment, but followed market trends and therefore the policy became heavily salary-driven. The quality of services, especially attitudes towards work, was not necessarily compatible with the level of award. In the 1990s, the lack of flexibility in civil service salaries and terms of employment became an obstacle to public sector reform and expenditure control. When crises happened (such as the cases of poor co-ordination and management of the new airport and municipal services departments), public respect for civil servants drastically decreased. There were voices from both the public as well as private sectors, demanding fundamental reform of the civil service system. The public began to raise doubts about whether senior bureaucrats were competent enough in managing the development of Hong Kong after 1997. The government also recognized the problems inherent in the system. The Chief Secretary for Administration, Anson Chan, for example, accepted that the institution should be restructured to suit environmental change. In August 1998, she admitted:

> For too long we have lived with a paradox. We are civil servants but have not always supported good service. We have controlled when we should have empowered. We have criticized when we should have motivated, and ignored good performance when we should have celebrated it. We must determine to change this, and change it soon, so that civil servants can give of their best because of the environment rather than in spite of it.[26]

The government chose the right time to propose civil service reforms. Yet the whole strategy of reform contained serious flaws. Messages from the government lacked coherence, and they gave the impression that the government was very much salary-oriented. An example was the proposal to introduce performance-related pay. Civil servants quickly claimed that monetary award was not the main factor to evaluate the commitment of public sector employees. Instead, they criticized the government for failing to value their contribution and moral commitment to public services.

How should the government manage the process of reforming the civil service? Valuing the people should be the starting point for any successful reform. Tony Blair, the British Prime Minister, for example, shared his experience with other government leaders in a speech delivered in January 1999:

> In the last 21 months, I have met many people across the public sector who are as efficient and entrepreneurial as any one in the private sector, but also have a sense of public duty that is awe-inspiring. Most of them could be earning far more money in business. But they don't and you don't. Why not? Because of a commitment to public service.... So let me say today, loud and clear — this government values public service; this government is proud of its public servants. What made you choose this career is what made me go into politics — a chance to serve, to make a difference.
>
> I want to launch a major new initiative. Not delivering a solution from on high, but starting from what public servants think, from your day-to-day experience, your successes and frustrations.... I want to start a conversation with public servants and others, about recruitment, retention and motivation. [27]

Towards the end of his speech, Blair outlined seven strategies for public sector reform in Britain. They were: (1) to invest in public services; (2) to focus on outcomes; (3) to devolve power to the front-line; (4) to value the public servants who succeed; (5) to encourage innovation; (6) to work across government boundaries, and (7) to organize around individuals. [28]

The contents of public sector reform in Britain were very similar to that in Hong Kong, but the strategies were dramatically different. The British experience showed that winning the commitment and participation of civil servants at all levels was crucial to the success of any process of major institutional or policy reform.

During public debates on civil service reform, several related issues have emerged: Should the public sector in Hong Kong remain small? Is the size of the civil service too big? Can public services be best provided with the participation of private sector management?

The doubts raised by the public debate show that everybody had high expectations of the government's performance. It is always much more desirable, however, for the government rather than the opposition to initiate the review of its own role and consciously keep it small and efficient. The Hong Kong government has long been regarded as a small and efficient system, but it is involved directly in providing and running a number of important services, such as schools, hospitals, public housing provision and management, and water supplies. Annex 3.3 shows the trends of civil service employment in six OECD countries and finds that most of them have gone through almost a decade of downsizing. If the trend of civil service employment in Hong Kong is compared to that of the six OECD countries, there is a clear sign of upward movement in the three years after 1996. By 1999, civil service employment (including 140,000 employees in the subvented and statutory organizations) accounted for about 10% of the labour force. The proportion of civil service employment in Hong Kong still remained small compared with other countries. Public sector expenditure was also relatively low, accounting for less than 20% of GDP in the 30 years between 1958–59 and 1997–98, compared with 31.4% in Australia, 50% in New Zealand, 43% in the UK, 31.4% in the United States and 60% in Sweden.[29] Even so, government expenditure has risen drastically since 1998–99 because of the economic recession. In 1999–2000, public expenditure went up for the first time beyond the 20% limit to 21.3%.

It was therefore necessary for the government to further control its size by continually reviewing its role. In Hong Kong, public opinion accepts in principle the limited role of government in policy making, legislation, monitoring, regulating, providing subsidies to the disadvantaged and weak, and ensuring a level playing field in the market. Service provision should be left to the private sector as much as possible. A series of initiatives to corporatize and privatize public services, such as the privatization of government shares in the Mass Transit Railway Corporation and the contracting-out of maintenance and management services in public housing estates were welcomed. The most critical issue that remained was to win the commitment of all levels of civil servants and communicate with them more effectively on the process of change. The problem is not whether there should be reform, but how to manage the reforms.

The grievances discussed above are related to the strategy of change management. The Hong Kong government is used to emphasizing financial control, rule of law and efficiency as the strategies of change management. The government is not accustomed to focusing on people to gain the hearts and minds of its staff as well as the recipients of public services. What is needed is a more systematic plan to conduct public consultation, and gradually develop public consent.

3.3 Problems of Accountability

As mentioned at the beginning of this chapter, public sector reform has had the effect of enhancing the degree of transparency and openness in the administrative system in the pre-1997 period, but at that time, the government failed to reform the management structure and human resources framework. In the first two years after 1997, however, accountability remained a problem. First, the delegation of authority to heads of departments was still inadequate. Second, internal monitoring mechanisms and procedures were too cumbersome, thereby discouraging the management to redeploy redundant manpower resources and under-performed staff. Third, hierarchies became complicated, thereby causing great difficulties to effective supervision. Fourth, citizens also felt that they did not have proper and effective channels to make complaints, except reporting to the media and publicizing the issues. By 1999, media commentaries began to call for the setting up of more independent complaint systems within government departments. A central Ombudsman was considered not adequate because her roles and functions were too narrow. Other departmental complaint systems were perceived as ineffective. A survey conducted to collect public opinion on the healthcare system, for example, revealed that citizens were quite concerned with the inadequate supervision of the hospital services and considered improving the complaint system as a reform priority.[30] For the time being, accountability is most effective by exposing cases to the media for public discussion. A more systematic strategy to encourage public involvement should be initiated by the government. The system of administrative accountability should also be enhanced as an important aspect of public sector reform.

What should the government do to enable public sector managers to continually and consciously review the use of their own resources and priorities to ensure that they are getting the most effective results? What should the government do to enhance the effectiveness of public communication and accountability? The government is in fact well aware that it should change the management culture by allowing greater career flexibility and enhancing the esteem of civil servants. It should also delegate more financial and managerial responsibilities to departments. The Secretary for the Treasury, Denise Yue, for example, has openly said that, "We must give our managers more flexibility by loosening our traditional control mechanisms," and that "We must empower our managers."[31] She elaborated that:

> We need managers to find their way round problems; to unleash their creativity and entrepreneurial spirit so that they can make the best use of the resources in "their business" to achieve results and meet community needs.... The challenge ahead is securing a permanent change in management culture.... In parallel we must engender a culture of robust and fair accountability in our managers.[32]

The economic recession should be seen as a favourable condition rather than an obstacle to civil service reform. People were critical primarily because they were generally unhappy with the economic and social environment. The government could not satisfy the demands for more social benefits, but had to control the resources tightly. The experience of the United States, for example, could be a good reference point. Vice-President Al Gore championed "reinventing government initiatives" in the first five years of the Clinton administration (1992–97). By December 1998, he claimed to have succeeded in eliminating 250 outdated government programmes, slashed more than 16,000 pages of regulations, cut more than 640,000 pages of internal rules, helped balance the federal budget for the first time in 30 years, and saved more than US$137 billion and cut more than 351,000 employees to create a more streamlined federal government.[33] The task of the HKSAR government is much smaller, but the direction is possibly the same as that in other developed countries — that is "to work better and cost less."[34]

4. The Way Forward

The task of public sector reform is to tightly control and if possible reduce the size of the public sector. This has already been the practice of similar reforms in other countries. In the first two years after 1997, the objectives of the HKSAR government were to ensure continuity as well as to effect changes in addition to budgetary control. The major mistakes committed were however not related to policy objectives, but the strategies and tactics of change management. The need to change the top-down management culture of the government was recognized as early as when the public sector reform programme was first initiated in 1989. The change has, however, been proceeding only very slowly in the first decade of reform. Entering the 21st century, the public sector should build up more skills and methods to positively encourage greater bottom-up commitment. The government should engage the line managers strategically in any institutional changes. Public service values should be openly debated in society, and built in as an integral part of the reforms. In addition, the government should also develop alliances with various sectors of society in the process of reform to ensure that its initiatives gain credibility and legitimacy. The greatest challenge is the management of people. It requires a visionary, open-minded and democratic leadership, as well as a high-quality and committed public sector workforce.

Notes

1. See Anthony B. L. Cheung, "Financial, Managerial and Political Dimensions of Public Sector Reform," in *Public Sector Reform in Hong Kong: Key Concepts, Progress-to-Date and Future Directions*, edited by Jane C. Y. Lee and Anthony B. L. Cheung (Hong Kong: The Chinese University Press, 1995), p. 42.
2. See Efficiency Unit, "Evaluation of Performance Pledges Programme," (leaflet) (Hong Kong: Printing Department of the Special Administrative Region, August 1998).
3. *Progress Report, The 1997 Policy Address*, "Overview" (Hong Kong: Printing Department of the Special Administrative Region, 8 October 1997).
4. *Progress Report, The 1998 Policy Address,* "Overview" (Hong Kong: Printing Department of the Special Administrative Region, 7 October 1998).
5. See Efficiency Unit, "Customer Services," *The PSR Forum: Continuous Improvement in Public Services* (Hong Kong: Printing Department of the Special Administrative Region). See http:/www.info.gov.hk/eu/psrhk/csp_com.htm.
6. See *Basic Law*, Article 100, "Public servants in all Hong Kong government departments … may all remain in employment and retain their seniority with pay, allowances, benefits and conditions of service no less favorable than before."
7. Jane C. Y. Lee, "Hong Kong-Mainland Relations after 1997," *China Review 1999*, edited by Chong-chor Lau and Geng Xiao (Hong Kong: The Chinese University Press, 1999), ch. 6.

8. In 1998, for example, the Labour Tribunal and Minor Employment Claims Adjudication Board handled a total of over 12,000 cases of labour disputes, which was about 60% higher than that of 1997.
9. *Building Hong Kong for a New Era.* Address by the Chief Executive, The Honourable Tung Chee-hwa at the Provisional Legislative Council meeting 8 October 1997, para. 151.
10. *From Adversity to Opportunity,* Address by the Chief Executive, The Honourable Tung Chee-hwa at the Legislative Council meeting 7 October 1998, para. 166.
11. The objective of the programme was to basically achieve the best value for money in government expenditure. Accordingly, government departments and agencies together with government-subvented organizations pledged to deliver productivity gains amounting to HK$818 million in 1999–2000. Resources made available for redeployment or savings in expenditure were to be achieved through a variety of measures. Controlling officers had to confirm and satisfy themselves that these measures would not undermine their respective policy objectives. About three-quarters of the productivity gains would be redeployed to provide more than 300 items of new or improved services in the year while the remaining one-third would be reflected in reduced expenditure. See *Enhanced Productivity Programme, 1999–2000* (leaflet) (Hong Kong: Printing Department of the Special Administrative Region, 1999).
12. *Onward with New Strengths, The 1999–2000 Budget,* Speech by the Financial Secretary, moving the Second Reading of the Appropriation Bill 1999 (3 March 1999), para. 133.
13. *From Adversity to Opportunity* (Note 10), para. 150.
14. Since 1998, the Education Department has changed its previous practice, which generally allowed school principals to continue their service after the retirement age of 60, subject to the recommendation of the school councils and a health certificate. In 1999, the Education Department attempted to enforce the retirement age to remain at 60 and did not grant all those applications for the extension of services after the retirement age of 60. Finally a principal fought against the decision of the Education Department and won the case to extend his services. See *Ming Pao Daily*, 26 June 1999.
15. *The 1999–2000 Budget* (Note 12), para. 107.
16. The Harvard Team, *Improving Hong Kong's Healthcare System: Why and For Whom?* (Hong Kong: Printing Department of the Special Administrative Region, April 1999).
17. Jane C. Y. Lee, "Healthcare Financing and Delivery Reforms in Hong Kong: An Analysis of Public Opinion," *Policy Bulletin* (July/August 1999).
18. The Housing Authority. *A Review of Private Sector Involvement in Estates Management and Maintenance Services.* A Final Report (February 1999), p. 8.
19. A mass protest was organized on 18 April 1999, in which 9000 civil service union

members participated to support the action of the union members of the Housing Department. See *Ming Pao Daily*, 19 April 1999. An Alliance of Housing Department Staff Unions called for the collective action of 30,000 members to sit-in on 5 May. See *Ming Pao Daily*, 30 April 1999 and 5 May 1999.

20. Civil Service Bureau, *Civil Service into the 21st Century — Civil Service Reform*, (Hong Kong: Printing Department of the Special Administrative Region, 8 March 1999).

21. The government froze all civil service recruitment in 1999, but allowed departments to recruit non-permanent staff at market rates, which were substantially lower than the standard norm then existing in the civil service. According to press reports the Social Welfare and Transport Departments had already begun doing so. Some of the ranks being affected were Executive Officer II, Assistant Labour Officer and Assistant Trade Officer. See *Hong Kong Economic Times*, 16 April 1999, and *Ming Pao Daily*, 18 April 1999.

22. It was reported in May 1999 that a group of more than 20 staff of the Urban Services Department had repeatedly neglected to clear dirty materials from water tunnels. The Department admitted that the staff involved would be punished accordingly. See *Ming Pao Daily*, 5 May 1999.

23. In March 1999, the Financial Secretary proposed to privatize a substantial minority share of the Mass Transit Railway Corporation through public offering and to list the company on the local stock exchange. See *1999–2000 Budget* (Note 12), para 89–94.

24. The Social Welfare Department had undergone a series of reviews to contract out some of its services. One of the plans was to contract out services for delivering the meals to the elderly at home. See *Ming Pao Daily*, 10 June 1999.

25. In a survey conducted by the Hong Kong Policy Research Institute in March 1999, 79.1% of the respondents agreed on the need for civil service reform. Only 14.4% disagreed, and 6.5% had "no opinion." See Press Release of 12 March 1999, http://www.hkpri.org.hk.

26. Anson Chan, "Continuity and Change," a speech given to the 14th Gordon Arthur Ransome Orathion at the 32nd Singapore-Malaysia Congress of Medicine, 13 August 1998.

27. Tony Blair, "Modernising Public Service," a speech given to a conference on Transforming Governments in the 21st Century, 18 January 1999, Washington, D.C.

28. Ibid.

29. *Measuring Public Employment in OECD Countries: Sources, Methods and Results* (Paris: OECD, 1997).

30. According to a survey conducted of key opinion leaders (business executives, district board representatives, advisers of the Hospital Authority), an average of 63.6% of the respondents considered that medical services should be given adequate supervision and monitoring. See Jane C. Y. Lee, "Healthcare Reform: A

Survey of Opinion Leaders," presented to a Healthcare Forum co-organized by the Hong Kong Policy Research Institute and the City University of Hong Kong, 25 June 1999.

31. Denise Yue, "Dynamic Public Sector Reform," a speech given to the 17th Graduation Ceremony of the MBA Programme jointly offered by Northwest Louisiana University and Shue Yan College, 16 January 1999, Hong Kong.

32. Ibid.

33. "Vice President Gore to Chair Global Forum on Reinventing Government," Office of the Vice President, The White House, 21 December 1998, http://www.21stcentury.gov/conf/index.htm.

34. Ibid.

Annex 3.1 The Changing Economic Context of Public Sector Reform

Year	Unemployment rate	GDP Real growth rate	Population (mid-year)	
			Size	% Change (Mid-Year)
1989	1.1%	2.7%	5,686,200	1.0%
1990	1.3%	3.4%	5,704,500	0.3%
1991	1.8%	5.1%	5,752,000	0.8%
1992	2.0%	6.3%	5,800,500	0.8%
1993	2.0%	6.1%	5,901,000	1.7%
1994	1.9%	5.4%	6,035,400	2.3%
1995	3.2%	3.9%	6,156,100	2.0%
1996	2.8%	4.5%	6,484,300[1]	—
1997	2.2%	5.3%	6,564,200	1.2%
1998	4.7%	−5.3%	6,645,600	1.2%
1999	6.3%	−3.1%	6,720,700	1.1%

Sources: DRI Asia Database, CEIC Data Co. Ltd.; *Hong Kong Annual Digest of Statistics*, Census and Statistics Department, HKSAR Government, various years.

Note: Since August 2000, the "resident population approach" has been adopted in place of the "extended de facto" approach for compiling population estimates and revised population figures back-dated to 1996 have been compiled.

Annex 3.2 Key Policy Reforms in 1998–99
(in Chronological Order)

Policy area	Reform document	Date of publication/ initiation
Legal	Consultation Paper on 1997 Legal Aid Policy Review	16 March 1998
Technology	The Chief Executive's Commission on Innovation and Technology's Report	15 May 1998
Telecommunication	Consultation Paper on the 1998 Review of Fixed Telecommunications	12 June 1998
Transport	Consultation Document on the Third Comprehensive Transport Study (CTS-3)	30 June 1998
Municipal services	Consultation Document on Review of District Organizations	31 July 1998
Education	Consultation Paper on Information Technology for Quality Education, Five-Year Strategy 1998/99 to 2002/03	31 August 1998
Telecommunication	"The 1998 Review of Fixed Telecommunications: A Considered View"	3 October 1998
Broadcasting	The 1998 Review of Television	3 October 1998
Education	Consultation on Review of Education Department	20 October 1998
Social Welfare	Report on "Review of the Comprehensive Social Security Assistant (CSSA) Scheme"	20 January 1999
Housing	A Review of Private Sector Involvement in Estate Management and Maintenance Services	February 1999
Education	Consultation on "Review of Academic System: Aims of Education"	6 March 1999

Annex 3.2 Key Policy Reforms in 1998–99
(in Chronological Order) (Cont'd)

Policy area	Reform document	Date of publication/ initiation
Banking	Consultation exercise on Banking Sector Consultancy Study	31 March 1999
Civil Service	Consultation Paper on "Civil Service into the 21st Century — Civil Service Reform"	March, 1999
Securities	Consultation Paper on Legislative Reform for the Securities and Futures Markets	6 August 1999
Health Care	Consultation Paper on "Improving Hong Kong's Health Care System: Why and For Whom?"	15 August 1999

Annex 3.3 International Trends on Civil Service Employment

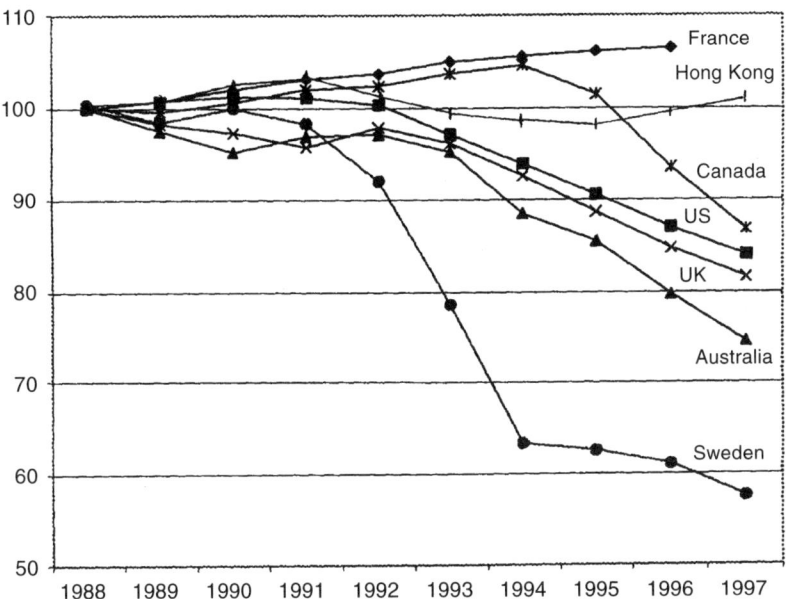

Sources: Compiled from *Structure of the Civil Service Employment in Seven OECD Countries*, http://www.oecd.org/puma/mgmtres/hrm/pubs/scs.htm; and homepage of Civil Service Bureau, the HKSAR government.

4

Are Hong Kong's Public Sector Reforms Converging with the International Trends?

Richard Common

Senior Lecturer, Department of Sociology and Applied Social Studies, London Guildhall University

For both practitioners and students of public administration, we are living in interesting times. A second major trend in public management is sweeping across the globe. Although it has been given various labels, the one that appears to have stuck the most is New Public Management (NPM). The first major trend was that of bureaucracy, and although it had its roots in Confucianism, and much later, in Cameralism, bureaucracy as an approach to public management took hold in industrializing Europe, and later North America, over a century ago. Colonial powers ensured that bureaucracy was exported from the West to much of Africa, Latin America and Asia. To this day, we can observe features of Weber's "ideal type" bureaucracy in all nations to varying degrees. Hong Kong is no exception, but now it is also displaying features of the second great international trend in public management: NPM. The question posed by the title of this chapter assumes that policy-makers in Hong Kong have deliberately embarked on a process of convergence with the international trend. However, this assumption can be misleading. Despite the claims of those who regard convergence on a single universal model of public management as inevitable, each nation-state has unique features and contexts that allow the possibility of divergence from apparently globally applicable models. Therefore, this chapter will take a critical view of the "one size fits all" approach of NPM and to make an assessment of the applicability of NPM to Hong Kong.

1. Policy Convergence

If we are discussing convergence on a global model of NPM, we need to define what is meant by policy convergence. Conceptually, policy convergence inevitably draws us towards a discussion of globalization. Globalization might be regarded as both a process and an ideology. As a process, many debates concentrate on its economic aspects, particularly the internationalization of capital. As an ideology, some regard globalization as destructive and exploitative whereas others see it as potentially beneficial. Problematically, what most perspectives share is the diminution of the role of the state as a primary actor in the international arena. A predominant view is that the end of the nation-state is the logical consequence of the processes of globalization and that the state is weakened by the increasing number of inputs into the policy process as a result of globalization. Moreover, domestic policy processes have been internationalized by a growing number of global actors, with both the state and society becoming more porous to international influence. Whichever view of globalization one takes, there is a general consensus that the exercise of political authority and bureaucratic power is no longer constrained by the boundaries of nation-states.

Although globalization does not mean convergence, at a simplistic level, convergence assumes that eventually all nation-states will adopt a similar model of governance. To accept globalization is to accept that states are becoming more alike in terms of how they react to and solve policy problems. The question is to what extent can globalization determine policy convergence? Convergence theory is "the idea that whatever their political economies, whatever their unique cultures and histories, the 'affluent' societies become more alike in both social structure and ideology."[1] This process of convergence occurs in concert with the globalization of capital "as market pressures force national institutions to adjust in ways which most effectively fit the international situation and optimally serve the national economies."[2] Furthermore, convergence becomes more likely with the homogenizing effects of technology, and thus education and wealth creation.[3] Convergence can also be formalized within the auspices of international institutions such as the European Union, the Organization for Economic Co-operation and Development (OECD) and the World Trade Organization (WTO). However, thus far, it appears that the weight of evidence is for economic convergence, rather than the convergence of political systems.

Although policy convergence can appear to occur independently of globalization where similar policies appear in diverse national settings, globalization serves to increase the likelihood of convergence. As Strang and Meyer observe, "rapid diffusion within the world system seems linked to the homogeneous cultural construction of contemporary nation-states" which are a pre-requisite "for the rapid diffusion of public policies and institutional structures."[4] However, it could be argued that this phenomenon is limited to what might be termed the "developed world" where structural similarities exist. Therefore, policy responses to similar problems in countries that are at a similar stage of economic development do indeed appear to be convergent. The globalization of nation-states and economic development only provide a small part of the explanation for convergence.

Another precondition for policy convergence is where nations are dominated by political elites with similar convictions and ideologies. For example, Waltman and Studlar concluded that policy convergence occurred to some degree between the Thatcher and the Reagan governments.[5] The ramifications of this political alliance were felt in a shift to orthodox free-market liberalism in Europe and North America. Although this thesis appears to be an attractive one, it fails to take into account the unique political contexts of individual nation-states and the homogenizing effects implicit in globalization. Therefore, it is more likely that if the administration of a particular country engages in reform strategies as a result of global socio-economic pressures impacting on administrative elites, policy convergence then apparently takes place in an ideological vacuum. In other words, policies are presented as pragmatic responses to these wider pressures. Castles called this the "paradox" of the convergence thesis. As the changing economic and technological environment imposes uniformity on systems of governance that dulls ideological inputs, the state struggles to accumulate power and sovereignty.[6] As Castles explains, "the convergence and 'end of ideology' theses are closely interlinked, not merely because both postulate increasing similarity in society, state and politics."[7]

Certainly, as states try and independently cope with policy problems it may appear that policy convergence is occurring. Harrop asserts that the importance of the nation-state could not be dismissed as:

> nations differ in the severity with which problems arise and in the range of solutions which it is feasible for them to consider. Fundamentally it is still national policy-makers who seek solutions, even if the problems are shared, and it is still national policy-makers who are accountable to

national electorates. Common problems do not mean common solutions; interdependence does not mean convergence.[8]

A comparative study of social policy in the UK, Australia and New Zealand would superficially appear to offer a "most similar systems" scenario where convergence might be comfortably predicted. In fact, Castles and Pierson found that although "economic internationalization" had impacted on domestic policy-making in each of these countries, they still found "three quite distinct trajectories of social policy development."[9] However, claims by the proponents of NPM that it is a model of universal applicability demand that we make some assessment of whether or not public sector reform in Hong Kong is converging with this particular international trend.

2. Pressures for Policy Convergence in Hong Kong

If policy convergence is the result of nation-states becoming more similar in structures and processes, then how can we determine that Hong Kong will start to become similar to elsewhere? This is a big empirical question, and Hong Kong would need to be compared with a range of other countries to properly test convergence theory. Furthermore, globalization defies measurement and cannot be neatly isolated as an independent variable. By testing whether or not policy convergence has taken place does not prove whether globalization is occurring, and this is not the concern of this chapter. However, in this section, I try to identify the pressures for both policy convergence and divergence within Hong Kong's political and economic context. As Kelly has noted, "a particular public bureaucracy or administrative structure is embedded within a particular political socioeconomic system."[10] This is important, because convergence does not occur independently of that context. Given the restrictions on space, the discussion is limited here to sketching out a few key determinants of policy convergence in Hong Kong.

2.1 Economic Globalization

One starting point for investigating policy convergence is the extent to which a country is integrated into the global economy. The consequence of a globalized economy is that it subsumes national "domains" of culture and politics. Globalization also forces economic and business integration;

"conventional wisdom has it that a more integrated world will be a more homogenous one."[11] This argument predicts "institutional isomorphism" will occur as a consequence of integration into the global economy. The thesis put forward by DiMaggio and Powell is that organizations become more homogenous due to two processes — institutional and competitive isomorphism.[12] Therefore, we might expect that globalization causes isomorphism on two counts: competition generating pressure for efficient organizations or turbulent political environments generating pressure for institutional legitimacy. In a globalized world of competitive markets, we might predict the latter occurs as organizations seek the most rational and efficient solutions to global economic challenges. The former assumes that organizations change to acquire legitimacy, rather than to enhance efficiency. If global competition creates pressure for efficiency, then the net result is the appearance of the "Competition State" that brandishes the NPM tool-kit.[13] As Rockman observes, it appears "the overall consequence of globalization is to produce a more limited state with a lighter hand on the economy."[14]

As a small state, Hong Kong is "more vulnerable to external economic and political forces."[15] Hong Kong's relative size, its lack of natural resources and its status as an entrepot port has exposed it to economic globalization, which it has weathered remarkably well and has turned to its advantage. Hong Kong's history as an entrepot for commerce within the former British Empire and the neighbouring region brought it into the global economy relatively early.[16] However, the development of global capitalism in the latter half of the 20th century brought with it a new set of opportunities for Hong Kong. Considering the "subregion" as a whole, Chiu et al argue "the advantageous position of Hong Kong in this emergent economic subregion lies in its status as a world city."[17]

The rapid economic development of Hong Kong has also been attributed to "laissez-faire" government. Scott feels that the description of Hong Kong's limited government is not accurate, and argues that the "Hong Kong government intervenes in the economy whenever it feels the need to do so," particularly in land use.[18] The public sector is well developed and carries out, or subsidizes, most of the functions found in liberal democracies. Islam and Chowdhury observe that the Hong Kong government "is very much Keynesian in nature and has never shied away from using its public expenditure programme to fine-tune the economy."[19] They gave the example of the Hong Kong government using its spending power to boost demand and increase public-sector wages to assuage uncertainty following the Tiananmen incident in 1989. In August 1998, the government intervened on the financial markets to protect the Hong Kong dollar "peg" to the US dollar. Where the government is minimalist is in terms of "sector- or industry-specific interventions."[20]

Hong Kong has achieved a high level of economic development in a relatively short space of time. As a former British colony, Britain's promotion of Hong Kong's economy was partly conceived with steering the colony away from conflict in China rather than a conscious attempt by the sovereign power to "modernize" the colony.[21] However, by 1997, Hong Kong was the eighth largest world trade entity, the busiest container port and the fourth ranking financial centre, as well as the main "gateway" to the People's Republic of China.[22] In terms of public sector reform, the level of development prompted the expansion of public services, particularly in health, education and housing. The government publication *Serving the Community* claimed that Hong Kong's economic success meant that people demanded "more and better public services." [23]

Often cited as a major impetus to administrative reform in the West, Hong Kong remained largely immune from the same sense of economic crisis that began to grip the West in the early 1970s that germinated NPM. From a more contemporary perspective, Ingraham regarded "the newly recognized need to compete effectively in the international market" as a spur to administrative reform.[24] Under the yoke of economic globalization, "all governments are obliged to bear down upon public spending."[25] In the case of Hong Kong, there was a general downturn in the local economy in the late 1980s. Growth in Gross Domestic Product (GDP) dropped from 14% in 1987 to 2.5% in 1989 and inflation was up from 5.7% to 10% in the same period, thus generating at least a perception of crisis.[26] The fiscal crisis of the 1980s appears to be small beer when compared with the crisis of the late 1990s. Hong Kong's GDP shrank by a record 7.1% in the third quarter of 1998.

Furthermore, within the civil service, a high proportion of staff on maximum point of pay scales combined with low wastage prompted reform calls in the late 1980s.[27] However, Chow's research in 1988–89 also revealed understaffing to be a serious problem along with civil servants joining the emigration bandwagon, as they began to fear the handover to China.[28] Writing a few years earlier, however, Scott argues that the relative "cheapness" of the Hong Kong civil service was due to a tall line hierarchy and low pay at the bottom of the hierarchy.[29] An expansion of the civil service between 1978 and 1982 had, by the 1990s, worked its way through in terms of staff reaching the maximum point of pay scales. In addition, Scott reports how, by the end of the 1980s, there were calls from the middle classes for an expansion of social services which "alarmed business pressure groups which have traditionally supported limited and cheap government," leading to the prediction that government will become more expensive "in real terms."[30] These concerns partially accounted for the key *Public Sector Reform* document of 1989. Despite these domestic pressures for change, Hong Kong remains vulnerable to the vicissitudes of the international economy.

2.2 Internationalization

Here, the emphasis is on the interaction of Hong Kong with the rest of the world. Unlike the homogenizing effects of institutions implicit in globalization, internationalization emphasizes social relationships that transcend national boundaries. Internationalization also depends on the relative power positions of individual states. For instance, the economic success of Hong Kong has meant it has never had to suffer the impositions of the international financial organizations, unlike some of its neighbours in the Asia-Pacific during the recent Asian economic downturn.[31] However, a further factor to consider here is that increasing interconnection with the international community comes with a better educated and more sophisticated population that is more likely to demand administrative reform. In Hong Kong, rising public expectations for services as a consequence of economic development acted as a further source of pressure for change.[32] Patten was sensitive to the pressure of the demands of a changing society and in his speech to the opening session of the 1992–93 Legislative Council he remarked: "an increasingly prosperous and sophisticated community quite rightly demands greater openness and accountability from the public sector which it pays for — and an official attitude of mind which regards the public as clients not supplicants."[33]

For many decades, Hong Kong has been subject to international influences in general, and Western influences in particular, and this has had an impact on the values of the bureaucracy. Economic prosperity has allowed Hong Kong people to receive higher education abroad. Moreover, many professionals receive their qualifications from the West or western countries, particularly, Australia, the UK, Canada and the US. Hook argues that there has been an "internationalization of the dominant section of the community and its way of life" and the "new Westernized elites were not content with the old arrangement that led to the administrative absorption of politics."[34] In the civil service, senior officials of deputy director rank are sent to Harvard University, and more junior administrative grades are sent to Michigan University. The Deputy Secretary for the Civil Service was reported as placing great emphasis on the importance of "leadership and strategic management" in attending such courses.[35] Generally, unless economic hardship severely curtails the travel opportunities of the Hong Kong people, this determinant of convergence is expected to remain influential.

2.3 Policy Learning

The opportunities afforded by improved communications and travel opportunities increases the scope for policy learning. Policy convergence does not necessarily presuppose policy learning, but policy learning can act as a process of convergence. As the attraction of management practices is increasingly shaped by globalization, then public sector reform may be explained by "policy learning" as a result of "wider socio-economic or technological forces."[36] Reform programmes then begin to appear across a range of political and administrative settings. Environmental pressures will then trigger reforms within governments, regardless of dominant political ideologies, and "modernizing elites within public administration" will respond to these pressures.[37] Thus "policy learning" produces the appearance of policy convergence or the perception by policy-makers that one system is starting to resemble another. However, policy learning may simply involve "the adoption of labels or buzzwords rather than thorough adoption of content in a specific package of institutional practice and behavior."[38]

The rhetoric of NPM appears as an attractive supplement to public sector reform aided and abetted by a public management epistemic community. Adler and Haas noted that "there are many paths by which learning occurs. For example, individual members of epistemic communities learn from their transnational encounters with one another and pass their lessons and advice on to the institutional bodies over which they have influence."[39] In addition, the availability of publications, the activities of international organizations and "change agents" officials and politicians sent on visits, secondments, study placements and tours, and interaction with academics and conferences, are among these many paths to policy learning. However, the impact of best-sellers such as Osborne and Gaebler, and conceptual models are more difficult to quantify on a global scale.[40] For example, Goffee and Hunt argue the "concept of a 'learning organization' is extremely complex; few would be confident in knowing they have seen one."[41]

As a recent British colony, Hong Kong has a long history of being influenced by British reforms. As Huque, Lee and Cheung observe:

> major reforms of the civil service since the Second World War drew lessons from British administrative reforms of the time; some were implemented simply with assistance from consultants or advisers recruited from the sovereign state.[42]

The McKinsey Review of 1973 appears to be the obvious place to begin when looking for evidence of borrowing management practices from the UK. There was some speculation that the UK Fulton Report of 1968 influenced McKinsey. As Cheung comments, "there was certainly some resemblance in the underlying 'managerialist' tones of their respective reform concepts."[43] However, like Fulton in the UK, McKinsey had little impact in Hong Kong. Harris observes that the lack of impact proved that managerial principles are not universally applicable: "the fact is the consultants were not talking about Hong Kong."[44] In other words, Hong Kong's unique context had been ignored.

It was also difficult to discern the influence of British "managerialist reforms" in the next attempt at civil service reform in Hong Kong despite certain similarities with the UK "Next Steps" initiative which aimed to make a clear separation between operations and management.[45] In addition, Hong Kong's *Public Sector Reform* (PSR) document focused on financial management reform in the same way as the Financial Management Initiative in the UK between 1982 and 1987. Furthermore, the notion of "trading funds" appeared to copy the UK 1973 Trading Funds Act. However:

> it would not be fair to say that Hong Kong follows exactly the footsteps of its sovereign state, but it should be quite clear that the underlying driving force, assumptions and expectations behind the two sets of reform strategies are of the same intellectual, if not ideological roots. This

is all the more plausible against the background of the rise of privatization and NPM as a prevailing international trend in public administration.[46]

Burns agrees that there are NPM underpinnings to Hong Kong's PSR but is surprised at its implementation given that NPM assumes a relatively stable and predictable administrative environment.[47] This cannot be said of the backcloth to Hong Kong's Public Sector Reform given the prospect of transition to Special Administrative Region status that was looming.

Lam also regarded public sector reform as being modelled on Britain after the arrival of Patten, especially the notion of a "service culture" manifested by the Performance Pledge initiative, which resembled the UK Citizen's Charter.[48] More generally, LeHerrisier notes that administrative change in Hong Kong was much less radical than that experienced by Britain or New Zealand and compared the incremental approach adopted in Hong Kong to the Canadian approach to administrative reform.[49] However, Cheung was sceptical of the role of policy learning in the case of Hong Kong: "the influence of external administrative or managerial ideas only played the cosmetic role of rendering the reforms more in line with the international trend."[50] NPM thus provided external legitimation for administrative change in the absence of political legitimation: the discourse or rhetoric of NPM is equally important to bureaucratic elites. Therefore Cheung argues that:

> by embarking on a reform programme that looks like an overseas reform movement, the local initiative can gain an added degree of acceptance and can downplay whatever political and bureaucratic implications that may arise from the reform.[51]

2.4 Transnationalization of the State

Policy convergence is also facilitated by the transnationalization of the state apparatus. This aspect of globalization involves the increasingly complex interpenetration of decision-making by nation-states by a variety of transnational actors. Cerny focuses on how the "transnationalization of the nation-state apparatus" results in the emergence of the "Competition State."[52] Cerny argues that globalization has caused state policies,

> to converge on a more liberal, deregulatory approach because of the changing structural character of the international system — its greater structural complexity and interpenetratedness — which in turn transforms the changing position of states themselves within that system.[53]

Globalization also assumes that the exercise of political authority and bureaucratic power is no longer constrained by the boundaries of nation-states. Public management now occurs in the context of an "interconnected" world as a result of global interdependencies. These interdependencies include "geographic connections" (crossing jurisdictional boundaries), "functional interdependence" (blurring traditional boundaries between government functions) and "temporal interconnectedness" (linking the past, present and future).[54] The public sector environment is thus characterized by "constant change" leading to uncertainty, complexity or even turbulence.

Hong Kong has never been a nation-state in terms of being a sovereign power, so its state apparatus has been "transnational" in the sense of being accountable first of all to the British, and then to Beijing. As a former British colony, inevitably British institutions were imposed on Hong Kong, but as Harris observed, a number of significant modifications were made, "in particular developing the apparatus of the administrative state."[55] In this respect, it was a fairly typical colonial government. With the transition from British colony to a SAR of China still very recent, the colonial influence remains powerful. According to Hook the crucial question for the British legacy "was the extent to which there could be continuity at the top of the civil service."[56] Moreover, Hong Kong represents an unusual decolonization; instead of the process being a preparation for independence, China replaced Britain as Hong Kong's sovereign power. However, it appears easy to overplay the importance of reunification with China on public administration as it left the structure of the civil service largely unaltered.[57] Furthermore, there appears to be no signs that public sector reform is converging with that of China, despite the increasing exchanges between Hong Kong officials and their mainland counterparts.

2.5 Pressures for Policy Divergence

There are a number of factors in the Hong Kong context that mitigate against policy convergence. The strength of local values and culture are an important consideration.[58] In particular, to what extent is the public sector shaped by the Confucian philosophy in Hong Kong? Clark and Chan point to the influence of Confucian culture on business and society in Hong Kong which needs to be considered here in the context of East Asian culture and values.[59]

It seems simplistic to overplay the importance of cultural differences to explain the lack of evidence in Hong Kong for more standard explanations of NPM found in the West. However, Chen asserts that "the West highly cherishes individualism while the East emphasizes communitarianism." He warned that we should be wary of making generalizations based on this dichotomy alone, but the differences are such that many NPM-type reforms may actually be infeasible in Hong Kong.[60] As NPM is related to Western notions of individualism and consumerism, there also appears to be a lack of western managerialist values. This may be partly ascribed to the persistence of "rule-governed hierarchies" that may, in fact, "fit" much more readily with the cultural norms of Asian countries than do the principles of NPM.[61] As Root points out, "the effectiveness of modern management techniques … is deterred by the persistence of traditional notions of social status and paternalism."[62] A backlash against the dominance of the American model of business management theory appears to have begun in Asia with the establishment of the Asia Academy of Management by mainly Chinese scholars and researchers. Lau Ching-ming, the Chair of the Academy, argued that many aspects of US management theory did not apply to Asia where there is less emphasis on individual performance and reward and "direct confrontation" did not work in the Asian context.[63]

To emphasize the poor fit between NPM and Asian public management, some insight is to be gained from Annex 4.1. In public management terms, attribute 1 in the table is similar in both the East and West. The notion of the "strong hierarchy" is largely the product of the imposition or the imitation of Weberian bureaucracies. However, the contrast between the rest of the attributes would appear to make NPM untenable in East Asia, in particular: professional vs. "social" managers, decentralization vs. centralization, diversity vs. unity, explicit control (performance indicators) vs. implicit control, and so forth. The main paradox here is that while the colonial imprint on the bureaucracy has been preserved and maintained in Hong Kong, local organizational cultures have been enhanced and strengthened. Hofstede showed how Asian countries (including Hong Kong) displayed more "power distance" in hierarchical settings when compared with "core NPM" countries such as New Zealand and the UK. The consequences for organizations are greater centralization with tall organization pyramids and so forth, features of "classic" colonial bureaucracies like that of Hong Kong.[64] Lachman et al. cited a study by Birnbaum and Wong, which argued that in Hong Kong, the cultural emphasis was on "power distance," so organizations tended to be highly centralized.[65] When added to the persistence of hierarchical relationships, in Hong Kong's civil service, we might predict some difficulty in implementing certain elements of NPM.

3. The International Trend of New Public Management

To account for policy convergence, we need a time-frame. Seeliger argues that political culture and policy style shape preferences for policy instruments and so convergence should be analyzed over relatively long time periods.[66] There may be a long gestation period between the adoption of a policy and its implementation. The diffusion of ideas also takes some time, and as Seeliger has pointed out "convergence over shorter periods of time might indicate efforts of lesson-drawing, whereas synchronous adoption of identical policies might indicate close international cooperation or even harmonization."[67] Given the above, the analysis will consider developments from 1989, a year after *Improving Management in Government* was published in the UK, which marked the intensification of the NPM trend.[68] The year 1989 also allows for the diffusion of *Government Management*, the New Zealand Treasury's briefing document to the incoming government of 1987, regarded as the "manifesto" of NPM.[69] Sankey's introductory chapter to this volume considers public sector reform initiatives in Hong Kong from 1989 onwards.

What is it that the public sector reforms in Hong Kong are supposed to be converging with? In the early 1980s, public sector reform involved a series of methods and techniques that acquired the NPM label, a label still employed as convenient shorthand to describe contemporary administrative change. The apparent diffusion of NPM across the world appears to be simply explained by the appeal of NPM as an attractive solution to the problems of big and inefficient government. The "promise" of NPM is that it will "modernize" public sector management, to make it more efficient, economical and effective. To accept the argument that a new international trend based on NPM is sweeping the globe, a key research problem is to explain why these reforms show striking similarities, given that they are taking place in different political and administrative contexts. The reforms share a commonality in that they are both couched in the language of management and import methods and techniques from the commercial sector. Commentators such as Dunleavy, Kettl and Massey have posited the globalization of NPM, but with the exception of Japan, the rest of the world, beyond the "core" NPM nations, is largely ignored in these discussions.[70] Moreover, these writers have a tendency to make extrapolations about the globalization of NPM based on the experience of a few Western countries (UK, US, Australia, New Zealand and Canada, with the addition of some other Western European countries such as the Netherlands and Sweden).

The main empirical problem is that NPM defies exact or precise definition. NPM is often used as a vague, encompassing term for a set of methods or techniques that are frequently part and parcel of any given public sector reform. There are a range of interpretations on offer: Hood provided one of the first distillations of "NPM" as a set of identifiable components, others provided normative accounts and produce lists of methods and techniques considered important in improving public administration.[71] Pollitt saw NPM as a "shopping basket" which countries chose from for a variety of reasons.[72] Others, at best, located NPM in theoretical frameworks based on management science and public choice theory.[73] These more sophisticated accounts of NPM attempt to identify theoretical justifications for public management reform, and writers such as Hood and Aucoin have struggled with the contradictions posed by managerialism and public choice theory. Terry regarded NPM as the product of the *liberation* management and *market-driven* management approaches to public management.[74] *Liberation* management points to "bad systems" for failure in public management and takes an optimistic view of management as a means of "liberating" managers from the constraints of their organizational environments. Terry quotes Al Gore who described public managers as "good people trapped in bad systems."[75] *Liberation* management draws its inspiration from Osborne and Gaebler and Peters and Waterman before them.[76] *Market-driven* management is guided by neo-classical economic belief in the primacy of markets and of private sector management. It is these varied standpoints on where NPM actually came from which mean that NPM is often so vaguely defined.[77]

Furthermore, NPM is heavily criticized by public administration academics. Rhodes singled out the lack of concern for interorganizational links, the managerialist obsession with objectives and the subsequent lack of trust, the focus on results which undermines the importance of managing in interorganizational networks, and the "contradiction between competition and steering at the heart of NPM."[78] Aucoin argued that these contradictions were the result of the uneasy blend of managerialism and public choice theory that underpinned NPM.[79] Furthermore, there is a danger that we are documenting a "fad." As with the drive for decentraliza-tion, Micklethwait and Wooldridge pointed cynically to "downsizing," "re-engineering" and total quality management (TQM) as fads sweeping through public administration.[80] As they pointed out, these are in fact, "mutu-ally incompatible." The result is that,

> a typical public-sector management reform involves keeping the old de-partmental structure, but hoping to do it with fewer people; worse, it introduces performance measurement in the crudest possible way. These days academics may be promoted for writing a lot of articles despite the fact they are all bunk, and surgeons can be demoted because so many of their patients die.[81]

Despite the problematic nature of defining NPM, we still need a method of assessing whether or not Hong Kong is converging with this interna-tional trend. It is assumed that the "market" model is the dominant model being adopted in a range of member countries of the OECD, then this model is clearly aimed at introducing competitive elements into public services.[82] The model presented below is presented as an ideal type. As Massey ob-served when debating the existence of a NPM paradigm, "models or 'ideal types' are employed as tools to aid understanding of these paradigms."[83] Indeed, Peters noted that,

> the method of ideal types has the virtue of providing a standard against which real world systems can be compared. Even if the "model" is rather ethnocentric (as Weber's certainly is), the comparison is meaningful. The danger, of course, is that the ideal type analysis is converted into a differ-ent type of ideal, with the assumption that the Western conceptions of "good" administration become normative standards rather than empiri-cal referents.[84]

The model as presented in Annex 4.2 is an "empirical referent" against which reforms in Hong Kong can be judged. However, there are poten-tially an infinite number of possibilities of types of public management "reform." Therefore, the model is not intended to epitomize "good" administration, rather it is presented here as an *accumulation* of NPM meth-ods and techniques. However, it should be noted that NPM is a cultural construct. By applying the NPM model beyond the core OECD reform countries, cultural variables that may explain policy divergence could be screened out of the analysis.

3.1 Structure

The first cluster of changes required by the model involves changes in organizational structure. A main ingredient of NPM reforms appears to be "decentralization," an ambiguous term that is used to describe a variety of managerial changes. More specifically, "organizational decentralization" refers to a set of changes aimed at devolving decision-making from the top or power centres of public organizations. Although Holmes noted that "there is no simple law which says that we should be centralized or decentralized, standardized or flexible," he concedes that there appears to be a tendency in public sector reform aimed at a "more decentralized or flexible operating environment."[85] Hoggett made a crucial distinction between "external" decentralization, or reforms aimed at contracting out or creating "quasi markets" in the public sector, and "internal" decentralization, which refers to the introduction of managerial techniques and "market values" into the public sector.[86] To move the discussion forward, NPM generally refers to the marketization of public services, usually facilitated by decentralization strategies that introduce, intentionally or unintentionally, market values into public sector management.

3.2 Process

Many of the NPM-type changes to government processes involve the introduction of private sector management techniques. Elements 8 to 18 have been grouped under the category of financial reforms ("budgetary process"). Here, Kettl described a profound shift in public management, "from a focus on *inputs* (how much should we spend?) to *outputs* (what activities do our inputs produce?)" leading "to a much more expansive view of budgeting by linking allocation decisions and their results."[87] Elements 19–23 have been grouped under the heading of 'Personnel' or to use the currently preferred terminology, "Human Resources." Elements 24–28 focus on changes in process that are more qualitative in nature, and reflect more mature NPM systems, certainly post-1990. The World Bank provided a neat summary of the rationale behind the appearance of such elements:

> Techniques for citizen and client consultation can introduce more openness and transparency into the system. As more people become aware of the performance of specific agencies or officials, they are more likely to exert collective pressure on the agency to perform better. At the same time public agencies will have less opportunity for arbitrary action.[88]

3.3 Functions

Under NPM regimes, the function of the public sector has shifted from one of a monopoly direct service provider to a function more akin to that of a commercial firm operating in the market place. In other words, the functions of the public sector have been "marketized," in line with the "Competition State." The NPM model does not assume a reduction in state intervention; it has "just shifted it from decommodifying bureaucracies to marketizing ones."[89] This shift has been achieved through wider liberalization and deregulation strategies as well as through privatization and contractorization programmes. Thus elements 29 and 30 are expected to give some indication of marketization is a consideration in the operations of the public sector in Hong Kong.

Clearly it is unlikely that all elements will be present in any one organization or system of organization. Many of the elements would contradict each other if introduced simultaneously. However, the appearance of any one of the above elements may indicate an attempt to implement NPM. The model as presented here provided the framework for a questionnaire that was sent to government agencies and departments in Hong Kong to assess the extent to which public sector reform has converged with the international trend.

4. Public Sector Reform in Hong Kong: Applying the NPM Model

The questionnaires were delivered by post to 59 Hong Kong government agencies and departments in August 1998, and 18 were returned (a return of 30 per cent).[90] Respondents were asked to score each NPM component on a 1 to 5 Likert scale. Each response was weighted 0 to 4, therefore the largest possible score for each component would be 4, when multiplied by each questionnaire return, it would give a figure of 72, indicating implementation of a particular NPM component across all 18 agencies. If a 72 were recorded for each component, this would indicate that Hong Kong would display extremely high NPM characteristics. However, because of the Likert scale, there may be uncertainty about the reliability in the range of the 1–3 scores, therefore, it would be possible to say that a "36" (18×2) may also indicate the implementation of a NPM characteristic. Overall, it should be safe to say that any component that scores 36 or over indicates NPM implementation. The results are shown in Annex 4.3.[91]

In sum, it appears that NPM has had a marginal impact on public administration in Hong Kong. Performance measurement and some attempts at decentralization were implemented, but the reforms have largely avoided the market approach favoured by western NPM countries. The model reflects two phases of administrative reform. The first being the attempts at introducing financial management by the drafters of Public Sector Reform; the second is the consumerist thrust of the Patten reforms. However, there are some nuances of NPM that are not picked up by the model, such as the emphasis on customer-friendly skills and the introduction of "core values."[92] Another feature is that the reforms have affected the centre of government, with the separation of policy and execution roles, and the creation of arm's length bodies, such as the trading funds, but the impact on line management appears to be minimal.

Certainly the highest scores (over 40) for elements 5, 6, 13, 22 and 27 appear to reflect the attempt by Public Sector Reform to introduce a management framework.[93] "Leadership" was highlighted as a key value. The kind of managerial accountability associated with NPM appears to be reflected in Hong Kong with respondents identifying with strong organizational leadership and strategic management, so there is little surprise they feel exposed to greater public scrutiny (28). Greater budgetary control (13 and 17) and the implementation of performance appraisal systems (22) commanded the other high scores. In his policy address of October 1998, Chief Executive Tung Chee-hwa announced the Enhanced Productivity Programme (EPP), which demanded that each government department and agency produces plans and targets to achieve a 5% productivity growth by 2002, without additional resources. This appeared to be a direct response to the perception of fiscal crisis when Hong Kong was buffeted by the wider economic crisis in Asia. There is also a move towards contract rather than permanent appointments in the civil service. Overall, EPP appears to have little to do with NPM and more to do with cost cutting.

Other scores (between 36 and 40) for elements 2, 7, 24 and 28 have a less consistent pattern. Elements 2 and 7, which suggest greater devolution in decision-making is consistent with the notion of greater accountability. Law argued that one of the central themes of administrative reform in Hong Kong was to delegate authority as close as possible to the point of delivery.[94] The rationale for this was to increase the responsiveness of departments to the community's needs and to delineate responsibilities and increase accountability, while allowing for flexibilities within a framework of control. Element 24 reflects the implementation of the CASCADE programme as a quality management initiative, and element 27 shows departments trying to improve by integrating service delivery through "one stop shops." However, there are no corresponding high scores for structural and functional change. This indicates that although there are changes in the management process, the structure and the service delivery function of the public sector remains largely unaltered.

Since the questionnaire was circulated in the late summer of 1998, the government in Hong Kong has made a fresh set of proposals to reform the civil service.[95] These reform proposals shifted the Human Resource Management elements, particularly element 21, closer to the NPM model. The wider implication of the Civil Service Bureau's proposals was to initiate a cultural change within the civil service more in tune with developments abroad where the public service is regarded less and less as a lifetime vocation. However, the Basic Law, Hong Kong's "mini-constitution," guaranteed continuity in the civil service system and conditions of service. The Basic Law has effectively frozen Hong Kong's civil service system and thus presents a considerable obstacle to present or future reforms.

In the absence of structural change, NPM appears to have been only half-heartedly applied in Hong Kong. However, the discourse of NPM has permeated and guided the debate about administrative change. Indeed, as Cheung observed, NPM (Cheung refers to "efficiency") "should be looked at more as an important persuasive power for change, providing the much-needed rhetoric to accommodate the politics making up the reform debate and process."[96] This view is echoed by Thrift who noted "the new managerialist discourse must be understood primarily as a form of rhetoric" which does not have to be "coterminous with organizational practice."[97] Therefore, it is unlikely that any civil service system, including Hong Kong, will display all the characteristics of a complete adoption of the NPM model. When assessing the extent of convergence with NPM in Hong Kong, it appears that imitating NPM is more important than its implementation. The attraction of NPM is that it encompasses fashionable ideas and theories. As Peters observes, "even if there are no clear benefits from some of these reforms, they are still likely to be picked up by governments" who wish to enhance, or be seen to enhance their performance.[98] Metcalfe hinted at the dangers of this kind of trend following by pointing to the difficulties in differentiating between public and private management. He argues that it "leaves government dangerously vulnerable to ideological fads and business management fashions — and the public are badly served."[99]

A considerable barrier to NPM in Hong Kong is the civil service's resemblance to a classical bureaucracy. As Scott argued, "if problems do arise, the first assumption is that there is a need for structural reform to improve the span of control or refine the hierarchy."[100] In particular, there is no expectation that junior civil servants will become involved in problem-solving, along with the kind of discretion and responsibility that is assumed by NPM. Therefore it could be argued that *any* administrative exercise could be greeted as successful in Hong Kong. As Lee and Huque observed, "the civil service demonstrates remarkable compliance with hierarchical loyalty. In such a situation, it is relatively easy to initiate changes from the top and get the new culture accepted by exploiting the sentiment of hierarchical loyalty."[101] The strong hierarchy associated with the bureaucracy assumes top-down implementation. NPM type reforms may be difficult to accommodate in a bureaucracy where civil servants are ready to accept orders from above, and hierarchical authority is "reinforced by strict bureaucratic rules and regulations which make violation of hierarchical orders punishable."[102]

Furthermore, the powerful elite that dominates Hong Kong's civil service would also be unlikely to welcome NPM. As Cheung explained:

> It would be inconceivable that the government, which is essentially led and run by civil servants, may want to constrict its own scope of activities and influence. The outcry for debureaucratization and rolling back the frontiers of the state is by no means prominent in the Hong Kong political scene. There are also no strong external demands for change towards such directions.[103]

5. Conclusions

Despite globalization, the state remains a powerful actor in international politics; Hong Kong is certainly no exception when displaying a mixture of convergent and divergent elements in its approach to public sector reform. Policy convergence does not offer an easy explanation of public sector reform in Hong Kong, or anywhere else. Moreover, the determinants of convergence in the Hong Kong context have been around for some time now and not just in the last ten years. Therefore, we should not be surprised that the survey findings support Cheung's view that Hong Kong is not a "trend-follower of NPM" but its reform strategy "has a more dynamic time- and context-relevant meaning."[104] The partial implementation of NPM in Hong Kong shows that the state is selective about which policy instruments it should adopt, without altering its basic structure. Huque, Lee and Cheung regarded Hong Kong as "an odd case in the current global trend of public sector reform," because it was not driven by the usual determinants; in fact they were largely "absent" in the Hong Kong case. The esteem with which the public held the Hong Kong civil service and the business community meant there were no perceptions of government failure to install NPM models.[105] Furthermore, in the Hong Kong context, reunification with China cannot be ignored. The fact that SAR status preserved Hong Kong's system of governance was, in the circumstances, acceptable to China. Government by civil servants, especially by those loyal to Beijing, was always going to be agreeable to the Chinese leadership. Therefore, the irony is that preservation of the colonial system facilitated a smooth transition to SAR status. Even Western NPM style reforms that emphasized efficiency "helped to depoliticize performance evaluation of public service, thus reducing the pressure for greater political accountability from elected politicians and the population at large."[106]

Therefore, rather than converging with a unified international trend, Hong Kong has witnessed the selective adoption of certain methods and techniques. NPM cannot be adopted wholesale, even in "similar system" scenarios. For instance, in his analysis of the transfer of the New Zealand model to Alberta, Canada, Schwartz pointed out Alberta's similarity to New Zealand, yet the transfer from New Zealand was dependent on political convenience to the ruling party in Alberta, which had quite different objectives from the New Zealand Labour government.[107] But as Chen noted when discussing the learning of management styles between Asian and Western companies, "it is ... better to borrow the strong points of the others to supplement one's own system than to abandon one's own system."[108] As convergence assumes that policies become more alike, regardless of the actions of state actors, it is perhaps better to describe Hong Kong's public sector reforms as the adoption of internationally popular policies and programmes in public management that are suited to the local context.

Notes

1. H. Wilensky, *The Welfare State and Equality* (London: University of California Press, 1975), p. xiii

2. M. Kluth and J. Andersen, "The Globalization of European Research and Technology Organizations (RTOs)," in *Beyond Master and Hierarchy: Interactive Governance and Social Complexity*, edited by A. Amin and J. Hausner (Cheltenham: Edward Elgar, 1997), p. 288.

3. R. Webber, "Convergence or Divergenc," *Columbia Journal of World Business*, Vol. 4, No. 3 (1969), pp. 75–83. Also, S. Ronen, *Comparative and Multinational Management* (New York, NY: John Wiley & Sons, 1986), p. 236.

4. D. Strang and J. Meyer, "Institutional Conditions for Diffusion," *Theory and Society,* Vol. 22, No. 4 (1993), p. 491.

5. J. Waltman and D. Studlar (eds), *Political Economy: Public Policies in the United States and Britain* (Jackson, Miss: University Press of Mississippi, 1987).

6. F. Castles (ed.), *The Impact of Parties: Politics and Policies in Democratic Capitalist States* (London: Sage, 1982).

7. Ibid., p. 27.

8. M. Harrop, "Comparison," in *Power and Policy in Liberal Democracies*, edited by M. Harrop (Cambridge, Cambridge University Press, 1992), p. 264.

9. F. Castles and C. Pierson, "A New Convergence? Recent Policy Developments in the United Kingdoms, Australia and New Zealand," *Policy and Politics*, Vol. 24, No. 3 (1996), pp. 242–43.

10. R. M. Kelly, "An Inclusive Democratic Polity, Representative Bureaucracies, and the New Public Management," *Public Administration Review*, Vol. 58, No. 8 (1998), p. 201.

11. J. Micklethwait and A. Wooldridge, *The Witch Doctors* (London: Heinemann, 1996), p. 243.

12. P. DiMaggio and W. Powell, "The Iron Cage Revisited: Institutional Isomorphism and Collective Rationality in Organizational Fields," in *The New Institutionalism in Organizational Analysis*, edited by P. DiMaggio and W. Powell (Chicago and London: University of Chicago Press, 1991).

13. See P. Cerny, "Paradoxes of the Competition State: The Dynamics of Political Globalization," *Government and Opposition*, Vol. 32, No. 2 (1997), pp. 251–74.

14. B. Rockman, "The Changing Role of the State," in *Taking Stock: Assessing Public Sector Reforms*, edited by B. Peters and D. Savoie (Motreal and Kingston: Canadian Centre for Management Development/McGill-Queen's University Press, 1998), p. 29.

15. I. Scott, "Administration in a Small Capitalist State: The Hong Kong Experience," *Public Administration and Development*, Vol. 9, No. 2 (1989), p. 185.

Citing P. Katzenstein, *Small States in World Markets* (Ithaca and London: Cornell University Press, 1985).

16. S. Chiu, K. Ho and T. L. Lui, *City-States in the Global Economy: Industrial Restructuring in Hong Kong and Singapore*, p. 168.

17. Ibid., p. 168.

18. I. Scott, "Administration in a Small Capitalist State: The Hong Kong Experience," in *Public Administration in Small and Island States*, edited by R. Baker (West Hartford, Conn.: Kumarian Press, 1992), p. 104.

19. I. Islam and A. Chowdhury, *Asia-Pacific Economies: A Survey* (London: Routledge, 1997), p. 192.

20. Ibid., p. 193.

21. A. Chun, "Discourses of Identity in the Changing Spaces of Public Culture in Taiwan, Hong Kong and Singapore," *Theory, Culture and Society,* Vol. 13, No. 1 (1996), p. 58.

22. M. Chan, "The Future of Hong Kong," *Annals of the American Academy of Political and Social Science*, Vol. 547 (1996), pp. 11–23.

23. Efficiency Unit, *Serving the Community* (Hong Kong: Government Printer, 1995). See commentary by A. S. Huque, G. Lee and A. Cheung, *The Civil Service in Hong Kong: Continuity and Change* (Hong Kong: Hong Kong University Press, 1998), pp. 47–48.

24. P. Ingraham, "The Reform Agenda for National Civil Service Systems: External Stress and Internal Strains," in *Civil Service Systems in Comparative Perspective*, edited by H. Bekke, J. Perry and Y. Toonen (Bloomington, Ind.: Indiana University Press, 1996), p. 250.

25. Castles and Pierson (Note 9), p. 234.

26. T. Lui, "Efficiency as a Political Concept in Hong Kong Government: Issues and Problems," in *Asian Civil Service Systems: Improving Efficiency and Productivity*, edited by J. Burns (Singapore: Time Academic Press, 1994), p. 27.

27. F. Law, "Hong Kong: The Challenge of Managing the Government's Human Resouces," in *Public Sector Reform: Critical Issues and Perspectives*, edited by I. Scott and I. Thynne (Hong Kong: AJPA, 1994), p. 138.

28. K. W. Chow, "Hong Kong Public Administration under Stress: The Significance and Implications of Management Paradoxes," *International Journal of Public Administration,* Vol. 15, No. 9 (1992), pp. 1633–63.

29. Scott (Note 15), p. 192.

30. Ibid., p. 195.

31. In particular, Indonesia, South Korea and Thailand sought IMF assistance.

32. Lui (Note 26), p. 18.

33. C. Patten, *Our Next Five Years: The Agenda for Hong Kong*, Address by the Governor at the opening of the 1992/93 session of the Legislative Council, 7 October 1992, Hong Kong, p. 26.

34. B. Hook, "British Views of the Legacy of the Colonial Administration of Hong Kong: A Preliminary Assessment," *The China Quarterly*, Vol. 151 (1997), p. 560.

35. M. Hon, "Officials in Need of Training," *South China Morning Post*, 9 October 1997.

36. C. Bennett, "How States Utilize Foreign Evidence," *Journal of Public Policy*, Vol. 11, No. 1 (1991), p. 31.

37. V. Wright, "Reshaping the State: The Implications for Public Administration," *West European Politics,* Vol. 17, No. 3 (1994), p. 107.

38. J. Bjorkman and C. Altenstetter, "Globalized Concepts and Localized Practice: Convergence and Divergence in National Health Policy Reforms," in *Health Policy Reforms, National Variations and Globalization*, edited by C. Altenstetter and J. Bjorkman (Basingstoke: Macmillan, 1997), pp. 14–15.

39. E. Adler and P. Haas, "Conclusion: Epistemic Communities, World Order, and the Creation of a Reflective Research Program," *International Organization,* Vol. 46, No. 1 (1992), p. 386.

40. D. Osborne and T. Gaebler, *Reinventing Government* (Reading, MA: Addison-Wesley, 1992).

41. R. Goffee and J. Hunt, "The End of Management? Classroom versus Boardroom," *Financial Times*, 22 March 1996, pp. 3–4.

42. Huque, Lee and Cheung (Note 23), p. 27.

43. A. Cheung, "Public Sector Reform in Hong Kong: Perspectives and Problems," *Asian Journal of Public Administration,* Vol. 14, No. 2 (1992), p. 120.

44. P. Harris, *Hong Kong: A Study in Bureaucracy and Politics* (Hong Kong: Macmillan, 1998), p. 138

45. Cheung (Note 43), p. 131.

46. Ibid., pp. 131–32.

47. J. Burns, "Administrative Reform in a Changing Political Environment: The Case of Hong Kong," *Public Administration and Development,* Vol. 14 (1994), p. 248.

48. J. Lam, "From a colonial to an accountable administration: Hong Kong's experience," *Asian Affairs,* Vol. 26 (1995), p. 310.

49. R. LeHerissier, "Implications of Overseas Experiences for Public Sector Reform in Hong Kong: Perspectives and Limitations," in *Public Sector Reform in Hong Kong*, edited by J. Lee and A. Cheung (Hong Kong: Chinese University Press, 1995), p. 205.

50. A. Cheung, "Efficiency as the Rhetoric: Public Sector Reform in Hong Kong Explained," *International Review of Administrative Sciences,* Vol. 62, No. 1 (1996), pp. 42–43.

51. Ibid., p. 42.

52. P. Cerny, *Globalization and the Changing Logic of Collective Action*, Working Paper No. 5, Department of Politics, University of York (September 1994).

53. P. Cerny, "The Dynamics of Financial Globalization: Technology, Market Structure and Policy Response," *Policy Sciences,* Vol. 24, No. 4 (1994), pp. 321–22.

54. J. Luke, "Managing Interconnectedness for Public Managers," in *Public Management in an Interconnected World,* edited by M. Bailey Timney and R. Mayer (Westport, CT: Greenwood Press, 1992), pp. 17–18.

55. Harris (Note 44), p. 4.

56. Hook (Note 34), p. 566.

57. Huque, Lee and Cheung (Note 23), p. 20.

58. G. Hofstede, *Culture's Consequences* (Beverly Hills, CA: Sage, 1980).

59. C. Clark and S. Chan, "MNCs and Developmentalism: Domestic Structure as an Explanation for East Asian dynamism," in *Bringing Transnational Relations Back In,* edited by T. Risse-Kappen (Cambridge: Cambridge University Press, 1995), pp. 122–23.

60. M. Chen, *Asian Management Systems* (London: ITP, 1995), p. 296.

61. B. Brewer, "Convergence in Public Sector Management," paper presented to *The State in the Asia-Pacific* conference (Hong Kong: City University of Hong Kong, 6–7 June 1998).

62. H. Root, *Small Countries, Big Lessons: Governance and the Rise of East Asia* (Hong Kong: Oxford University Press [China], 1996), p. 159.

63. H. Johnstone, "Asia Academy seeks to tackle US dominance," *Sunday Morning Post* (Money), 27 December 1998, p. 1.

64. Hofstede (*Culture's Consequences*, p. 98) uses "power distance" as a measure of inequality in organizations. Thus "Power Distance is a measure of the interpersonal power of influence between B and S as perceived by the less powerful of the two." Also see the discussion on p. 135.

65. R. Lachman, A. Nedd and B. Hinings, "Analyzing Cross-National Management and Organizations: A Theoretical Framework," *Management Science,* Vol. 40, No. 1 (1994), pp. 40–55. p. 46, citing P. Birnbaum and G. Wong, "Organizational Structure of Multinational Banks in Hong Kong from a Culture-Free Perspective," *Administrative Science Quarterly,* Vol. 30 (1985), pp. 262–77.

66. R. Seeliger, "Conceptualizing and Researching Policy Convergence," *Policy Studies Journal,* Vol. 24, No. 2 (1996), p. 299.

67. Ibid., p. 300.

68. Efficiency Unit, *Improving Management in Government: The Next Steps* (London: HMSO, 1988).

69. J. Nagel, "Radically Reinventing Government: Editor's Introduction," *Journal of Policy Analysis and Management,* Vol. 16, No. 3 (1997), p. 351.

70. P. Dunleavy, "The Globalization of Public Services Production: Can Government be 'Best in World'?" *Public Policy and Administration,* Vol. 9, No. 2 (1994), pp. 36–64; D. Kettl, "The Global Revolution in Public Management: Driving Themes, Missing Links," *Journal of Policy Analysis and Management,* Vol. 16,

No. 3 (1997), pp, 446–62; and A. Massey (ed.), "In Search of the State: Markets, Myths and Paradigms," in *Globalization and Marketization of Government Services* (Basingstoke: Macmillan, 1997).

71. C. Hood, "A Public Management for All Seasons?" *Public Administration,* Vol. 69, No. 1 (1991), pp. 3–19; and see example, E. Ferlie, L. Ashburner, L. Fitzgerald and A. Pettigrew, *The New Public Management in Action* (Oxford: Oxford University Press, 1996) and M. Holmes and D. Shand, "Management Reforms: Some Practitioners Perspectives on the Past Ten Years," *Governance*, Vol. 8, No. 4 (1995), pp. 551–78.

72. C. Pollitt, "Justification by Works or by Faith: Evaluating the New Public Management," *Evaluation,* Vol. 1, No. 2 (1995), p. 133.

73. For example, P. Aucoin, "Administrative Reform in Public Management: Paradigms, Principles, Paradoxes and Pendulums," *Governance,* Vol. 3, No. 2 (1990), pp. 115–37; Hood (Note 71); C. Pollitt, *Managerialism and the Public Services,* 2nd ed. (Oxford: Blackwell, 1993), and R. Rhodes, "The New Governance Governing without Government," *Political Studies*, Vol. 44, No. 4 (1996), pp. 652–67.

74. L. Terry, "Administrative Leadership, Neo-Managerialism, and the Public Management Movement," *Public Administration Review,* Vol. 58, No. 3 (1998), p. 195.

75. Terry (Note 74), citing A. Gore, *From Red Tape to Results: Creating a Government that Works Better and Costs Less* (Washington, DC: National Performance Review, 1993).

76. P. Light, *The Tides of Reform* (New Haven: Yale University Press, 1997), p. 36, refers to D. Osborne and T. Gaebler, *Reinventing Government* (Reading, MA: Addison-Wesley, 1992) and T. Peters and R. Waterman, *In Search of Excellence* (New York: NY: HarperCollins, 1982).

77. See the discussion in C. Hood, "Contemporary Public Management: A New Global Paradigm," *Public Policy and Administration*, Vol. 10, No. 2 (1995), pp. 104–17.

78. Rhodes (Note 73), pp. 663–64.

79. Aucoin (Note 73).

80. J. Micklethwait and A. Wooldridge, *The Witch Doctor* (London: Heinemann, 1996), p. 330

81. Ibid.

82. B. G. Peters, *The Future of Governing: Four Emerging Models* (Lawrence, Kansas: University Press of Kansas, 1996).

83. Massey (ed.) (Note 70), p. 3.

84. B. Peters, "Theory and Methodology in the Study of Comparative Public Administration," in *Comparative Public Management*, edited by R. Baker (Westport, Conn.: Praeger, 1994), p. 82.

85. M. Holmes, "Public Sector Management Reform: Convergence or Divergence?", *Governance*, Vol. 5, No. 4 (1992), p. 477.

86. "A New Management in the Public Sector," see also J-E Lane, *The Public Sector* (London: Sage, 1993), p. 147.

87. Kettl (Note 70), p. 449.

88. World Bank, *World Development Report* (New York, NY: Oxford University Press, 1997), p. 27.

89. Cerny (Note 13), p. 266.

90. Only 3 questionnaire respondents indicated that they were willing to be interviewed. As this constituted an insignificant percentage of Hong Kong government departments and agencies, it was decided not to conduct interviews. See Appendix 1 for a full list of responding departments and agencies.

91. "High" scores (36+) in bold.

92. Chief Secretary, "The Hong Kong Government Serving the Community," Briefing to Legislative Council Members on 10 February 1995.

93. Haque, Lee and Cheung (Note 23), p. 48.

94. Law (Note 27), p. 137.

95. Civil Service Bureau, Hong Kong Special Administrative Region Government, "Civil Service into the 21st Century — Civil Service Reform" (Hong Kong: Government Printer of the SAR, March 1999).

96. Cheung (Note 50), p. 32.

97. "The Rise of Soft Capitalism," p. 37, citing N. Nohria and J. Berkley (1994), "The Virtual Organization: Bureaucracy, Technology and the Implosion of Control," in *The Post-Bureaucratic Organization*, edited by C. Hecksher and A. Donnellon A (Thousand Oaks, CA: Sage, 1994), pp. 125–26.

98. B. Peters, "Policy Transfers Between Governments: The Case of Administrative Reforms," *West European Politics,* Vol. 20, No. 4 (1997), p. 78.

99. L. Metcalfe, "Public Management: From Imitation to Innovation," in *Modern Governance*, edited by J. Kooiman (London: Sage, 1993), p. 177.

100. Scott (Note 15), p. 195.

101. G. Lee and A. S. Huque, "Hong Kong: Administrative Reform and Recent Public Sector Changes — The Institutionalisation of New Values," *Australian Journal of Public Administration,* Vol. 55, No. 49 (1996), p. 18.

102. Haque, Lee and Cheung (Note 23), p. 25.

103. Cheung (Note 43), p. 136.

104. Ibid., p. 137.

105. Haque, Lee and Cheung (Note 23), p. 47.

106. A. Cheung, "Rebureaucratization of Politics in Hong Kong: Prospects after 1997," *Asian Survey,* Vol. 37, No. 9 (1997), p. 727.

107. H. Schwartz, "Reinvention and Retrenchment: Lessons from the Application of

the New Zealand Model to Alberta, Canada," *Journal of Policy Analysis and Management,* Vol. 16, No. 3 (1997), pp. 405–22.

108. Chen (Note 60), p. 298.

Annex 4.1 Comparison of Western and East Asian Management Styles

Western	East Asian
1. Hierarchical, egalitarian command, segmented concern	Free-form command, roles loosely defined, holistic concern
2. Professional manager, position related to function	Social leaders often with high-sounding titles for low-ranking jobs
3. Particularism, specialized career path possibly with rapid evaluation and promotion, individually orientated	Non-specialized career paths, slow evaluation, regimented promotion, socially orientated
4. Decentralization of power	Centralization of power
5. Mobility	Stability
6. Diversity	Unity
7. Direct approach	Indirect approach
8. Systematic analysis, standardization, categorization, classification, conceptualization, precision.	Ambiguity, reaction, adaptation
9. Long-term set planning	Often lack of formal set planning, high flexibility in adjustment
10. Explicit control mechanisms	Implicit control mechanisms
11. Organizations and systems adapt to change	Leaders/managers adapt to change

Source: D. Waters, *21st Century Management: Keeping Ahead of the Japanese and Chinese* (Singapore: Prentice-Hall, 1991) p. 196, cited in *Asian Management Systems*, p. 298.

Annex 4.2 New Public Management Model

Reform	Meaning
STRUCTURE 1. Separate policy from operations 2. Greater operational control 3. Territorial/geographical decentralization 4. Reduce number of departments/ agencies	Organizational decentralization Horizontal decentralization Shift to emphasis on executive functions Vertical decentralization Streamline organizational structure
PROCESS 5. Corporatization/strong organizational leadership 6. Strategic management 7. Decisions made close to/at point of service delivery	Introduce private sector management techniques "Hands on" management enjoying greater visibility, accountability and discretion. Business and corporate planning Managerial decentralization
Budgetary Process 8. Financial performance measurement 9. Creating internal markets 10. Cost-centre creation 11. Use of cost rather than expenditure 12. Ending annuality 13. Use of budgets for planning/ control 14. Use of output measures and volume targets in budgets 15. Cost-saving incentives 16. Greater evaluation through audit 17. Bulk budgeting 18. Deregulation of purchasing	Stress on and use of outputs (or outcomes) Separation of purchasing and providing functions Devolved budgeting Focus on actual costs rather than volume budgeting Freedom to retain savings Rational budgeting More detailed budgetary scrutiny Encouraging managers to make efficient use of resources Establishment of independent auditing bodies Greater flexibility within budgetary parameters Avoiding central procurement agencies

Annex 4.2 New Public Management Model (Cont'd)

Reform	Meaning
Human Resource Management (Personnel)	
19. Changing reward structure	Pay to reflect "market" conditions
20. Performance related/merit pay	Pay to reflect performance
21. Performance contracts	Tenure determined by performance
22. Appraisal based on performance	
23. Personnel deregulation	The elimination of a range of civil service controls.
Quality	
24. Quality management	Deprofessionalization (consumer orientation)
25. Programme review	Systematic analysis of costs and benefits of individual programmes.
26. PR and marketing	Establishing market identity for public organizations
27. Integrated service delivery	"One stop shops" and case management
28. Foster greater transparency	More public scrutiny
FUNCTIONS	"Marketization"
29. Privatization	Sale of publicly owned enterprises, goods, assets etc.
30. Contracting out (market testing)	Creating and managing competitive environments

Sources: Designed with thanks to Normal Flynn, who provided useful comments
when the model was being drafted. The model also builds upon the
following works: *The Future of Governing: Four Emerging Models*;
B.G. Peters, "Theory and Methodology," in *Civil Service Systems in
Comparative Perspective*, edited by H. Bekke, J. Perry and T. Toonen
(Bloomington, Ind: Indiana University Press, 1996); "The Globalization
of Public Services Production: Can Government be 'Best in the
World'?", "Reshaping the State: the Implications for Public
Administration," "Management Reform: Some Practitioner Perspectives
on the Past Ten Years," in J. Ukeles, *Doing More with Less: Turning
Public Management Around* (New York, NY: AMACOM, A Division of
American Management Association, 1982).

Annex 4.3

Reform	Meaning
STRUCTURE	Organizational decentralization
1. Separate policy from operations	18
2. Greater operational control	**37**
3. Territorial/geographical decentralization	30
4. Reduce number of departments/agencies	24
PROCESS	Introduce private sector management techniques
5. Corporatization/strong organizational leadership	**51**
6. Strategic management	**50**
7. Decisions made close to/at point of service delivery	**39**
Budgetary Process	
8. Financial performance measurement	16
9. Create internal markets	34
10. Cost-centre creation	28
11. Use of cost rather than expenditure	25
12. Ending annuality	12
13. Use of budgets for planning/control	**50**
14. Use of output measures and volume targets in budgets	32
15. Cost-saving incentives	20
16. Greater evaluation through audit	28
17. Bulk budgeting	**38**
18. Deregulation of purchasing	30
Human Resource Management (Personnel)	
19. Change reward structure	29
20. Performance related/merit pay	20
21. Performance contracts	20
22. Appraisal based on performance	**52**
23. Personnel deregulation	20
Quality	
24. Quality management (continuous quality improvement)	39
25. Programme review	34
26. PR and marketing	23

Annex 4.3 (Cont'd)

Reform	Meaning
27. Integrated service delivery	**38**
28. Foster greater transparency	**53**
FUNCTIONS	"Marketization"
29. Privatization	9
30. Contracting out (market testing)	28

PART TWO

Departmental/Agency Reforms:
Progress and Review

5

Post Office Trading Fund

P. C. Luk

Postmaster General

1. Introduction

The Post Office has operated as a Trading Fund since 1 August 1995. The Post Office Trading Fund was established under the Trading Funds Ordinance of 12 March 1993. This Ordinance provided for the Legislative Council, on the recommendation of the Financial Secretary, to establish a Trading Fund to manage and account for the operation of a government service where the government has the financial objective of that service funding itself from its own income.

The Trading Fund is designed primarily for improving the efficiency and quality of service of government departments which have the capacity to meet expenses and to finance liabilities from their own revenue. All revenue generated by the services provided by the department is paid into the fund and all expenditure, including capital, incurred in the provision of services is paid out of the fund. This accounting framework provides a higher degree of flexibility in resource management for the departments concerned, with a higher degree of financial accountability and management responsibility.

The basic criteria of a trading fund operation are that:

- the revenue consists principally of receipts in respect of goods and services provided in the course of the fund's operation;

- financing by a trading fund would improve the management efficiency and effectiveness of the operation;
- it is essentially providing a commercial or quasi-commercial service; and
- the operation should be able to break even and make a profit.

2. The Post Office

The Post Office has an exclusive privilege under the Post Office Ordinance to provide a local and overseas letter service in Hong Kong. This exclusive privilege comes with a social obligation, which requires the Post Office to maintain a universal postal service in Hong Kong and charge all customers basically the same postage rates. The government's policy has always been to provide an efficient and effective universal postal service at reasonable and affordable prices to meet the needs of the community and to fulfil Hong Kong's international postal obligations. Any price increases have been kept broadly in line with inflation.

The Post Office is the first public certification authority in Hong Kong providing full public certification services to facilitate secure electronic transactions and to authenticate the identities of participants in e-commerce. The initiative is part of the government's commitment to foster an environment conducive to a flourishing e-commerce sector in Hong Kong. It is built on the basis of the Post Office's high status as a trusted third party.

The Post is a HK$3.7 billion highly labour intensive industry currently employing some 5,800 full time permanent staff. Its wage bill represents over 60% of total operating costs. It is a big business with structured systems and practices: a business which needs to continue to remain profitable in the face of rising competition.

The core businesses operated by the Post Office are essentially:

- Letters and packets;
- Parcels;
- Speedpost and Local Courier Post;
- Retailing of postal related products through counter outlets and appointed agents;
- Philatelic services and issue of stamp products;
- Agency services for government departments, public bodies and public utilities;

- Certification Authority services;
- Remittance services;
- Logistics services.

In addition, the Post Office provides a range of miscellaneous services set out in the Post Office Regulations, such as leasing of private post boxes, certifying posting of mail items and so on. In its efforts to better meet demands of individual groups of customers, it also provides different forms of value-added services.

The postal business is one of the world's oldest infrastructural businesses. In its original form it was the mechanism that enabled individuals to exchange documents and goods nationally and internationally. This is still the main feature today — the acceptance, transport and delivery of documents and goods. Despite the predictions of a declining market of document and letter transactions in the face of technology, growth in the traditional business areas has continued to be buoyant over time with a total 1,280 million mail items handled in 1999–2000 compared with 1,054 million items in 1993–94 — an overall increase of 21% over six years. In the four years leading up to the establishment of the Trading Fund in 1995 (from 1990–91 to 1993–94) traffic overall grew by 18% (from 891 to 1,054 million items) per annum.

Growth of this order has naturally created demand for additional resources in order to maintain consistent quality service at affordable prices. At the same time, the postal service has had to face increasing competition from private operators who are aggressively competing in the city/business area of documents and goods as they are for the international courier and airmail business. This environment demands the creation of new value-added services and new products as well as venturing into new markets, in order to expand the business and to sustain it into the future.

Prior to the establishment of the Post Office Trading Fund, all surplus revenue was required to be paid into the government's general revenue with operational funding being governed through the government's annual Resource Allocation Exercise. Thus, while the total revenue from the Post Office's various activities had, in the years leading up to 1995, been more than adequate to cover operating costs and provide a modest profit, any surplus could not be deployed automatically by the Post Office towards operational expenses or to improve services to the community.

In this regime, the Post Office had to contend with conflicting pressures on it to restrain expenditure, to maintain service standards, to meet increasing demands, and to achieve agreed financial targets. While the Post Office was able to obtain additional resources from the annual Resource Allocation Exercise, these had not been sufficient to keep pace with the growing demand for services. As a result, the Post Office found itself in the unenviable situation of having to cut back on certain services such as ceasing the remittance service, reducing the deployment of services on the profitable Speedpost service and shortening the operating hours of some branch offices. Service performance generally suffered and management certainly were not motivated to think innovatively.

3. The Post Office Trading Fund

Early in 1993 the Public Services Policy Group of the Government directed that a postal policy review should be undertaken to develop a strategy for the Post Office, in particular to examine the case for operating the department as a trading fund. The Economic Services Bureau (then Economic Services Branch) together with the Post Office, Finance Bureau (then Finance Branch), and the Efficiency Unit undertook the review. The issues covered, among other things, the role of the Post Office and the option of a Post Office Trading Fund.

3.1 Role of the Post Office

In recognition of the need to maintain a universal letter service the view was that the Post Office's role was to provide a reliable, efficient, comprehensive and universal postal service at an affordable price that responds to Hong Kong's postal needs and accords with Hong Kong's international postal obligations. To do this it was seen as important that the Post Office should keep itself abreast of its markets and establish close relationship with its customers in order to respond quickly to their needs, to improve the quality of service and to develop new products and services to suit the market.

The review concluded that to improve its financial performance and keep pace with changing market needs, the Post Office should not only be required to maintain its existing core services but should also be encouraged to introduce new services and improve existing services, provided:

- it could demonstrate that it would be able to meet its universal service obligation up to agreed standards after the introduction of the new services;
- it can self-finance these new activities; and
- the services are provided in response to proven demand or to achieve better utilization of resources.

The review recognized that there was an unmet demand in a number of areas and suggested that the Post Office should, provided that resources were available, meet such demand and generate additional revenue to finance further new or improved services. These include services such as the expansion of the Speedpost service, philatelic product ordering service, parcel delivery service to the New Territories and the introduction of vending machines and agency services for other organizations or government departments within Post Office premises.

The review also recognized that the main problem faced by the Post Office was that while it had the potential to finance from its annual profits, improve productivity and expand services to meet demand, and maximize revenue, it was simply not being afforded the opportunity or the flexibility to do so. It noted that the Post Office had consistently failed to secure the necessary funds in the annual Resource Allocation Exercise because of the priority claim of other competing government programmes.

3.2 Option of a Post Office Trading Fund

The outcome of the review was clear. Ways had to be found to enable the Post Office to be able to respond more effectively to changes in its market and operating environment and to enable it to improve productivity, cost efficiency and customer service standards by having greater flexibility in resource management. It was considered that these issues and the problems faced by the Post Office should be dealt with by moving the department onto a trading fund operation, giving it the ability to plough back a portion of its profits into the business to enable it to upgrade services generally.

The staff of the Post Office had been consulted during the course of the review and had not indicated any objection to the proposal. Under the trading fund operation, all staff would remain civil servants subject to the normal civil service terms and conditions of service. This consultation process was quite thorough. Letters were sent to all staff by the Postmaster General at regular intervals, keeping them informed of the developments and meetings were held with union and staff association representatives.

The criteria for operating as a trading fund having been met, the Legislative Council passed a resolution at its sitting on 19 July 1995, to establish the Post Office Trading Fund with effect from 1 August 1995. The resolution set out the services that may be provided, the assets appropriated to the Fund, the net value of fixed assets and the funding arrangements. The net value of the assets was assessed at HK$3,001.4 million and was represented in the Capital Investment Fund by HK$900.4 million as a loan to the Post Office and by HK$2,101 million as a contribution of trading fund capital (the government's investment in the trading fund). The loan is repayable by ten equal annual instalments of HK$90.04 million due on 1 August each year (1996 through to 2006) with loan interest payable annually in arrears at a rate equal to the average of the best lending rate quoted by the continuing members of the Committee of the Hong Kong Association of Banks. Dividend on trading fund capital is payable having regard to the projected annual surplus and the long-term funding requirements of the trading fund. The assets remain the property of the government.

Under the Trading Funds Ordinance the Post Office Trading Fund is obliged to achieve a reasonable rate of return, as determined by the Financial Secretary, on the fixed assets employed. Also under the Ordinance, the Financial Secretary designated the Postmaster General as the General Manager to control and manage the Post Office Trading Fund, accountable to the former for the operations of the Fund. The Ordinance sets out a general manager's responsibilities in managing a Fund, the accounting and reporting requirements, and the rules governing trading fund monies surplus to requirements. A general manager may not vary the services undertaken by a trading fund other than in accordance with the Legislative Council resolution, except that the Financial Secretary may authorize a general manager to undertake additional operations under a trading fund that are incidental to the trading fund's prescribed services.

4. Framework Agreement

Prior to the 1 August 1995 Post Office Trading Fund vesting date, a regulatory framework in the form of a Framework Agreement was agreed between the Secretary for Economic Services and the Postmaster General.

This was put in place with the purpose of ensuring that the Post Office exercises its increased autonomy responsibly and to safeguard the interests of its customers. The Framework Agreement sets out the role and responsibilities of the Secretary for Economic Services and the Postmaster General, the functions and objectives of the Post Office, the financial planning and control arrangements, pay and personnel matters, and the interface arrangements with other government departments and the use of their services.

The Agreement calls for the Postmaster General to prepare each year a medium range corporate plan and an annual business plan setting out the short and longer-term strategies for achieving the business and policy objectives.

The medium range corporate plan sets out:

- the main policy aims, financial objectives and performance targets;
- management and organization;
- demand analysis and forecasts;
- assumptions in relation to external factors affecting the incomes and business plans of the Post Office;
- the quality and standard of service;
- forecast revenue, including the basis of prices for new services and proposed changes to existing charges;
- manpower and other resource assessment;
- the proposed capital investment programme;
- the funding required (if any) from the Capital Investment Fund in the form of loan or trading fund capital;
- forecast results, balance sheets and cash flow statements; and
- forecast performance against financial and other targets.

The annual business plan outlines the plans for the following financial year, including budgeted results, financial and performance targets, and the assumptions on which they are based.

In addition, the Postmaster General is required to submit statements of the annual accounts of the trading fund prepared in accordance with generally accepted accounting principles for auditing by the Director of Audit and for the subsequent tabling in the Legislative Council together with the annual report on the operation of the trading fund by the Financial Secretary.

Proposals for changes in postage rates or to the level of fees and charges continue to be handled by the Postmaster General within the framework of the Post Office Ordinance (Cap. 98). However, the Framework Agreement requires the Postmaster General to discuss them with the Secretary for Economic Services for agreement during the formal planning process set out in the annual business plan.

Under the Framework Agreement, the Secretary for Economic Services assumes the role of the regulator of postal services and is responsible for, *inter-alia*:

- formulating and reviewing government's policies and aims for postal services;
- setting policy objectives of the Post Office;
- setting performance targets for the Post Office in consultation with the Postmaster General;
- ensuring timely consideration and approval of the Annual Business Plan and the medium range Corporate Plan;
- speaking for the administration on policy matters relating to the Post Office;
- price fixing mechanisms not governed by the Framework Agreement.

The Postmaster General is also responsible to the Secretary for Economic Services for:

- managing and operating the business of the Post Office and achieving the performance targets of the Post Office;
- responding to questions and queries on matters relating to the day-to-day management of the Post Office;
- advising the Secretary for Economic Services on policy, legislative and operational matters relating to the business of the Post Office; and
- providing information as and when requested, on any matter relating to the Post Office.

The Framework Agreement gives the Postmaster General authority to:

- incur expenditure in accordance with the approved Annual Business Plan with due adjustments in response to changes in customer demands and services;
- invest in and dispose of assets or individual items approved in the Annual Business Plan (any other items being subject to separate discussion with the Secretary for Economic Services and the Secretary for the Treasury);

  - borrow from the Capital Investment Fund or by way of temporary overdraft facilities as may be approved by the Secretary for the Treasury under the Trading Funds Ordinance in order to finance fixed assets and working capital; and
  - invest cash balances which are surplus to immediate requirements in accordance with any instruction issued by the Secretary for the Treasury under the Trading Funds Ordinance.

5. Post Office's Performance in the Trading Fund

As previously discussed, the aim of the trading fund is for the Post Office to provide better services, while making reasonable profits. The financial flexibility provided by the trading fund has enabled the Post Office to do so. New skills have been developed, new and improved services have been introduced, decision making is quicker and a new customer service culture is emerging.

The change to trading fund status has spurred the Post Office to review how it can best serve Hong Kong and its customers. It has developed a new vision, mission and values in early 1996 through a series of seminars and workshops, commencing with senior management and then cascading to the entire management grade, and to union and staff representatives. Each level made its own specific contributions, with senior management focusing on the vision and mission, the management grade focusing on the values, and the union and staff representatives helping to shape the final version. The Post Office considered that as many people as practicable should be involved, to ensure wide understanding and support as the concepts are cascaded to others in the department. Thus some 300 people were involved in the initial stages.

In serving the community, the Post Office has a vision to be recognized in Hong Kong as an outstanding service organization and worldwide as an outstanding postal service.

Its mission is to have a highly motivated, satisfied and valued workforce, achieve high levels of customer satisfaction, be a viable business with sufficient resources to invest in the future and anticipate and meet changing needs.

The values are to care about customers and staff and to team up for excellence and continuous improvement.

The vision gives the overall direction, defining the kind of organization the Post Office should be. The aim is to compare favourably with outstanding service organizations in Hong Kong, and to be a world class postal administration. The mission sets out the areas to concentrate on to turn the vision into reality. The values define the way in which staff at all levels should work, or the culture of the Post Office. The culture is to care for those the Post Office deals with, and to work together for better results.

Measures have been developed to monitor customer feedback through various channels including customer liaison groups, collection of customer suggestions, market research and public perception survey. Staff feedback has been monitored through regular meetings with staff representatives and union representatives and the staff perception survey. There are also other measures on performance, viability and meeting changing needs. The public perception survey indicates that customers are increasingly satisfied with the service provided by the Post Office. The staff perception survey also indicates that the staff are generally satisfied with the management of the Post Office.

Some of the more notable achievements that have been made since the establishment of the Post Office Trading Fund is shown in Annex 5.1 and details are found in Hongkong Post's *100 Projects for Better Services 1997– 98 to 1999–2000.*

A great deal has, therefore, been achieved by the Post Office in the trading fund environment within a comparatively short span of time. The efforts expended in service improvement and promotion have paid off and the business has been expanded. It would have been almost impossible to do this under the traditional government department regime that applied prior to 1995 and certainly not within the same time span.

6. Operational Constraints

Despite the increased financial flexibility provided to the Post Office through the Trading Fund Framework Agreement, there are still a number of operational constraints affecting the Post Office's ability to address the challenges of technology substitution, globalization, growing customer sophistication and competition both domestically and internationally.

The main operational constraints include:

- limited discretion over fees and charges;
- limited scope under the existing legislation to expand business;

- high staff cost and lack of authority to determine terms and conditions of staff;
- insufficient commercial skills to cope with diversification of postal business; and
- no legal entity to enter into partnership and joint ventures with the private sector to exploit commercial opportunities.

The target rate of return expected to be met by the Post Office Trading Fund in due course (as determined by the Financial Secretary) is 10.5% on the average net value of fixed assets. In each of the first three years of operation under the trading fund, the financial targets have been exceeded, the return on average fixed assets being much higher than projected. This was to a large extent due to an overwhelming demand for Hong Kong postage stamps experienced during the period of sovereignty transition in 1997.

However, during the recent two years, as a result of economic downturn and increasing competition in both the local and international postal markets, the volume of mail handled has declined. Furthermore, burdened by its operational constraints, coupled with the interest in Hong Kong stamps stabilizing and the fact that postage rates have not been revised since 1996, the Post Office has suffered operating losses in the 1998–99 and 1999–2000 financial years. This is a clear indication that the current trading fund operation has not given the Post Office sufficient commercial flexibilities to cope with the present challenges.

During the five-year period operating as a trading fund, the Post Office has returned to the government a total of HK$1,236 million in dividends and another HK$535 million by way of taxation (key financial performance see Annex 5.2)

7. The Way Ahead

The regulatory framework of the trading fund has brought about a new level of commercial thinking and sense of urgency to the Post Office. Post Office staff have become more innovative and responsive to customer needs and are today better equipped to provide new and improved services and products. But the organization is still tightly bound, through the Trading Funds Ordinance and the Post Office Ordinance, to the protocols of a government department rather than to those of a trading enterprise. In reality the Post Office does not have full autonomy or authority as a true commercial concern would have to introduce new service concepts or to react quickly to change — whether this be in response to "environmental" issues or to exploit opportunities in the market place. It is also obliged to adhere to some government department procedures which are not appropriate to those of a postal trading enterprise in the modern world. Certainly decision making within the Post Office is now quicker than in bygone days but the overall process can still often be hampered because of the need to follow bureaucratic processes which are perceived as debilitating by the enterprise as a whole.

Like any commercial enterprise the Post Office will face ever increasing demands and pressure in the year's ahead to adapt its operation to take account of new processes, new technology, movements and shifts in traffic patterns affected by economic cycles and increasing competition both in the local and international market, and to act in a competitive way — returning a reasonable dividend to its owner (the government). It will be hard pressed to do this effectively and efficiently as it does not have complete freedom to act commercially and to trade competitively.

As it presently stands, the Post Office Trading Fund has provided the Post Office with more financial flexibility than that available to a traditional vote-funded government department. It has given its staff a stronger market orientation and a sharper customer focus. However, management's ability to exploit business opportunities, to expand the business and to take it forward into the future, will be hampered if it is obliged to operate under the existing rules of the fund and while it is still bound by civil service salaries and conditions and other government rules and regulations. These are not appropriate for a trading entity in today's increasingly competitive world and, in the long term, will preclude the Post Office from meeting its committed aims and obligations. If the Post Office is to survive and prosper as a profitable and efficient trading organization into the next millennium, more exemptions from existing government rules and regulations, and greater flexibilities in other areas such as staff matters, procurement and business diversification would be required.

Annex 5.1 Notable Achievements Since the Establishment of the Post Office Trading Fund

- Established a Business Development Branch to ensure that customer's needs are being given priority
- Established a Customer Service and Sales Division to focus on account management and regular visits to major customers
- Established a telesales team to improve customer service
- Opened a new and fully mechanized Air Mail Centre
- Introduced new design and layout for new and reprovisioned counter offices
- Provided composite counter at new post offices
- Purchased culler-facer-canceller machines to enhance productivity in letter processing
- Opened a post office in Discovery Bay
- Opened Sheung Tak Post Office
- Set up Postal Gallery
- Introduced Local Bulk Economy service
- Introduced Freepost service
- Introduced e-Post service
- Introduced Direct Entry service
- Introduced Surface Airlifted service
- Introduced postage paid envelopes
- Introduced Transshipment service
- Introduced Mail Order service for postal souvenirs to local and overseas customers
- Introduced Take-one Box service for business customers
- Introduced Local Consignment service for business customers
- Introduced Local CourierPost Standard and Premium service
- Introduced Logistics service
- Introduced one-stop-shop service for private souvenir covers
- Provided photocopying service at selected post offices
- Launched postal remittance service with China Post and Philippine Post
- Launched PayThruPost service at all branch offices
- Introduced a new millennium series of postal souvenirs to the public

Annex 5.1 Notable Achievements Since the Establishment of the Post Office Trading Fund (Cont'd)

- Launched Certification Authority (CA) service
- Implemented pilot Public Key Infrastructure application with major companies and organizations to test the ease of use, performance and reliability of the Hongkong Post Certification Authority services
- Collaborated with the University of Hong Kong to bundle the Strong Cryptographic Library Client Suite (e-Cert Edition) software with Hongkong Post e-Cert service to promote locally developed cryptographic technology
- Established the Hongkong Post e-Cert Gallery at 1/F of the General Post Office to enhance public understanding of security on electronic transactions and the Hongkong Post CA services
- Set up the Hongkong Post e-Cert Promotion and Support Centre at the DigiHall 21 of Hong Kong Productivity Council to promote the Hongkong Post e-Cert services to small and medium enterprises
- Attained 99% next day delivery for local letters, up from 96.4% in 1993/94
- Extended the next day delivery service standard to local mail other than Permit and Hongkong Post Circular service items
- Improved the delivery standard for parcels addressed to major commercial and industrial areas to within two working days of posting/arrival
- Extended door-to-door parcel delivery service to the Central District and the New Territories
- Provided door delivery for bulk parcels
- Provided evening delivery of registered items, parcels and large packets in residential areas on an ad hoc basis
- Increased frequency of mail collections for street posting boxes in the New Territories from once to twice a day
- Resumed collections from street posting boxes on Sundays and public holidays
- Provided evening collections for street posting boxes in major commercial and industrial areas
- Provided posting boxes at some MTR stations
- Extended the facilities of mail rooms at major commercial buildings to accept Speedpost and privately franked mail items including registered articles and parcels

Annex 5.1 Notable Achievements Since the Establishment of the Post Office Trading Fund (Cont'd)

- Enhanced the Speedpost service, including the introduction of new size Speedpost packs and insurance service, the provision of new credit arrangements for customers, the establishment of a one-stop-shop hotline service for pickup orders, the extension of pick-up time to 8 pm and to include Sunday on request, the acceptance of items up to 30 kg and the introduction of a track and trace system to enable customers to obtain delivery information either through the telephone interactive voice response system, or fax, or through the internet
- Accepted and delivered parcels up to 30 kg and extend compensation to include all ordinary parcels
- Enhanced the Bulk Air Mail service
- Enhanced the Local Standing Order service for philatelic products
- Established additional philatelic offices
- Accepted payment by credit card
- Introduced Internet ordering of philatelic and PostShop products
- Introduced a new local postage rate structure to offer more choice, discounts and services to bulk mail
- Sold postage stamp booklets through additional private agents
- Introduced overnight operations at General Post Office and International Mail Centre to improve work efficiency
- Started Sunday opening for the Airport Post Office
- Arranged Joint Stamp Issue with other postal administrations
- Enhanced Hongkong Post Circular service by extending its delivery coverage to commercial areas and upgrading its service standard
- Extended bulk acceptance facility to more post offices
- Extended cut-off time for acceptance of postage prepaid items to 3 pm
- Revised all letter delivery beats to improve productivity and efficiency of letter delivery
- Extended the installation of document posting boxes
- Implemented an on-line system for Speedpost customers to place orders for stationery and pick up through Internet
- Extended the acceptance hours of Speedpost service at selected post offices
- Provided time certain delivery of Speedpost to major destinations

Annex 5.1 Notable Achievements Since the Establishment of the Post Office Trading Fund (Cont'd)

- Introduced Speedpost Bulk Bargain promotion programme
- Extended the sale of PostShop items and introduced the sale of magazines to selected post offices
- Extended the service hours of Post Office Boxes at selected offices
- Provided virtual Post Office Boxes for renting at over-subscribed post offices
- Introduced the sale of stationery items and greeting cards to selected post offices
- Expanded the distribution network of stamps and Speedpostpacks cartons through the management offices of selected private housing estates and industrial buildings
- Improved and upgraded the franking machine service and streamlined the operational control procedures
- Licensed new and enhanced models of the franking machine with remote telemeter resetting capability
- Enhanced the Post Office Box Information System to provide one-stop service in processing new applications for boxes and to introduce the autopayment facility
- Introduced new logo/image and new staff uniforms, including uniforms for counter staff
- Published Hongkong Post Chinese homepage on the Internet
- Completed Customer Service Training for all staff
- Commissioned Track and Trace system for Speedpost, Parcels and Registered articles
- Extended Internet mail tracking enquiry for parcel and other mail services
- Installed facilities at selected post offices to enable public access to government services via the Internet
- Established business case on introducing postcode
- Enhanced Telephone Enquiry Bureau by installing voice mail box for customer inquiry outside normal office hours
- Opened all two-men post offices during lunch breaks
- Improved customer service by reviewing the mail tracing operation
- Improved customer service by introducing customer retention schemes
- Implemented the customer complaint/feedback management system

Annex 5.1 Notable Achievements Since the Establishment of the Post Office Trading Fund (Cont'd)

- Conducted customer satisfaction survey on counter, delivery and telephone hotline services
- Improved customer service by reviewing the Speedpost recovery system
- Introduced "Postal Consultancy" service at pilot post offices

Annex 5.2 Key Financial Performance of Post Office Trading Fun

(Unit: in HK$ million)

	1995–96*	1996–97	1997–98	1998–99	1999–2000
Revenue	2,376	4,964	4,930	3,519	3,516
Expenditure	2,075	3,341	3,697	3,669	3,593
Profit /(Loss) from operations	301	1,623	1,233	(150)	(77)
Other income[1]	22	70	269	252	127
Finance cost	53	69	72	63	48
Tax charge/(credit)	45	274	240	(1)	(23)
Profit after tax	225	1,350	1,190	40	25
Dividend	68	540	595	20	13
Retained earnings	157	810	595	20	12
Return on average net fixed assets	9.0%	47.8%	41.0%	3.1%	2.1%

* For eight months ended 31 March 1996.

Note: 1. Other Income includes interest income and HK Profits Tax rebate, which was received in 1998–99.

6

Management Enhancement Programme in the Housing Department

Tony Miller
Director of Housing

Every historian knows the temptation to impose an order on the past. In reality the unfolding of events may suggest a pattern, but it rarely follows even the best laid plan. So it is with public sector reform. What starts with instinct and a perception that is common only to the extent that things are felt to be not quite right, may through brainstorming and analysis evolve into a more formal plan, but what happens thereafter depends far more than the textbooks suppose on opportunity and accident. Nothing is inevitable, least of all the outcome of a programme of reforms, because, as in a journey abroad, each step along the road of reform is part of a process of discovery.

Two things in particular contribute to the uncertainty. First, the policy landscape is rarely fixed and more usually dynamic. Thus in the Housing Authority's case the reforms were conceived at a time when key psychological barriers on both a more rational allocation and a more market-friendly means of providing housing assistance were yet to be scaled. Second, the human factor is always present, and in the Housing Authority's case ranged from the aspirations of its 3 million customers, through the hopes and fears of the Housing Department's 15,000 loyal and hardworking staff, to the ambitions of several newly energetic private sector service industries.

So in describing the origins of the Management Enhancement Programme at the Housing Authority, I will consciously try to avoid any order other than the roughly chronological. It has been an evolutionary process. At time of writing (March 1999) it has reached a critical stage, and success is by no means a foregone conclusion. The potential for improvement is huge, but the risks are not small.

1. The Organizations

The Housing Authority traces its origins to the great fire at Shek Kip Mei on Christmas Day 1953, which first prompted the government to commence a crash programme of emergency housing for the huddled masses of refugees sheltering in flimsy shacks on the hillsides surrounding the city. However, the current institutional structure, a Housing Authority comprising appointed non-officials with a Government Department as its executive arm, dates from a major governmental reform in April 1973.

That was the year when the Urban Council was given its autonomy, its chairmanship passed from official to non-official hands and its previous responsibilities for housing were passed to a newly constituted Housing Authority.[1] Prior to this, responsibility for the provision of housing and housing services was fragmented, shared between the Housing Division of the Urban Services Department, the Resettlement Department and the Public Works Department. The establishment of the new unified Housing Authority with sole responsibility for provision of public housing was designed to give a proper impetus to the recently announced Ten Year Housing Programme. However, this merging of responsibility for the various different types of assisted housing — Cottage Areas, Licensed Areas, Resettlement Estates, Government Low Cost Housing and the old Housing Authority's Estates — is of particular interest from the point of view of early departmental culture.

The newly formed Housing Department brought together four previously separate groups. The first three were: the staff of Government's Resettlement Department responsible for Squatter Control and Clearance and the Management of the Resettlement Estates, most of whom were non-professionals, the professional Housing Managers and staff of the old Housing Division of the Urban Services Department, and the professional architectural, engineering and related staff of that part of the Public Works Department which had previously been responsible for construction of most estates. The fourth group of staff included many former members of the

Urban Council's Hawker Control Force, which was being dis-established at that time. Many of these latter were redeployed as Estate Assistants, a position in which, no doubt, it was felt their previous experience in controlling illegal hawkers would be useful.

Four years after these disparate groups were brought together, one decision was taken which was to have a lasting and, in retrospect, unhelpful impact on the quality of services. In an effort both to upgrade maintenance standards and, allegedly, to minimize the opportunity for corrupt practices, responsibility for management and maintenance functions in the estates was deliberately separated.

The common cultural denominator, which all groups brought with them from two decades of dealing with periodic waves of mass migration, was a self-reliant "can-do" spirit. This was nurtured by the pressure of the government's new Ten Year Housing Programme. No demand was too much for them: miracles could be accomplished quickly, the impossible would take a day or so longer. However, many of the internal splits, inter-grade rivalries and on-going arguments over manning scales and delineations of duty have their roots in 1973's arranged marriage.[2] Today staff of the department comprise 103 different grades and divide themselves for consultative purposes into 30 different Unions or Staff Associations. The 1,590 staff of the Estate Assistants Grade are represented by no fewer than 5 grade–specific associations and 2 general unions.

By any standards the Housing Authority is big. It has housed nearly half Hong Kong's population in public rental flats or homes built for subsidized sale. It is tasked to build a steady average of 50,000 new flats a year. It has a combined annual budget of over HK$100 billion including capital expenditure accounting for 16% of public spending and nearly half of total government capital expenditure. The Housing Department which serves it is also very large; it is now the third largest government department. One does not have to look far for a reason. To a constant drum beat emanating from Upper Albert Road — More, Better, Faster, More, Better, Faster — production rose, the quality and sophistication of design constantly improved, allocation standards increased, stock under management constantly grew, and the department expanded. An establishment of 6,600 in 1973 increased to 11,790 in 1983 and 12,930 in 1993. It peaked at just over 15,000 in 1997, but as will be seen later, zero growth has since been self-imposed under the Management Enhancement Programme.

2. The Policy Context

The birth pangs of the Management Enhancement Programme coincided with a growing realization that the stock of public rental housing was increasingly misallocated. Its development has straddled the preparation of, consultation on and progress in implementation of a revised Long Term Housing Strategy.[3] Inevitably there has been an interplay between both processes of change, most significantly manifest perhaps in the consequences of re-channelling subsidies to transform tenants into owners.

Since the early 1980s the Housing Authority had attempted to encourage tenants who had prospered to purchase flats built under the Home Ownership Scheme and to vacate their Public Rental Housing units for those who needed them more. However, by the early 1990s it was becoming clear that for many families the attractions of retaining cheap rental accommodation virtually in perpetuity outweighed those of surrendering this "right" in exchange for a subsidized sale unit with a ten-year restriction on re-sale. The Comprehensive Redevelopment Programme (CRP) under which the Authority's older estates were demolished and replaced with new, higher standard rental accommodation compounded the problem. With the clarity of vision which comes with hindsight, the Authority missed an opportunity. The package of incentives devised to ease the clearance of the old estates encouraged tenants to wait for modern low-rent accommodation rather than opt for subsidized ownership.

Recent years have thus seen the adoption of policies which aim to reverse this trend and facilitate a more rational allocation of public housing resources.[4] These essentially comprise carrot and stick in equal measure: incentives to encourage and enable those who want to get their feet on the first rung of the ownership ladder, and disincentives in the form of means tests and market rents to persuade those who no longer merit public housing assistance to make way for those who do.

Several psychological barriers have had to be overcome along the way, both regarding what had come to be viewed as "rights" as well as how housing benefits are best provided. The abolition of the automatic transfer of public rental tenancies from one generation to the next is perhaps the best example of the former; the Tenants Purchase Scheme the best of the latter. Both were included in the Long Term Housing Strategy consultative document released in January 1997, both provoked intense discussion, and both were finally adopted in the Long Term Housing Strategy published in

February 1998. In the meantime, the in-coming Chief Executive Tung Chee-hwa had given both endorsement and momentum to this new policy direction in his inaugural address on 1 July 1997 and his first policy address in October of the same year.

The Tenants Purchase Scheme is of particular significance in the context of the Management Enhancement Programme from two perspectives. First, previous proposals of this sort had been opposed by the department's professional housing managers in the sincere belief that mixed tenure, which is the norm in private residential developments, would be unmanageable in public or ex-public housing estates. Secondly, transformation of public tenants into private owners would simultaneously require managers to transform from landlord's agents into owners' employees, a radical and potentially traumatic change in both the legal and psychological relationship.

3. The Origins of the Management Enhancement Programme

A foretaste of that fundamental change was already discernible at the beginning of the 1990s. Increasing education, greater prosperity and greater community participation in public affairs progressively confronted staff of the department with a paradox. Hong Kong's public housing programme was a success. It was internationally recognized as such. The stream of visitors from around the world coming to learn from Hong Kong's example never slackened. And yet at home the department was the subject of increasing criticism in District Boards, in the Legislative Council, in the media. The contrast between its proud, professional self-image and its public one could not have been starker, nor staff frustration more keenly felt at all levels.

When frustration peaked in 1995 — no coincidence that it was an Election year — a period of intense introspection began. In order to give greater definition to the general perception of both staff and customer dissatisfaction, parallel independent surveys were commissioned in mid-1995. In retrospect both proved invaluable because they represent that watershed between denial and admission of a problem which must be overcome before solutions can be explored.

Staff were directly involved from the start and the Director took a personal lead.[5] The employee survey was designed by a group comprising both staff representatives from all areas of the department and consultants.

Coverage was comprehensive. In the event some 10,741 staff, that is over 80% of the then establishment took part, and the findings were made available to all. They were very revealing.[6]

While 40% of staff were satisfied with working at the Housing Department, only 13% felt proud and committed. Few were content with the way work was organized and performance appraised. Concern at the lack of clarity of purpose and dissatisfaction with senior management were equally pronounced. There was a broad consensus on the areas which needed to be improved in order to have a significant impact on both staff dissatisfaction and service culture. The top five were:

- Supervisor's consistency in enforcing policies and standards.
- Management's consistency in communicating service policies.
- Flexibility in applying Housing Department procedures.
- Ability to work as a team to solve customer problems.
- Improving the level of customer service skills.

The design of the customer satisfaction survey was similarly a joint effort by staff representatives and the consultant. During the summer of 1995, some 1,305 tenants of rental estates and a further 922 owners of Home Ownership and Private Sector Participation Scheme flats were surveyed. The results were consistent, but not encouraging. On a scale of seven points, tenants rated the department at 4.57 and owners at 4.52, indicating something between "mixed feelings" and only "slight satisfaction."

Again there was a broad consensus on areas where improvement would have the most significant impact on customer satisfaction. These were:

- Maintenance — response time, quality and willingness to do minor repairs.
- Cleansing — thoroughness of refuse collection and cleansing of common areas.
- Handling of enquiries and complaints — responsiveness, courtesy and follow-through.
- Security — quality.
- Community Services — types of shops and markets near estates.

Underlying both surveys was the problem of staff attitudes towards customers which had remained frozen in time even as customers' awareness of their rights had increased. Too many still saw themselves primarily as representatives of the landlord, responsible for the control of both the property and the people privileged to live there and enjoy government's generous subsidies. The response of service contractors was similarly revealing. Maintenance workers regarded the contractor's foreman as the client. The foreman regarded the Housing Department's Clerk of Works as the client, and so on. Few regarded tenants as the customer.

To address these problems, structured soul-searching went on in parallel with the survey work. Senior management organized a whole series of internal workshops and brainstorming sessions at various levels. Consultations with customer groups were arranged, including service contractors. All aimed at achieving a greater self-awareness. From this process their gradually emerged a consensus on the department's Vision, Mission and Values (Annex 6.1), and from it flowed the commissioning of a consultancy tasked with devising the programme of internal reforms required to translate the Vision, Mission and Values into reality. Thus began the Management Enhancement Programme.[7]

4. The Management Enhancement Programme

The consultants were initially asked to produce a set of strategies aimed at helping the Department achieve its customer service and public relations goals. When they presented their recommendations in May 1996, it was decided to fold these into other corporate strategy and human resources related initiatives which had emerged from the process of self-examination. From this point onwards the Management Enhancement Programme has become truly comprehensive in scope.

The aims of the Management Enhancement Programme as set out in the relevant Housing Authority Paper were to secure:

- enhancement of organizational effectiveness;
- better clarity of organizational objective;
- more systematic approach to corporate and business planning;
- more informed basis for decision making;
- more effective financial control;
- more efficient and responsive services to customers; and
- more rewarding working environment for staff.

In developing the strategy for achieving these aims, four key dimensions, or "pillars," were identified for strategic purposes: Corporate Strategy and Organization, Service Delivery, Culture and Communications.

Under these 13 initiatives were selected for priority treatment (Annex 6.2) and a master plan for implementation was then developed. These were duly presented to and adopted by the Housing Authority at its meeting of 2 January 1997.[8]

Work proceeded apace, simultaneously and across a very broad front. It is not my intention here to catalogue all that which led up to, in some cases paralleled, or flowed from the endorsement of the Management Enhancement Programme. However, to give a flavour of what went on and what is still going on under the Programme's umbrella, I will select some illustrative examples.

4.1 External Communication

The boldest and most successful of the cultural reforms was the establishment of Estate Management Advisory Committees (EMACs). Although Mutual Aid Committees (MACs) had been formed in most Public Housing Estates since the 1970s under the auspices of the Home Affairs Department, there was never any formal functional link between them and the Housing Department.[9] Starting in 1995,[10] however, as part of a conscious campaign to improve customer responsiveness and service quality, Estate Management Advisory Committees were formed, with the estate Housing Manager as Chairman and Members drawn from Mutual Aid Committees and shop tenant representatives. Meetings were called regularly to discuss estate affairs and members were consulted on not only the standard of cleansing and security services, but also on improvements and priorities for maintenance. A modest budget was made available for EMACs to spend at their discretion.

This purposeful involvement of tenants in the management of the estates in which they live has broken many old barriers and provided the estate management staff with considerable assistance in focusing their work. Representatives of cleansing and security contractors as well as other government departments are now regularly invited to attend to facilitate discussion. By 1998 EMACs had been formed in almost all of the Authority's over 150 estates, and their existence has fundamentally altered the character of the Authority's relationship with its principal customers.

A second reform which has been well received was the publication in October 1997 of a leaflet detailing rights and responsibilities for all of the Housing Authority customers, be they purchasers of Home Ownership

Scheme flats, tenants of rental accommodation, commercial premises or applicants for any form of housing assistance. This was far more than a simple compilation of standard eligibility criteria and the like. It was a document which involved intensive prior discussion with customer representatives and Members of the Housing Authority and its various Subcommittees. The latter in particular devoted a great deal of time in informal session to ensuring not only that the information given was both comprehensive and accurate but that the tenor of the language was appropriately balanced. Workshops were also held to ensure that staff of the department bought in to the concept. The document was approved by the Housing Authority on 26 September 1997 and was given a wide distribution.[11]

These two examples of greater customer involvement and greater Housing Authority transparency are by no means isolated illustrations. They have provided both a pattern and a standard for the future. It was notable that during the consultation period on the Long Term Housing Strategy, and in the development of initiatives arising from the strategy, this greater openness and willingness to exchange ideas, in advance of formal decisions being taken, reaped dividends.

4.2 Internal Communication

Communications within large organizations are always fraught with rumours usually running ahead of all more formal messages. Since the commencement of the Management Enhancement Programme, much has been done both to ensure rapid dissemination of departmental news as well as to encourage a two-way flow of information.

A common complaint of front-line staff earlier, was that they read about policy changes in the newspapers long before they became officially aware of them. The demands of confidentiality inevitably prevent dissemination of some information ahead of Housing Authority and Committee decisions. Nevertheless, weekly internal newsletters are now issued after the weekly Heads of Businesses meeting to alert front-line staff to impending changes and other matters of key interest to them. The newsletter message is e-mailed to all estate offices and out-stations, where it is printed and pinned on notice boards for general review. More often than not the newsletter is accompanied by a "Message from the Director."

Following on the earlier customer survey, an "MEP Ambassador Programme" was launched in May 1997. Nineteen middle-ranking staff from a variety of grades and professions were selected as "Ambassadors." After being briefed on the role they were expected to play, they were let loose to visit estates and other front-line stations to talk to staff and more importantly to listen to what staff had to say. In particular, they were asked to listen for sources of frustrations and any staff suggestions for improvement.

Their first report was as remarkable for the very large number of small irritants which they reported, as for the small number of more generalized frustrations. Removal of such sand in the shoe was made a priority. In most cases, it was completed before the same ambassadors visited the same estates for a second time. One interesting by-product of this 6-month exercise was that those involved became more aware of the full extent of the Housing Authority's activities and gained greater sympathy for the difficulties faced by their colleagues in other divisions. It is an exercise which will be repeated.

In addition to this more formal exercise, the senior directorate were encouraged to spend more time on informal visits to the front-line and outstations and to meet informally with unions and other staff representatives. As part of this, a series of "Open Forum" was launched. Attendance was open to all staff of the department on application, on a first-come-first-served basis. The Director and senior staff would speak reasonably briefly on one or two topical issues related to the Management Enhancement Programme, but most of the session was reserved for no-holds-barred questions and comments from the floor. This informal dialogue has provided a useful vent for frustration as well as a channel for more direct and personal communication on sensitive issues.

Another exercise in breaking down grade and divisional barrier similar to the Ambassador Programme was carried out at the junior directorate levels. Individual staff at this level were co-opted to serve on the Management Enhancement Programme Steering Committee, chaired by the Director, and each was given a specific task involving cross-cutting issues generally unrelated to their immediate sphere of work or experience. They responded enthusiastically and, in the process, almost all came up with new and unexpected insights into problems. The senior directorate led by example. Thus one Deputy Director, an architect by profession, turned super-salesman and took on the sole responsibility for driving development of the detailed arrangements for the Tenants Purchase Scheme through to implementation of Phase I.

4.3 Human Resource Management

Happily enough, this process of loosening up coincided with the emergence through the ranks of talented representatives from several of the professional minorities to challenge the traditional dominance of the architect and housing management grades. This has facilitated the gradual "opening up" of the directorate. Where previously most directorate posts were reserved as promotion posts for specific professional grades, the directorate is now open from D2. Since early 1999, applications for promotion to vacancies at that level have been open to application by all regardless of professional qualification or experience.

This more open approach would not have been possible without much internal discussion on what was previously wrong with the organization and what was needed to put it right. Most of these strategic ideas were brain-stormed in day-long workshops outside the department and attended by almost all directorate staff. These sessions paved the way for some of the structural reforms which will be described later, and were an essential part of securing investment by staff in the process of change. In a typical session, 60 or 70 persons were divided into half a dozen teams, tasked with designing an organization for the new decade, specifying the mix of skills which would be required for the future, or proposing solutions to other problems which they themselves had identified. Subsequent team presentations, while often hilarious, sowed many seeds.

Such sessions were underpinned by the nitty-gritty process of developing core competencies for the directorate and for specific grades, as well as a complete redesign of the grade management system and the development of a comprehensive human resource plan. The Human Resources Committee of the Authority has been kept busy, has been warmly supportive and has provided astute advice. Where the requisite skill sets were not readily available within the civil service, the Committee has sanctioned the replacement of government grades by Housing Authority contract staff.[12] It has agreed to lift the training budget from 1% of payroll in 1997–98 to 3% a year in the year 2000–01. It has endorsed zero growth in establishment since 1997, where the actual strength has been allowed to shrink through natural wastage and recruitment occurs only where necessary and only on Housing Authority agreement terms since 1998. Such disciplines have helped focus minds on both the need for change and the relative cost efficiencies of established ways of doing things.

4.4 Process Redesign

Clumsy procedures were singled out as a source of staff frustration early on in the programme. In most cases, arrangements originally designed to ensure against slippage in product delivery had, over time, become so institutionalized that in one case, the close of one quarter's monitoring meeting marked the start of drafting papers for a cycle of preparatory meetings which would continue all the way through to the next quarter's monitoring meeting. In other cases, the routing of files and correspondence through a long chain of command, up one silo and down another was creating delays, inefficiency and complaints of buck-passing and non–co-operation between staff of different divisions. Staff were given a free hand and encouraged to look for short cuts whenever these made sense. Where matters were more complex, systematic business process re-engineering (BPR) was followed. A considerable number of these were instituted. Regardless of scope or scale, staff were encouraged to approach them in a competitive spirit and to show off their results in gatherings of directorate staff and peer colleagues.

One macro level example of such BPR is provided by the production process for public housing. Each step, from site acceptance through planning, design, and tender to construction was subjected to rigorous examination, as a result of which the delivery time, was cut from a previous standard 62 months to 47. Most of the reduction in time was attributable to simplification of planning and design discussions and approval. At the same time, the opportunity was taken to introduce a project management system modelled on private sector practices.

At a micro level, short cuts were agreed for the handling of all complaints and enquiries. Thus, a letter to the Director would be logged and acknowledged and then sent straight to the front-line officer responsible, and draft replies would then not be passed through every intervening supervisory layer as in the past, but go through the central Complaints Division for vetting before signature. In common with all other department activities published Performance Pledges[13] applied. Thus correspondence was required to be dealt with within 14 days. Vetting by the Complaints Division also allowed correlation and analysis for feedback to the Business Directors as one means of identifying areas for improvement to service quality.

4.5 Service Delivery

A similarly robust approach to brainstorming and solving traditional problems was applied to service delivery. Maintenance provides perhaps the best example.

Following serious problems with a number of older blocks in the 1970s and earlier 1980s, the Department had introduced comprehensive programmed maintenance. This has been steadily improved and all housing stock is now subject to a regular cycle of inspection and repair under the "CARE" programme.[14] With a view to further future streamlining, the Maintenance Division had begun as early as 1991 to examine Information Technology solutions to long-standing programme management and financial control problems. Fortuitously work on the "MISIS" system,[15] which covered both major, term maintenance as well as minor, day-to-day work, was coming to fruition as public complaints began to build. In mid-1994, it was decided to combine the proposed systems in such a way that tenants would have access to a quick and efficient one-stop service.

Thus the proposals on minor maintenance which were finally submitted to the Authority at the end of that year included the concept of Customer Service Assistants. These were to be stationed in the entrance foyer of estate offices. Equipped with a desk-top computer terminal they would be able to register complaints or requests for minor maintenance. Using a system, similar to those used by utility companies, they would steer the customer through a simple questionnaire aimed at identifying the probable cause of any particular problem and the type of service most appropriate. A time for a visit to the customer's home would then be agreed and logged, confirmation would be automatically sent to the customer's home by phone or fax, and the necessary works order issued.

The new system went live on 1 April 1995 in 35 estates. Once the initial bugs had been removed, it proved a great success in improving the response time and customer satisfaction in most cases, and it was rolled out progressively to all other estates thereafter. In parallel went a programme of office refurbishment aimed at giving offices a friendlier feel, a sizable investment in customer service training and a major overhaul of the maintenance contract award, service delivery and quality assurance systems. An integral part of the latter was a programme aimed at getting contractors and other service suppliers to buy in to the culture change.

However, a common complaint amongst Housing Managers which persisted even after the system was installed was that they were the ones who were always in the firing line when things went wrong even though the source of the problem was beyond their control. As suggested at the beginning of this chapter, this had its roots in the separation of management and maintenance functions in the late 1970s. Essentially, the managers' complaint was that they had no direct control over either the department's maintenance staff or the maintenance contractor. The latter would take instructions only from the maintenance staff (who were not normally stationed on the estate), but residents of the estates expected the managers (who were) to ensure that maintenance work was done quickly, and to their satisfaction.

The problem presented by this three-horse chariot arrangement was solved pragmatically by merging the management and maintenance functions and delegating full responsibility and authority for everything which went on in each estate to the Housing Manager. A trial scheme in the Western New Territories which lasted six months attracted sufficient support from both tenants and staff involved to allow the scheme to be rolled out territory-wide in 1998, albeit not without some kicking and screaming from die-hard "separatists" in the respective grades.

Emphasis in this and other related reforms was on giving front-line staff greater authority and independence. Individual initiatives and responsibility had in the past been frustrated by fragmented control, a multi-tier hierarchy, over-concentration of authority at the centre and over-reliance on voluminous departmental instruction manuals. The impression gained by junior staff over time was that it was better not to report a problem, or at least avoid making a mistake, than to exercise any initiative.

To assist the process of cultural change, individual initiatives and inter-estate competitions were encouraged, often in consultation with the EMACs. Ideas generated by enterprising individuals in one estate would be rewarded, advertised and, where practicable, shared with other estates. Again Members of the Housing Authority supported this process and involved themselves in adjudication of such competitions. Inevitably, this process also gradually uncovered practices or deviations from established policy which might otherwise have gone undetected. Embarrassing though this may be, staff have been encouraged to come forward with such problems so that these can be dealt with expeditiously, along with similar problems in other estates. The Internal Audit Section and Technical Audit Unit in the Director's office have been given a free hand to follow up on this type of problem.

4.6 Reorganization

Accountability requires clear lines of responsibility. Cost consciousness requires that people know how much things cost. The degree to which both are absent in any public sector body almost invariably flows not from the failings of individual staff or their general quality, but from the way in which they are organized. The previous organization of the Housing Department and its relationship with the various Committees of the Housing Authority provide a textbook illustration of this point.

A series of deliberately forward looking directorate workshops in late 1996 and early 1997 helped to surface senior staff frustrations with the existing structure. Mixed teams of professionals from the various divisions of the department were confronted with similar problems and invited both to analyze weaknesses in existing systems or structure before devising solutions. The "SWOT" (Strengths, Weaknesses, Opportunities and Threats) analyses showed remarkable consistencies, especially as regards the weaknesses: responsibility not matched by ability to deliver; overly long chains of command with too many layers; having to secure the approval of more than one Housing Authority committee for the same thing; responsibility not matched by delegation of authority; communications from one front-line team to another having to be routed up one silo and down another, and so on.

The accompanying, often passionate discussions revealed also a lack of sympathy and trust between rivalrous divisions: housing managers and maintenance crews complaining that they had to take the blame for the shoddy work accepted by colleagues on the "Works" side; the latter demoralized by a project monitoring system which chained them to an endless cycle of paperwork and meetings at the expense of "real work"; all fed up with a blame culture which constantly found fault and failed to recognize the good things they achieved. Running throughout was a feeling of frustration with constant public criticism and a sense of powerlessness that no matter how hard they tried things just seemed to get worse.

About this time the Director found himself in a somewhat embarrassing position. He was due to appear before the Establishment Subcommittee of the Legislative Council's Finance Committee in January 1997 to justify a request for three additional directorate posts. Unfortunately the committee paper included an organization chart (Annex 6.3) which it was increasingly obvious bore little relation to what now seemed likely to come out of the workshop process, but which was still far from agreed! He will always be indebted to Honourable Members for their trust. In answer to the question where did he think the process of reform would have taken the department in three years time, he said that he did not know. Remarkably, this was accepted, the staff request was approved and he was asked to report back three years thence.[16]

Things came to a head at the workshop held on 5 March 1997, during which the various teams of directorate staff were tasked with designing the organization they thought most appropriate to the needs of the Housing Authority in the first decade of the new millennium. There were several common threads e.g. the desire to move from a direct provision to a facilitation of housing role, as well as some new and radical ideas. The Director must have done less than justice to the latter because his summing up was greeted by a raucous comment from the floor that it was time we stopped talking about reorganization and got on and did it. It was a case of striking when the iron was hot. He took a deep breath and undertook to firm up the details of the new structure within a month, with a view to introducing it as early as possible in the new financial year.

The key feature of the reorganization was the separation of the Authority's work into four "core businesses" and the nomination of a single "Business Director" to take independent charge of each. In addition, two other Directors were charged with responsibility for providing supporting Finance and Corporate services (Annex 6.4). The four core businesses identified were: Development, Ownership, Rental and Commercial. While each business was made independent, the relationship between the businesses was clearly identified. Thus, for example, Ownership and Rental were both "clients" of Development; it was for each of the former to agree the financial viability and quality standards of projects for the latter to deliver. Where appropriate it was agreed that cross-business service agreements would be drawn up.[17]

Two other elements of the new structure are worth highlighting. These are the role of the two Deputy Directors and the Corporate Strategy Unit. While the former retained in their titles the traditional split between "Works" and "Management," they were deliberately given no formal, functional link with any of the businesses. One, nominally, had oversight of the

Development and Sales businesses, the other over the Rental and Commercial businesses. However, in practice they were deliberately lifted above day-to-day supervisory functions in order to free them up for a more strategic role. Their real and most valuable function was to trouble-shoot and brainstorm the development of cross-cutting policy issues. As mentioned earlier, for example, one of them drove the Tenants Purchase Scheme through to implementation.

The Corporate Strategy Unit was completely new and was put in place in response to a need, frequently voiced in the directorate workshops, for a single point of reference for coordinating and monitoring the implementation of new and old policies alike, and for analytical studies. As will become evident later, the unit also played a key role in coordinating the drawing up of the Business and Corporate Plans.

The new organization was put in place in large part on 15 April 1997. With the tolerant agreement of Housing Authority Members to the tail wagging the dog, the terms of reference of the Housing Authority's committees were subsequently scrutinized with a view to securing the same clarity of purpose and accountability. Where necessary they were amended so as to align each committee with a single business and to ensure as far as possible that there were no overlaps of responsibility. The resulting amendments were formally approved by the Authority in September.[18] The relationship between the Committees and the Business Directors is illustrated in (Annex 6.5). It is worth noting that while the Director of Housing and one Deputy remain members of the Committees, the individual Business Directors were deliberately denied membership to underline the fact that they were to be answerable to their respective Committees.

4.7 Corporate and Business Plans

The next and vital step was the development of business plans. This we again did backwards, but not without purpose. Ideally, the process should have started with the setting of objectives by the Authority at the corporate level. However, this would have wasted a year, so instead we opted for a bottom-up approach, using the existing policy framework as a proxy reference.

Staff and budgets had already been divided between the core businesses at the time of reorganization. Each of the Business Directors was then tasked, subject to broad guidelines on format, with preparing his own

Business Plan independently and presenting it to the new "Executive Board," comprising the Director and his two deputies, the Finance Director, Director of Corporate Services, Head of Corporate Strategy Unit, Legal Adviser and Assistant Director of Information and Community Relations. As with the adoption of the title "Business Director" this structure was deliberately modelled on the private sector to reinforce the notion of cost consciousness. It was also designed to institutionalize risk management and the adoption of best practices.

Apart from ensuring consistency, the Board performed two important tasks. Their first task was to vet and approve the objectives identified by each Business Director and the performance targets offered by him for the coming year. It was accepted that, in future, this would form part of the formal annual budgetary process. Their second and more difficult task was to meld the substance of the four Business Plans, together with the separate Finance and Corporate Services Plans, into a first attempt at a Corporate Plan for the Housing Authority.

The first Business Plans were presented by Business Directors to their respective Committees in the latter part of 1997. Each was given a thorough scrutiny, and there were many suggestions for improvement, particularly as regards bench-marking, but overall the new process, the greater clarity of objectives and the increased financial transparency were very well received by Members. Production of the first Corporate Plan fell behind schedule, however it was finally put to the Housing Authority for endorsement on 4 June 1998. In introducing it, the Director took the opportunity to summarize the benefits which would flow from these reforms:

- Firstly, the clarification of aims and responsibilities makes it possible to delegate authority and accountability further down the organization than was possible before, thus allowing more rapid and more efficient response to customer needs;
- secondly, the higher quality of financial information now available will make it easier to identify and eradicate waste and inefficiency; and
- thirdly, we will be able to take a more rational view of the relative levels of subsidy which we provide to different groups in need and the cost-effectiveness of the various forms these subsidies take.[19]

The Authority endorsed the Corporate Plan and instructed that it be published for general information.

Inevitably, doing things backward in this fashion proved a little messy, but it also proved enormously helpful in clarifying thinking. At the level of the individual Business, costs which had previously been obscured or confused because of cross-subsidies were immediately brought into much sharper focus. This in turn sparked a process of questioning about why certain functions existed and how certain services were provided. A new cost-consciousness came into being, which was nowhere more evident than in the haggling between Business Directors over the share of central overheads allocated to them.

The less immediate, but at least as valuable, result has been a progressive refining of costs across the whole spectrum of the department's work and at every level of operation. To take a simple example, the manager in charge of an individual housing estate was previously blissfully unaware of whether or not his estate broke even or whether commercial facilities in the estate made a profit or a loss. He would have been aware of in-comings in the form of rent, but he would not know, indeed he was not required to know, how much was spent on his estate for management, maintenance and improvements. As part of the initial business planning exercise, accounts were constructed for each business and each estate and the manager of each estate was required to draft a business plan for his estate. In future the review of the estate level plans will form an integral part of the annual planning and budgetary process. The results so far have been encouraging. Provided with data they previously did not have, the managers are now thinking about and raising questions they previously never asked.

Another example relates to the planning of new projects. The Corporate Strategy Unit is now responsible for conducting both a technical and a financial viability study on each site made available by the government to the Housing Authority, in order to establish the optimum development mix for the site. This it does in conjunction with the Business Director Development and his three clients, the Business Directors of Sales, Rental and Commercial. Viability studies are put to the Strategic Policy Committee of the Authority for approval and form the basis of the project budget for each development. The result has been the emergence of a much harderheaded and better informed decision making process by the Authority on the one hand, and far more rigorous cost-control by project managers on the other.

Further evidence of this came with the preparation of the second set of Business Plans and the second edition of the Authority's Corporate

Plan. The level of discussion provoked by the draft Business Plans in their respective Committees was very gratifying. However, more work still needs to be done in one particular area and that is in devising and using a satisfactory and comprehensive set of corporate and business level Key Performance Indicators.

The consequences of greater clarity and transparency exemplified by the estate level action plans has its counter-part at the centre. Costs which were previously obscured have been brought into much clearer focus and anomalies have no place to hide. One such anomaly is the department's unduly high corporate overheads.

In the public sector such overheads are generally inversely proportionate to the number of lower-level front-line staff. Thus the ratio is relatively high for a small department such as the Observatory and relatively low for an organization such as the Police Force. The Housing Department for some reason is near the top among government departments. Finding out why this is so and trimming the overhead back was therefore flagged as a priority during discussion of the 1999–2000 budget.

Similarly the relative costs and effectiveness of different forms of housing assistance have also been thrown into sharper relief. A comparison of the real life-time cost of the various types of housing assistance shows Public Rental Housing at the top, Home Ownership Scheme housing in the middle, and Home Purchase Loan Scheme assistance at the bottom. In very rough terms at current land prices, for the real cost of an average Public Rental Housing unit, the Authority could make loans available to four separate families. This sort of comparative subsidy cost data raises some fairly obvious questions about the correct policy mix for the future, but it also begs the question as to whether we could do what we are already doing cheaper and more efficiently.

In one area of service delivery, namely the management and maintenance of estates, examination of this latter question has been precipitated by a fundamental change in the choice of housing assistance offered to tenants.

4.8 Quality and Safety

Quality and safety both deserve a special mention. They also merit a chapter all of their own. In both areas, the department has made and continues to make a special effort to drive its own ethics up stream to the private sector partners on whom it depends. This is particularly but not exclusively the case with the construction industry.

Pressure for delivery of the product on time and to budget will always be there, but these goals cannot be met at the expense of either quality or safety. The design can be perfect, but if the customer is not happy with the finished product then all effort has been wasted. Cutting corners puts the Authority's reputation at risk. It can also put life and limb at risk. I do not intend to elaborate here on all the measures taken to enhance both, and to get the industry on board. However, I would not like the reader to assume that we have neglected this hugely important aspect of cultural and service delivery reform.

5. Interplay between Policy and Reform

I commented at the beginning of this chapter that the policy context is rarely static and that changes of policy inevitably impact on reforms and vice versa. The process now underway of restoring the housing market after 45 years of very direct government intervention provides a vivid example of this interplay.

Where the government previously offered those in need of housing no option other than public rental accommodation, it now offers in addition a range of ownership options to suit all but the poorest of the poor. Over time, the effect of the Home Ownership, Tenants Purchase and Home Purchase Loan Schemes, taken with the new Buy-Or-Rent Option for families on the Waiting List, will be to radically reduce both the proportion and the absolute number of families living in rental dependency on the state.

The social, political and economic benefits are obvious. People for whom home ownership was an improbable if not impossible dream have been given new hope. Released from the bureaucratic control which comes with being a tenant of the state, their self-esteem will be restored. As the bottom third of the market (essentially subsidized public rental housing) is unfrozen and more and more properties trade freely at real market prices, more and more people will live where they choose to live rather than where chance and bureaucracy almost randomly placed them. The community's long-term subsidy burden will be reduced and the economy stimulated by the freeing up of resources inefficiently deployed.

5.1 Estate Management and Maintenance Services

There is, however, one other inevitable consequence. Much of the bureau-cratic apparatus which previously serviced these families' housing needs will need to be dismantled. Taking the example of the management of the estates, this will require care. The private sector cannot double its capacity overnight. It will also need human resources. The 9,000 loyal staff of the Department until now responsible for the management and maintenance of these estates cannot simply be discarded. Hence the arrangements presently under discussion for phased transfer to the private sector.

The management of Home Ownership Scheme courts is already contracted out to private companies. In 1995 the Housing Authority tested the extension of this form of private sector involvement to new rental estates as a means of curbing staff growth and cutting costs, by taking advantage of the greater efficiency and service flexibility offered by the rapidly growing property management services sector. Since 1997, the management of all new rental estates has been contracted out. However, the successful implementation of the Tenants Purchase Scheme from January 1998 has introduced a whole new dynamic and forced a fundamental re-think of the Authority's continuing direct involvement in delivery of management and maintenance services.

Under the Scheme, as with private sector developments, the new owners acquire the right to choose who manages their property. In Phase I of the Scheme three-quarters of tenants opted for ownership. The government has pledged to offer no fewer than 25,000 rental units for sale to tenants each year for the next ten years. That is a total of no fewer than 250,000 units, or over one-third of the existing public housing rental stock. Staff of the Department must now confront head-on the question of what happens if the new owners choose not to retain their services.

Since the Scheme was launched, the senior directorate, in formal and informal meetings with staff at all levels, in Open Forums and in public speeches, have drawn staff attention to this question bluntly and repeatedly. It is not a pleasant prospect and staff have been unsettled by it, but it has been necessary to repeat the message in order to prepare staff psychologically for the inevitability of change in this area. They are also, very naturally, resentful that having invested a great deal of effort over the last few years on improving the quality of the services they provide, their career development prospects are now threatened.

Consultants were engaged to examine the opportunities for greater private sector involvement in the Authority's work generally, and to explore possible solutions to the problem presented by the rise of ownership in particular. They have concluded that given the likely savings and more flexible services which private companies would be able to offer the tenants-turned-owners, most of the latter are unlikely to want to retain the Housing Department's services. However, recognizing both the scale and speed of the privatization of public housing now underway, the difficulty which the private sector would have digesting the potentially huge volume of new work and the human problems of the Department's staff, the consultants have recommended a "phased transfer" of management and maintenance functions to the private sector.[20]

On the one hand this would involve the government offering staff a package which facilitates the transfer of those willing to leave into the private sector. On the other it would involve the Authority negotiating a new form of contract with private companies which would require them to take on significant numbers of Housing Department staff as part of an open bidding process for the management of groups of estates. The consultants have recommended that this process be phased over a period of five to seven years. They have also recommended that the Authority should not rule out the possibility of assisting staff who are interested in forming their own company.

Following consideration of the submissions received on the consultant's recommendations, the Authority at its meeting on 6 May has decided to adopt phased transfer as the broad direction for outsourcing management and maintenance services, but the pace and phasing of the service transfer, as well as the arrangements for staff will be further examined by a special Task Force set up under the Authority. At time of writing, the Task Force is at the point of finalizing its recommendations for report to the Authority in early 2000. This will be a watershed period for both the Authority, its customers, staff of the Housing Department, and the property management services industry.

5.2 Corporate Governance

The process of reform and restructuring has surfaced not only problems of detail, but also wider issues of principle. For example, the drafting of the Corporate Plans and the Business Plans has forced all involved to focus on and clarify objectives, to ask hard questions about the real costs of various activities, to question why the Housing Authority is involved in these activities,[21] and to query the traditional way in which things are done. These questions in turn force a higher level of questioning about the relationship between the Authority and its traditional executive arm, about whether or not the latter provides value for money, about accountability and all those related issues which come under the general heading of "corporate governance."

At the beginning of this year, in the Housing Authority meeting to discuss the budget, we have flagged the need to deal with what appears to be unreasonably high overheads.[22] Similarly, in the second Corporate Plan we have signalled our intention of giving greater attention to measuring value-for-money of services provided direct by the Department. Preliminary work on tackling corporate governance framework issues is just getting underway and should be driven to first conclusions by the end of the financial year 1999–2000.

6. Lessons for Public Sector Reform

This chapter set out to trace the course of a single albeit complex programme of public sector reform. The tools and techniques are transferable, but no two such programmes will be the same and how to proceed will always depend on the circumstances of the individual case. However, there are some larger lessons which can be derived from dealing with particular problems, and before closing I would like to offer a couple of prescriptive thoughts on prevention rather than cure.

The natural instinct of those in charge of any organization is to expand, to demonstrate their abilities by greater activity. However, what may be a virtue in the private sector can become a vice in a public sector counterpart. If government's intrusion in the economy is to be kept small, then doing more in the public sector is only virtuous when the "more" is something the private sector cannot do equally well. When interests become entrenched, and this applies to recipients and provider agencies alike, the problem of creating the political climate for the acceptance of reform becomes more complex. What is needed are institutional arrangements which enforce regular review both of the continuing need for services and of their mode of delivery.

In an expanding economy, guidelines which link aggregate public spending to trend growth are convenient at the macro level, but they can result in both unintended inefficiencies at the micro level and greater adjustment trauma when times are tougher. This is particularly the case where finances are tightly controlled at the centre, and the absence of delegated authority discourages saving and redeployment. In Hong Kong's case, the annual Resource Allocation Exercise (RAE) pits Policy Secretary against peers in haggling over the division of the relatively small increase in the size of the spending pie. It does not involve any fundamental examination of how the original pie was divided. The relative shares remain largely fixed and arguments over anything other than marginal increments are rare.

Until very recently, the authority of most Heads of Departments to vire funds from one highly specific use to another was almost non-existent, and savings were required to be surrendered to the centre.[23] There was incentive neither to save nor to think. More recently, Policy Secretaries have been granted some discretion in re-allocating funds, but the failure to delegate any meaningful financial authority to Heads of Department means that they have no incentive to volunteer any such redeployment. Their eyes remain firmly fixed on squeezing just a little bit more out of the RAE next year.

To be successful public sector reform should be a continuous process. This demands both effective institutional arrangements for policy review and incentives to comply with them. The simplest way of introducing incentives is to delegate authority such that those who are responsible for spending public funds are not simply accountable for that spending, but also have a clear stake in ensuring that funds are well spent. A Head of Department who has the authority to shift funds from one area of activity to another, and who has the authority to decide whether to provide a service direct or to contract it out to private sector delivery, will be more inclined to ask intelligent questions about what his department is doing and how it is doing it, than one who has no such authority.

The fact that under a financially autonomous Housing Authority the Director of Housing has such authority has made it possible to implement reforms under the Management Enhancement Programme at a speed which would be unthinkable in an ordinary government department. As part of the reforms we have taken this process one stage further by cascading the same authority to each of the Business Directors. This is already reaping rewards.

While necessary at the departmental level, such incentives are not in themselves sufficient. They must be matched by institutional arrangements at the centre which require periodic rejustification of services and how these are delivered. As part of the budgetary process, Policy Secretaries and their Heads of Department should be required regularly to review each service for which they are responsible and to answer the following simple checklist of questions:

- What are our core businesses?
- Why have we become involved in them?
- Do we still need to be involved in them?
- Is there scope for greater private sector involvement?
- What are the real costs of what we are doing?
- Are there more efficient ways of doing it without compromising on service standards?
- Are there things we should and could be doing if we were not tied up this way or could free up resources?

The questions are deceptively simple. They raise the difficult issue of how to change if change is deemed desirable, but the answers can open new avenues of thought as well. What is important is that they are asked and that a clear view is then taken of what is desirable. Deciding where one really wants to get to makes even a difficult journey easier.

7. Final Reflections

"Conclusion" seems somehow not the right note on which to end the diary of an on-going journey; perhaps "reflection" would be more appropriate. So in closing this chapter allow me a few reflections on how we have got to where we are now, and the challenges and opportunities which still lie ahead.

From this vantage point, it is possible to pick out some of the landmarks passed along the way. Because they stand out and are of some interest, I have described a few of them. But it would be wrong to infer that they are entirely representative of the country through which we have passed. There has been a lot of foot-slogging across rough ground before any new vistas opened before us. There have been pauses for breath on steep climbs as we searched for the best path.[24] And there have been a few dangerous passes. A few words on foot-slogging, on pauses for breath and on risks.

The hardest and yet the most important part of the slog is getting to grips with the data, especially the financial data. In a large organization which has grown amoeba-like with every new policy accretion, much becomes hidden and uncovering the rationale behind oddities in the system requires skill, patience and tact. The unsung heroes of this odyssey are thus those who undertook and supervised this task and persuaded others whose interests lay elsewhere to help rather than hinder the process. Which brings me to pauses for breath.

Getting people started on a journey is not easy; keeping them going when it gets rough is harder. It is sometimes necessary to force the pace, but equally it is necessary to stop periodically, to rest, to let the stragglers catch up and to take fresh bearings. It is also necessary to accept that wrong turnings can be taken on a path, that steps may need to be re-traced, and that, when someone suggests that the party is headed in the wrong direction, he is given a fair hearing. At the same time, a sense of direction must be agreed on by those responsible for leading the way and they in turn must convey it to those following.

A sense of adventure is also helpful. I have mentioned a few examples of things we did backwards. Short-cuts are always risky, but they can also save time. Similarly, breaks in the weather offer opportunities which may not come again for some time. Consultants may urge caution; they are right to do so, but if the mood of the wagon train is for letting things roll, no one will thank you for hesitating and it may be twice as hard to make the same distance if enthusiasm is allowed to cool.

At this point, I think it right to pay tribute to all staff of the Housing Department for their courage and professionalism. Not all understand or are committed to the MEP to the same degree, but all have contributed. At a time when the twin burden of implementing a number of major housing policy reforms and of cranking up the building programme to record levels has been particularly heavy, they have also tolerated considerable and sometimes radical organizational change without complaint and without interruption to the services they render day-in day-out to customers. The community has been well served by them.

The author is also happy to acknowledge the debt he owes to his predecessors and colleagues past and present. None of this would have been possible without the tolerance, wise advice and firm but gentle encouragement of the Members of the Housing Authority, and the many hours which they have spent in informal workshops of one sort or another helping us think through the issues and devise new solutions.

Notes

1. Previously the members of the Urban Council sitting with the Director of Public Works, the Commissioner for Housing and the Commissioner for Resettlement had formed a "Housing Authority." A "Housing Board" comprising senior Government Secretariat officers provided policy coordination, and was in the immortal words of former Director of Housing, Bernard Williams, "a sort of toothless Secretariat talking-shop." See *Hong Kong and Me / From Shelter to Home — 45 Years of Public Housing Development in Hong Kong* (Hong Kong Housing Authority, 1999).

2. References in the official literature to the human problems involved in merging the professional staff of the old Housing Authority with the rougher diamonds of the Resettlement Department are sparse. However, Frank Carroll, the Director at the time, has recently allowed a rare glimpse of the divide between what came to be termed the Group A and B estates, in his reminiscence for the Housing Authority's 45th Anniversary Publication: "There had been even before then (1973) some liaison between the staff of the Housing Authority and that of the Resettlement Department with a view to getting the resettlement estates up to the same standards of management as those of the Authority, and this now became much more urgent. It was a tremendous task, given the different backgrounds of both tenants and staff, and initially the two were kept separate, each under a professionally qualified Assistant Director, while integration of policies, methods and personnel proceeded inevitably slowly, with a large quota of pain and misunderstandings on all sides." See *Hong Kong and Me / From Shelter to Home*, ibid.

3. *Long Term Housing Strategy — Homes For Hong Kong People: The Way Forward, Hong Kong Government*, January 1997, *and Long Term Housing Strategy — Homes For Hong Kong People: Into the 21st Century* (Hong Kong Government, February 1998).

4. Community debate on this issue was deliberately stirred by the Housing Authority's release in December 1995 of a consultative document, *Safeguarding Rational Allocation of Public Housing Resources*. Measures implemented following publication of *Safeguarding Rational Allocation of Public Housing Resources — Report on Final Recommendations* in April 1996 were strengthened two years later subsequent to consultation on the Long Term Housing Strategy.

5. Fung Tung, Director of Housing in his "Dear Colleague" letter to all staff of 9 May 1995, informing them of the appointment of consultants and encouraging staff participation in the Employee and Customer Satisfaction Surveys.

6. On 1 July 1996, the results of the Employee and Customer Satisfaction Surveys were distributed to all staff in a booklet incorporating a "Dear Colleague" letter from the Director. Follow up surveys have been similarly handled.

7. It is difficult to put a precise date on when the Management Enhancement

Programme (MEP) became a conscious plan. As is often the case with public bodies the paper work lagged behind the translation of wish into action. Thus the term was first used as the title for a Senior Management Workshop held on 22 January 1996, by which time it had become clear that several disparate initiatives needed to be pulled together. (Simon Li Pak-ho, the then Senior Assistant Director/Management is credited with coining the term at the directorate meeting which preceded this.) The Director of Housing first promulgated the draft Vision, Mission and Values and announced the intention to establish an "MEP Office" in his "Dear Colleague" letter of 3 April 1996. The Chairman of the Finance Committee refers to the MEP as an established fact in his report to the Housing Authority tabled at the Housing Authority's meeting of 6 June 1996 (HA Paper EFC 44/96). However, the formal papers setting out the detailed proposals for the MEP were not discussed by the Housing Authority until its meeting of 26 September 1996. (HA Paper 62/96: Management Enhancement Programme refers)

8. Housing Authority Paper HA Paper HA 83/96: MEP Master Action Plan, refers.

9. In the mid-1970s when MACs were first formed in the estates as part of government's community building programme, the Director of Home Affairs had proposed such a link. However, his counterpart in the Housing Department had rejected the idea on the grounds that it might undermine the authority of the Housing Manager as landlord's representative.

10. The decision to establish EMACs was taken by the HA in November 1994. Housing Authority Paper 59/94 refers.

11. *Rights and Responsibilities* (Hong Kong Housing Authority, October 1997). Close on 2 million copies of this were printed and distributed to customers.

12. The first example of this was the wholesale replacement of Government Information Services staff by private sector recruits beginning in 1995.

13. The Housing Authority published its first pamphlet detailing Performance Pledges in July 1993.

14. The "CARE" programme — Condition, Appraisal, Repair and Examination — was introduced in 1993.

15. MISIS is the acronym for the "Maintenance Information System and Infrastructure Support."

16. Establishment Sub-Committee of Finance Committee of the Legislative Council Committee Paper ESC (96-97) 51 and Minutes of Meeting ESC 22/96-97 refer.

17. About one year after the reorganization it became clear that the original distribution of some of the common service functions which had been designed to even out the relative "weight" of the BD posts, would require an excessive number of cross-business agreements. It was therefore agreed to re-distribute in a manner which minimized the number of such agreements. These refinements to the reorganisation were introduced progressively in 1999.

18. Informal discussion with HA Members on the revision of terms of reference, as

well as the proposed corporate planning process took place in July 1997. Amendments were formally adopted on 25 September 1997. Housing Authority Paper HA 61/97 refers.

19. Housing Authority Paper HA 30/98, minutes of the Housing Authority meeting on 4 June 1998, and the first Housing Authority Corporate Plan 1998/99 refer.

20. PriceWaterhouseCoopers: *A Review of Private Sector Involvement in Estates Management and Maintenance Services*, presented to the Housing Authority on 4 March 1999.

21. For example, the Housing Authority's commercial properties comprise about 13% of Hong Kong's retail space. This is a curious position for a non-interventionist Government to be in.

22. Housing Authority Budget and Corporate Plan 1999/2000, passed on 28 January 1999 refer.

23. Ironically, the need for greater delegation of financial authority was clearly identified by McKinsey & Co in the consultancy study they did prior to the last major bureaucratic reform in 1973. (*The Machinery of Government: A New Framework for Expanded Services*, Hong Kong Government 1973 refers.) The first successful challenge to the rule that savings must accrue to the centre was mounted by Yeung Kai-yin as Secretary for Education and Manpower, when he volunteered to scrap the Student Travel Subsidy Scheme, but only on condition that he could divert the savings to new policy initiatives.

24. In pursuing these reforms, the author has done much of his thinking out-loud, in speeches to various professional and academic organisations. They include: *Housing Department: Towards a Better Tomorrow*, address to the Hong Kong Institute of Surveyors/Royal Institute of Chartered Surveyors (Hong Kong Branch) on 28 May 1997; *Major Issues of the Enhancement Programme of the Housing Department*, address at the Centre of Urban Planning and Environmental Management, University of Hong Kong on 18 November 1997; *The Changing Role of Public Sector Housing* Management, address to the Housing Conference of the Hong Kong Institute of Housing on 23 October 1998; and: *Public Sector Reform : The Housing Authority Example,* address at the Hong Kong Institution of Engineers, Group 1 Seminar on 22 February 1999.

Caveat

The views expressed by author in this chapter are entirely his own and should not be interpreted as reflecting the policy of either the Hong Kong government or the Housing Authority.

Annex 6.1 Vision, Mission, and Values

Our Vision Is
– To be the community's pride as a professional team striving for continuous improvement in the provision of public housing and related services.

Our Mission Is
– to provide affordable housing and quality management, maintenance and other housing related services to meet the needs of our customers in a proactive, progressive and caring manner;
– to ensure cost-effective and rational use of public resources in service delivery and allocation of housing assistance in an open and equitable manner;
– to engender a competent, dedicated and performance-oriented team under an inspiring, dynamic and forward-looking leadership.

Our Core Values Are
– The "3 Cs" : Caring, Customer-focused, Committed.

Annex 6.2 Management Enhancement Programme: Key Initiatives

Corporate Strategy and Organization
– Corporate Direction
– Corporate Planning
– Corporate Information Systems
– Organization Structure

Service Delivery
– Service Measures and Targets
– Process Re-design
– Contractor Management
– Customer Feedback

Culture
– Leadership Development
– Human Resources Management
– Competency Development

Communications
– External Communication
– Internal Communication

Annex 6.3 Organization Structure of Housing Department, 1996

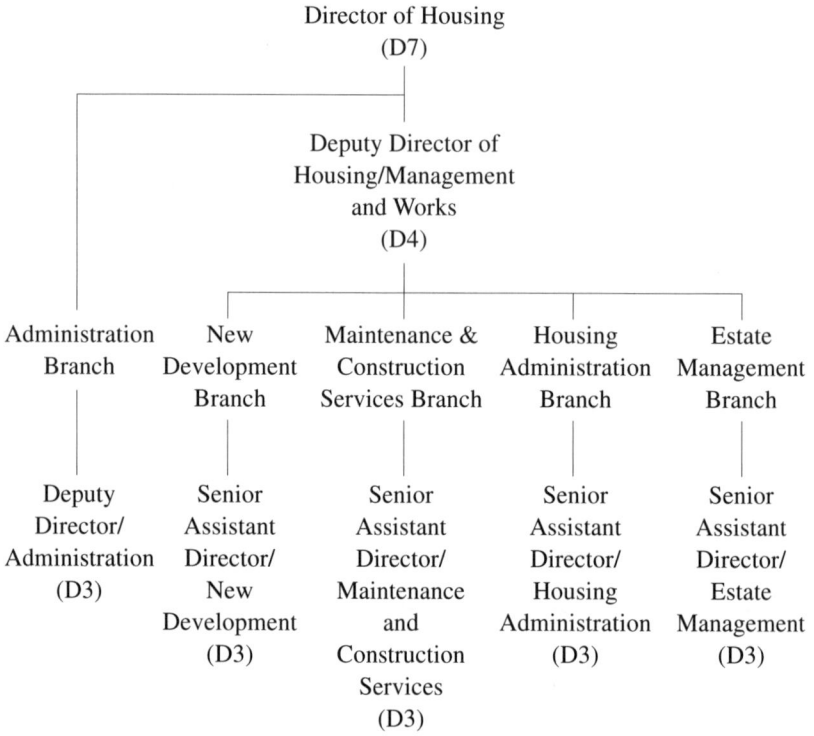

Director of Housing
(D7)

Deputy Director of
Housing/Management
and Works
(D4)

Administration Branch	New Development Branch	Maintenance & Construction Services Branch	Housing Administration Branch	Estate Management Branch
Deputy Director/ Administration (D3)	Senior Assistant Director/ New Development (D3)	Senior Assistant Director/ Maintenance and Construction Services (D3)	Senior Assistant Director/ Housing Administration (D3)	Senior Assistant Director/ Estate Management (D3)

Annex 6.4 Reorganization of Housing Department on Core Business Lines, April 1997

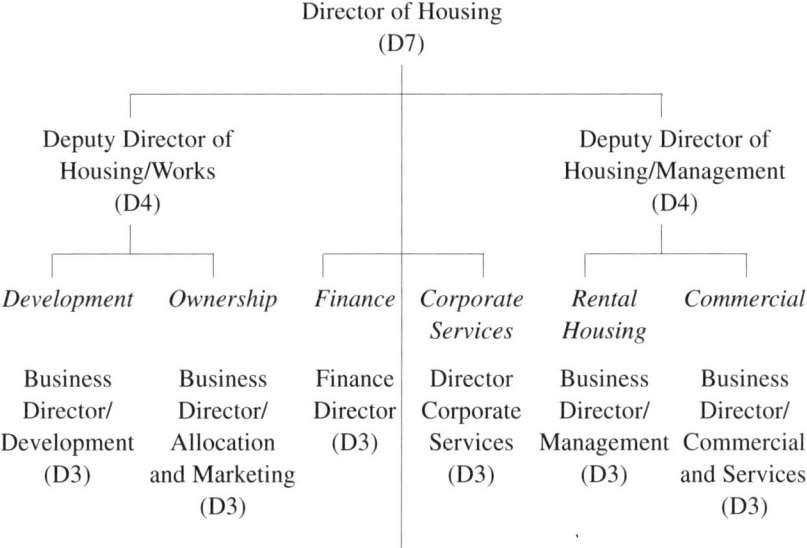

Director of Housing
(D7)

Deputy Director of
Housing/Works
(D4)

Deputy Director of
Housing/Management
(D4)

Development *Ownership* *Finance* *Corporate Services* *Rental Housing* *Commercial*

Business Director/ Development (D3) Business Director/ Allocation and Marketing (D3) Finance Director (D3) Director Corporate Services (D3) Business Director/ Management (D3) Business Director/ Commercial and Services (D3)

Corporate Strategy Unit

Head, Corporate Strategy Unit
(D2)

Annex 6.5 Relationship between Housing Authority's
Committees and Core Businesses

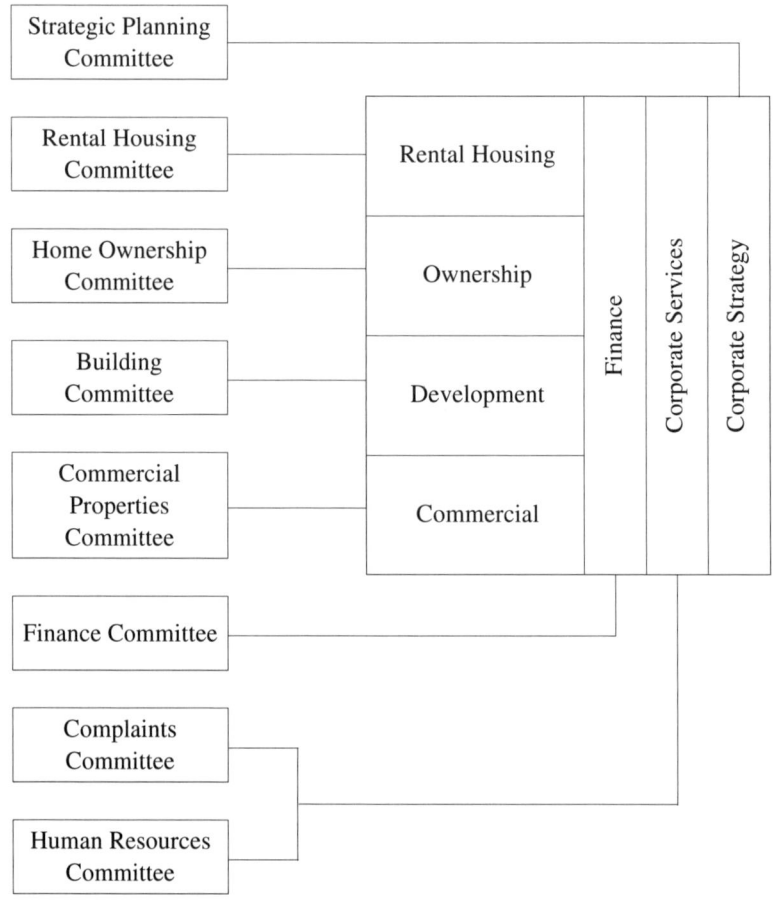

7

Management Reforms in the Police Force

Ki-on Hui

Former Commissioner of Police

1. Introduction

The Hong Kong Police Force, hereafter referred to as "the Force," is one of the largest government departments in Hong Kong, with over 28,500 sworn policemen and women, 6,000 civilians and 5,500 part-time auxiliary police officers. The Force is commanded by the Commissioner of Police, who is responsible to the Chief Executive for its administration and operational efficiency. The Commissioner of Police is assisted by two deputies: a Deputy Commissioner of Police (Operations) and a Deputy Commissioner of Police (Management). The structure of the Force may be thought of in terms of Force Headquarters and the Regions. Force Headquarters comprises five departments — Operations; Crime and Security; Personnel and Training; Management Services; Finance, Administration and Planning. The Finance, Administration and Planning Department is headed by an Administrative Officer, and the other departments by Senior Assistant Commissioners of Police. Annex 7.1 graphically illustrates the present day organization of the Force.

For day-to-day policing, the Force is divided into six regions: Hong Kong Island (HKI), Kowloon East (KE), Kowloon West (KW), New Territories South (NTS), New Territories North (NTN) and Marine (MAR). Each Region, commanded by a Regional Commander in the rank of Assistant Commissioner, is largely autonomous in its day-to-day operation and management matters. Regions are divided into districts and divisions and in a few cases sub-divisions. Currently there are a total of 23 districts in the Force.

Regional police are the front-line force serving the community round-the-clock. With a strong emphasis on enlisting community support, they play the traditional constabulary role of preserving life and property, preventing and detecting crime, keeping the peace, and responding promptly to calamities in times of emergency. Each of the five land regions has a headquarters comprising an Operations Wing, an Administration Wing, a Regional Crime Wing and a Traffic Wing. The Marine Region follows a broadly similar structure, minus the traffic component. The structure of a land Region is set out in Annex 7.2.

To ensure that the organization and management of the Force responded to growing demands for its services from the public, and was able to properly justify the government funding necessary to provide that service, a series of reviews were conducted throughout the 1990s with a view to improving the quality of service given by the Force. The Force's long term aims were to develop a police force that is accountable, lives within its means, manages for performance, and is service-oriented. To achieve these aims, the Force has pursued a dual approach under the broad headings of Service Quality and Performance Management.

2. Service Quality

2.1 Reasons for Change

Throughout the late 1980s and early 1990s, it became apparent that the people of Hong Kong had increasingly high expectations of how Hong Kong should be both governed and policed. The people wanted a user-friendly government and police force. A review of the Force's top command structure, conducted by management consultants in early 1992, reflected public opinion and recommended that the Force adopt a more customer-oriented approach. Governor Chris Patten, in his October 1992 inauguration policy speech, urged government departments to regard the public as clients not supplicants. In his 1994 Policy Address, Patten gave a commitment to develop a customer-based service culture in the public service.

In a free society like Hong Kong, it is crucial that the police operate with the consent and trust of the people. To maintain the support of the people of Hong Kong, which the Force had worked hard for many years to obtain, it became apparent that the Force had to: stop doing what it should not be doing; improve what it was already doing well; redesign what it was doing badly; and start doing what it was not doing but should be doing.

2.2 Force Strategy on Quality of Service

On 1 May 1994 the Force created a new body, Service Quality Wing (SQW), as a result of recommendations made in a review of the Force's top command structure. Headed by an Assistant Commissioner of Police, SQW was responsible for, among other things, bringing about a change in culture and work attitudes within the Force. To start such a change SQW launched the Force Strategy on Quality of Service (FSQS) in March 1995. FSQS sought to develop a culture that involved officers, at all levels, continually striving for improvement to ensure that services provided by the Force were effective, efficient and economical. Such an approach also required that the Force met the expectations of its internal and external customers, in regard to the quality of the service it provided. FSQS is best explained in terms of its component parts, namely: the Force Vision and Statement of Common Purpose and Values; Living-the-Values; Surveys; Consultancy Support; Customer Service Improvement Project; Staff Suggestion Scheme; and Best Practices.

2.2.1 Force Vision and Statement of Common Purpose and Values

To bring about the desired changes in the way Force was run, it was considered necessary to let everyone serving in the Force know exactly what was expected of them. To this end in April 1996, a draft Force Vision was formulated along with a draft Statement of Common Purpose and Values, with a view to fine-tuning both through extensive consultations throughout the remainder of the year. The consultation process required every member of the Force from Chief Superintendent downwards, including both civilians and members of the Hong Kong Auxiliary Police Force, to attend peer-based discussion groups. The rationale behind this approach was to involve and commit officers at all levels to providing genuine feedback on the draft package.

As a result of the support and co-operation of the entire Force, a final version of both the Vision and the Values was developed, and officially launched on 7 December 1996. The Force Vision and Statement of Common Purpose and Values, which are commonly referred to in the Force as "the Values," are set out in full at Annex 7.3. For the first time in the Force's history, everybody could see exactly what the Force stood for and what it expected from those serving within its ranks.

2.2.2 Living-the-Values

The launch of the Force Vision and Statement of Common Purpose and Values was never envisaged to be a one off exercise. For such an important initiative to succeed, it was considered essential that it was followed up by a programme that would give life to the vision, common purposes and shared values that the Force had collectively agreed to work for. As a result, "Living-the-Values" was born.

In the first wave of the Living-the-Values campaign, all members of the Force attended in-house seminars at which they discussed the relevance of the Values to their daily work. These meetings highlighted areas and issues that prevented or made it difficult for police officers to live up to the Values. As a result of this feedback, improvements were made that overhauled the Force's system of internal communications, an area that concerned an overwhelming majority of staff. Examples included: better use of notice boards, news flashes, training days, staff suggestion scheme, staff opinion survey, and Senior Directorate visits. However, although initiating such structural changes was relatively easy, the Force still had to bring about change among individual officers and their culture. Therefore, a second wave of the campaign was initiated in 1999 to address such concerns.

The second wave of Living-the-Values, which commenced at the time of writing, was intended to take a more focused approach, concentrating on three core issues: honesty; trust; and internal communications. Throughout 1999, workshops were run to help clear the air on matters of honesty and trust for both senior and junior staff, by creating an atmosphere that encouraged people to suggest where more trust could be given. Emphasis was also given on making it clear to senior police officers that, where possible, they must pass on information of staff interest at the earliest opportunity.

The theme that runs through this entire approach is a desire by the Force to move away from an autocratic command and control style of management, to a more modern managerial style of leadership. By giving police officers greater trust, the Force hopes to save time and money, as well as to develop a more productive and professionally competent work force.

2.2.3 Surveys

One of the key elements in providing quality service is the ability to understand the needs and expectations of the Force's clients, both external, i.e. members of the public, private bodies and other government departments, and internal, i.e. disciplined and civilian staff working in the Force. It was decided that the most effective way to find out what such external and internal customers thought of the Force was to ask them, by using surveys conducted by accredited private consultants. Three types of survey were initiated: on public opinion, customer satisfaction and staff opinion.

A starting out point in the service quality initiative was the commissioning of the Force's first independent public opinion survey, conducted in December 1995. The general purpose was to determine how the public rated the quality of the services the Force provided, and to establish a base for further similar surveys. The results were very encouraging. Of the more than 2,000 people interviewed, 78% considered the Force's overall performance worthy of praise, whilst only 3% thought poorly of it. A second survey was conducted in November 1997 and the results were again encouraging; 73% of respondents considered the overall performance of the Force good, with only 5% voicing criticisms.

To complement the public opinion survey, which canvassed public perceptions, a customer satisfaction survey was conducted in 1997 to measure the satisfaction of persons who had called upon the police for some form of service or help. The survey revealed that over 70% of respondents considered that the Force's standard of service was quite good or very good. Many useful suggestions were made, such as that officers could arrive more quickly to the scene when called by the public, and be more polite in their dealings with the public. The survey helped provide a focus for future strategies to improve the quality of service provided to the public, for example: improvement in efficiency in handling cases; better reception processes for telephone calls and visits to police report rooms; and improvement in police officers' close contact with the public.

The first ever staff opinion survey of serving disciplined and civilian members of the Force was launched in 1997, to ascertain what issues most concerned them. A majority considered the Force to be a good employer that operates with a high degree of efficiency. Recognition, respect, a corrupt-free police force and confidence in the future were some of the areas perceived by staff to be important and of high satisfaction. Areas of concern included the misuse of the Complaints Against Police Office by members of the public, and internal communications.

The information elicited in these surveys was of immense value in formulating management strategies to overcome problems identified. With the experience gained, the Force recognized the potential benefits of integrating and co-ordinating all such surveys to provide continuous and complementary feedback from its internal and external customers. As a result a Force survey strategy was formulated to make the best possible use of this important management information. In addition, it was determined that a management survey was required to supplement the staff opinion survey, in order to gauge views of managerial staff on issues such as financial, developmental and programme management.

The Force's survey strategy has three main objectives, namely integration; standardization and co-ordination. Integration involves using the findings of different surveys to match police and public perceptions on Force performance and priorities on law and order issues. Standardization requires confirmation of the scope, methodology, rating scale and frequency of surveys, to facilitate future comparison and cross-referencing. Finally, co-ordination is provided by SQW which is responsible for the scheduling, tendering and management of all Force level surveys. Annex 7.4 indicates the schedule and frequency of the four surveys that constitute the Force survey strategy.

2.2.4 Consultancy Support

Early on it was realized that external management consultants would bring a high degree of professionalism, objectivity and impartiality to the change process. Support for using consultants was forthcoming from the government's Efficiency Unit, which agreed to fund a project related to front-line service delivery. The management consultants commenced a one-year consultancy support project on 6 October 1997, with the objective of supporting the implementation of a customer service improvement programme as well as Force-wide culture change initiatives. This consultancy was subsequently extended until April 1999 for the Station Improvement Project, and until October 1999 in general support of the

Force culture change programme.

The consultants were required to support the Performance Review Branch of SQW in the delivery of its projects programme. Specifically, the consultants were to provide advice and support in four areas, beginning with a customer service improvement project at North Point Police Station to create a benchmark for Force service quality standards. The starting point for this project was a review of the delivery of report room services, but based on lessons learned, the improvement process was extended to other areas of police/public interface including the crime and property offices. Similarly, the consultants were to implement a series of customer service and culture change initiatives focusing on programmes such as: using work improvement teams to develop and implement best practices; developing and managing customer focus measurements through surveys; facilitating the development of the Staff Suggestion and Motivation Scheme; developing a support network to enhance communications within the Force; and conducting skill transfer sessions and designing other relevant training programmes to reinforcing the impact and momentum of the proposed changes. Based on what was learned from these programmes, the consultants were to devise and implement a Force-wide rolling out of the above initiatives, as well as to assist and contribute to the production of regular reports on progress.

To co-ordinate the work involved, a full time consultant worked from an office in SQW as a member of the Performance Review Branch team, and reported on a day-to-day basis to the Chief Superintendent in charge of the Branch. In so doing, the consultant provided specialist technical input not readily available within the Force, and helped transfer necessary skills and techniques to officers in SQW.

2.2.5 Customer Service Improvement Project

The Customer Service Improvement Project was initially focused on changing staff culture and attitude towards the way the public are treated. This resulted in the identification of the need to review processes and procedures and also to examine the physical environment in which the police/ public interface takes place. In order to address these issues a Station Improvement Project was initiated.

The Station Improvement Project at North Point Police Station initially focused on the provision of report room services but was subsequently extended to both the crime and property offices, as well as other areas of interface with the public. Signage was designed to indicate to members of the public what they can expect when making a report. This was complemented by the introduction of a well-organized reception procedure that prioritized reports by their significance, and ensured a proper queuing system. Similarly, a series of information packages were developed that give the public detailed information as to how the Force will handle different types of report. In addition, the scheme successfully introduced self-reporting of minor cases, such as lost property, by fax.

Physical improvements were made to the layout of the public areas of the Station, to make them less intimidating and more user-friendly to the public. Similarly, physical improvements were also made behind the scenes for the benefit of staff members. For example, a resource centre with computers linked to the internet and air-conditioned changing rooms were introduced to enhance the working environment.

Technological improvements came with the introduction of an Artificial Intelligence Crime Analysis and Management System (AICAMS), developed jointly by the Force and the Chinese University of Hong Kong. AICAMS is a touch-screen computer system that permits beat officers and police managers to analyze crime patterns, as well as prepare identikit drawings of suspects. In future this system will also incorporate facial recognition, speech recognition and a variety of communication and map-based techniques. The success of the Station Improvement Project was recognized by the Chief Executive who announced, in his 1998 Policy Address, that it would be extended to all of the Force's 57 police stations.

2.2.6 Staff Suggestion and Motivation Scheme

The Staff Suggestion and Motivation Scheme, launched in 1994, aimed at promoting efficiency, productivity and positive management within the Force. Cash and other awards are presented to individuals whose suggestions can bring about improvements to work processes, utilization of resources, quality of service, working environment, Force image or staff morale. Some useful suggestions received include: improvements to forms and procedures to make them more user-friendly; publication of a newsletter at each police station to enhance staff cohesiveness; and installation of Staff Suggestion Boxes.

2.2.7 Best Practices

At all levels, the Force has pursued a strategy of seeking out and widely publicizing best practices. This allows tried and tested quality practices to be implemented throughout the Force, as well as identifying bad practices that should be eliminated. To facilitate this approach SQW have conducted extensive research on management best practices in the public and private sectors, both locally and internationally. Work improvement teams have been encouraged at Divisional level to utilize the experience and knowledge of junior staff in devising good work procedures. Through the sharing of knowledge that already exists but which had not been properly disseminated, the Force hopes to reduce duplication of effort and in so doing become more effective and productive. Ultimately a best practices directory will be made available to managers at all levels through the Force's own intranet. Not only will this provide a forum for sharing best practices across formation lines and specialization in the Force, but should also help reduce time wasted reinventing the wheel.

2.3 Resistance to Change

To overcome anticipated resistance to the changes highlighted above, workshops have regularly been held for officers of all ranks to discuss the concepts of service quality and living-the-values. A bilingual video, newsletters, bulletins and booklets have also been used to spread the message and complement the workshops. Much effort has been made to follow up problems highlighted during workshops, to demonstrate that the Force is fully committed to living-the-values in respect of its staff.

2.4 Strategic Directions

Following the development of the Force Vision and Statement of Common Purpose and Values, consideration was given as to how the standards and beliefs expressed therein could be put into practice in the day-to-day management and operation of the Force. The key business issues that may affect or impede the pursuit of the Values were therefore identified, and agreement reached on the appropriate responses to them. Similarly, specific goals were developed against which to measure progress in achieving the Values.

The first set of Strategic Directions were published in December 1996 to govern the management and operation of the Force, and subsequently revised to take into account changes that occurred within both the Force and Hong Kong. The revised Strategic Directions are set out in full at Annex 7.5. To ensure that the core business of the Force is properly prioritized, scheduled and co-ordinated, it was realized early on that it was necessary to translate the Force's Strategic Directions into programme plans under the heading Performance Management discussed below.

3. Performance Management

3.1 Background

As part of the Force's initiative to improve its quality of service, it was considered essential that the existing planning and management structures were re-organized. The purpose of such a re-organization was to lay the foundations for improving service throughout all levels of the organization by establishing a clear and consistent process for developing objectives and monitoring progress. This process, commonly referred to as Programme Management, sought to categorize the core business areas of policing into a number of clearly defined programme plans, each managed by dedicated programme managers. These programme plans provide a link between the overall strategic direction of the Force, as set out in the Commissioner's Strategic Directions, and the day-to-day actions of various formations throughout the organization.

The duties of the Hong Kong Police Force are laid down in Section 10 of the Police Force Ordinance, Cap 232. These have been interpreted, through the Force Vision that Hong Kong remains one of the safest and most stable societies in the world, to define the Force's core business as: upholding the rule of law; maintaining law and order; preventing and detecting crime; safeguarding and protecting life and property; working in partnership with the community and other agencies; striving for excellence in all that we do; and maintaining public confidence in the Force.

3.2 Relationship with Government

In conducting its core business, the Force provides a variety of services and the government provides resources. Its services and related resource levels are enumerated annually in the Controlling Officer's Report which delineates the Force's contribution to Government Policy Area 9 : Internal Security. Resources are acquired through a series of annual exercises, for example: estimates giving the recurrent expenditure for the next financial year; estimates of the Force's provisional baseline and forecast of recurrent expenditure; capital works and capital non-works resource allocation exercises (RAE).

Six problems were identified in respect of the way in which the Force's interface with government operates. First, although the Force planning cycle should be easy to synchronize with the government cycle, the government has, in the past, brought forward the RAE on several occasions. Since these exercises are generally conducted on a one-off basis the result has been hurried submissions. Second, the Force had viewed the RAE as an opportunity to acquire new money to implement new projects whilst maintaining existing services. This was a partial misconception as, since only 1% of government expenditure is new money, even the best presented and argued bids cannot significantly increase the Force's slice of the pie. Third, this misconception tended to externalize the Force's perspective on resources by turning to government for new money rather than determining how it could better use existing resources. Fourth, the system did not encourage better and more flexible use of resources. The attitude of use-it-or-lose-it remained prevalent because unused resources were returned to government, and financial regulations made it difficult to vire savings from one area to new expenditures in another. As a result there was little incentive to achieve savings. Greater financial autonomy for the Force and more financial devolution within the Force are required. Fifth, the passage of information among committees was only achieved by a great deal of haphazard cross-membership. This resulted in certain officers, notably Assistant Commissioners, being members of many committees. Lastly, below Assistant Commissioner level only informal channels for planning and resource allocation existed in most formations.

3.3 Force Committee Structure

What passed for programme management in the Force was conducted through committees or conferences at all levels, some of which had a primary decision making role whilst others only existed to pass information. However, in terms of a programme management structure, it was also necessary to identify which committees should deal with planning activities.

This proved difficult because even committees that seemed to have narrow operational remits, often turned out to have long-term planning and resource implications.

At Force level, 27 committee down to Assistant Commissioner level were identified as having planning or resources implications. It was not unusual for officers of Assistant Commissioner rank to be members of six to eight committees at Force level, as well as to participate in meetings that did not have resource implications and meetings within their own major formations. This undoubtedly allowed them to pass and receive information from a large number of sources but, given the amount of time and effort in being physically present at such meetings and in preparing briefs beforehand, such a system was hardly efficient. A study of the function and membership of the aforementioned 27 committees, revealed that although the Force had a lot of committees, it did not have a committee structure as such.

The committee structure within Regions was much simpler than that at Force level. Meetings tended to be cloned at each command level, for example Regional Commander's Conference, District Commander's Conference, and Divisional Commander's Conference. In membership terms, these regional committees provided a suitable forum for both decision making and information dissemination. However, they tended to be backward looking, studying retrospective performance figures and passing on relatively dated information. Few of the meetings involved forward planning or discussion of plans and activities.

Within Regions no formal system of prioritizing resource bids existed. Bids for the various resource exercises were channelled from unit and formation commanders to the Regional Commander who prioritized them. Such a system was not effective for a number of reasons. Formations received little prior direction on bids, which would have cut out many unrealistic bids at source and reduced wasted effort at all levels of the system. Major Formations lacked a frame of reference to compare competing bids from Formations. Formation Commanders lacked a forum to argue the case for their bids against competing bids from other Formations. Few bids were actually rejected at Formation and Major Formation levels, but those given lower priorities had practically no chance of acceptance. Formations and units received little feedback on why their bids received the priority they did, which led to the tendency of trying again next year, resulting in more wasted effort.

District and Divisional commanders had little financial autonomy, and as a result there was no incentive for them to make savings on planned expenditure. Since commanders did not control their major expenditures, such as salaries and allowances, police officers were not deployed solely on a value-for-money basis. In the main, police officers were deployed on an operationally effective basis. This was not necessarily a bad thing, but it meant that at District and Divisional levels, financial planning was a purely paper exercise.

Furthermore it was apparent that whilst some Regions and Districts had their own stated aims and objectives, that followed the Commissioner of Police's Law Enforcement Policies and Priorities, this was by no means universal. Similarly, such aims and objectives were not examined and updated regularly.

The Force's initial approach was to establish what elements of the existing command and management structure could be used, or modified, to produce a programme management structure that met its needs. Although much of the existing structure was of use, it was far from being perfect. Unless the defects were corrected, superimposing a programme management structure on top of the existing command and management structure would have merely resulted in more bureaucracy with little benefit to show for it.

3.4 Responsibilities of Decision Makers

Given its disciplined nature, the Force has a tendency to defer responsibility to rank. Very often decisions which could be made at a lower level are passed up the chain of command. Whether this is because of excessive control from the top or because of a lack of confidence at the bottom, the effects are the same. High level commanders end up dealing with minor items instead of devoting proper attention to the issues that they really should be dealing with at their level. Similarly, a slow and inflexible paperwork system had evolved, where requests were passed up and orders passed down. Finally, there was a widespread lack of motivation at the bottom of the chain. If officers cannot take responsibility for their actions they cannot take credit for them either. The system has turned them into bureaucrats who conform, rather than police officers who initiate.

It was therefore realized that it was crucial to clarify the decision making process so that officers know which issues should be dealt with at specific levels. Although it may be easy to make such specifications, it was realized that there will often be cases where the impact of a decision cannot be finely judged, or where a potential decision may have such an impact on the Force or the public that consideration and endorsement outside the decision maker's area of responsibility is necessary. This highlighted the importance of meetings such as the Commissioner's Monthly Meeting with Assistant Commissioners and above, and similar meetings within Departments and Major Formations, as a forum for information exchange and the discussion and endorsement of decisions when necessary.

3.5 Purpose of Meetings

Committees and meetings in the Force exist for two purposes, passing information and making decisions. By far the largest proportion of the business conducted in most of them relates to information passing. It must therefore be considered whether a meeting is the quickest and most accurate way to pass information and whether or not the information is relevant to the members. Furthermore, where committees do make decisions they face the same problems as individual decision makers, i.e. are they making decisions appropriate to their command level?

There was therefore a need to clarify the role of committees and to distinguish between what was for information, what was for discussion and what was for decision, and why. It was believed that this could best be achieved by introducing terms of reference for meetings and sticking to them. Similarly it was also necessary to clearly establish where a committee or meeting fits into the programme management structure. Who does it report to and when? Who reports to it, and when? By making these relationships clear the cross-membership of the meetings could be rationalized, and the workload of individual officers reduced.

Within the existing structure most meetings spent the greatest proportion of their time reviewing past events, usually in terms of reports tabled by members. This had a number of drawbacks. The information was inevitably out of date by at least a few weeks, and where performance information was used for comparison purposes it was invariably against past performance, rather than against future objectives. Depending upon the frequency of the meetings, the time intervals were often too short for any changes in reported performance to be meaningful. For instance monthly variations in figures may be attributable to many factors and may not represent a trend. In many cases reports were tabled solely for the information of the chairman, and had little relevance to other members. The preparation of meeting briefs took much time and effort, yet many officers frankly admitted that they rarely read every brief tabled at a meeting.

Although there is undoubtedly a role in a programme management structure for reviewing progress towards set objectives, the essence of such a system must be forward looking, concentrating on planning, prioritization and resource allocation. Therefore, if the new programme management structure was to use the existing Force meeting structure, the role of many of the meetings had to be revised. Clearly, stating duties in the terms of reference of meetings would not be enough to achieve this because there was a real danger that the meetings would just take on the new workload without dropping the old. It was believed that such a change would require the Force to determine what performance indicators were required for each programme area and report them in a meaningful way. The existing workload of meetings had to be reduced by removing any performance reviews that were not required to support the programme area. Similarly, performance reviews had to be timed so that they were meaningful, whilst the amount of meeting time devoted to passing information that was better transmitted by other means had to be reduced.

3.6 Resource Allocation

One of the main purposes of any programme management system is the rational allocation of scarce resources. In the Force this entails allocating resources where they will produce the greatest operational benefit and derive the best value for money. However, resource allocation was often made on very scanty information. Those seeking resources were not required to demonstrate what benefits would be derived and how those benefits were to be measured. Therefore those allocating resources could not make rational judgments about competing resource bids. This situation was largely attributable to the informal resource allocation structure at Assistant Commissioner level and below.

To enable resource allocators to make rational choices, the bidding system has to be enhanced with the introduction of internal service level agreements, whereby the bidder offers a return for the allocation. Resources could therefore be allocated on the basis of the best return. In this respect, the track record of the bidder in reaching his own targets on previous bids would be an important consideration. Commanders who made the best use of resources should not be penalized by having their resources cut. It should be a basic principle of a programme management system that a commander who saves resources has the first call on those savings.

Commanders at all levels have also to be encouraged to make the best use of their resources by maintaining a wish list of projects that they would like to undertake and a slack list of activities they could do without. Wish list projects could then be funded by savings from other sources or by trade-offs from the slack list. Only when this cannot be done would the wish list projects be put up as a bid for additional resources.

3.7 Programme Management Structure

The Force's new programme management structure is based on four assumptions. First, the Force would pursue three operational programme areas, namely crime prevention, public order and crime control, along with three support programmes, namely human resources, management services and administrative services. Second, as programme areas may change in the future, the structure has to be flexible enough to cater for this. Third, the overall structure of the Force and its interface with government, would remain unchanged. Lastly, the level of decision making is not to be determined by the rank of the decision-maker alone, but by the forum in which the decision is made.

The aim of the new programme management structure is to use the existing Force structure to provide a continuous flow of command directions and resources down the structure, and a return flow of feedback and resource bids. This envisages a top-down, bottom-up approach. Top-down: strategic directions are set at Force and programme manager level and are converted into plans at Assistant Commissioner level and activities at Formation Commander and Divisional level. Bottom-up: resources are allocated at various command levels to implement such plans and activities, whilst the outcomes of these activities and resource allocations are monitored; feedback is sent up the system so that plans, policies and strategic directions can be evaluated, reviewed, re-assessed and revised as necessary.

Within the Force structure there are four decision-making levels, each making different types of decision. These are illustrated in Annex 7.6. Translated to the Force structure the decision making process develops as follows: The Commissioner with his Deputies, supported by the Senior Directorate collectively, are responsible for the strategic thinking. The Senior Directorate collectively, supported by programme managers individually, are responsible for long-range planning. Based on the above, Assistant Commissioners, Formation Commanders and unit commanders are responsible for operational and tactical planning.

3.8 Performance Indicators

The proper design and use of performance indicators and measurements was considered essential to provide the feedback necessary to develop plans, monitor performance, and identify problems or pressure areas that require action or slack areas where resources could be saved. In addition to internal use, it was also appreciated that the Force required indicators for external consumption, for example those for the Secretary of Security's Key Result Areas, the Controlling Officer's Report, and crime and traffic statistics.

As far as possible, it was thought desirable that the raw data used in indicators should already be available from the statistics produced in the normal course of police duties. For example, large amounts of data on establishment, development, productivity, financial resources and outcome opinions were already available, supported by data freely obtainable from external sources. Only in exceptional cases, where a well-defined problem has been identified, should indicators that require special collection of data be used. It was realized that failure to keep to such guidelines could result in vast tracts of redundant paper checks being initiated that created work rather than help reduce it. Therefore, when deciding upon which indicators to use to monitor an activity, it was advised that design criteria, content, use and presentation be all considered.

3.8.1 Design Criteria

The performance indicator must flow from, and serve to implement, the strategy, so that there is a coherent hierarchy of indicators at different levels in the programme management structure. There has to be a realization that in each programme area there can only be a limited number of key indicators for each level.

3.8.2 Content

Performance indicators must measure inputs and workloads, outcomes and outputs. They should be balanced to cover internal and external measures and be easily understandable. The value of the data used for performance indicators should be more than the cost of collecting it. Finally, performance indicators must be given meaning by being expressed as comparisons and rates rather than crude figures.

3.8.3 Use

Performance indicators should be capable of, and used for, internal (same unit, different time) and external (different unit) comparisons. They should be used to align effort and behaviour with the intended objective, and be used as the basis for informed action. They should be dynamic, changing and improving over time as objectives and circumstances change. Thus they must be deleted if no longer relevant.

3.8.4 Presentation

As far as possible, performance indicators should be presented in graphics rather than as tables, and be consistent for ease of comparison over time.

3.9 Performance-Related Bidding

Performance-related bidding offers a rational method of allocating resources. At Force and programme area levels, performance-related bids must be able to rely on the performance indicators for that programme area, albeit these may require fine-tuning to adequately reflect the benefit that is expected of a successful bid. At Assistant Commissioner and lower levels, it has been necessary to introduce specific indicators to match specific, small scale bids. Performance-related bids are subject to review in forums such as the Secretary for Security's pre-Star Chamber Reviews for Force bids and in the Programme Managers Quarterly Meetings for internal bids.

3.10 Force/Government Planning Interface

The elements that make up the Force/Government Planning Interface, such as the resource allocation exercises and draft estimates, may be complex but they are predictable. Therefore it was possible to tie the Force resource planning and allocation exercises into the government cycle by clearly identifying when things have to be done at all command levels from division upwards. This broke down a complex procedure into a series of simpler procedures and produced a smooth, continuous cycle of resource requests, allocation and monitoring, as opposed to the spasmodic and often rushed system in place previously. In order for the system to work commanders are made aware of their own deadlines in the annual cycle, as well as what they require from those below them and what is required by those above them. Like the programme management structure, this model may be tailored to suit the requirements of specific programme areas.

3.11 Revised Force Committee Structure

The programme management structure calls for the creation of an additional tier of meetings, namely the Programme Manager's Quarterly Meetings. The structure and the Force/Government interface also call for existing meetings at all levels to be used for planning and resource issues. The imposition of these requirements on top of the previous structure with its recognized workload was unlikely to be effective. For the structure to function effectively, the workload of the committees had to be reduced by at least as much as programme management would impose, but preferably more. Consequently, it was necessary to start at the top of the existing Force Committee Structure to determine what improvements or deletions could be made. It was perceived that changes made at the top would have a knock-on effect down the system.

The programme management structure envisages the Commissioner of Police and the Senior Directorate meeting and operating collectively at two levels, namely Tier One and Tier Two. Tier One stipulates that the Commissioner of Police and his Deputies are responsible for strategic thinking and the approval of annual resource exercises. However, Tier Two solely involves the Senior Directorate, without the Commissioner of Police, in long-range planning and quarterly reviews of programme areas. In conjunction with the meetings that such a system requires, the Commissioner's Monthly Meeting with Assistant Commissioners and above is retained as is the Commissioner's Weekly Meeting with the Senior Directorate. Both meetings provide a forum for the exchange of information and ideas, rather than as decision-making vehicles. The two Quarterly Major Formation Commander's Meetings were dispensed with in favour of the Programme Manager's Quarterly Meetings, the only new meetings introduced. As a result, the five programme managers hold quarterly meetings that cover the six programme areas set out in Annex 7.7. Within Major Formations, no changes were made to the structure of meetings, although there were changes in content. In general the lower the level the less time is needed to be spent on resource bidding and allocation, and planning functions.

3.12 Force Plan

In order that managers at all levels were aware of their role in the programme management structure, it was considered necessary to collate all levels of planning into a Force Plan that mirrored the programme structure. The plan that was formulated consists of six component parts or levels. At level one, the Force Vision and Statement of Common Purpose and Values are set by the Commissioner of Police in conjunction with the Force and are only very rarely changed. Level two deals with both the Strategic Directions and Programme Structure, which are set by the Commissioner of Police together with the Senior Directorate. These directions and structure are reviewed annually and changed only occasionally. Programme Plans follow on at level three, with the Programme Manager allocating resources, prioritizing sub-programmes, and setting targets. Programme Plans are reviewed and updated quarterly and changed as necessary. At level four are the Assistant Commissioner's Plans that implement the Programme Manager's priorities, as well as setting their own priorities funded by their own resources, setting indicator measurements, and consolidating performance data. These plans are reviewed and updated quarterly, and changed as necessary. Formation Plans are formulated at level five. They implement both the Programme Manager's and Assistant Commissioner's priorities, as well as setting priorities from their own resources, and collating and assessing performance data. Formation Plans are reviewed and updated quarterly and changed as necessary. Finally, at level six are unit level plans. They implement the Programme Manager's, Assistant Commissioner's and Formation Commander's priorities, as well as setting priorities from their own resources, and collecting performance data. They are reviewed and updated quarterly and changed as necessary.

The Force Plan provides a useful tool for improving Service Quality by allowing for benchmarking among units, formations and major formations and by facilitating inspections.

3.13 Overview

Programme Management provides a structured approach to the management of Force activities by dividing them into six programme areas that reflect the core business of the Force. This establishes a clear and consistent process for developing objectives, implementing plans and monitoring progress throughout the Force. Each programme area is each under the responsibility of a Programme Manager at Senior Assistant Commissioner of Police or equivalent civilian rank.

Each programme area has a defined purpose. These definitions allow the programme to be further broken down into sub-programme areas. The programme area definitions and sub-programmes are set out in Annex 7.8. Within these areas, Programme Managers and the Senior Directorate are responsible for setting strategic directions which are aimed at fulfilling the Force Vision and Values in that programme area or at overcoming obstructions to fulfilling the Force Vision and Values. These are implemented through programme plans which provide a link between the overall strategic direction of the Force and the day-to-day actions of units. The plans are developed and implemented through a Programme Management Structure which is designed to do four things:

- Define the Force programme areas and clearly identify responsibilities.
- Translate the strategic directions established at Force level for each programme area into plans at major formation commander level. These plans are, in turn, translated into activities at formation and unit level.
- Provide feedback on the effectiveness of the programmes, strategic directions, plans and activities. This feedback will usually be in the form of operational and/or financial performance indicators.
- Interface the feedback with the programme planning process by providing assessments of the effectiveness of the programme area and plans.

The Force Programme Management Structure consists of six interrelated elements: (i) A decision making and planning structure that mirrors the Force's command structure from unit level to Commissioner, provides a continuous flow of command directions and resources down the structure; a return flow of feedback and resource bids up the structure. (ii) The Force

planning and resource allocation exercises are integrated by clearly identifying when things have to be done at all command levels from unit upwards.
This breaks down a complex procedure into a series of simpler procedures
to produce a smooth, continuous cycle of resource requests, allocation and
monitoring. (iii) The system has the flexibility to match resources with
operational needs through the one-line-vote and the ability to vire funds
and create or delete posts. This is based on the principle that formations
which make savings will have first call on using the surpluses created for
their own needs. (iv) A structured system of meetings and committees
emphasizes the use of existing meetings at all levels for planning and
resource issues, by integrating the terms of reference of committees and
meetings in the Force Committee Structure. (v) The Force Plan, produced
in the form of a dynamic working document, illustrates the link between
the Force's Vision and Values, and the activities by which the Force delivers its service to the community. The Force Plan also provides a concise
summary of the Force's plans down to unit level, gives an overview of the
costs involved in meeting the Force's goals and activities in terms of
resources, and shows how the Force is actually performing. (vi) Finally,
performance indicators are used to provide feedback on the implementation of plans at all levels.

4. Lessons Learned

The process of change initiated in the Force's service quality journey is not
over. From a management perspective the Force has learned a lot and expects to continue to do so. Nevertheless there are six major management
lessons that have been learned so far.

- Bringing about change in a large organization requires total commitment from managers at the highest levels. Only those at the very
  top have the clout and influence to mobilize the necessary resources
  to ensure that proposed changes last and are adopted by all. It is
  essential that high level decision makers personally exercise this
  authority, as such a commitment instils confidence that the change
  process will be seen through to its conclusion and ensures appropriate resource allocation.
- Employees believe what they see and not what they hear. Managers,
  particularly those at the top, must realize that it is simply not
  enough to make speeches, publish papers and run a few courses. If

employees do not believe that management at all levels are practising what they are preaching, they will not accept change and consider it to be an imposition.

- It is best to consult staff before announcing changes that effect how they are expected to perform their duties. Failure to do so is likely to result in lip-service being paid to such changes. By getting the staff involved and committed from the outset, and seeking inputs from them, it is more likely that they will help the change process rather than hinder it.

- All organizations have their own language and management must ensure that they are speaking the same language when communicating changes. It was difficult for the Force to define service quality in a police context, and as a result this initially led to confusion and scepticism. The lesson learned from this is that management jargon should be avoided. Wherever possible, simple language that conveys the same message and achieves the same effect should be used.

- From a police perspective it is only when officers believe that they are working for the community that they are policing, will they approach their duties with a service-oriented approach. To foster such an approach it is necessary to emphasize the importance of living up to the values and beliefs that are publicly espoused to be the values of the organization.

- Putting theory into practice has ramifications that are hard to predict, and may lead an organization into areas not previously contemplated. For example, the Force's Customer Service Improvement Project started out as a culture change programme, but resulted in a major Force-wide initiative to improve the physical environment within police stations. Organizations must therefore recognize that putting theory into practice will inevitably result in unforeseen consequences that they will have to manage.

During the change process certain limitations have been identified which act as barriers to reform. Of particular note are:

- Management initiatives targeting efficiency savings, which hit staff in the pocket. These are unpopular and quickly become significant morale issues within the groups affected. It is, therefore, necessary for management to clearly explain the wider benefits of such initiatives to staff. For example, savings from overtime expenditure as a result of revised policies, had been used to fund a pay revision for Junior Police Officers and to establish additional posts.

- Fundamental changes to organizational culture, such as the change from an enforcement culture to a service culture, are not easy to implement. Some officers buy in, some do not, and some never will. Management needs to recognize that such problems exist and take steps to encourage participation.
- Even if an organization has a master plan, because of changes in the business environment outside of its own control, it may not be able to implement it. For example, the Hong Kong government's Enhanced Productivity Programme (EPP) and Capitalized Service Reform have resulted in changes to the system of acting allowances, a recruitment freeze and changes in the conditions of service for new recruits. Staff would feel frustrated with unanticipated changes as it appears that the goal posts are constantly moving. They do not always appreciate the distinction between these internal motives and external factors.

It is therefore vital to have effective internal communication and to engender a culture of loyalty and positive participation amongst staff. One of the strengths of the Hong Kong Police Force is the "can do" attitude of its staff, which has in the long term been reflected in their acceptance of and participation in the change process.

5. The Future

The management changes initiated by the Force, were introduced when both the Force and Hong Kong were experiencing good times. These have proved to be of immense benefit in light of the recent economic downturn in Asia and the Chief Executive's annual policy address in October 1998. The Chief Executive stated that the civil service must operate more efficiently and cost-effectively, while at the same time maintain its high standard of service to the people. To this end he announced that the civil service would implement an Enhanced Productivity Programme, to save five percent from each government department's operating expenditure between 2000 and 2003.

All government departments were required to put forward proposals for new and improved services without incurring additional cost. EPP thereby seeks to improve productivity across the civil service with a view to releasing resources to ensure that money is spent on priority areas, as well as creating new initiatives. However, the government does not aim to achieve cuts in overall expenditure, as normal RAE will continue and new money will continue to be allocated if justified.

The Force's programme management structure, which has now been running for two years, provides the ideal mechanism for ensuring that the Force delivers the required savings. This is illustrated in the savings already achieved by the utilization of this management system by the Force. For example, in 1996–97 the Force reduced the Auxiliary Police Quota by HK$50 million to fund 258 regular Police Constable posts. In 1997–98 a revision of Marine Region's duty shift patterns saved HK$64 million in overtime payments and thereby helped finance 314 additional Police Constable posts. The 1998 amalgamation of the Field Patrol Detachment with Border District yielded a further HK$48 million savings in overtime payments, which funded 235 new Police Constable posts. With this success in mind, the five Programme Managers are working to identify a series of fresh initiatives that are expected to yield significant savings, as well as to improve the day-to-day management of the Force. The accent is on how the Force can utilize existing resources to better perform its core business, and at the same time save money.

The government has recognized the Force's commitment to managing its resources properly, by allowing it to operate a one-line-vote system with effect from 1 April 1999. Essentially this means that financial responsibility for the Force's annual budget is fully devolved to the Force. Once the annual budget has been allocated it is now up to the Force as to how it spends that money. This allows the Force to vire money to and from different votes as and when such reallocation becomes necessary, without having to seek permission from the Finance Bureau to do so, as happened previously. Such a system ensures greater flexibility and efficiency in the management of Force finances. The only downside is that the government will not come up with any more money on top of that which has been annually allocated.

How successful the Hong Kong Police Force will be in achieving the aims of EPP, and managing the one-line-vote, remains to be seen. However, the management reforms discussed in this chapter have given the Force a solid and reliable mechanism to face the challenges of the next few years with confidence.

Annex 7.1 Force Organization

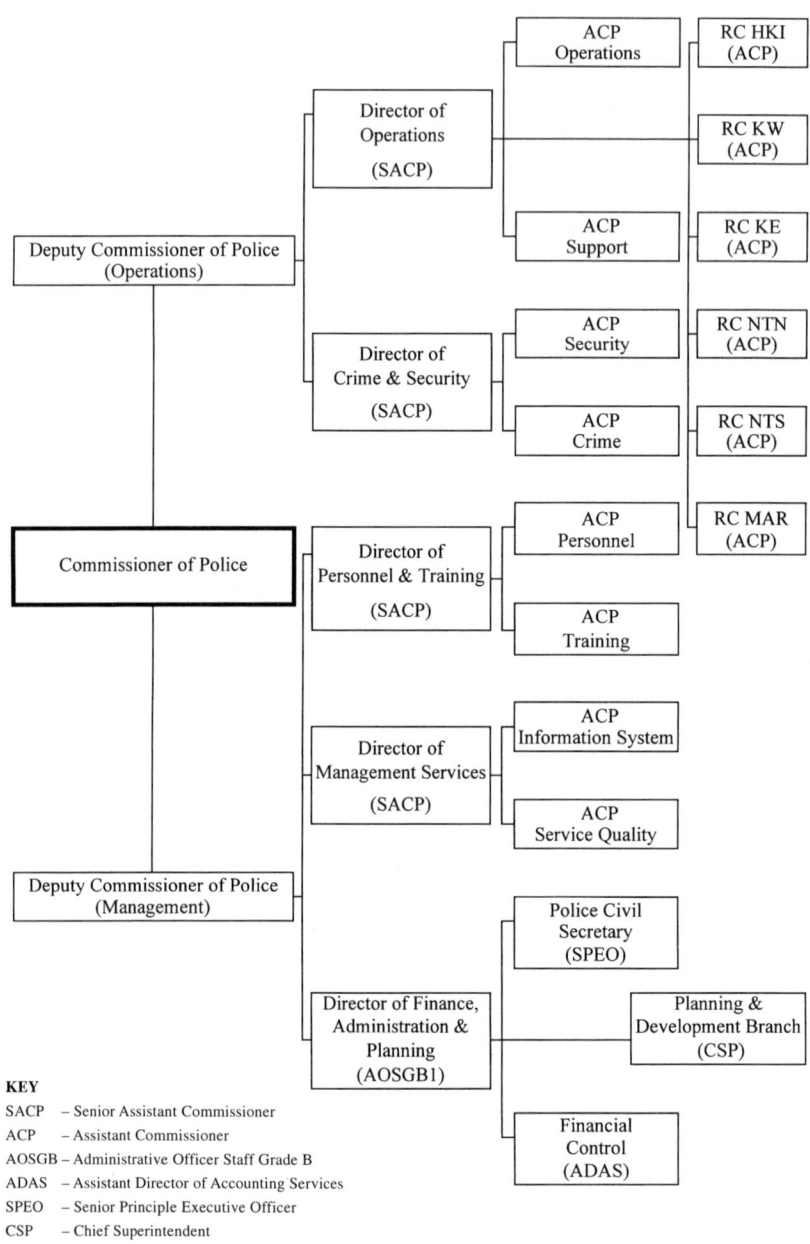

KEY

SACP – Senior Assistant Commissioner
ACP – Assistant Commissioner
AOSGB – Administrative Officer Staff Grade B
ADAS – Assistant Director of Accounting Services
SPEO – Senior Principle Executive Officer
CSP – Chief Superintendent
RC – Regional Commander

Annex 7.2 Regional Organization

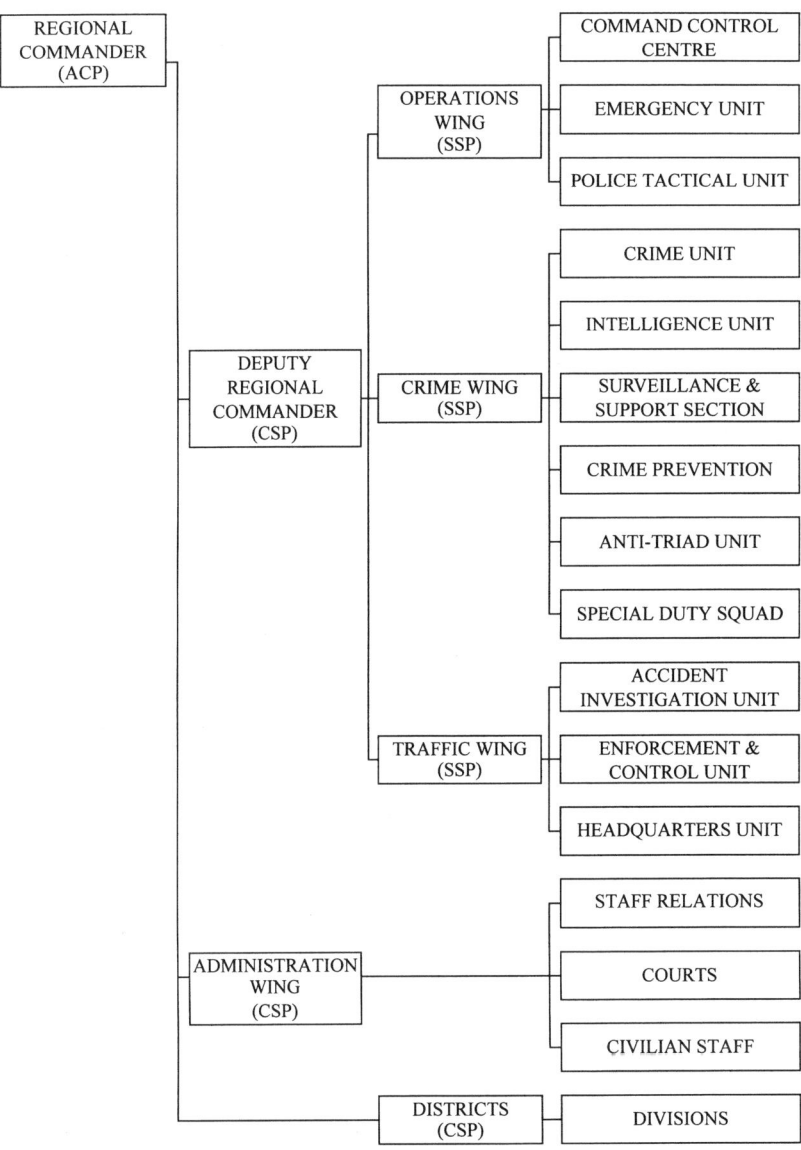

KEY
ACP – Assistant Commissioner
CSP – Chief Superintendent
SSP – Senior Superintendent

Annex 7.3 Force Vision and Statement of Common Purpose and Values

Vision
– That Hong Kong remains one of the safest and most stable societies in the world

Our Common Purpose
The Hong Kong Police Force will ensure a safe and stable society by:
– upholding the rule of law
– maintaining law and order
– preventing and detecting crime
– safeguarding and protecting life and property
– working in partnership with the community and other agencies
– striving for excellence in all that we do
– maintaining public confidence in the Force

Our Values
– integrity and honesty
– respect for the rights of members of the public and of the Force
– fairness, impartiality and compassion in all our dealings
– acceptance of responsibility and accountability
– professionalism
– dedication to quality service and continuous improvement
– responsiveness to change
– effective communication both within and outwith the Force

Annex 7.4 Schedule and Frequency of Surveys

Survey	Frequency	Schedule			
		Year 1	Year 2	Year 3	Year 4
Public Opinion Survey	Biannual	✔		✔	
Customer Satisfaction Survey	Biannual		✔		✔
Staff Opinion Survey	Annual	Core[1]	Full[2]	Core	Full
Management Survey	Biannual	✔		✔	

Notes: 1. The Core Staff Opinion Survey is to assess staff views only on Force performance of key police functions.
2. A Full Staff Opinion Survey includes staff concerns generated from focus group discussions.

Annex 7.5 Commissioner's Statement of Strategic Directions: Policing Beyond 2000

1. Introduction

Eighteen months ago I issued my first statement of Strategic Directions which formulated a set of initiatives to govern the management and operation of the Force. We have now reviewed these Strategic Directions to take into account changes that have occurred which affect both the Force and Hong Kong.

The Force must look ahead to dealing with the policing problems of the next millennium. Although the present Asian economic turmoil makes identifying trends and anticipating changes difficult, such trends and changes are inevitable. In these circumstances the Force must continue to emphasise its value of "Responsiveness to Change," so that we can sustain our vision of Hong Kong as one of the safest and most stable societies in the world.

2. Key Thrusts

2.1 Force-wide Initiatives

The Force needs to address a number of issues that affect its immediate future and ongoing development as an effective police force.

- We need to reinforce the values that underpin our efforts to prevent corruption, reduce complaints, and enhance service oriented policing.
- We must review the current arrangements for resource allocation and management, recognizing that pressures on government spending are growing and that our share of the budget is unlikely to keep on increasing. This requires a response at two levels :
  - To develop a blueprint for increased financial autonomy that enables us to maximize existing resources; and
  - To review opportunities for streamlining processes and more effective use of technology in order to achieve better value for money and greater efficiency.

3. Operational Initiatives

We are fully resolved to maintain our present rapid and effective response capability, and to enhance our professionalism in preventing and controlling crime.

We recognize the need to strengthen our relationship with the public and the importance of the public in helping us to successfully fight crime. This requires us to improve the way in which we deal with people on the street, in police stations and on the telephone. It also involves improving our capability to

Annex 7.5 Commissioner's Statement of Strategic Directions: Policing Beyond 2000 (Cont'd)

receive and process information from the public by enhancing our command, control and communication systems.

We will focus on developing a sense of civic responsibility among young people, by working in collaboration with other agencies to develop a comprehensive educational package covering crime prevention and drug abuse. Our aim is to prevent today's problem child from becoming tomorrow's criminal.

The initiatives in crime control focus on improving and enhancing our capabilities in three main areas:

- access to and use of crime information;
- the pursuit of criminals and management of crime cases; and
- the procedures for dealing with witnesses and suspects.

With respect to public order, our focus is on continuing to prevent illegal immigration and on regulating public order events in accordance with the law.

We will also play our part in easing traffic congestion by rationalizing our approach to damage only traffic accidents and by upgrading the equipment used in traffic enforcement.

The role of the Hong Kong Auxiliary Police will be reviewed to optimize its management and operational deployment.

4. Management Initiatives

Operational policing will be supported by a series of management initiatives to promote our values through: wider use of modern technology; a greater focus on human resource management; open communication; and better management of resources. These initiatives will be directed at managing the continual improvement of the people who make up the Force, the equipment we use and the service we provide.

Despite the proliferation of modern technology, people remain at the core of our operations. We need to continue to develop our capabilities to manage and motivate staff. We also need to continue to improve our performance appraisal and promotion systems, develop appropriate training and engender a healthier lifestyle.

I have already emphasized the importance of resource management and value for money in achieving our future goals. This will be supported by an improved system of financial planning and management, and the provision of relevant training. Value for money will be the benchmark for a coherent

Annex 7.5 Commissioner's Statement of Strategic Directions: Policing Beyond 2000 (Cont'd)

planning mechanism that links the management of resources to the achievement of objectives.

5. Implementation

The implementation of the Strategic Directions will be controlled and monitored by the Programme Managers.

The Strategic Directions are intended to provide a focus and impetus for the more detailed programme plans which will support the allocation of resources, and the development of plans at formation and divisional level. These in turn will feed back into the continuous process of aligning the Strategic Directions with the needs of the Community and the Force. To accurately determine these needs, the Force has embarked upon a series of integrated surveys to measure public opinion, customer satisfaction and staff opinion.

6. Conclusion

The Force has identified a vision for the future and a set of specific goals to realize that vision. We are continuing to pursue initiatives that will achieve these goals.

My role, and that of the Senior Directorate, will be to steer this work by sustained commitment to the objectives that we have agreed, in conjunction with regular and rigorous progress reviews.

I look forward to the continued support of the public and to a personal commitment from everyone in the Force to work together towards achieving our goals in the coming years.

Annex 7.6 Force Decision Making Levels

– Level One: Commissioner and Deputies	Decisions that go beyond the Force
– Level Two: Senior Directorate (i.e. Deputy Commissioners and Senior Assistant Commissioners)	Strategic decisions
– Level Three: Programme Managers (Senior Assistant Commissioners) and their Assistant Commissioner	Policy decisions
– Level Four: Assistant Commissioners and their Formation and Unit Commanders	Planning decisions

Annex 7.7 Programme Areas

Programme Manager	Programme Area
Director of Operations	– Public Order – Crime Prevention
Director of Crime and Security	– Crime Control
Director of Personnel and Training	– Human Resource Management
Director of Management Services	– Management Services
Director of Finance, Administration and Planning	– Administrative Services

Annex 7.8 Programme Area Definitions and Sub-programme Areas

	Operational Programmes			Support Programmes		
	Crime Prevention	Public Order	Crime Control	Human Resources	Management Services	Administration Services
	Prevention of crime through deterrence, effective legislation, public education and involvement	Preserving public order by preventing illegal immigration, reducing traffic accidents and congestion, regulating crowds and dealing with emergencies including threats to internal security	To control crime by focusing on target activities, crime areas and groups, detention and dealing with suspects and investigations	Providing and managing the HRM framework to manage the Force supported by human resource planning, performance management, staff relations, remuneration and conditions of service, and training and development	Provision of management skills and knowledge and modern technology to support the operations and management of the Force	Providing information guidelines and a control framework to ensure that Force resources are deployed effectively
Sub Programme Areas						
	– Deterrence – Effective Legislation – Public Education – Public Involvement	– Prevention of Illegal Immigration – Reduction of Traffic Accidents and Congestion – Crowd Control – Internal Security Readiness	– Focus on Target Activities, Crime Areas and Groups – Detention and dealing with suspects – Investigations	– Human Resource Planning – Performance Management – Staff Relations – Remuneration and Conditions of Service – Training and Development	– Use of Modern Technology – Ethics and Integrity – Culture Changes – Management Knowledge and Skills	– Finance – Stores Management – Administration – Planning and Development

PART THREE

Academic Studies and Critiques

8

The "Trading Fund" Reform in Hong Kong: Claims and Performance*

Anthony B. L. Cheung

Professor, Department of Public and Social Administration,
City University of Hong Kong

1. Introduction

One of the main initiatives by the Hong Kong government to transform the operation of public services under the 1989 *Public Sector Reform*[1] is the introduction of a new mode of "trading funds" premised on a commercial and self-financing basis. Since the passage of the Trading Fund Ordinance in March 1993, six trading funds have been established, namely: Companies Registry (August 1993), Land Registry (August 1993), Sewage Services (March 1994), Office of the Telecommunication Authority (OFTA) (June 1995), Post Office (August 1995) and Electrical and Mechanical Services (August 1996). Of the six, the Sewage Services Trading Fund was the only one not created out of an existing government department. It was also by far the most controversial, being heavily criticized by the Legislative Council for its high capital and operating costs and by the public in general for the escalating new "sewage charges" and "trade effluent surcharges" levied on both domestic households and industrial units to pay for the trading fund's expenditure. In October 1996 during a Legislative Council debate on a motion calling for a comprehensive review of all

---

* This is a revised version of an article first published in *Public Administration and Policy*, Vol. 7, No. 2 (1998), pp. 105–23.

trading funds, the Secretary for the Treasury, while defending the efficiency of existing trading funds, replied on behalf of the government that no more new trading funds would be set up in the foreseeable future. The government also produced the first ever report on the review of the operation of the trading fund scheme.[2] In March 1998 the Sewage Services Trading Fund was abolished as a result of persistent legislative objection to raising sewage charges.

This chapter examines the features of the trading fund mode within the Hong Kong context. Using the existing six trading funds as case-studies, it explores whether, and if so to what extent, trading funds can improve efficiency and generate benefits to consumers at large. In discussion, it questions the efficiency claims of trading funds, and suggests that the new approach may have in effect benefitted management most, leaving the central agencies pondering about the extent of any efficiency gain and the consumers at a loss as to whether they themselves, rather than producer efficiency, have paid for any improvement in service quality. Although the data used in the case-studies were only up to 1996–97, the doubts raised still remain generally valid as the observations in Chapter 5 on the Post Office Trading Fund have corroborated.

2. Nature and Legislative Framework of Trading Funds

The 1989 public sector reform programme has resulted in a new typology of agency modes within the public sector, comprising traditional departments, trading funds, public corporations and non-departmental public bodies. The choice of agency type is broadly determined by three factors: (a) the type of service to be delivered; (b) the degree of freedom from government control that is desired; and (c) the pricing strategy to be applied to the service, as indicated in Annex 8.1.

Trading funds are accounting entities established by law which provide services on a commercial or quasi-commercial basis with the objective of recovering cost. They do not have separate legal existence but remain to be part of the civil service establishment, unlike public corporations (such as the Mass Transit Railway Corporation) or non-departmental public bodies (such as the Hospital Authority) which enjoy a fully autonomous status. As illustrated in Annex 8.2, trading funds are similar to traditional departments in terms of the staffing regime, being still staffed by civil servants who are subject to centrally-defined terms and conditions of service, but are given much greater financial flexibility since they depend on business revenue rather than tax revenue.

Under the Trading Funds Ordinance, trading funds may be established by resolution of the Legislative Council on the recommendation of the Financial Secretary (section 3). The Financial Secretary designates a General Manager (normally head of the "converted" department) to control and manage the trading fund, who is accountable to the former for its operation. The general perimeters given to the Trading Fund General Manager are (section 6):

- to provide an efficient and effective operation that meets an appropriate standard of service;
- within a reasonable time, to meet expenses and to finance liabilities out of the income of the trading fund;
- to achieve a reasonable return, as determined by the Financial Secretary, on the fixed assets employed.

More detailed performance and pricing targets are to be set in "Framework Agreements" agreed between the General Manager and the relevant Policy Secretary of the government. The General Manager can invest any surplus and borrow for the trading fund with the approval of the Financial Secretary. However, the Financial Secretary can also plough back into the government's general revenue part of the trading fund's surplus funds if he considers that "any surpluses in the nature of distributable profits disclosed in the certified statements are in excess of the reasonable requirements for the provision of the service including the repayment of loans" (section 10 [1]).

3. Features of Trading Funds and Their Perceived Benefits

The idea of "trading fund" was first introduced to Hong Kong by the management consultants Coopers & Lybrand who helped prepare the 1989 *Public Sector Reform* report[3] and explained the idea by saying that "although this concept has been widely applied in the UK it would be an innovation in Hong Kong which has always operated a centralized cash accounts system."[4] The traditional vote-funding system of the government was characterized as being: annualized; cash-based accounting; cash balances returning to general revenue; expenditure limited by budget; and resource consumption-oriented. Trading funds, on the other hand, would operate on an ongoing, accrual basis, continuing year to year, with cash balances retained or ploughed back, and be financial-performance–oriented, being self-financing with the need to break even.

Apart from commercial services such as Water Supplies Department and the Post Office, the consultants considered that trading funds could be appropriate for both government core services on a partial or full cost recovery basis *and* those support services where a charge could be levied for the services provided. Indeed, the trading fund mode was seen as a premise for turning support services more pricing-oriented in order to promote "a more economical use of the service, particularly where no charge has been raised in the past" and "greater efficiency, by exposing the service to competition or to proxy competitive pressures through price comparisons and cost consciousness on the part of the user."[5] Ultimately it was expected that the service can be reoriented to a customer-led rather than producer-driven organization and culture.

Under the inter-departmental charging regime newly introduced in the late 1980s, which restored resource allocation to user departments instead of supplier departments as in the past, it was assumed that a real customer-supplier relationship would develop. Such a relationship could be extended into the private marketplace where both the service supplier could provide services to private firms *and* the user department could turn to new private sector suppliers for services if they are competitive.

As summarized in the Legislative Council Brief on the Trading Fund Bill 1992, the main benefits that can be derived from the setting up of trading funds to operate government services are that: (a) this could develop a customer-led rather than producer-driven system; (b) the need to face competition or quasi-commercial pressure could stimulate cost-consciousness and promote efficiency; and (c) the elimination of various accounting and funds restrictions could facilitate more effective management that is more responsive to customer needs.[6] These being the claimed benefits, they should form the criteria for assessing the actual performance of the trading funds so far established.

The importance of the trading fund reform initiative in Hong Kong should also be seen within the context of the present public sector reform programme which is an all-embracing package of reforms transcending both human resource management and financial resource management, covering such initiatives as privatization, commercialization, performance pledges and new cost-recovery regimes. Of these reform initiatives, the trading funds are by far the most visible embodiment of the new approach to public services management. Although still retaining a civil-service workforce that serves to maintain their institutional link with the government, trading funds are empowered both legislatively and administratively to adopt a more flexible and market- (as well as customer-) oriented management framework which should in principle enhance the impact of the economic forces of demand on production and decision-making processes within the service organization. Trading funds are supposed to embody all those flexibilities, new regimes of incentives and sanctions, and other efficiency virtues which may not otherwise be possible within the existing civil service framework. If trading funds prove to be successful they could serve as the main organizational vehicle to spearhead the rest of public sector reform and to bring about a new culture of efficiency and cost-effectiveness in the management of public services. As such trading funds form a most strategic part of the overall public sector reform process.

However, like the 1989 public sector reform package which had received minimal attention in the public domain,[7] there was also only luke-warm support for trading funds within the community at large, not because the public was necessarily against the direction of reform but more because the reform had failed to generate sufficient public interest in it. When the trading fund legislation and various enabling resolutions for establishing the six trading funds were debated in the Legislative Council, legislators' attention was mainly focused on how to ensure that fees and charges would not get out of control as a result of the organizational change, that Legislative Council's power of scrutiny would not be weakened, and that the staff's welfare would not unduly be affected.[8] As the following analysis shows, the perceived benefits that can be gained from the trading fund scheme are not as evident as the concept implies. Such doubts about their benefits will also likely strengthen the scepticism which already exists in the community about the impact of trading funds.

4. Claims versus Realities

4.1 Management Flexibilities — How Flexible?

The main attraction of a trading fund mode to departmental managers is the kind of managerial autonomy that they can enjoy in the new framework.

As explained earlier, trading funds are accounting entities and have full powers to deploy their business revenue so long as the general financial targets (such as the required rates of return on net fixed assets) and performance standards set by the government are met. In practice this means trading funds can retain their revenue surplus for further investment which can bring about greater returns/profits in the longer term. For those trading funds set up so far, they belong to departments which previously were small departments with only limited political clout within the civil service bureaucracy and thus were unable to compete with big departments (like the Police and the Works departments) and those departments dealing with more publicly debated policies areas (like health, education, welfare and housing) in the intra-bureaucratic resource allocation process. Even if they were revenue-earning departments (as in the case of the Post Office), their surplus income in the past all went back to the Treasury while they very often lost out in their bids for new spending allocations. One of the major achievements through conversion into a trading fund is to free such revenue-earning departments from the restrictions imposed by the civil service budgetary process and to let them have full access to the surplus they accumulate. Revenue surplus retention is probably the most visible gain that has persuaded departmental managers of the benefit of reform. The ability to exploit its surplus-retention capacity provides an incentive for trading funds to restructure their management organization, reorientate their organizational culture and diversify product lines so as to earn greater revenue and hence more surplus. Other flexibilities result from the freedom to adopt commercial procurement and marketing practices which would likely expand business opportunities and hence revenue income.

However, two important constraints still remain, namely restrictions on pricing policy and the fact that trading funds continue to be staffed by civil servants.

Despite the claim to greater marketization and competition, trading funds set up so far do not have the power to determine their fees and charges. Partly because of the need to address public concern about the impact of decontrol of pricing that might lead to excessive charges, and partly because most of the trading funds are still monopolies of some kind and thus should not be left to their own to impose their price levels, the pricing mechanism has remained essentially unchanged from that which prevailed while they were still government departments. For the Land Registry, Companies Registry, OFTA and Sewage Services Trading Fund, fees and charges are subject to scrutiny and endorsement by the Legislative Council in the form of subsidiary legislation. For the Post Office, while legislative approval is not required, fees and charges have to be approved by the Chief Executive-in-Council.[9] Only the Electrical and Mechanical Services Trading Fund is "free" to fix fees and charges but it is a service provider for government users and, to be further explained below, has no reason to be excessive in pricing because it faces the impending threat of competition from private sector suppliers and has been protected from such competition through special arrangements in the first three years of establishment.

As regards staffing, there is a limit to flexible management because the staff of trading funds remain part of the civil service and are subject to uniform pay structure and conditions of service which apply service-wide. Pricing of the goods and services of trading funds (apart from the regulatory restriction just mentioned) and departmental sales income therefore bear only a limited relationship to the actual performance of staff or the cost structure (as labour rates continue to be exogenously determined by centrally determined civil service rates and practices). The only flexibility available is for trading funds to make greater use of temporary and contract staff other than civil servants. There was also suggestion in the past of allowing trading funds to introduce some kind of performance-related pay regime for their senior staff,[10] but it was not followed up in practice. Operating within civil service staffing regime rigidities, it is difficult to contemplate (even in the logic of competitiveness and incentives) that trading funds can be easily reoriented towards a market-/customer-led system. Trading funds can at best be conceived as a half-way option which should eventually lead to taking the operations out of the civil service system entirely. Either the civil service sector can become marketized (thus a trading fund is no more than an self-accounting device which can be applied to ordinary government departments), or the agency concerned has to be further restructured into a public corporation or non-departmental public body (thus reinforcing the transient nature of a trading fund).

4.2 Competitiveness — How Competitive?

One of the ironies of the trading fund experiment in Hong Kong is the fact that the majority of the trading funds is of a monopoly nature which implies a minimum impact of the market discipline. Four of the six trading funds established were monopolies supplying statutory services which the customers must consume (i.e. company registration, land registration, telecommunication regulation, and sewage services). For the Post Office, with the rapid expansion of private sector activities in parcel delivery services and the greater use of telephone, fax and electronic communication in lieu of postal communication, it can be argued that the kind of monopolistic status enjoyed by this trading fund has become somewhat diluted. However, as pointed out later, the Post Office is still in a position to generate monopolistic revenue in the issue of stamps. It is not unreasonable to suggest that it was precisely these trading funds' monopolistic (and also statutory) nature and the resultant guaranteed profitability which had convinced the government of the low risk involved in the reform, and which had helped to persuade management and staff alike of their trading viability in the first place. Such trading fund "pioneers" may perhaps stand a greater chance in performing and operating in a marketized environment, however their "success" is not sufficient proof of the viability of the trading fund mode for *any* commercial or quasi-commercial services of the government.

Indeed in the case of the Electrical and Mechanical Services Trading Fund (EMSTF), staff unions petitioned both the government and the Legislative Council against hiving-off the main bulk of the previous Electrical and Mechanical Services Department (EMSD) into a trading fund for fear of redundancies and other forms of career casualties (such as reduction in promotion opportunities). In the event the government had to alleviate staff anxieties by agreeing that "government departments and statutory bodies will still be obliged to use EMSD's services for the first three years following the setting up of the EMSTF."[11] Whether the lifting of such protective practices in 1999 will see this trading fund in firm footing to compete in the market in the long-run has yet to be ascertained,[12] but the concession is certainly not strengthening the argument for competition. In another way the Sewage Services Trading Fund was set up in 1994 as a wishful-thinking type solution to raising funds to embark on an ambitious sewage improvement programme. The financial viability of the trading fund had remained in question until its dissolution in March 1998. Prior to then, the legislature had repeatedly refused its support to the trading fund increasing sewage charges significantly in order to self-finance its vast capital and operational costs and had instead called for the injection of some form of government finance or subsidy (e.g. Legislative Council motion debate, 10 July 1996).

4.3 Cost Control and Pricing — How Effective?

The logic of the competitive market being able to stimulate cost-consciousness and producer-efficiency seems to be straight-forward. In the absence of genuine competition for most of the trading funds, however, cost-consciousness and producer-efficiency have to depend on sufficient managerial incentives within the new system. In theory it can be argued that given financial targets imposed by the central agencies in the form of stipulated rates of return and given price ceilings imposed by legislative and other forms of regulative scrutiny, if the trading fund is to meet such targets and to live within its means it must improve efficiency and reduce costs. Besides, the launch of reform would have encouraged higher customer expectations about improved service quality.

In practice, however, there is as yet insufficient evidence to suggest that the trading funds have established an effective cost control regime. Trading funds continue to be able to increase their overall level of fees and charges broadly in line with inflation. If business continues to boom given there is little effective market competition *per se* for most of them, trading funds will not have the structural incentives to review their basic cost structures. Besides, as can be seen from Annex 8.3, all of the trading funds are staff-intensive in cost (staff cost takes up 70% or more of the operating cost of the Companies Registry and OFTA, and some 60% in the case of the Land Registry, Post Office and EMSTF), except the Sewage Services Trading Fund which by nature is capital-intensive. Since staff remain to be part of the civil service structure, the scope for major restructuring which may result in redundancies is quite limited. The case of the EMSTF also illustrates the difficulty (both politically and in terms of staff relations within the civil service) to lay off staff in order to rationalize the cost structure and to improve competitiveness. Indeed, staff cost by and large continued to rise at a significant rate (at times higher than the rate of inflation) over the years in most trading funds.

The government seems to be satisfied with the fact that the pricing levels of trading fund services are in line with inflation, using that as an indicator of performance.[13] However such "performance" represents more an attempt by all trading funds to seek price increases broadly up to the ceiling (i.e. the inflation rate) which politically would have been acceptable to the Legislative Council or the Executive Council, *than* necessarily a result of cost control. The political "capping" effect on fee increase would have applied to such services even if they were supplied in the traditional departmental mode anyway.

It should also be noted that while the fees of some trading funds have been kept below inflation, those for some selected services have gone up quite drastically under service repackaging and high fees are introduced for new services, even though the overall fee increase level for the trading fund as a whole is in line with inflation (refer to discussion on individual trading funds below).

It is therefore doubtful if the customers have really benefitted in terms of price from the trading fund mode of operation. For new services or improved services (sometimes brought about by automation or reprogramming of operating procedure), new and often higher fees are charged so that it is not unreasonable to suggest that it is the customers who have paid for such service improvements rather than the trading fund's internal cost control efforts. There is even the worry, for example by legislators, that some trading funds might have tended to provide high-profit services so as to meet the relatively high rate-of-return targets set by Finance Branch, to the extent that customers help to bear the burden of the financial performance of the new trading funds. The concern raised by some public opinion[14] and by legislators has driven the Secretary for the Treasury to play down the impact of financial targets on fees and charges by saying that those were targets intended to provide trading funds with some objective benchmarking, and were not expected to be met every year as this would have been unrealistic (see his reply speech to Legislative Council, 30 October 1996).[15] However, most trading funds have managed not only to meet but to exceed the target rate of return (see Annex 8.4). How to ensure that while there are sufficient cost-control incentives, the costs (and thus financial and even quality improvements) have not been "externalized" to the paying public remains an open question which has not been sufficiently answered by identifiable efficiency gains in practice.

5. Performance of Individual Trading Funds

5.1 Land Registry and Companies Registry

The Land Registry and Companies Registry are the first two trading funds, both established in August 1993. Both have been credited by the government to have achieved service improvements. For example the 1996

Finance Branch Review reported that the Land Registry had reduced the time required for certification, registration and search of documents by 17%, 9% and 17% respectively since its establishment.[16] Similarly the Companies Registry managed to improve its document registration time from 33 days in 1993–94 to 16 in 1995–96, against an original target of 20 days.[17]

Such service improvements have to be put in perspective. In the case of the Land Registry, the Direct Access Service was introduced in September 1994 to enable customers to make on-line searches for land records and to place on-line orders for copies of documents through their own computers. From July 1996 a Document Imaging System (DIS) has been implemented so that all incoming land documents are converted into electronic images for on-line retrieval. These and other computerization projects have certainly improved service efficiency which is borne out by official service improvement statistics. However, over the period staff number was on the rise too, from 614 permanent posts in 1993–94 to 760 in 1995–96,[18] an average increase of some 9% per year. There are no separate statistics to show how unit costs have improved correspondingly. Fees and charges had an overall increase in real terms of 3.6% over three years, due to "the very large investments in projects designed to improve service quality and enhance efficiency in response to customer demand, with consequential increase in depreciation charges."[19] Fees for major services increased much more drastically, e.g. those for "registration of agreement for sale and purchase or for mortgage" and "registration of lease, agreement for a lease, or renewal or surrender of lease" increased by 33% in 1995 and 133% in 1996. With higher fees for major services and a booming property market in those few years, Land Registry was able to generate a comfortable level of revenue and to meet the set financial target (its 1995–96 and 1996–97 rates of return being 14.7% and 29.1% respectively, both in excess of the 10% target rate). There was a clear indication of customers footing the bill for service improvement.

The Companies Registry has similarly improved its services through computerization. While overall increase in its fees and charges was broadly in line with inflation, fees for some individual services registered a much higher increase. Major revenue-generating services included the incorporation of companies and registered trustees and the registration of trust companies and limited partnerships,[20] and the corresponding fee for "registration of a company having a share capital" increased by 23.1% in

1993 and 11.5% in 1994. In 1995 though registration fee was reduced by 9.7%, a new fee for submission of document was added thus making an overall real increase of 9%. Over the period, despite some significant decrease in business output, with numbers of companies incorporated, charges registered and searches made down by 43.9%, 14% and 4.4% respectively from 1993–94 to 1995–96, and with documents received for filing only up by a mere 3.1%,[21] the operating cost of the Registry had however increased by some 38% and full-time staff number from 335 in 1993 to 395 in 1996.[22] Even if some service improvement targets had been achieved, it is difficult to conclude that there was improvement in producer-efficiency.

5.2 Post Office

Historically the Post Office did not enjoy good commercial viability. Although it was able to maintain an operating surplus for the 10 years prior to its conversion into a trading fund in August 1995 (except in 1991 and 1995), its operating surplus (as well as rate of return on turnover) had by and large been on the downward trend.[23] However, the Post Office is now arguably the agency most committed to the trading fund vision, setting the example for other trading funds. It announced a long series of programme and service improvements in May 1996 in a consolidated plan *100 Projects for Better Services 1996–97*. It is the only trading fund so far to publish unit cost statistics (but only for local handling cost).

According to a report made to the Legislative Council Panel on Economic Services on 13 January 1997,[24] the local handling cost per evaluated postal item increased from HK$1.27 in 1993–94 to HK$1.43 in 1995–96, against a slight decrease in the index on inflation-adjusted cost (using CPI (A) (1983=100)) from 118.1 to 113.3. The index was however expected to rise to 117.5 by 2001–01 with HK$2.08 per item. Staff establishment was on the upward trend. It increased from 5,325 posts in 1993–94 to 5,788 posts in 1996–97 and was expected to rise to 6,544 posts by 2001–02.[25] Target productivity index and target postal traffic were both expected to rise by 24% and 2.5% respectively between 1995–96 and 2000–01,[26] but there was little statistical evidence to show that such an increase was possible or realistic. Actual postal traffic growth and productivity both fell behind planned targets (see Annex 8.5).

Even the Post Office had to admit that "the local handling cost per evaluated item is projected to increase, after discounting the effect of inflation, by some 5.7 points over the period to 2000–01 [such increase being] largely due to assumptions that staff costs, which comprise some 80% of the total local handling cost, will continue to rise at a faster rate than inflation."[27] Major postal services had had a rather dismal business out-turn (letters and postcards, up 0.6%; printed papers and small packets, up 5.4%; registered articles, down 6.3%; speedpost, down 1.4%); only parcel services had a higher increase of 10.5%.[28] In terms of the rate of return on average net fixed assets, it was estimated to be 8.3% in 1995–96 (against a target of 10.5% revised downwards from an original 12%) and expected to remain below target throughout the next five years except 1999–2000.

The viability of the Post Office is therefore not without question, especially given its very labour-intensive cost structure and the continuing rise in staff numbers, despite various automation programmes. Given the political difficulty to increase postal rates beyond the rate of inflation,[29] and some competition from private delivery agents particularly in parcel and bulk delivery and the increased use by the public of telecommunication and electronic mail in lieu of postal services, the Post Office has to stay viable as a commercial entity by expanding into profitable services such as special stamps and philatelic services. In 1996–97 its philatelic revenue exceeded HK$1.3 billion, some 11 times that of the previous year and constituting one-quarter of that year's total revenue.[30] Accordingly the rate of return has shot up to a much unexpected 47.8% in 1996–97[31] (see also Annex 8.4). The year 1997 may be an exceptional year for philatelic activities because of Hong Kong's transfer of sovereignty to China and philatelic income may not experience a similar boost in subsequent years. However, it is clear that without a more market-led approach in philatelic business it is difficult for the Post Office to maintain its commercial revenue.

5.3 Sewage Services Trading Fund

The Sewage Services Trading Fund was by far the most controversial trading fund. Established on 11 March 1994, it did not begin full operation until 1 April 1995 when a scheme of charges for sewage services was introduced by the government. Because of the controversies surrounding the imposition of a community-wide charging scheme for sewage services that previously had been provided free, the trading fund's target rate of return was set at 0%, requiring it to break even only in nominal terms. In 1995–96 the trading fund achieved an operating surplus of HK$76 million on net fixed assets of HK$2,311 million.[32] In 1996–97, there was an operating deficit before depreciation of HK$3.6 million.[33] The deficit resulted from the government's repeated failure to obtain the Legislative Council's approval to increase sewage charges, despite efforts having been made to defer the commissioning of Stage 1 of the Strategic Sewage Disposal Scheme and to make other cost reductions.

Because of political opposition to raising sewage charges the overall financial viability of the trading fund was very much called into question. In the 1996 Finance Branch Review, the government had to admit that even if it were able to persuade the legislature to approve increase in sewage charges, "... with all the extra costs of running the improved facilities, it will take some years before ... the trading fund will break even," and that it might need to "revisit the original financial principles behind the Strategic Sewage Disposal Scheme for the longer term."[34]

The original financial principle was based on the "polluter-pays" principle first introduced into government's policy thinking in the 1989 White Paper, *Pollution in Hong Kong: A Time to Act.* Since then the government had adopted a new strategy to improve Hong Kong's outdated sewage system through a series of Sewage Master Plans (SMPs) and a Strategic Sewage Disposal Scheme (SSDS). In October 1992 the Governor announced a High Priority Programme (HPP) comprising Stage 1 of SSDS and six SMPs. Following a public consultation on introducing charges for sewage services in late 1993, the Legislative Council voted in favour of the polluter-pays principle and the government then proceeded to establish a trading fund to take over sewage services, to be financed by the new sewage charges. From the very beginning the Sewage Services Trading Fund was not conceived out of a clear picture of financial viability. The government emphasized that setting up the trading fund would facilitate the "timely and cost-effective implementation" of the sewage programme.[35] A legislator even suggested that "[u]nlike the Trading Funds set up for the Land Registry and Companies Registry which are to enable existing departments to operate under commercial regimes, this Trading Fund is really a construction fund of a sewage service scheme ...."[36] Another legislator claimed in an earlier Legislative Council debate that "the former Secretary for Planning, Environment and Lands told this Council that, given a tight budget, it would be extremely difficult, if not impossible, for the Government to finance the sewage scheme through the normal channel of public funding under the

Public Works Programme."[37] It is clear that the Sewage Services Trading Fund was not proposed out of commercial viability and efficiency considerations, but more out of a motive to bypass normal budgetary procedures in obtaining funds for SSDS which amounted to HK$20 billion in capital investment. The launch of the scheme took place during a time when there were tense relations between the British and Chinese governments over political reform in Hong Kong. The fear that SSDS might be dragged into Sino-British negotiations as happened to the Airport Core Programme projects might have also contributed to the decision to turn SSDS into a trading-fund–financed project.

The levying of sewage charges and "trade effluent charges" remained controversial. The Legislative Council passed a motion on 10 July 1996 calling on the government to drop the target of seeking full cost recovery for sewage services by the year 2000, to extend the break-even period and to inject further funds from general revenue into the trading fund. The government was in a dilemma. On the one hand it was under no illusion that increasing sewage charges could overcome public and legislative opposition. On the other hand injecting funds from general revenue would defeat the whole philosophy of a trading fund which was supposed to be self-financing. Senior officials began to contemplate the option of reverting the trading fund into departmental mode.[38] On 19 November 1997, the Secretary for the Treasury formally sought the approval of the post-1997 Provisional Legislative Council to close the Sewage Services Trading Fund on 31 March 1998 and to re-establish sewage services on a vote-funded basis.[39] In the event, the case for the efficiency and financial viability of sewage services failed to be established.

5.4 Electrical and Mechanical Services Trading Fund

As pointed out earlier, the Electrical and Mechanical Services Trading Fund was set up out of the Electrical and Mechanical Services Department despite widespread staff opposition. Staff were mainly concerned that setting up the trading fund could lead to redundancies. In particular they were worried that the trading fund would not be able to compete successfully with private sector service suppliers and "are sensitive to any programme of "untying" [i.e. the department's users within government being given the freedom to "untie" and to go to alternative suppliers for services supplied by EMSD] being included in the Corporate and

Business Plan."[40] In order to alleviate staff fears, the government finally gave the specific reassurance in the EMSTF Framework Document that full use would be made of redeployment and natural wastage to deal with any identified staff surpluses. Furthermore, the trading fund would be "protected" for three years in respect of its government business, in order to allow it to improve its capacity to compete for clients in the open market.

While there might be good policy reasons to convert EMSD (except its regulatory function) into a trading fund (so as to force it to improve productivity and efficiency because in the past the Department was rather notorious among its user departments as being unresponsive and over-charging for its services), the fact remained that it was not yet ready for it in terms of commercial viability. The use of protective arrangements pointed to the difficulties in practice to cut staff cost when this was precisely the crux of the efficiency problem.

5.5 Office of the Telecommunication Authority

Office of the Telecommunication Authority is both a statutory regulatory body to license and monitor telecommunication operators. It also provides some limited consultation services to government departments and public organizations. Because of the rapid expansion of the telecommunication industry resulting in escalating demands for its regulatory services, OFTA basically faces no business risk. The relatively high fee level regime which it inherited from its vote-funded predecessor also meant that it would not need to increase its fees for the next five years. Although its rates of return came to 42.4% and 43.8% respectively for 1995–96 and 1996–97, much in excess of the target rate of 14.5%, OFTA's financial viability was more a result of design than efficiency *per se*.

6. Conclusion

Summing up, because of the lack of real competition or the power to freely determine their price levels based on costs or customer demands, most trading funds set up in Hong Kong continue to operate as monopolies or near-monopolies not fully sensitive to the "market" disciplines. Discipline comes in the form of financial targets prescribed by the central agency (i.e. Finance Branch) and political pressures imposed on pricing by the

Legislative Council and Executive Council which in turn are influenced by public opinion. Since the objective is to recover the full cost of providing services, customers have some influence on service decisions in the sense that new and improved services will be introduced (e.g. express services in the Companies Registry and Land Registry and philatelic services of the Post Office) so long as there is demand for them and users are willing to pay for them. However, since most trading fund services are statutory or at least essential ones, customers have no alternative suppliers to turn to. Customers, rather than producers, are likely to bear the cost of service improvements. If they are not satisfied with the services, whether in terms of quality or prices, they have to still rely considerably on political pressures to induce improvements. A clear example is the Sewage Services Trading Fund which was unable to charge full cost for its services because of continuous political opposition and was finally reverted into a tax-funded department. In the case of EMSTF where market competition from private sector suppliers was feasible the government had to provide it with protective arrangements for the first three years of operation for fear of the trading fund being out-competed once user departments were allowed to go for private sector services.

Most trading funds use some general performance standards to demonstrate their improvement in service quality, such as standard processing times, much similar to the practice already adopted in all government departments and public organizations through "performance pledges."[41] Unit cost statistics are not available nor are they known to be monitored, except in the Post Office. Operating cost, particularly staff cost, continues to rise at a pace even higher than the rate of inflation. There do not exist any effective mechanisms to contain or reduce cost, though recent "enhanced productivity programme" (EPP) measures imposed service-wide by the Finance Bureau have created some pressure for departments, including trading funds, to be more cost-conscious. Given that trading fund staff remain to be civil servants subject to government-wide terms and conditions of service, and the need to maintain good staff morale and stable staff relations, trading funds are in practice reluctant to critically identify redundant manpower. One way to keep surplus staff is to launch into new business but this option is not necessarily available to all trading funds. Besides, within the present framework, so long as trading funds continue to generate sufficient business revenue to meet financial targets, there is no pressure from the central agencies for them to be more cost-sensitive. *The original objectives of creating a customer-led rather than producer-driven system and of promoting cost-consciousness and efficiency through competition or quasi-commercial pressure do not seem to have been borne out in operation.*

Trading funds are not without their merits. They have certainly become more cost- and revenue-conscious than in the past, given the new financial performance targets, and have more incentives to respond to demands for quality improvement and product diversification. Management flexibilities and surplus-retention, together with the lifting of some accounting and financial restrictions, have indeed enhanced the operating autonomy of the managers. They are now no longer required to look to central agencies for budgetary resources or for funds to finance redevelopment and further investment. A self-accounting device has of course enabled trading fund "monopolies" to free themselves from bureaucratic quagmire, but may also represent a nightmare to a trading fund like EMSTF which has to face competition eventually. Notwithstanding such merits it is still arguable if these are only obtainable if a department is turned into a trading fund. On the contrary, as for performance pledges, the government is already pushing for budgetary devolution and greater managerial flexibilities in departments anyway. A reform of the accounting regime whereby departments can all be given separate accounting entity status and be allowed to have some surplus-retention capacities is in theory possible.[42] *So what is so special about the trading fund?* So far managers have gained because of the newfound flexibilities, but the benefits available to customers are as yet uncertain.

Finally the question is begged as to whether the trading fund reform represents a means to induce commercial viability and producer efficiency on the part of the agency concerned (as in the case of EMSD) *or* it is an outcome of design to prove such viability by selecting those services which are monopolistic and have high revenue-earning capacity as the target of reform (such as Companies Registry and Land Registry). If it is the former, then the case of EMSD is not an encouraging sign. If it is the latter, then the trading fund claim to efficiency and customer-responsiveness is more of a myth or rhetoric than a proven case. The fate of the Sewage Services Trading Fund all the more illustrates the failure of the "result by design" strategy when the government underestimated the politicalness of *public* services particularly if these affected the population at large and not just some selected sectors.

Notes

1. Finance Branch, *Public Sector Reform* (Hong Kong, February 1989).
2. Finance Branch, *Report on the Review of the Operation of the Trading Fund Scheme* (Hong Kong, February 1996).
3. Finance Branch (Note 1).
4. Ibid., p. 13, The UK *Trading Fund Act* of 1973 made possible the funding of certain government activities outside normal parliamentary supply, so that the enterprise concerned would not be dependent on annual budgetary appropriations for its expenditure. The *Government Trading Funds Act* of 1990 amended the 1973 legislation and provided greater flexibilities and enabling powers to trading funds including that to borrow. Under the new Act, a Minister, with the concurrence of the Treasury, may order the establishment of a trading fund where (a) the operations are suitable to be financed by a fund, and in particular to be so managed that the revenue of the fund would consist principally of receipts in respect of goods or services provided in the course of those operations; and (b) it would be in the interest of improved management efficiency and effectiveness (section 1).
5. Ibid.
6. Efficiency Unit, *Legislative Council Brief: Trading Fund Bill 1992* (EUCR 11/92) (Hong Kong, February 1992).
7. Anthony B. L. Cheung, "Public Sector Reform in Hong Kong: Perspectives and Problems," *The Asian Journal of Public Administration*, Vol. 14, No. 2 (December 1992), pp. 115–48.
8. See, for example, Democratic Party, *What Price Efficiency? A Review of Hong Kong Trading Funds* [in Chinese] (Hong Kong, October 1996), ch. 2.
9. That is, the Chief Executive in consultation with his Executive Council.
10. According to a former Deputy Secretary for the Civil Service in discussion with this author in 1993.
11. Secretary for Works, *Reply Speech on the Establishment of the Electrical and Mechanical Services Trading Fund* (Hong Kong: Legislative Council, 22 May 1996).
12. According to the Finance Branch Review, EMSTF has achieved a higher rate of return in the first eight months of operation than earlier expected (11% against 9.2%) See Finance Branch, *Review of the Trading Fund Operation: Update as at March 1997* (Hong Kong: Government Printer of the Special Administrative Region, April 1997), p. 9.
13. See the review in Finance Branch, *Report on the Review of the Operation of the Trading Fund Scheme* (Hong Kong, 1996), p. 5.
14. See, for example, "Commercialization of Five Government Departments" [in Chinese], *Hong Kong Economic Times*, Hong Kong, 28 October 1996, p. 2.
15. Secretary for the Treasury, *Reply Speech on the Motion to Review Trading Funds* (Hong Kong: Legislative Council, 30 October 1996).

16. Finance Branch (Note 2), p. 6.
17. Ibid., p. 8
18. Land Registry, *Land Registry Annual Report 1993–94* (Hong Kong: Government Printer, 1994); Land Registry, *Land Registry Annual Report 1995–96* (Hong Kong, 1996).
19. Finance Branch (Note 2), p. 5.
20. Companies Registry, *Companies Registry Business Plan 1996–97* (Hong Kong, 1996), p. 4.
21. Companies Registry, *Companies Registry Annual Report 1995–96* (Hong Kong, 1996), p. 17.
22. Companies Registry, *Companies Registry Annual Report 1993–94* (Hong Kong, 1994); and Note 21.
23. The Treasury, *Hong Kong Government Utilities Operating Accounts for the Year Ended 31 March 1995* (Hong Kong: Government Printer, 1995), p. 15.
24. Post Office, *Presentation to the Economic Services Panel of Legislative Council* (Hong Kong, 13 January 1997).
25. Ibid.; Post Office, *Hong Kong Post Office Annual Report 1996–97* (Hong Kong, 1997), p. 21.
26. Post Office (Note 24).
27. Post Office, *Hong Kong Post Office Annual Report 1995–96* (Hong Kong, 1996), p. 19.
28. Ibid., p. 53.
29. Postage rates were in fact frozen in 1997–98 because of the unexpected revenue from philatelic income. They were frozen for a second year in 1998–99 because of Hong Kong's current economic downturn (*Hong Kong Standard,* 27 July 1998).
30. "Philatelic Income Making Up 25% of Revenue" [in Chinese], *Hong Kong Economic Times*, Hong Kong, 18 July 1997, p. A18.
31. Post Office (Note 25), p. 20.
32. Finance Branch (Note 2), Annex H.
33. Sewage Services Trading Fund, *Sewage Services Trading Fund Annual Report 1996–97* (Hong Kong, 1997), p. 21.
34. Finance Branch (Note 2), p. 16.
35. Works Branch, *Paper on Sewage Services Trading Fund presented to a Joint Meeting of the Environmental Affairs Panel and Financial Affairs Panel of Legislative Council* (Hong Kong, 14 January 1994).
36. Peter Wong, *Legislative Council Hansard* (9 April 1994), Hong Kong, on the motion to set up the Sewage Services Trading Fund.
37. Leong Che-hung, *Legislative Council Hansard* (1 December 1993), Hong Kong, on the motion on sewage charging policy. Leong's allusion was corroborated by the remarks made by the Development Manager of the Drainage Services Department, P. G. Winder, to the Legislative Council Sub-Committee to study the

motion to establish the Sewage Services Trading Fund: "it was a better alternative to fund the programme of such a magnitude than by means of Capital Works Reserve Fund because by setting aside the necessary funds at the outset it would not be necessary to compete annually with other projects under the CWRF for future funding" (see Legislative Council Notes of Meeting on 3 February 1994, Subcommittee to Study the Motion to Establish the Sewage Services Trading Fund (LEGCO Paper No. 1733/93–94).

38. See "Proposals to Increase Sewage Charges to Be Resubmitted to Legislature Shortly" [in Chinese], *Ming Pao*, Hong Kong, 25 October 1996; "Government to Review the Prospect of Sewage Services Trading Fund" [in Chinese], *Ming Pao*, Hong Kong, 26 August 1997.

39. Secretary for the Treasury, *Speech Moving the Motion to Close the Sewage Services Trading Fund* (Hong Kong, Provisional Legislative Council, 19 November 1997).

40. Works Branch, *Legislative Council Brief: Electrical and Mechanical Services Trading Fund* (WB(CR)10/81/01(95)IV) (Hong Kong, 17 January 1996).

41. See this author's discussion in Anthony B. L. Cheung, "Performance Pledges — Power to the Consumer or a Quagmire in Public Service Legitimation?" *International Journal of Public Administration*, Vol. 19, No. 2 (February 1996), pp. 233–59.

42. In the UK government departments have begun to adopt an accrual accounting system in place of the traditional cash accounting system since the publication of the 1995 White Paper on *"Better Accounting for the Taxpayer's Money."*

Annex 8.1 Typology of Agency Choices under Public Sector Reform

Type of service	Degree of government control	Pricing strategy	Mode of agency	Examples of service activity
Core services	Direct control	Free	Traditional department	Law and order
Core services	Direct control	Partial or full cost recovery	Trading fund	Vehicle registration
Core services	Arm's length control	Free or partial cost recovery	Non-departmental public body	Hospital services
Core services	Arm's length control	Full cost recovery	Public corporation	Urban renewal
Support services	Direct control	Full cost recovery	Trading fund	Data processing
Support services	Arm's length control	Full cost recovery	Public corporation	Property services
Commercial services	Direct control	Partial or full cost recovery	Trading fund	Tunnel operations
Commercial services	Arm's length control	Partial or full cost recovery	Public corporation	Public transport

Source: Finance Branch, *Public Sector Reform*, Hong Kong, 1989.

Annex 8.2 Staffing and Financing Regimes of Different Agency Modes

Civil service–staffed
(More rigid staffing regime)

Traditional
Departments   Trading Funds

Financial
dependence   Financial
(Tax-financed   autonomy
regime)   (Business-
                                              financed regime)

Non-
departmental   Public
Public Bodies   Corporations

Non civil service–staffed
(More flexible staffing regime)

Annex 8.3 Increase in Operating and Staff Costs of Trading Funds

(in HK$ million)

		1993–94**	1994–95	1995–96	1996–97
Land Registry (1.8.93)*	Operating cost	135.2	230.1	288.8	370.1
	Operating cost increase rate (%)		13.5	25.5	28.2
	Staff cost	97.7	163.0	180.1	203.8
	Staff cost increase rate (%)		11.2	10.5	13.2
	Staff cost as % of operating cost (%)	72.3	70.8	63.4	55.1
Companies Registry (1.8.93)*	Operating cost	77.1	140.5	159.8	168.7
	Operating cost increase rate (%)		21.5	13.7	5.6
	Staff cost	58.9	102.9	120.0	131.1
	Staff cost increase rate (%)		16.5	16.6	9.25
	Staff cost as % of operating cost (%)	76.4	73.2	75.1	77.7
Sewage Service (11.3.94)*	Operating costΔ			639.0	723.0
	Operating cost increase rate (%)				13.2
	Staff cost			314.3	370.3
	Staff cost increase rate (%)				17.8
	Staff cost as % of operating cost (%)			49.2	51.2
OFTA (1.6.95)*	Operating cost			136.2@	178.1
	Operating cost increase rate (%)				9.0
	Staff cost			110.2@	147.9
	Staff cost increase rate (%)				11.9
	Staff cost as % of operating cost (%)			80.9	83.0

Annex 8.3 Increase in Operating and Staff Costs of Trading Funds (Cont'd)

		1993–94**	1994–95	1995–96	1996–97
				(in HK$ million)	
Post Office (1.8.95)*	Operating cost			2075.2#	3340.8
	Operating cost increase rate (%)				7.32
	Staff cost			1210.3#	2010.5
	Staff cost increase rate (%)				10.7
	Staff cost as % of operating cost (%)			58.3	60.2
Electrical and Mechanical Services (1.8.96)*	Operating cost				1477.3+
	Operating cost increase rate (%)				
	Staff cost				900.0+
	Staff cost increase rate (%)				
	Staff cost as % of operating cost (%)				60.9

Source: various annual reports.

* Date in brackets denotes date of establishment of trading fund.

** August 1993–March 1994.

Δ No operating cost was recorded in the Sewage Services Trading Fund Annual Report 1994–95, presumably because the Fund was not in full operation until the Sewage Service Charge Scheme was established in April 1995.

@ June 1995–March 1996.

August 1995–March 1996.

+ August 1996–March 1997.

Annex 8.4 Rates of Return of Trading Funds

	Target#	Actual			
		1993–94	1994–95	1995–96	1996–97
Land Registry (1.8.93)*	10%	9%	10.3%	14.7%	29.1%
Companies Registry (1.8.93)*	10%	6.2%	8.1%	6.5%	19.8%
Sewage Services (11.3.94)*	0%	–	–	–	–
OFTA (1.6.95)*	14.5%	–	–	42.4%@	43.8%
Post Office (1.8.95)*	10.5%	–	–	8.8%	47.8%
Electrical & Mechanical Services (1.8.96)*	13.5%	–	–	–	16.8%

Source: annual reports of above trading funds (various years).

* Date in brackets denotes date of establishment of trading fund.

Target rate of return is based on averaged net fixed assets.

@ According to the government, "given the relatively high fee level regime that OFTA inherited from its vote funded predecessor, and because of strong demand in the telecommunication sector for its services, it somewhat predictably over-achieved its target in 1995–96 ..." (Finance Branch, 1996). *Report on the Review of Operation of the Trading Fund Scheme*, Hong Kong, p. 17). Since the government undertook that OFTA would not increase its fees for five years after setting up and would transfer all operating surplus in excess of the target return to a development reserve so as to reduce the requirement for future fee increases, and in view of the effect of inflation over the years, lower rates of return were to be expected in subsequent years.

Annex 8.5 Postal Traffic Growth and Productivity in Post Office

	Postal traffic growth		Productivity index	
	Target	Actual	Target	Actual
1995–96	4.5%	1.7%	109	108
1996–97	5.4%	2.7%	109.5	108

Source: Post Office annaul reports (1996; 1997).

9

The School Management Reform in Hong Kong: Administrative Control in a New Cloak of Managerialism*

Joan Y. H. Leung

Associate Professor, Department of Public and Social Administration, City University of Hong Kong

Ho-mun Chan

Associate Professor, Department of Public and Social Administration, City University of Hong Kong

1. Introduction

In line with the global wave of reform which swept through the public sector in the past two decades, numerous efforts were occurring in different parts of the world to improve the school system as well. David de Ferranti, Vice President of the Human Development Department of the World Bank, observed that "as part of education and public sector reforms, many countries are decentralizing the financing and administration of education services to regional, local and school levels."[1] In Hong Kong, as in other countries, there were reforms which aimed to encourage self-management in school decisions. The School Management Initiative (SMI) programme, for example, was announced by the Education and Manpower

* This chapter has drawn on findings of a research project, "Decentralization Reform in Public Management: A Case Study of the School Management Initiative (SMI) in Hong Kong," funded by a strategic research grant of the City University of Hong Kong. The investigators were Joan Y. H. Leung (Principal), H. M. Chan and Norman Flynn (External).

Branch (EMB) in March 1991. The programme has been actively pushed by the Education Department since 1992. In September 1997, the Education Commission Report (ECR) No. 7 which outlined the proposals of Quality Education in Hong Kong suggested that the School-Based Management (SBM), in the spirit of SMI, would be put in place in all schools by 2000.[2] Moreover, to encourage participatory decision-making, the School-Based Management Consultation Document released in February 2000 proposed to include teacher and parent representatives in the school management committees (SMCs).[3] Indeed, the principles of school-based management are in accord with the global trends of public sector reforms which emphasize decentralization, de-regulation, autonomy to manage, client-oriented, objective-focused and result-based management. This set of specific beliefs and practices has been named differently by various scholars. C. Pollitt referred it as "managerialism"[4] while C. Hood identified the emerging doctrines as the "New Public Management" (NPM).[5] Other scholars, such as D. Osborne and T. Gaebler, referred the shift as a "reinvention" in the government and claimed that a new "global paradigm" has emerged.[6] Undoubtedly, the effectiveness of the traditional model was questioned and there have been world-wide reforms in the public sector. Nonetheless, as C. Hood points out, it is less certain that the "shift" to NPM has become a "global paradigm."[7] Using the education sector as an example, this chapter argues that the Hong Kong school management reform is, in essence, a rediscovery of "administrative control" in a new cloak of "managerialism." Dressed up in a trendy cloak of "school-based management," the SMI or SBM reforms were managerial measures to re-regulate the relationship between Education Department (ED) at the central level and the aided schools sponsored by varieties of voluntary bodies. The monitoring role of ED was reinforced and strengthened through the programmes proposed in the SMI document (1991), the ECR No. 7 (1997) and the School-Based Management Consultation Document (2000). Rather than "decentralization," "de-regulation" or greater "teacher participation" in school decision-making which should be the guiding principles of school-based management, the main goal of ED was to streamline its school governance — through a series of indirect controls — in the aided-school sector. The SMI programme, renamed as the SBM in the ECR No.7, has adopted some techniques of new managerialism in the handling of financial and human resources. However, the financial autonomy granted to schools has been very limited. Most critically, it failed to empower the teachers, the key and front-line workers who were responsible for the delivery of service or the parents who were the consumers. Originally, the SBM proposal to introduce participatory decision-making into SMCs was to be formally enacted by an amendment to the Education Ordinance in early 2001. Yet, because of the strong opposition from some influential school-sponsoring bodies, it is likely that the reform plan has to be delayed.[8] Undeniably, the existing school system in Hong Kong is far from satisfactory and is in need of reform. However, if reform were to be effective, it has to be implemented with the full support and active involvement from both the school management and rank-and-file teachers. In order to understand the obstacles in the implementation of the SMI/SBM scheme, it is necessary to revisit its initial rationales as outlined in the SMI document (1991) and the objectives of the government in pushing for management reforms in the aided-school sector.

This chapter first gives a brief review of the major differences between the "old paradigm of administration" and "new paradigm of management." It then re-examines the key features of the SMI scheme which was introduced in the context of Public Sector Reform and was implemented by more than 110 aided secondary schools when the authors conducted a survey in 1998.[9] Based on the research findings, we argue that there has been no "paradigm shift" in the school management system. An analysis of the SMI management framework, for example, shows that there is no real decentralization of power to the school level. Similarly, the discretion granted to schools under the new funding arrangements is very limited. In addition, our research findings clearly showed that there was no major difference in the management style between SMI and non-SMI schools in terms of participatory decision-making or the empowerment of front-line teachers. In both groups, authority remained concentrated in the hands of the principal and senior teachers. Most of all, in contrast to the general assumption that a liberal and open management is conducive to better school performance, our findings showed the contrary. Better student academic results were associated with a tighter control and closer supervision by the principal and the board of directors or school council. Based on these findings, it is clear that if there were a "shift" to the new paradigm, it has yet to be a change in both the values and style of management in the school system.

2. The Old and New Models of Governance

Since the mid-1980s, the traditional approach of governance has been discredited as rigid, hierarchical, bureaucratic and ineffective. Numerous efforts have been made in the public sector, especially in the OECD (Organization for Economic Cooperation and Development) countries to improve organization effectiveness by managerialism.[10] Essentially, there are three key differences between the "old public administration" and the NPM.[11] First, under the old paradigm, the bureaucracy is the direct provider of public services. The NPM advocates, however, believe in decentralization rather than monopolistic provision by a single supplier. Public interest is best served if public services are provided by multi-centres through market competition, voucher or franchising. Second, the old paradigm focuses on legality, rules, regulations, structure and safeguards. On the contrary, the NPM emphasizes de-regulation, delegation, flexibility, innovation and the empowerment of front-line managers and workers. To achieve organization effectiveness, greater autonomy should be given not only to the management at the site level, but it is equally important that the front-line and lower echelon employees participate in the decision-making process. Third, the traditional model is more concerned about formal procedures, due process and legal responsibilities while the new model focuses on results, performance and outcomes.

In the school sector, accordingly, there has been a pervasive belief in the idea of self-managing school or SBM. A key concept of SBM is to provide the key stakeholders — including the school sponsoring body, the school management committee (SMC),[12] the principal, teachers, parents and the past student association — a locus of responsibilities and involvement in school decisions. In particular, teachers, who are in direct contact with students, are regarded as having a great deal of insight and expertise about how to provide good services. Their participation in decision-making is, therefore, highly contributory to school performance and effectiveness. Similarly, the clients of the service, the parents, should also play a part in school decision-making. Thus, a crucial component and manifestation of a "shift" to the new paradigm in school governance is a "decentralization" of authority to the site level as well as an empowerment of the front-line teachers. The remainder of this chapter discusses the school management reform in Hong Kong and analyses its changes with reference to the three key features of NPM mentioned above.

3. School Expansion in the 1970s and the Need for Administrative Reform

According to the NPM doctrines, a monopolistic provision of school service by a single supplier is undesirable because it is rigid, ineffective and unresponsive to parental choice. Yet, this has not been a serious problem in Hong Kong where the delivery of school service was already decentralized and supplied by multi-centres of voluntary bodies. Traditionally, the government operates only a small number of schools directly. Although the state remains the key provider, it has always been its policy to deliver school service through the aided sector where school places were less costly than provided in government. Less than 10% of the primary and secondary schools in Hong Kong are directly run by the government.[13] The majority of schools are run by multi-suppliers, including religious bodies, voluntary agencies, welfare organizations and trade associations, but with full government subsidies. Instead of formalism or rigid legislation, the main problem faced by the government was, in fact, a lack of clearly defined roles and responsibilities throughout the education system, from the EMB and ED to schools.[14] The problem was particularly acute in the aided-school sector. The legal framework which regulated the monitoring role of ED and the school system — including the Education Ordinance and Regulations, and the Codes of Aid — was outdated. It was originally devised for an environment where most schools were privately operated and the aided sector was relatively small. However, with the provision of six years of free primary education introduced in 1971 and its extension to junior secondary education (nine years) in 1978, there was a tremendous increase in the number as well as types of non-government bodies involved in the provision of school service. In 1991, for example, there were 221 voluntary bodies of different varieties — including religious bodies (Catholic, Protestant, Buddhist and Taoist), welfare organizations, clans, rural, alumni, Kaifong, or trade associations — sponsoring a total of 830 aided schools which provided 80% of the school places in Hong Kong.[15] The main requirements for an aided-school sponsor were its corporate status as a non-profit making body with educational objectives. However, the responsibility and accountability of the sponsoring bodies were not clearly defined. Thus, with the rapid expansion of the aided sector, the government was faced with the problem of quality control in school education. The publication of the Public Sector Reform (PSR) document by the Finance Branch in 1989 provided the government a "policy window" to redefine the relationship between ED and the aided sector.[16] In the drive for efficiency and accountability, a study to redefine the responsibilities and relationship between the EMB, ED and schools would be a good case to test the principles set out in the PSR report.[17] The SMI document, a report of the PSR pilot study, was released in 1991. Consequently, its recommendations to reform the school management system have been implemented by schools which voluntarily joined the scheme. In 1997, the ECR No. 7 identified the SMI/SBM measures as process indicators to enhance quality school education in Hong Kong.[18] It also recommended all schools to practise these measures by the year 2000.

4. A Reformulation of the Management Framework

Indeed, the government has repeatedly referred the SMI measures as a kind of school-based management.[19] Nevertheless, a scrutiny of the following aims outlined in the *SMI Handbook* shows the contrary:

- to define clearly the roles of sponsors, managers, supervisors, principals and Education Department to ensure greater effectiveness and accountability;
- to provide for greater participation of teachers, parents and past students in school decision-making and management;
- to encourage more systematic planning and evaluating of schools' activities and reporting their performance; and
- to give schools more flexibility in the use of resources in meeting their defined individual needs.[20]

Rather than a "school-based management," the primary objective of SMI, as indicated in the first and third aims listed above, was to reconstruct a management framework so as to ensure accountability and control in the school system. The original SMI document also explicitly stated that the main target of the programme was to "clarify roles, reallocate responsibilities and strengthen management throughout the [school] system."[21] In Chapter 2 of the document, it described in great detail the problems identified in the aided-school sector. The main concerns of the government were inadequacies of the management structure and an absence of effective programme review, result evaluation and performance measures.[22] For example, it pointed out that there was no specification on the composition or the minimum size of an aided school SMC, and so a SMC could legally consist of a single manager.[23] In addition, it reported that some principals run their schools like little emperors with dictatorial powers while others take minimal interest in the running of the school.[24] Also, it expressed apprehension that many schools did not have formal staff reporting procedures and teachers were simply left "to do their own thing with minimal accountability to the management."[25] In sum, the system of school management in Hong Kong was unsatisfactory. The crux of the problem, as described in the SMI report, was the inadequacy of the legal framework, not the rigidity of legislation. The main focus of management reform, therefore, was not so much to promote teacher and parental participation in school decisions, but to reinforce effective monitoring and public accountability in the aided-school sector.

Moreover, it was most unsatisfactory that although there were "detailed stipulations of the Codes of Aid," they failed to ensure that schools operate effectively.[26] Traditionally, efficiency has been an important value of Hong Kong government and there were institutional and procedural safeguards to ensure financial accountability in the administration.[27] The ED, for example, had firm control on the financial management of aided schools, including staffing, funding and equipment. It exercised detailed controls on items, such as staff establishment, payments to teachers, amounts to be collected from students' fees, ceiling for fee remission, types of recurrent grant, items on which recurrent grants may be spent, a standard list of equipment and even tendering procedures. Such a funding framework was devised to prevent frauds, corruption or abuses in resource management, yet it failed to ensure quality and effective performance in schools. With the growth in both the number of aided schools and social complexities in the last few decades, the funding framework which gave little discretion to front-line managers at the school level was indeed outdated, inflexible and ineffective. Hence, the problem faced by Hong Kong government was different from those in other countries where the state is both the provider as well as the direct supplier of school service. The key problem in Hong Kong, as explicitly expressed in the SMI document, was that "the government has not developed a framework of responsibility and accountability, which would ensure that these [sponsoring] bodies could do their job properly with the minimum of detailed controls."[28] In fact, the government was faced with a paradox. On the one hand, there was a pressing need to delegate financial management to the school level, yet, on the other hand, it had to ensure accountability and to monitor performance in schools. The SMI scheme, a self-managing model, was a reinvention to re-establish central steering and effective monitoring through indirect controls. We argue that the SMI programme did not meet the spirit of self-management because it failed to empower the school management with the freedom or the necessary financial discretion to manage. Neither did it facilitate a decentralized power structure and a participatory environment, which are characteristics of the new model of public management. Rather than an enhancement of self-management, schools teachers were faced with double-whammy.[29] In essence, it was a reinforcement of administrative control in a new cloak of managerialism. There is no paradigm shift in the school management system.

5. The Weberian Structure of Control and Limited Financial Discretion

Administratively, schools joining the SMI scheme had to adopt formal procedures for planning, budgeting and evaluating school activities. Step by step, SMI schools were expected to introduce the following measures over a period of three years:

- prepare a formal *constitution* for the SMC;
- issue an *Annual School Plan* (A *Summary of School Plan* will be distributed to the parents);
- evaluate the school activities at the end of a school year and write up an *Annual School Profile*;
- develop its formal *Staff Appraisal System*;
- produce its *School Policy and Procedure Manual*; and
- set up its *Parent-Teacher Association* and its *Alumni Association*, and elect their representative(s) to the SMC.[30]

The above measures aimed to develop accountability in the aided-school sector with the assistance of a more formal structure and specific procedures. A formalization of the management structure and a systematization of the planning, budgeting and monitoring of school activities were returns to the rule-bound approach which attempted to give predictability, regularity and continuity to the school management system. Given the inadequacies of clearly defined roles and responsibilities in the aided-school sector, the Weberian system, based on rational-legal authority, might be the most suitable tool for restoring an organized and systematized accountable system in schools. Rather than decentralization or de-regulation, the main target of the SMI reforms was, therefore, a reformulation of central steering and control through a system of regular structures and consistent procedures. The ECR No. 7 identifies these SMI practices as SBM that could develop and enhance quality school education. Accordingly, it recommends that all schools should practise SBM and there will be no more distinction between SMI and non-SMI schools by 2000.[31]

Financially, aided schools which had been in the SMI/SBM scheme for more than a year could exercise some discretion in spending their Block Grant. The Block Grant was a combination of the School and Class Grant, Administration Grant, Recurrent Furniture and Equipment Grant, and the optional Substitute Teacher Grant.[32] Aided schools are fully funded by the government and are provided with various kinds of grants. Before the introduction of the SMI scheme, each type of grant had a tightly defined scope and virement between grants was not allowed. The new arrangement gave schools more flexibility in the use of their funds to meet their needs. Under the SMI scheme, schools might choose to freeze unfilled teaching vacancies up to 5% of the total teaching establishment. The savings could be used for purposes acceptable to other elements under the Block Grant. In addition, SMI schools were allowed to collect charges from students for specific purposes, such as air-conditioning in the school hall and paying for instructors' fees for various cultural activities. Compared with the old arrangement, the SMI scheme did provide schools some adjustability in their spending pattern. However, the flexibility granted was, in fact, very limited. The limitation was noted in the ECR No. 7. It, therefore, recommends greater flexibility in funding arrangements, including the provision of block subject grant, the retention of savings, and the approval of collection of special fees.[33] Accordingly, it recommends that —

- all schools which have put in place SBM should be allowed to enjoy the management and funding flexibility under the SMI. That is, the Block Grant should be granted to all schools;
- schools should be allowed to freeze not more than 10% (it was 5% only under the SMI scheme) of the teaching establishment;
- schools should be given a block allocation for all subjects (the existing arrangement does not allow schools to use interchangeably the money allocated by ED to individual subjects);

- schools should be allowed to retain savings of not more than 12 months' provision in the Block Grant (the present arrangements for SMI and non-SMI schools are about 4 and 3 months' provision respectively); and
- schools should be allowed to collect fees from students for specific school-related purposes and the approved limits be adjusted annually. (At present, the limits are fixed at HK$200 and HK$150 per year for each secondary and primary school student respectively).[34]

No doubt, compared with the pre-SMI system, the above-mentioned recommendations will provide schools a greater extent of discretion in the use of resources, yet the flexibility is still inadequate to encourage schools to take *initiatives* and to achieve *individuality* according to their needs. Primarily, schools have no discretion on the largest grant, the Salaries Grant, which takes up about 85% of the school funding. Since the salaries of staff are tied to the civil service pay, the degree of the school's financial autonomy is practically very limited. Nevertheless, the link to civil service pay is a crucial factor contributing to the recruitment of quality teachers and parents' confidence in school performance. As the teachers' salaries are fixed and taken care of by the government, schools do not have to worry about the implications on their budget and could recruit the best teachers for the job. Also, it helps maintain continuity, stability and expertise of the teaching staff in schools. Yet, since schools are funded according to standard patterns and procedures set by ED, the resources given are not linked to performance. Accordingly, the exercise of financial discretion by front-line managers as an incentive to promote effective performance — an important guiding principle of new managerialism — is not applicable to the school management reform in Hong Kong.

Apart from the non-discretionary Salary Grant, the main non-salary grant is the School and Class Grant, but this is also fixed according to the type and size of the school. Thus, despite its merger with the other grants into one bloc, schools have been constricted to deciding how the total budget should be allocated to meet their individual needs. In practice, they could only exercise discretion at cost margins. However, the exercise of discretion by the front-line managers — that is, the freedom to manage based on the idea of empowerment — is a crucial component of the spirit of managerialism. The rationale behind this principle is the promotion of human initiative and creativity, both in the setting of the organization goals and objectives as well as the flexibility to meet individual needs. Unless there is a merger of salary and non-salary grants and a linking of the resource allocation to school achievement, there will be no shift to the new paradigm. However, such a shift would be too drastic for the Hong Kong community. Neither the government nor the aided-school sector is prepared for such a radical change. Without a decentralization of authority or an empowerment of decision makers at the site level with sufficient financial autonomy to achieve innovation and individuality, the SMI or SBM measures would be far from being an authentic kind of school self-management. A shift towards the NPM has yet to be established. Given the limited discretion in financial management, the main aim of the SMI/SBM reform was to strengthen the transparency and public accountability of school management in the aided-school sector.

6. A Research Study on School Management in Hong Kong

The main positions made in this chapter were supported by findings of our research project conducted in 1998. The study aims to investigate the differences between the SMI and non-SMI schools in school management and the relationship between school management structure/style and students' academic performance, civic consciousness, learning motivations, self-esteem, and so on.

In the research project, a non-random matched group sampling method was used in conducting our surveys. Letters were sent to all SMI schools (148) to invite them to participate in our project. Fifteen (10.1%) of them were interested. Letters were then sent to 73 selected non-SMI schools with characteristics similar to the SMI schools participating in the project. These characteristics included banding, years of establishment, religious affiliation, district and school type (co-education, boys' or girls' school). Among those 73 schools, 14 (19.2%) agreed to participate in the project. The total number of schools joining the project was thus 29.

Two surveys were conducted. In the first survey in June–July 1998, all teachers (1,583) of the 29 schools were invited to complete a questionnaire about the management of their schools. Teachers' perception to some extent reflects the management structure and style of the school. A total of 1,325 valid responses were received giving a return rate of 83.7%.

The second survey was conducted from October to November 1998. All Forms 6 and 7 students (3,925) of the 29 schools were invited to complete a questionnaire on their Hong Kong Certificate of Education Examination (HKCEE) results, civic consciousness, extra-curricular activities, learning motivations, self-esteem, attitude towards teachers, family background and so on. There were 3,757 valid responses, representing a return rate of 95.8%.

7. No Decentralization but Administrative Control

Our research findings indicated that there was no decentralization of authority from ED to the school level. Neither was there any decentralization within the school from the senior management to junior teachers. Teachers in the SMI schools sample, as compared to the non-SMI schools sample, felt a higher degree of external control from ED (see Annex 9.1). This finding was contradictory to the spirit of school-based management but it was not surprising. The SMI programme was a top-down reform introduced by ED. Schools joining the SMI scheme were *required* to submit annual school plans and school profile, and to set up a structured managerial framework as specified by ED, an outside authority representing the government at the central level. Apart from the external control, the perception of control from the internal administration was stronger in SMI than in non-SMI schools (Annex 9.2). For example, a larger proportion of teachers in SMI schools than those in the non-SMI schools believed that the Board of Directors was influential in the decision-making. In addition, more SMI school teachers agreed that their schools had a lot of rules about how to work, that their principal had a close monitoring on the work of the teachers and that all important decisions are taken by the principal. Hence, contrary to the principles of school-based management, the SMI programme had not facilitated a decentralization of authority or a participatory decision-making in schools. Most teachers did not regard the SMI scheme as a school-based development conducive to effective teaching and learning. They had great reservations in joining the scheme. Even after seven years of continuous persuasion by ED, only 111 out of a total of 346 (32%) aided secondary schools had voluntarily joined the programme by 1997.[35]

Nevertheless, the practices of the SMI were repackaged as school-based management (SBM) under the label of quality school education and all schools were expected to adopt a more structured management framework and a systematized planning of their activities.[36] In 1998, those schools which had not joined the SMI scheme were required to submit their 1998–

99 school annual report and the 1999–2000 school plans. In addition, all schools should have set up their own constitution of school management committee and staff appraisal system between 2001 and 2002. Clearly, these procedural measures and management structures are formalized frameworks to strengthen the system of accountability and control rather than a move to decentralize authority or to encourage initiative development at the school level. Thus, the reform is in effect an attempt to rebuild the Weberian structure of old public administration. There is no evidence of a shift towards the new paradigm of de-regulation or a delegation of power to the school site-level in the management of its major resources.

8. Persistence of Authoritarian Culture and a Lack of Teacher Participation

Apart from a restoration of the management structure, another recommendation of the SMI reform was to promote participation in decision making. In order to improve the delivery of education and school effectiveness, it required the involvement of key stakeholders, including the principal, the SMC, teachers, and (to an appropriate degree) parents and students in the decision-making process.[37] The idea that a participatory management is beneficial to organization effectiveness has its intellectual tradition in the human-relations theorists, such as Argyris and Lihert.[38] In the 1990s, the old ideas of job expansion and organization participation have been redis-covered and dressed up in the new language of empowerment.[39] Guy Peters observed that greater participation by the employees and clients of public organizations was an emerging model of future governance.[40] The fundamental assumption is that participation and communication of all members of the organization are valuable to quality and productivity be-cause they help to inculcate job satisfaction and a sense of commitment to the organization. On the contrary, hierarchical rule-based structures are impediments to organization effectiveness because they tend to discourage human initiatives and independent decisions on the job. Also, the manage-ment will find it difficult to legitimate its actions without active public involvement. The empowerment of front-line workers is a key feature of NPM. The participation of teachers and involvement of parents are, therefore, essential components of the ideas of school-based management.

Our findings indicated that most schools remained hierarchically structured and there was still a high concentration of power and decision-making at the top. After seven years of implementation, the level of teacher participation in SMI schools was not significantly higher than that of the non-SMI schools. Although SMI school teachers are more involved in school management and have expressed agreement on how to promote teaching and learning in school (Annex 9.3), they might have been "drafted" into involving in the management process. Also, parents and alumni seemed to be more influential in SMI schools because of the requirement of setting up Parent-Teacher Associations and Alumni Associations (Annex 9.3). Yet our research findings indicated that their influence was very limited. There was no significant difference between the styles of management in SMI and non-SMI schools (Annex 9.4). Even if one can argue that teachers, parents, and past students did involve more in the management of SMI school, these changes had emerged in the context in which school management had become more structured and directed from the top. The management culture of SMI schools was not more participatory than that of non-SMI schools (Annex 9.4). There was no sign that there was wider consultation or that teachers in SMI schools felt it easier to discuss issues with their seniors or the principal. Although, as we have seen, teachers in SMI schools felt more involved in school management, their sense of contribution to the decision making process was not stronger than that of their counterparts in non-SMI schools. This supports our claim that the SMI teachers might have been "drafted" formally to be involved in the management process. Finally, our findings also indicated that teachers in SMI schools in general did not have stronger agreement on more shared values about school management than teachers in non-SMI schools.

Such findings are not surprising because participatory management style — based on the principle of equality and a contractual relationship between the boss and the subordinates — is culturally alien to a Chinese society like Hong Kong. The idea of self-managing schools has its roots in western societies which emphasize the "self." Countries such as Australia, the United Kingdom, the United States and Canada were amongst the pioneers which took the initiative to increase the autonomy of schools within publicly-funded systems of education.[41] The model was copied by Hong Kong as an attempt to improve school effectiveness when it introduced the SMI scheme.[42] Yet, Hong Kong society differs sharply from the Anglo-American culture which has a strong tradition in individualism. In spite of its high level of economic development, the Chinese community in Hong Kong seems to have retained considerable elements which support a hierarchical power relationship between the seniors and juniors. Hofstede, for example, characterized Hong Kong culture as similar to East Asian communities in that it has large power distance, implying that subordinates feel dependent on their supervisors, and their employment relationship is an autocratic or a paternalistic rather than a contractual style.[43] Since management is culture-bound, it would be unrealistic to expect top-down structural reforms will effectively induce an attitudinal change in organizations. If reforms are to be successful, they require a strong commitment and a change of values and attitudes on the part of both the leaders and subordinates. Organization culture can be changed, but very slowly.[44] If the relationship between the principal and teachers in most schools remains to be hierarchical and authoritarian it would be too far-reaching to expect the school authorities to allow parents, whom were considered as uninformed outsiders, a bigger say in the running of schools. Not unexpectedly, the government proposal to include parent representatives in the SMCs met strong opposition from some big school-sponsoring bodies.[45]

9. Performance Indicators and Output-oriented Assessment

On the one hand, the school management reform fails to empower the frontline educators. On the other hand, it adopts the NPM techniques of performance indicators and output-oriented assessment. To measure school performance, the ECR No. 7 introduced the concepts of value-added achievement, self-evaluation and external assessment. It suggested to use quality indicators to measure and monitor the delivery of education service by schools. For example, it aimed to achieve quality education by adopting the NPM strategies of "setting clear and commonly accepted goals" and by "translating the goals into *achievable, observable and measurable* (emphasis by the authors) quality indicators for self-evaluation and external assessment."[46] The report also recommended to use a framework of indicators, including the school context and profile, the process indicators and output indicators which would take into consideration both the academic and non-academic performance.[47] Nonetheless, it is expected that the focus of assessment would incline to lean toward the output, measurable and academic indicators. Plausibly, the school context and profile would only be used as a pretext to justify or explain the unsatisfactory performance of weak schools. Likewise, the process indicators — namely, the school culture and ethos, the school-based management, the teaching and learning process, the personal growth and development of students[48] — are not the ends but the means or facilitators to achieve the output performance. Pragmatically and practically, most schools would concentrate on the academic achievement of their students which are the measurable, concrete and substantial evidences of schools' performance.

Our data analysis showed that school management styles only had impact on students' academic performance but virtually had no significant relation to non-academic dimensions of the student profile, including civic consciousness, sense of morality, self-esteem, learning motivations, attitude towards teachers, and others. This finding indicated that, on the one hand, schools in general devoted their utmost efforts to improving students' academic performance which was their paramount goal of management; on the other hand, students' academic performance could conversely be regarded as an indicator of the effectiveness of school management in Hong Kong. Based on this working assumption, our data analysis showed that an open management was not conducive to school effectiveness and better student academic results were associated with a management style of tight control and close supervision (Annexes 9.5, 9.6 and 9.7). The academic performance of the students was measured in terms of the total score for the best six HKCEE subjects in our survey.

The results in Annex 9.5 indicated that ED might have taken the right move to strengthen the control of the board of directors, and the management and monitoring framework within the school, but it should not *rhetorically* coin the reform in terms of *participation*. Also, Annexes 9.6 and 9.7 showed that students in a school with an open/participatory system and strong shared culture without too many rules might not perform better academically. Such findings are thought provoking. It seems that the SMI/SBM measures — which aim to develop a more structured management — are the appropriate remedies in tackling the problem of a lack of accountability and control in the school system. Nevertheless, it is a misnomer to refer these managerial strategies as a school-based quality reform which aims to enhance the "participation and [innovative] contribution of frontline educators."[49]

Moreover, it is important to note the differences between close monitoring by the principal and hierarchical structures in schools. Although schools with close supervision under the principal had better student performance, our findings also showed that rigid and hierarchical structures in schools would not facilitate better academic performance (Annexes

9.8 and 9.9). It can be argued that administrative measures which aim to tighten the management structure *per se* could not enhance school effectiveness.

10. Are School and Family Backgrounds Intervening Factors?

One may suggest that our research findings are compatible with a rival hypothesis, namely, it is a kind of school or family background that makes students more likely to attain better HKCEE results; and it is the same factor that makes schools more prone to adopt a management style with tighter control and closer supervision. If this rival hypothesis were to be confirmed, it would be difficult to establish the result that such a management style is conducive to better student academic achievement in terms of HKCEE results, because the better performance is a result of some intervening school or family background factor.

However, we have found no evidence to support the above rival hypothesis. Our student survey showed that the total score for the best six HKCEE subjects was significantly related to students' social economic background and their school bands. It was found that students in schools with lower banding[50] tended to perform better in HKCEE. In other words, students in schools with higher academic standing in general got better results in HKCEE. Also, we found that the total score for the best six HKCEE subjects was positively related to parents' education level and students' living environment. Nevertheless, these findings do not lend ready support to the rival hypothesis for the reason below.

There was no general trend that schools with lower banding tended to adopt a management style with tighter control and closer monitoring. As an illustration, it was found that these schools did not tend to have higher mean scores on the following three items as listed in Annex 9.5:

- All important decisions are taken by the Principal.
- The Principal has a close monitoring on the work of the teachers in this school.
- Our board of Director/School Council is influential in the decision making of this school.

Hence, the significant relationship between a management style with tighter control and closer monitoring and better student academic performance cannot be explained in terms of school bands. As for the factor of socio-economic background, again there was no evidence that styles of school management were systematically related to parents' education background and students' living environment. All in all, we can only conclude that apart from the academic banding of a school and the family background of students, a management style with tighter control and closer monitoring is another factor that can have significant positive effect upon students' academic performance.

11. Job Satisfaction and Staff Appraisal System

Although a systematic management framework is conducive to school effectiveness, it means additional administration for teachers. Teachers generally felt that the implementation of SMI increased their workload.[51] Most teachers believed that it would be more beneficial if they spent the time on preparing lessons, teaching and counselling of students than on administrative work. Ideally speaking, the involvement of teachers in setting school goals and formulating school plans would create a shared vision and mission, and better understanding of the needs of their students. In face of heavy workload, however, some teachers would tend to copy from samples of other schools or make cosmetic changes and minor trimmings annually.[52] Accordingly, the drafting and compiling of school plans and budgets have become merely paper exercises. Also, hierarchical control and heavy workload would have adverse effect on teachers' job satisfaction. Our findings indicated that although tightening up the control of the school system had positive relationship with students' academic performance, teachers working in a more open and participatory environment were more satisfied with their jobs. For example, our stepwise multiple regression analysis showed that answers to the following questions could explain a significant portion of the variance of teachers' job satisfaction ($r^2 = .418$, $F = 68.507$, $p < 0.001$):

- I feel free to raise issues with the senior teachers ($\beta = .252$).
- I go to see the principal whenever I like to discuss any issue with him/ her ($\beta = .191$).
- The staff in this school share values about how the school should work ($\beta = .143$).
- I do contribute to decision making process in our school ($\beta = .164$).

 – The subject panels are important part of how the school is run (β = .096).
 – There are a lot of rules about how we work (β = –.071).
 – The management committees in this school are an important part of how the school is run (β = .071).[53]

In sum, our research findings indicated that the old model of formalized structures and administrative control, if exercised at an appropriate level, was supportive and conducive to school performance. Although our study also showed that a more free and open style of school management was favourable to teachers' job satisfaction, there was no evidence that such a style was an important element contributory to school effectiveness. On the contrary, our findings showed that there was a negative relationship between a free and open style of school management and students' academic performance in terms of public examination results. As such, the new cloak of manageralism would lead to a paradoxical situation where school effectiveness could be enhanced by a reinforcement of administrative control but at the expense of making teachers less satisfied with their jobs.

According to the ECR No. 7, all schools are required to set up a formal staff appraisal system. Theoretically speaking, the implementation of a fair and systematic appraisal system is supportive and beneficial to staff development. No doubt, it is a key element of a school-based management. However, many teachers are sceptical of its effectiveness. They do not have trust in the system and do not consider that the appraisal could help their professional development. In order to build the confidence and trust among staff, it is important to have an open and participatory management. Teacher participation in the decision making is, therefore, an essential prerequisite for the implementation of a constructive and effective staff appraisal system. Their involvement can help reinforce a sense of commitment and collective identity which has been threatened by more individualistic appraisal, evaluation and reward. The lack of involvement will create misunderstanding, suspicion and alienation among staff. To be effective, a school-based management has to enhance teacher participation in decision-making. An authoritarian management structure with tight control and additional administrative workload would be a deterrent to job motivation, school performance and quality education.

12. Conclusion

After seven years of implementation of the SMI scheme, there was still no paradigm shift in the school management. Instead of decentralization, deregulation and delegation, the SMI/ SMB reforms in fact attempt to restore the traditional principles of administration, that is, central steering, regulation, and controls. Meritocracy and authoritarian-centralism are still the dominant values prevalent in most school culture. Moreover, our research study reveals that there is a paradoxical relationship between teachers' job satisfaction and students' academic performance, both of which are indicators of quality of education. The discussion in this chapter argues that the SMI/SBM measures in Hong Kong are a mix of both the old and new styles of management. In the quest for school effectiveness, it is expected that the management reforms would bring tensions and stresses to the school system. Paradoxes and contradictions are likely to persist despite the drive for quality school education.

Postscript

The main part of this chapter was written before the publication of the "School-Based Management Consultation Document" in February 2000.[54] The main proposal of the Consultative Document, which outlines the structure and composition of the SMC, confirms the authors' argument that the key objective of the SBM is to restore a systematized accountable framework in schools by a strengthening of administrative controls. The Consultative Document, for example, proposes that all schools in Hong Kong will each establish its SMC in which the school sponsoring body could nominate up to 60% of its total membership. The other members include the principal (an ex-officio), teacher manager (two or more), parent managers (two or more), alumni managers (one or more) and independent member (one or more) nominated by the SMC from the community.[55] The proposed SMC will provide a structured framework to ensure the participation and involvement of various stakeholders. It also specifies the requirements, qualifications, roles and responsibilities of the SMC and the key stakeholders. Moreover, the proposal to include an independent member from the community helps increase the transparency and public accountability of the management system. A formalization of the management structure, embodying both internal controls and external monitoring, is a rational-structural approach to ensure school quality. That is, it would be achieved by administrative measures, such as internal self-evaluation through school annual planning (with performance targets) and review, and external inspections by the ED based on a set of performance indicators.[56] However, as pointed out in the chapter, unless there is a change of leadership style and a decentralization of authority in schools, a reformulation of the management structure alone will not bring about a participatory decision-making. Neither will it enhance the job satisfaction and professionalism of teachers which are important indicators of quality education.

Notes

1. See C. Gaynor, *Decentralization of Education, Teacher Management* (Washington: The World Bank, 1998), p. v. The note was made by David de Ferranti in the "Foreword" of the book.
2. Education Commission, *Quality School Education*, Education Commission Report No. 7 (Hong Kong: The Government Printer), p. xiii. In this chapter, we have reservations that the School-Based Management programme is a truly school-based approach. Hence, the term School-Based Management (SBM) is used to refer to the reform introduced by the Hong Kong government while "school-based management" is used as a generic name of a school management style.
3. Advisory Committee on School-Based Management, *Transforming Schools into Dynamic and Accountable Professional Learning Communities, School-based Management Consultation Document*, (Feburary 2000).
4. C. Pollitt, *Managerialism and the Public Services*, 2nd ed. (Oxford: Blackwell, 1993).
5. C. Hood, "A Public Management For All Seasons?" *Public Administration*, Vol. 69, (1991), pp. 3–19.
6. D. Osborne and T. Gaebler, *Reinventing Government: How the Entrepreneurial Spirit Is Transforming the Public Sector* (New York: Penguin, 1992).
7. C. Hood, "Beyond 'Progressivism': A New 'Global Paradigm' in Public Management?" *International Journal of Public Administration*, Vol. 19, No. 2 (1996), pp. 151–77. See also Anthony B. L. Cheung, "Understanding Public-sector Reforms: Global Trends and Diverse Agendas," *International Review of Administrative Science*, Vol. 63 (1997), pp. 435–57.
8. Q. Chan, "A Bigger Stake for Parents?" *South China Morning Post*, 8 November 2000.
9. Information obtained from the Education Department. The figure does not include the government schools which joined the SMI scheme. The scheme also covered primary schools. However, this study focuses only on aided secondary schools.

10. O. E. Hughes, *Public Management and Administration* (Houndmills: Macmillan Press, 1998), pp. 1–21. For details, see OECD, *Public Management: OECD Country Profiles* (Paris: Public Management Service [PUMA], OECD, 1993); OECD, *Public Management Developments Update* (Paris: Public Management Service [PUMA], OECD, 1995a); and OECD, *Governance in Transition: Public Management Reforms in OECD Countries* (Paris: Public Management Service [PUMA], OECD, 1995b).

11. There is a rich literature on this area. See, for example, Jan-Erik Lane, "Will Public Management Drive Out Public Administration?" *The Asian Journal of Public Administration*, Vol. 16, No. 2 (1994), pp. 139–51; Owen E. Hughes, *Public Management and Administration,* 2nd ed. (New York: Macmillan, 1998), pp.1–80; and B.G. Peters, "Models of Governance for the 1990s," in *The State of Public Management*, edited by D. F. Kettl and H. Brinton Milward (Johns Hopkins University Press, 1996).

12. In Hong Kong, there has been a diversity of management structures in schools. For example, schools belonging to the same sponsoring body have a common School Council/ Board composed of representatives of the sponsoring body and school principals. Internally, most schools set up their own management committees composed of the principal and senior teachers. The main role of the School Council/ Board is to guide the overall vision and development of the school while the task of the internal school management committees is to oversee the operational management in the school. Hence, the nature and composition of the pre-reform school management committee is different from the School Management Committee (SMC) proposed under the SBM scheme. For details, refer to the postscript.

13. For details, see H. M. Chan and J. Y. H. Leung, "Education," in *Social Policy in Hong Kong*, edited by Paul Wilding, Ahmed Shafiqul Huque and Julia P. W. Tao (Cheltenham: Edward Elgar, 1997), pp. 57–59.

14. Education and Manpower Branch and Education Department, *The School Management Initiative* (Hong Kong: Government Printer, 1991), p. 4.

15. Ibid., p. 12.

16. Finance Branch, Hong Kong Government, *Public Sector Reform* (Hong Kong: Government Printer, 1989). The term "policy window" is borrowed from J. Kingdon. It means an opportunity for policy advocates to put on the agenda their ideas or programmes. See J. Kingdon, *Agendas, Alternatives and Public Policies* (Boston: Little Brown, 1984).

17. C. D. Godwin, "Pilot Study One: The School Education Programme: Redefining the Relationship between Policy Branch and Department" in *Public Sector Reform in Hong Kong*, edited by Jane C. Y. Lee and Anthony B. L. Cheung (Hong Kong: The Chinese University Press, 1995), p. 89.

18. *Quality School Education,* Education Commission Report No. 7 (Note 2), p. 11.

19. See *The School Management Initiative* (Note 14), pp. 27–32; Education Department,

School Management Initiative (SMI) Handbook, p. 2; and *Quality School Education, Education Commission Report No. 7* (Note 2), pp. xiii, 11 and 23–29.

20. *School Management Initiative (SMI) Handbook*, ibid., p. 2.
21. Ibid., p. 1.
22. *The School Management Initiative* (Note 14), pp. 9–24.
23. Ibid., p. 12.
24. Ibid., p. 14.
25. Ibid., p. 15.
26. Ibid., p. 17.
27. T. T. Lui, "Changing Civil Servants' Values," in *The Hong Kong Civil Service and Its Future*, edited by Ian Scott and John P. Burns (Hong Kong: Oxford University Press, 1988), p. 137.
28. Ibid., p. 10.
29. The term double whammy was used by C. Hood. See C. Hood et al., *Regulation inside Government: Waste-Watchers, Quality Police and Sleaze-Buster* (Oxford: Oxford University Press, 1999).
30. Education Department, SMI Section, *School Management Initiative (SMI) Handbook*, (September 1996), pp. 9–11. (1) A **School Management Committee Constitution** specifies its composition, its manner of operation and functions, as well as defining the roles, authority and responsibilities of the parties concerned in school decision-making. (2) An **Annual School Plan** should set out the aims and values of the school, its objectives, the programmes of activities through which the objectives will be achieved, budget allocation, and procedures for assessing performance. (3) A **Summary of the Annual School Plan** has to be issued to parents at the beginning of a school year. It should cover mission statements, major concerns for the current year with brief descriptions. (4) The **School Policy and Procedure Manual** should list out the policy of a school and its working procedures (e.g. admission of pupils, extra-curricular activities, reward and punishment of pupils, etc.). (5) The **Annual School Profile** is a document to be issued annually by SMI schools to parents and other interested people with a variety of information about the school, its resources, its success, and the areas in which improvement is needed. (6) The **Staff Appraisal System** is a set of formal procedures used by a school to make regular assessment on the performance of staff.
31. *Quality School Education,* Education Commission Report No. 7 (Note 2), p. 17.
32. Ibid. For information on flexibility in the funding arrangements described in this paragraph, refer to pp. 5 and 19.
33. *Quality School Education,* Education Commission Report No. 7 (Note 2), p. 24.
34. Ibid., pp. 24–29.
35. Information obtained from the Education Department. The figure does not include the government schools which has joined the SMI scheme. The scheme also covered primary schools. However, this study focuses only on aided secondary schools.

36. *Quality School Education,* Education Commission Report No. 7 (Note 2), p. xiii.
37. *The School Management Initiative* (Note 14), p. 37.
38. See C. Argyris, *Integrating the Individual and the Organisation* (New York: Wiley, 1964); and R. Likert, *New Patterns of Management* (New York: McGraw-Hill, 1961).
39. B. G. Peters, *The Future of Governing: Four Emerging Models* (Kansas: University Press of Kansas, 1996), p. 50.
40. Ibid., pp. 47–71.
41. B. J. Caldwell and J. M. Spinks, *The Self-managing School* (London: Falmer Press, 1998).
42. *The School Management Initiative* (Note 14), pp. 25–32.
43. G. Hoftede, *Cutlures and Organizations* (New York: McGraw-Hill, 1997). The book was first published in 1991.
44. Hofstede's scholarly study on work-related values of more than 10,000 employees of a multinationa (IBM) in 40 countries was conducted in the 1970s. In 1993, Lowe replicated Hofstede's study in Hong Kong and the UK. His study found some but no great change in the cultural environment in these two countries. There was still a large power distance (PDI) in Hong Kong culture. The PDI score (1993) in Hong Kong was 53 (68 in 1972) compared to 16 (35 in 1972) in the UK. See S. Lowe, "Hermes Revisited: A Replication of Hofstede's Study in Hong Kong and the UK," *Asia Pacific Business Review,* Vol. 2, No. 3 (1995), pp. 101–19.
45. Refer to Note 9.
46. *Quality School Education,* Education Commission Report No. 7 (Note 2), p. xi.
47. Ibid., p. 10.
48. Ibid., p. 11.
49. Ibid., p. 15.
50. Based on their academic results in the scaling test of Secondary School Place Allocation, Form 1 students are classified into bands, ranging from Band 1 (strongest) to Band 5 (weakest). The banding of the school in the year when the student subjects were admitted was used in the data analysis.
51. K. C. Wong, "Organizing and Managing Schools," in *Schooling in Hong Kong,* edited by Gerard A. Postiglione and W. O. Lee (Hong Kong: Hong Kong University Press, 1997), p. 88.
52. The information is based on informal contacts and conversations with teachers.
53. For the definitions of r^2, F, p and β, see David C. Howell, *Statistical Methods for Psychology,* 3rd ed. (Boston: PWS-Kent, 1992).
54. Advisory Committee on School-based Management, *Transforming Schools into Dynamic and Accountable Professional Learning Communities: School-based Management Consultation Document* (February 2000).
55. Ibid., p. 12.
56. Ibid., p. 18.

Annex 9.1 Teachers' Perception of External Control in SMI and Non-SMI Schools

	SMI	Non-SMI	F	p
The Education Department is influential in our school management	3.38	3.16	17.088	<.001

Note: A 5-point response scale was adopted in the teacher questionnaire, with 1 = "strongly disagree" and 5 = "strongly agree." *F* and *p* are respectively the test value and significance level of analysis of variance (ANOVA).

Annex 9.2 Teachers' Perception of Internal Control in SMI and Non-SMI SXchools

	SMI	Non-SMI	F	p
Our Board of Directors/School Council is influential in the decision making of this school	3.33	3.20	6.163	<.05
The Principal has a close monitoring on the work of the teachers in this school	3.32	3.14	11.855	<.001
All important decisions are taken by the Principal	3.95	3.74	12.329	<.001
We have a lot of rules about how we work	3.56	3.32	23.535	<.001

Note: A 5-point response scale was adopted in the teacher questionnaire, with 1 = "strongly disagree" and 5 = "strongly agree," *F* and *p* are respectively the test value and significance level of analysis of variance (ANOVA).

Annex 9.3 Teachers' Perception of Involvement of Teachers, Parents and Past Students in the Management of SMI and Non-SMI Schools

	SMI	Non-SMI	*F*	*p*
Most of the teachers are involved in our school management	2.72	2.55	10.914	<.001
Most of the staff agree about how to promote teaching and learning in this school	3.13	3.02	4.769	<.05
The parents have a significant influence in our school management	2.68	2.45	18.403	<.001
The Past Students' Association has a significant influence in our school management	2.10	1.93	4.501	<.05

Note: A 5-point response scale was adopted in the teacher questionnaire, with 1 = "strongly disagree" and 5 = "strongly agree." *F* and *p* are respectively the test value and significance level of analysis of variance (ANOVA).

Annex 9.4 Teachers' Perception of Participation of Teachers in the Management of SMI and Non-SMI Schools

	SMI	Non-SMI	F	p
The management committees in this school are an important part of how the school is run	3.64	3.71	1.595	Ns
There is wide consultation before important decisions are made	2.77	2.74	.217	Ns
I feel free to raise issues with the senior teachers	3.15	3.16	.027	Ns
I do contribute to decision making process in our school management	2.89	2.85	.710	Ns
I go to see the Principal whenever I like to discuss any issues with him/her	3.11	3.22	2.772	Ns
Most of the staff agree about how the school should be managed	2.85	2.78	2.057	Ns
The staff in this school share values about how the school should work	3.06	2.99	1.903	Ns

Note: A 5-point response scale was adopted in the teacher questionnaire, with 1 = "strongly disagree" and 5 = "strongly agree." F and p are respectively the test value and significance level of analysis of variance (ANOVA). Ns refers to non-significance of the F value.

Annex 9.5 Results of Oneway Analysis of Variance Show That Students in Schools Which Score *High* in the Following Questions Have *Better* Performance in HKCEE (Total Score for the Best Six Subjects)

	High	Medium	Low	*F*	*p*
All important decisions are taken by the principal	18.84	16.47	17.59	73.864	<.001
The principal has a close monitoring on the work of the teachers in this school	18.78	15.71	18.21	141.519	<.001
Directors/school council is influential in the decision making of this school	18.75	17.56	16.72	56.736	<.001

Note: For each question of the teacher questionnaire, a tripartite split was used on the mean response to rank each school as "high," "medium," or "low." *F* and *p* are respectively the test value and significance level of analysis of variance (ANOVA).

Annex 9.6 Results of Oneway Analysis of Variance Show That Students in Schools Which Score *Low* in the Following Question Have *Better* Performance in HKCEE

	High	Medium	Low	F	p
There is wide consultation before important decisions are made	16.62	17.43	17.76	6.298	<.01
I feel free to raise issues with the senior teachers	18.00	16.44	18.64	72.821	<.001
I go to see the Principal whenever I like to discuss any issues with him/her	15.90	18.03	18.99	144.845	<.001
Most of teachers are involved in our school management	17.69	16.22	18.95	107.925	<.001
The staff in this school shares values about how the school should work	17.68	17.15	18.07	11.795	<.001
Most of the staff agree about how to promote teaching and learning in this school	17.73	17.00	18.04	30.974	<.001
Most of the staff agree about how the school should be managed	17.73	15.96	19.42	177.703	<.001

Note: For each question of the teacher questionnaire, a tripartite split was used on the mean response to rank each school as "high," "medium," or "low." F and p are respectively the test value and significance level of analysis of variance (ANOVA).

Annex 9.7 Results of Oneway Analysis of Variance Show That Students in Schools Which Score *High* in the Following Questions Have *Lowest* Performance in HKCEE

	High	Medium	Low	F	p
We do not need many rules because we all know what to do	16.54	18.60	17.42	57.779	<.001

Note: For each question of the teacher questionnaire, a tripartite split was used on the mean response to rank each school as "high," "medium," or "low." *F* and *p* are respectively the test value and significance level of analysis of variance (ANOVA).

Annex 9.8 Results of Oneway Analysis of Variance Show That Students in Schools Which Score *Low* in the Following Questions Have *Better* Performance in HKCEE and *vice versa*

	High	Medium	Low	F	p
The management committees in this school are an important part of how the school is run	16.91	17.14	18.80	59.358	<.001
The subject panels in this school are important part of how the school is run	16.26	18.21	18.44	78.290	<.001
Education Department is influential in our school management	17.35	17.69	17.89	4.159	<.05

Note: For each question of the teacher questionnaire, a tripartite split was used on the mean response to rank each school as "high," "medium," or "low." *F* and *p* are respectively the test value and significance level of analysis of variance (ANOVA).

Annex 9.9 Results of Oneway Analysis of Variance Show That Students in Schools Which Score *High* in the Following Question Have *Lowest* Performance in HKCEE

	High	Medium	Low	*F*	*p*
I have to report frequently the progress of my work to the senior teachers	16.92	18.59	17.31	41.936	<.001

Note: For each question of the teacher questionnaire, a tripartite split was used on the mean response to rank each school as "high," "medium," or "low." *F* and *p* are respectively the test value and significance level of analysis of variance (ANOVA).

10

Human Resource Management Reforms in the Hong Kong Government

Brian Brewer

Associate Professor, Department of Public and Social Administration, City University of Hong Kong

1. Introduction

Opinions differ about the distinction between human resource management (HRM) and personnel management. HRM is regarded generally as a re-source-centred concept concerned with management needs for the provision and deployment of human resources. There is an emphasis on planning, monitoring and control. Personnel management, on the other hand, is workforce-centred and involves all aspects of "managing" an organization's employees.[1] In considering specifically the case of civil service organizations HRM is often identified with macro-level policies and procedures, cutting across different departments and agencies, while personnel management has to do with the human resource activities of a particular organization. The foregoing distinction has been applied to the following discussion, even though the terms "HRM," "human resources" and "personnel management" are used interchangeably in the interest of enhancing readability.

This chapter focuses on the HRM aspects of public sector reform in Hong Kong. Of course human resources issues are one part only of an extensive package of reforms undertaken by the Hong Kong government in recent years. Confining the analysis to one aspect of the reform process is, inevitably, a somewhat artificial exercise, but this degree of isolation permits a more in-depth treatment of key points.

The relationship between new public management and human resource management is the first topic addressed in this chapter. Hypotheses about the launch of public sector reform in Hong Kong precede an outline of the Hong Kong government's most recent initiatives. This is followed by an analysis of the four major subjects addressed in the Civil Service Bureau's *Civil Service Reform Consultation Document* (March 1999) and discussion about the private sector orientation of the reform proposals.

2. New Public Management and Human Resource Management

A new model of public sector management has been emerging in most industrialized countries since at least the beginning of the 1990s. Various labels have been attached to this phenomenon,[2] but its essential characteristics include a shift from bureaucratic to market-oriented decision-making, attempts to improve the quality of public management, an emphasis on reducing the scope and cost of government services and the privatization of public enterprises. Key aspects of traditional public administration such as accountability have become the focus of systemic changes. Thus, government departments and agencies have become engaged in redefining what they are accountable for, how they are to be held accountable, to whom they will be held accountable and the ways in which accountability can be internalized by public sector employees. Included, as an integral feature of new public management (NPM), is enhancing organizational accountability to service recipients or "customers."[3] Many NPM ideas have been embodied in the concepts and strategies of the Hong Kong government's public sector reform initiatives over the past 10 years.

HRM is an integral part of public management.[4] A large portion of government costs is related directly to maintaining the civil service establishment. Indeed, the public personnel function can be regarded as not only *the* key administrative process for creating, supporting and maintaining a quality public service,[5] but it is also likely to be a significant factor influencing the success or failure of public sector reform. After all,

> The reforms place considerable demands on staff: They must manage scarce resources, be productive, become accountable for results, learn management techniques, incorporate the concerns of customers and users, comply with legal requirements and ensure the proper use of public funds, all at the same time.[6]

It is logical therefore to raise the question of where HRM fits within the framework of public sector reforms and the development of new public management. An answer can be found in a comprehensive theoretical model based on an aggregation of NPM methods and techniques.[7] It positions HRM within a "process" category, together with budgetary reforms and the development and maintenance of quality service delivery. Five specific personnel reforms are identified. Civil service pay features in two of the reforms, namely changing the reward structure to ensure that pay reflects "market" conditions and introducing performance-related or merit pay to reflect on-the-job achievement. The determination of tenure through the specification of goals in performance-related contracts and performance-based appraisals are two further reforms. General deregulation of personnel management through the elimination of a range of civil service controls constitutes the fifth reform element. Thus, the extensive changes in the traditional practices of HRM, which are required as NPM principles are applied and are evident in this model, reinforce the point that human resources have a key role in the ultimate success of public sector reform in Hong Kong and elsewhere.

3. Background and Impetus for Reform

Within Hong Kong there was considerable uncertainty about the future in the years leading up to the 1997 transfer of sovereignty and there were, in particular, a number of critical issues affecting the Hong Kong civil service.[8] There were increased wastage rates for both newly recruited and more experienced personnel, particularly within the police and in key occupational groups such as doctors, nurses and social workers. Between 1992 and 1994 the administration, under the leadership of the last British-appointed governor, Christopher Patten, was embroiled in a bitter row with Beijing over electoral reforms. Fears were raised about the interference of Beijing officials in Hong Kong affairs once the Special Administrative Region (SAR) government was established and there were concerns about whether or not the government, for either political or financial reasons, would honour its pension commitments to retired civil servants. The pace of localization and succession planning were issues, as was the cumulative effect of losing a large number of senior officers in a short period of time. There were problems, particularly for the senior government officials, in coming to terms with the new accountabilities arising from a political system now characterized by a partially directly elected, and increasingly critical, Legislative Council (LegCo). Directorate grade staff regarded LegCo as "too politicized" and "immature."[9] The pressure on the civil service was such that in October 1994 the Chief Secretary Anson Chan Fang On-sang, in a speech before the Legislative Council, felt it necessary to defend vigorously the public service, telling legislators that their constant criticisms were undermining staff morale in government departments.[10]

Such an environment would not appear to be conducive to the introduction of major changes and different explanations have been given about what has driven the reforms in Hong Kong. It has been suggested that neither economic nor social problems, nor a widespread perception of inefficiency within the civil service were the forces behind the government's initial reform initiatives. Rather, the reforms were a strategic response to enhance administrative credibility and re-legitimate traditional bureaucratic power in a changing environment where politicians were becoming increasingly important actors in the political process.[11] Hong Kong's political reforms have also been explained as a substitute for more radical political reform. They have been the means whereby the government has attempted to deal with the dilemma created by demands for increased state intervention arising from global economic re-structuring, the 1997 change of sovereignty, and the rising political consciousness within Hong Kong society. While there has been pressure for the government to act, its institutional and financial capacity have been constrained by the provisions of the Basic Law (Articles 107 and 108) and the interests of Hong Kong's powerful economic and business elites.[12]

In addition, it seems apparent that the reform initiatives reflect a diffusion into the Hong Kong system of ideas concerning public services management that came to the fore in the United Kingdom (UK) following the 1979 election to government of the Conservative Party under Margaret Thatcher's leadership. Given the nature of the colonial relationship between Hong Kong and the UK, senior government officials and even Hong Kong's business leaders could not have failed to be familiar with the general philosophy, and even many of the details, of the Thatcher government's reform initiatives. Clearly Christopher Patten's blueprint for reform, including the impetus to develop a service culture within the public sector, was influenced directly by his own first-hand knowledge about the British civil service reforms carried out under successive Conservative governments throughout the 1980s and the early 1990s.

The considerable credit garnered by the civil service for its stabilizing role in the uncertain days prior to the change of sovereignty on 1st July 1997 was undermined rapidly within the next year. The civil service became involved in a series of major fiascos,[13] and there was evidence that a substantial proportion of the general public was now dissatisfied with the "low efficiency of civil servants."[14] Increasing public discontent concerning performance within the civil service was heightened still further in early 1999 when the Director of Audit criticized three government departments for their under-performing employees, citing in particular a failure to provide adequate work supervision.[15] Additional problems were highlighted by the Public Service Commission's findings on over-grading in appraisal reports. In some departments 60 to 70 percent of the staff were identified as "outstanding" for the purposes of promotion.[16]

The general sense of a non-productive civil service and, in particular, the belief that the public sector was filled with individuals whose levels of incompetence were related inversely to their job security and generous employment-related benefits grew in the year and a half after the change of sovereignty. It is an impression that fits neatly with popular stereotypes. Since the early 1980s public sector shortcomings, both real and imagined, have ensured that managerialist reforms have become a prominent feature on the political agendas of Anglo-American governments from across the political spectrum. It should however be kept in mind that the issue of problem employees is not exclusive to the public sector. It is estimated that between 80 and 90 percent of supervisory time is consumed by the 10 to 20 percent of the workforce who under-perform.[17] In North America alone companies spend up to $100 billion a year in worker's compensation, health insurance and benefit costs for problem employees.[18]

4. Recent Reform Initiatives

Civil service reform in Hong Kong was initiated officially in 1989 when the Finance Branch released its document on *Public Sector Reform*. In recent years the government's "Serving the Community" campaign (1995) designed to encourage a more customer-oriented service delivery in the public sector, was followed by the Target-based Management Process (TMP) to enhance results-oriented management. This, in turn, was followed by Chief Executive Tung Chee-hwa's announcement, in his 1998 Policy Address, of a government plan to launch an Enhanced Productivity

Programme (EPP). Its goal is a five-percent reduction in operating expenditures without any reduction in service quality by 2002–2003.

Within the framework of these programmes the government has targeted specifically the civil service personnel management structures and processes. In a speech to the Legislative Council on 14 January 1999, the Chief Executive outlined plans to improve the efficiency of the civil service by reviewing and reforming the entire management system. These plans included reviews of permanent and pensionable term appointments, of salary levels, fringe benefits, and starting salaries to ensure consistency with those of the private sector, and an examination of the feasibility of linking pay to performance in a manner similar to commercial organizations. Disciplinary procedures were to be streamlined, and the speech highlighted the need for strict enforcement of disciplinary actions "to ensure that an effective reward and punishment system is maintained in the civil service." Finally a results-driven and customer-oriented management culture was to be fostered through improvements to the performance appraisal system and the strengthening of professional training and individual development at all levels in the civil service.[19]

In his 1999–2000 Budget Speech the Financial Secretary, Donald Tsang Yam-kuen, reiterated the government's intention to implement the foregoing measures.[20] He also announced a hiring freeze to accomplish, by the end of 1999–2000, a reduction of 8,000 in the strength of the permanent civil service. Positions could only be "unfrozen" on a case-by-case basis and the recruitment of more contract and temporary staff was anticipated.

5. Proposals for Further Reform

In early March 1999 the Civil Service Bureau issued a consultation document on HRM reform within the civil service.[21] The stated reasons for the review were the negative impact on the Hong Kong economy of the Asian economic turmoil, increased unemployment, and rising community expectations towards the government at a time when the government's handling of some specific incidents and the efficiency of certain departments had been criticized. In line with the Chief Executive's January 1999 announcement to LegCo, the review outlined initial thinking about entry and exit mechanisms, pay and fringe benefits, disciplinary procedures, and performance management, professional training and personal development.

Following a three-month consultation the government planned to frame a more detailed package of proposals for additional consultation and gradual implementation over an 18-month period.

6. The Reform Philosophy and Principles

The Hong Kong government's most recent reform initiatives are focused on human resource issues and will affect more directly the HRM functions of the general civil service than have the previous reforms. The points outlined in the consultation document are not yet government policy and, at the time of writing this chapter, these skeletal proposals need to be fleshed out before their full impact can be assessed. Nevertheless, the document serves as a blueprint to indicate quite clearly the direction in which the government is heading and to support an analysis of the philosophy and principles guiding this phase of the reform process.

One approach to the discussion of the Hong Kong government's reform philosophy would be to examine the extent to which these reform proposals signify a shift towards market principles as opposed to publicly planned and delivered services. This discussion however focuses more directly on the nature of the reforms from a management perspective. Ideas from McGregor's classic management theory[22] are used to frame an analysis of the philosophical ideas and management principles supporting the HRM reform proposals.

McGregor's theory is based on the premise that pervasive assumptions about human nature underpin managerial decisions and behaviours. Two dichotomous approaches are identified. One labelled Theory X and the other Theory Y. The Theory X approach to management favours, as a central organizational principle, direction and control through the exercise of authority. This is required because the average human being is seen to dislike work, to prefer directives over autonomy, and to contribute adequately to the achievement of organizational goals only when coerced or threatened with punishment. In comparison, Theory Y assumes that people will exercise self-direction and self control to achieve objectives to which they are committed. Employees can be encouraged to utilize their potential more fully by the selective adaptation of organizational forms that facilitate the integration of personal and organizational goals, rather than a single absolute form of control. Given the right circumstances the average human being will seek responsibility and expand his/her own efficacy at work.

Despite being somewhat stereotypical these ideas provide an appropriate explanatory framework for the analysis of NPM strategies.[23]

In the *Civil Service Reform Consultation Document* each of the four chapters focuses on one substantive aspect of HRM reform in the Hong Kong civil service. The following discussion examines these chapters in turn, beginning with entry and exit to the public service. Next, pay and conditions of employment, conduct and discipline are each addressed, with the final topic being performance management, training and development.

6.1 Public Sector Employment: Entry and Exit

Traditionally the Hong Kong civil service has been a career service based on a system of permanent employment. Following recruitment into entry-level positions, most public sector employees could expect to develop their career through step-by-step promotions up the hierarchy. Loyalty and faithful service have represented important organizational norms, unlike Hong Kong's competitive private sector where there has been little stigma attached to changing jobs frequently in pursuit of personal gain. At the same time the opportunity costs associated with lost pension benefits have tended to discourage corrupt practices. Together these factors have helped to maintain a relatively stable public sector workforce, even in the years just prior to 1997 when the rate of early retirement increased. Despite their advantages, these entry and exit arrangements have resulted in an unhealthy rigidity in HRM management and have provided next to no opportunities for personnel exchanges between the public and private sectors.

In order to enhance flexibility the government has proposed to replace permanent and pensionable terms with fixed-term agreements for all basic rank civil servants. Supervisory ranks would be filled through a competitive appointment system, instead of the current promotion system. Normally, competition between basic rank employees and outside candidates would be used when vacancies occur. Upon appointment into the supervisory ranks basic rank civil servants could be offered new permanent terms, whereas outside candidates would be appointed on fixed-term agreements. Experienced civil servants who had left the service would be allowed to rejoin. The current retirement benefits scheme would be replaced by a Civil Service Provident Fund scheme to allow for compatibility of retirement protection between the civil service and the private sector.

The proposals are designed to enhance significantly the flexibility of HRM in the public sector. They are consistent with the proposals of Joseph Nye, dean of Harvard University's John F. Kennedy School of Government who, in a speech to the Singapore civil service, argued the need for places like Singapore and Hong Kong "to think through ... the idea of having a totally segregated class of people who are public servants."[24] He went on to suggest a "break with tradition" to allow for more lateral recruitment into the public service, including experienced people from the private sector in their 40s and 50s. The Hong Kong government's reform proposals are very much in line with these ideas. An individual's career development is envisaged as a process whereby he/she moves between the private and public sectors or develops a career spread among private, public, subvented and corporate organizations. Indeed the Hong Kong government has begun the process already by appointing, with effect from September 1999, Yeoh Eng-kiong, the Hospital Authority chief, as Secretary for Health and Welfare.

A positive, though little recognized, feature of Hong Kong's system of colonial administration was the regular recruitment of overseas officers. This introduction of people into the system, largely without local connections and who could resist pressure from special interests with relative ease, gave an element of "objectivity" to the public sector.[25] Interpreting what was in the "public interest" could be done relatively free of tendencies towards bias or favouritism that can, quite naturally, arise when individuals have long-established links within the local community. At the same time, these individuals brought with them ideas based on their training and experience overseas, albeit primarily from the UK, into the relatively closed civil service system.

This advantage can be recaptured through greater flexibility in the hiring of mid-career managers and professionals. These civil service reform initiatives would allow the public sector to "import" expertise in specialist areas such as finance and information technology together with the most up-to-date techniques and strategies from the private sector. Research on poorly performing organizations, where new management teams are put in place, has found they contribute strategies developed in their previous work experience that facilitate organizational change.[26] Thus, by recruiting experienced personnel outside the bounds of the civil service, the Hong Kong public sector stands to gain in terms of the introduction of new perspectives and expertise into the system. It can be anticipated there will also be a greater propensity for "new blood" to push forward different ideas and to engage actively in change processes.

Besides, the exchange of personnel will be reciprocal. Not only does the public sector stand to gain; the private sector would have the benefit of employing staff with public sector experience. Such individuals can contribute their greater understanding about the nature of government operations, the constraints under which public policies are made and implemented, and the strategies needed to "get things done" in government. Given the collaborative or "joint venture" nature of many large projects in Hong Kong, with extensive involvement by both public and private organizations, any HRM practices that enhance opportunities for a cross-fertilization of ideas between sectors can only be regarded as a healthy development.

A Theory Y approach to HRM can be discerned in these proposals concerning public sector employment. There is an underlying theme of job enrichment through job rotation across employment sectors. Individuals would be given opportunities to accept new responsibilities and to test themselves in relation to a variety of challenges. In line with Theory Y assumptions people are seen to be self-motivating and will respond positively to changes allowing them to gain additional work experience.

Of course, any attempt to maximize flexibility must be undertaken with some degree of caution. The civil service is far from being a homogenous entity. It is comprised of a wide variety of departments and agencies whose mandates concerning policy development, regulation, and/or service delivery differ substantially. In fact, within days of the consultation document's release, Secretary for the Civil Service Lam Woon-kwong acknowledged there were strong views about imposing contract terms on new recruits across the entire service. In particular, the disciplined services argued for an exemption from the government's proposals. Such organizations need to maintain strong command-and-control hierarchies in order to make critical decisions quickly,[27] and in fact the Hong Kong government admitted that, where issues of law enforcement and public safety are a direct concern, it might be inappropriate to phase out permanent appointments and pensions.[28]

A fine balance must be struck between achieving a reasonable amount of flexibility, while maintaining sufficient expertise within the public sector to ensure the smooth delivery of services. Vacancies will need to be filled expeditiously to ensure the government is capable of providing uninterrupted services across a broad range of policy areas. Furthermore, the proposals may not be as cost-effective as anticipated. The continuous recruitment, selection, training and monitoring of large numbers of new entry-level staff can be an expensive process, even when their reduced starting salaries are taken into account. In addition, substantial costs can be incurred in the administration of large numbers of fixed-term contracts.

It is also important to ensure that what began as flexibility does not turn into instability. In recent years Hong Kong has had one of the highest employee turnover rates of the major economies world-wide.[29] Even though this is much the same for other economies in the region such as Singapore, Thailand and Malaysia, and given the likely reduction in turnover rates as a consequence of economic slowdown of the late 1990s, this issue does need to be considered carefully. Once the current economic downturn is over, then increased turnover rates may very well return. And when a plan for the transfer of pension benefits between employers and across sectors has been approved, the deterrent factor of lost pension benefits associated with movement out of the civil service will no longer operate as it has done in the past.

6.2 Pay and Conditions

The consultation document has outlined support for the principle of fair remuneration as perceived by both civil servants and the public, though there is to be broad comparability with the private sector. The government reiterated its commitment to the use of the Pay Trend Survey but conceded the necessity of considering how it could be modified and improved to be consistent with a performance-based pay system. It also expressed its continued support for a movement away from the provision of fringe benefits in kind towards a "total remuneration" concept. For both pay and fringe benefits the practices and arrangements in the private sector are regarded as appropriate points of reference.

The government's criticism of the existing pay system has arisen on two counts. First of all, pay scale increments have not been closely linked to performance. Secondly, accelerated promotion has been the reward for good performance, even though promotion opportunities may be limited depending upon the individual's grade or department's vacancy situation. The proposed solution supports the principle of rewarding better performers with higher pay rises. Performance based pay systems are seen to be the norm in the private sector and part of an accelerating trend in public sector systems overseas.

Certainly the salary and fringe benefits available currently to Hong Kong civil servants must be regarded as generous by international standards. In the final years of the colonial administration relatively liberal remuneration was one way to try to ensure their continuing loyalty in the face of an uncertain future. It can also be seen to have been a mechanism to boost the retirement packages of those who were destined to leave the public sector just prior or subsequent to the change of sovereignty. During this period the voices of opposition to these upward adjustments were muted by Hong Kong's general economic prosperity. The commercial sector was making substantial profits while, at the same time, expecting the "good times" to continue indefinitely.

The trend towards "pay for performance" has been identified in both the private and public sectors and it can be regarded as re-emphasizing merit over considerations such as cost of living or seniority.[30] The idea of performance-related pay has tremendous general appeal as it implies a guarantee of value-for-money in the employment of human resources. However, empirical evidence suggests that the chances for success of any performance management scheme, of which performance-related pay may be one aspect, is probably organization-specific.[31] The adoption of a single strategy or scheme may not be appropriate for the variety of organizations and agencies that comprise the civil service. Besides, the government will need to consider very carefully the involvement of staff in the formulation and implementation of any performance pay scheme. Case study research[32] has demonstrated the positive impact, for both acceptance and success, when employees participate actively in the development process.

Performance-related pay, used as a key management tool to enhance motivation, has a strong Theory X philosophical bias in the assumptions it makes about human nature. It is important to keep in mind that, in line with Theory Y assumptions about managing people, this is but one form of reward. Motivation can be secured by other means. The effective motivation of employees may be as much a function of personal managerial skill as the characteristic of any performance related scheme.[33] Recently, in discussions about the transformational challenges facing the public sector it has been argued that there is a strong case for motivation derived "... from understanding and recognition — the need for which is too often ignored, but which is of particular importance in the public domain...."[34]

6.3 Conduct and Discipline

The government has proposed to establish jointly a task force with the Independent Commission Against Corruption (ICAC) to review the rules and regulations on conduct and discipline and to assist departments to strengthen their guidelines and procedures concerning potential staff conflict of interest. Streamlined and more effective disciplinary mechanisms and procedures are to be developed, including the setting up of an independent standing secretariat to process disciplinary cases for all civil servants, except for those in the disciplined services whose procedures are subject to their own legislation. The centralized processing of disciplinary cases is designed to bring to bear the expertise of a pool of experienced officers separated from departments. This is to ensure a more expeditious handling of cases and a greater degree of consistency in deciding on the level of punishment.

It appears that assumptions very much in accordance with the Theory X approach to management underlie the Hong Kong government's reform proposals on discipline. A central organizing principle derived from Theory X is the use of authority to direct and control.[35] The consultation document proposals suggest clearly a more centralized and tightly controlled disciplinary process.

A Theory Y approach to discipline would not be so inclined to define exclusively the individual as the source of the problem. There would be more emphasis on the responsibility of managers to encourage staff, to ensure they receive appropriate skills training and that the tools they need to do their jobs are in place. There would be seen to be little need for coercion or adversarial interactions. Discipline, from a Theory Y perspective, is an organizational task shared by employees and supervisors, both of whom take responsibility for personal actions and share a commitment to learning from their interactions. The process is imbued with a sense of personal integrity concerning conduct, behaviour and performance.

Of course discipline, which may involve punishment and corrective action, is a set of difficult and uncomfortable activities that most supervisors do not want to do. The centralized processing of disciplinary cases ought to spare supervisors the need to take corrective actions, or to institute a set of penalties that could ultimately lead to dismissal. While this is likely to reduce the trauma experienced by individual supervisors it does raise the question of whether individual employees will be in a position to explain adequately their particular circumstances. It undermines the autonomy of individual supervisors and may, in effect, reduce the responsibility they feel for motivating their own staff. A Theory Y approach would regard supervisors much more as facilitators exercising strategies for encouraging efforts towards organizational objectives not based primarily on external control and threat of punishment.

Support for the adoption of a Theory X approach to discipline may have more to do with the government's desire to meet goals on its political agenda than with management principles. In light of the events referred to at the beginning of this chapter the general public in Hong Kong is likely to support a "get tough" line with the civil service. Evidence of this can be gauged from the public's reaction to a high profile disciplinary case in the civil service, subsequent to the consultation document's release.

In August 1999 the government demonstrated its determination to adopt a tough approach towards officials falling foul of civil service guidelines when it terminated the contract of Commissioner of Inland Revenue Wong Ho-sang. He was also required to forfeit his gratuity. A report by the Director of Audit, who had been ordered by Tung Chee-hwa to investigate Mr. Wong's investment in his wife's taxation firm, concluded that a proper declaration had not been made and the civil service regulations had been breached. The issue was raised originally by a report in the *Apple Daily* newspaper on 17 June 1999 and was concluded with the Inland Revenue Commissioner's dismissal on 19 August 1999.

Despite falling short of a full disciplinary inquiry, as advocated by the Democratic Party, the government's swift and decisive actions in the taxation chief's case were well received in the community.[36] Without doubt the credibility of the government was enhanced by this show of toughness against one of its senior officials. That high status or seniority would not deter disciplinary actions, when warranted, was the clear message to the civil service rank and file. Outside of the public sector this decisive contract termination provided tangible evidence of the government's determination to take seriously disciplinary matters and to rid the system of its "bad elements."

6.4 Performance Management, Training and Development

The individual-based performance management system, recommended in the reform document, would continue to leave the report of staff performance in the hands of reporting officers, but the grading would be determined by an assessment panel formed by senior members of the department. Across-the-board inflated ratings are to be avoided by reforming the performance appraisal culture and standardizing grading with the possible introduction of an indicative benchmark for grading distribution to guide departmental managers. Continued support for a result-oriented management culture at the organizational level would be further developed through the system that has already been established, in conjunction with the Efficiency Unit, to design performance measurement systems for departments.

Training and development are expected to continue to help enhance the overall efficiency and effectiveness of the civil service. Wider use of tailor-made training plans would be encouraged at the departmental and individual level with departmental management expected to be more proactive in using training and development strategies to meet goals and objectives. Inter-departmental exchanges and a greater interface with the private sector are seen to be mechanisms to help civil servants to either develop their professional knowledge or to gain experience.

In this section of the reform document a Theory X philosophy comes through strongly. Ideas about direction and control are implicit in most of the recommendations. Far less attention is given to mechanisms for enhancing the potential of staff to increase their self-control and commitment to the achievement of civil service objectives. Training and development issues are addressed in purely instrumental terms, designed with a focus limited to enhancing efficiency and generating greater productivity. Even the reference to tailor-made training plans does not appear to support a commitment to continuing education and the self-development of individual employees. There is no reference to developing teamwork and inter-disciplinary communication which are congruent with Theory Y assumptions about human motivation.[37] Overall, little consideration has been given to the education and development of public sector employees. By way of comparison, Singapore's PS21 (Public Service for the 21st Century) initiatives highlight continuous learning with an explicit commitment that every public employee will spend not less than five percent of his/her total working time (or 12.5 days a year) on training.[38]

According to the reform document it is HRM practices drawn from the private sector that form the cornerstone upon which the government's plans rest. However, some of the more positive private sector developments, and the ones consistent with a Theory Y approach to management, appear to have been overlooked. A commitment to employee welfare is difficult to discern in what the Hong Kong government is proposing. For example, Employee Assistance Programmes (EAPs) are an increasingly common feature of corporate life. Developed originally to help employees with substance abuse problems many have expanded their scope to include assistance with a range of personal and family issues that can impact on the ability of employees to do their jobs properly. Helping to retain experienced and knowledgeable employees, rather than just dismissing them, facilitates organizational learning. With the increasing complexity of the public services, experienced staff are required more than ever before. However, these reform proposals seem to have largely overlooked that "… the best private employer around the world look on their employees as assets, not costs. They focus on their people as the most important tool to serve their mission."[39]

When the four major areas of the Hong Kong government's proposed HRM reforms — entry to and exit from employment, pay and conditions, conduct and discipline, and performance management, training and development — are considered *in toto*, a mixture of Theory X and Theory Y assumptions and approaches can be discerned. There does, however, seem to be a bias towards Theory X management practices. Less emphasis is given to ideas based on Theory Y principles. As a starting point for major changes in HRM practice in Hong Kong this is somewhat disconcerting, given that amongst the stated aims is the creation of a system characterized by an enabling and motivating environment and a proactive responsible culture.

Even when, as a part of NPM, a Theory Y approach to personnel is espoused, there is evidence from outside Hong Kong that Theory X management practices are actually employed. As a consequence, there is little likelihood of creating the environment of trust crucial to any change designed to engage successfully the talents and support of employees.[40] The formal commitment to a Theory Y philosophy and approach is already limited in the *Civil Service Reform Consultation Document*. What then will be the case when the reforms are actually implemented? Especially considering that the current political agenda in Hong Kong tends to favour a Theory X approach to civil service management.

7. Private Sector Orientation

There is a high degree of consistency between the values inherent in Hong

Kong's public sector reform initiatives and those that have underpinned reforms in Anglo-American countries overseas. Key among these values is a strong preference for private sector management practices and strategies over those characteristic of the traditional bureaucratic model of public administration. Therefore, in discussion about NPM and public sector reform the unique aspects of public and non-profit organizations are often either neglected or they are assumed not to exist.

It is however, well to remember that organizations in the public sector seek to achieve public as opposed to private goals. Rather than a single success criterion, namely profitability, success is measured by a number of criteria including effectiveness, efficiency, fairness, equity and inclusiveness. The public sector is also subject to different constraints than the private sector in terms of the legal framework within which it must operate, the nature of its financial arrangements and need to satisfy accountability and transparency requirements.[41]

Career civil servants are often regarded as a part of the problem with government,[42] even though this "bureaucracy-bashing" perspective tends to cast public servants in the role of helpless victim. Metaphorically, civil servants are perceived to be caught within a sticky web of red tape spun by a tenaciously hidebound bureaucracy.[43] Whatever the actual case, the widespread adoption of private sector values and management practices is regarded as the logical solution to streamlining government services and enhancing productivity.[44] NPM and the reinventing government movement, certainly within the Anglo-American context of Australia, Canada, New Zealand, the UK and the United States (US), has been based firmly on a premise of inherent business superiority *vis-à-vis* the public sector.

Although the interests of business and government do not always coincide, the Hong Kong government has been generally sympathetic to the views of the business community. Lines of communication between the government and business have been relatively open. Senior corporate managers have often been appointed to the Executive Council and business people have made up a large proportion of the members of the government's approximately 400 non-statutory committees that give advice on a range of public policy issues.[45]

It should not be surprising then to see a private sector bias reflected in the Hong Kong government's latest reform initiatives. They are designed to reformulate the relationship between the state and its citizens to be similar to that existing between private enterprise and its customers. However importing unmodified private values into the public sector is not the only, nor necessarily the most appropriate, basis for reform. There are other bases upon which public management reform can take place. For example, in the Scandinavian countries of Sweden and Finland, the general perception of the state is that, even though it may be somewhat unresponsive and slow, it is an integrative force within society and there is not a taken-for-granted assumption about the superiority of business.[46]

There are indeed arguments for preserving the integrity of the bureaucratically organized public organization. Hierarchy, specialization and standardization — the important dimensions of bureaucratic organizations, are essential to good public management.[47] They facilitate a high degree of consistency across thousands of individual decision-making episodes and ensure that the state upholds equity and fairness values with respect to its citizens. They can be seen to be an integral part of good governance as "… public sector hierarchies are as much accountability devices as management tools."[48]

It is also worthwhile to reiterate the obvious point that the public service is not a homogeneous organization. Its responsibilities vary enormously across departments and agencies and this has to be accounted for in any reform proposals. Command-and-control hierarchies are necessary where quick decisions are expedient not only from an efficiency perspective, but in extreme emergencies. They may even mean the difference between life and death. Law enforcement agencies, corrections, fire and marine services are obvious examples. Indeed, government has a moral responsibility to ensure the risk-taking behaviour found in the private sector does not become the norm in many of the administrative actions for which the public sector is responsible.[49]

8. Lessons from Overseas

When the Hong Kong government's ambitious plans for HRM reform are compared to overseas experience it appears that, even when differences in government structure and environment are taken into account, some important learning points seem to have been ignored. For example, the Civil Service Reform Act of 1978, which represented a comprehensive reform of the US federal civil service, bears striking similarities to what is being proposed for Hong Kong's public sector. The Theory X assumptions related to developing private sector "efficiency" by using business methods and an emphasis on performance appraisals for the distribution of rewards and punishments underpinned the US reforms, even though this was criticized as likely to have a negative impact on public service morale and programme implementation effectiveness.[50]

Nevertheless the 1978 legislation was followed by a whole series of pay for performance strategies and these basic principles have continued as an important component of the US government's HRM strategy. This has occurred despite the widely held view that these initiatives have been a failure. The resources needed for their full implementation have been less than adequate and there continues to be a lingering impression that they have failed to ensure improvements in poor performance. However the most damning criticism of all, must be the agreement amongst scholars that pay for performance has never been empirically proven to operate effectively as a tool for motivating employees.[51] Yet, the Hong Kong government has chosen a narrowly-based reform model consistent with the US approach where plans have often been adopted on the basis of political ideology rather than more research-based managerial and organizational strategies.

9. Conclusion

Human resource management is an integral part of public management and changes in the philosophy and techniques of HRM are an important aspect of new public management. They now figure largely within the on-going civil service reforms in Hong Kong that, during the mid to late 1990s, have been taking place within an environment where the public sector has come under increasing scrutiny and been subjected to increasing criticism.

In the Civil Service Bureau's *Civil Service Reform Consultation Document*, a much greater flexibility in civil service staffing, with increased opportunities for the movement of personnel between the public and private sectors has been proposed. This is in line with Theory Y ideas about encouraging individual self-development through a variety of work experiences. The proposals concerning pay are more restricted. A narrow alignment between pay and performance casts this reform proposal much more in the philosophical mold of Theory X. The same holds true for disciplinary matters, which are framed in terms of centralized processes designed to mete out punishment expeditiously. Even the proposals concerning performance management and training and development are oriented more towards the measurement and control of individual behaviour rather than personal development within the context of supportive and facilitative management structures.

Like NPM developments overseas, those in Hong Kong reflect a preference for initiatives that align more closely public sector HRM practices with those in the private sector. In the case of the consultation document's proposals, there has been a tendency to identify for adoption initiatives oriented much more towards a Theory X philosophy of human nature. As the discussion in this chapter suggests, such an approach may not provide the most appropriate foundation upon which to build the human resource management policies and practices needed for the Hong Kong civil service to function at maximum effectiveness in the initial decades of the 21st century.

Notes

1. This issue is discussed in D. Torrington and L. Hall, *Human Resource Management*, 4th ed. (London: Prentice-Hall, 1998).
2. For example, O. E. Hughes, *Public Management & Administration: An Introduction*, 2nd ed. (London: Macmillan Press, 1998) has identified a number of different labels used to describe the phenomenon of new public management: "managerialism," C. Pollitt, *Managerialism and the Public Services: Cuts or Cultural Change in the 1990s*, 2nd ed. (Oxford: Basil Blackwell, 1993); "new public management," C. Hood, "A Public Management for All Seasons," *Public Administration*, Vol. 69, No. 1 (Spring, 1991), pp. 3–19; "market-based public administration," Z. Y. Lan and D. H. Rosenbloom, "Public Administration in Transition?" (Editorial), *Public Administration Review*, Vol. 52, No. 6 (Nov./Dec. 1992); "post-bureaucratic paradigm," M. Barzelay, *Breaking Through Bureaucracy: A New Vision for Managing in Government* (Berkeley and Los Angeles: University of California Press, 1992), and "entrepreneurial government," D. Osborne and T. Gaebler, *Reinventing Government: How the Entrepreneurial Spirit Is Transforming the Public Sector* (New York: Penguin, 1992).
3. D. Osborne and P. Plastrik, *Banishing Bureaucracy: The Five Strategies for Reinventing Government* (Reading MA: Addison-Wesley, 1997), p. 41.
4. C. Ban and N. M. Riccucci (eds), *Public Personnel Management: Current Concerns, Future Challenges*, 2nd ed. (White Plains, NY: Longman, 1997).
5. L. M. Lane and J. F. Wolf, *The Human Resource Crisis in the Public Sector: Rebuilding the Capacity to Govern* (New York: Quorum Books, 1990), p. 16.
6. OECD, *Performance Management in Government: Performance Measurement and Results-Oriented Management*, Public Management Occasional Papers No. 3 (Paris: OECD, 1994), p. 76.

7. R. Common, *Global Impacts on Public Administration in Hong Kong*, Occasional Paper Series, No. 1 (Hong Kong: City University of Hong Kong, Department of Public and Social Administration, 1998).

8. For a topical discussion of these issues as they were emerging refer to A.B.L. Cheung, "The Civil Service," in *The Other Hong Kong Report 1990, 1991, 1995, 1996*; K. W. Chow, "The Civil Service," in *The Other Hong Kong Report 1992*; J. C. Y. Lee, "Civil Servants," in *The Other Hong Kong Report 1994*; and F. Wong, "The Civil Service," *The Other Hong Kong Report 1997*. *The Other Hong Kong Report* was published by The Chinese University Press, Hong Kong.

9. For a complete discussion of this piece of research refer to J.C.Y. Lee, *The Other Hong Kong Report 1994*, pp. 39–59.

10. *South China Morning Post*, 27 October 1994.

11. A.B.L. Cheung, "Efficiency as the Rhetoric: Public-Sector Reform in Hong Kong Explained," *International Review of Administrative Sciences*, Vol. 62, No. 1 (March 1996), pp. 31–47.

12. E.W.Y. Lee, "The Political Economy of Public Sector Reform in Hong Kong: The Case of a Colonial-Developmental State," *International Review of Administrative Sciences*, Vol. 64, No. 4 (December 1998), pp. 625–41.

13. "While the economy turned sour, the civil service staggered from one disaster and mistake to another, with the avian flu, occasioning the slaughter of millions of live chickens, a massive red tide which heavily damaged the fish farming industry, a dramatic drop in tourism following a bungled tourism advertising campaign, and repeated and gross health authority errors plaguing it through the fall and winter." M. DeGolyer, "The Civil Service," in *The Other Hong Kong Report 1998* (Hong Kong: The Chinese University Press, 1998), p. 86.

14. Ibid.

15. *South China Morning Post*, 4 January 1999; 11 February 1999.

16. *South China Morning Post*, 20 February 1999.

17. W. Bruce, *Problem Employee Management* (New York: Quorum Books, 1990), p. 1.

18. M. Boyd, "One Bad Apple," *Incentive*, August 1994, p. 64.

19. "Issues Under Consideration": Extract from a speech by the Chief Executive HKSAR to the Legislative Council, 14 January 1999. http://www.info.gov.hk/eu/best/cs_con.htm (15 February 1999).

20. The 1999–2000 Budget *Onward With New Strengths*, Speech by the Financial Secretary the Hon. Donald Tsang, 3 March 1999. http://www.info.gov.hk/bdgt/1999–2000/english/eindex.htm, 7 March 1999.

21. Civil Service Bureau, *Civil Service Reform Consultation Document* (March 1999).

22. D. McGregor, *The Human Side of Enterprise* (New York: McGraw-Hill, 1960).

23. See for example A. Lawton and A. G. Rose, *Organisation and Management in the Public Sector* (London: Pitman, 1991); G. Zajac and A. Al-Kazemi, "Reinventing

Government and Redefining Leadership: Implications for Personnel Management in Government," *Public Productivity and Management Review*, Vol. 20, No. 4 (1997), pp. 372–83.

24. *South China Morning Post*, 10 January 1999.

25. M. J. Enright, E. E. Scott and D. Dodwell, *The Hong Kong Advantage* (Hong Kong: Oxford University Press, 1997).

26. W. Boeker, "Strategic Change: The Influence of Managerial Characteristics and Organizational Growth," *Academy of Management Journal*, Vol. 40, No. 1 (February 1997), pp. 152–70; and W. Boeker, "Executive Migration and Strategic Change: The Effect of Top Manager Movement on Product Market Entry," *Administrative Science Quarterly*, Vol. 42, No. 2 (June 1997), pp. 213–36.

27. Zajac and Al-Kazemi (Note 23), p. 276.

28. *South China Morning Post*, 10 March 1999.

29. Enright (Note 25).

30. R. F. Adie and P. G. Thomas, *Canadian Public Administration: Problematic Perspectives*, 2nd ed. (Scarborough: Prentice-Hall, 1987), p. 56.

31. Refer to C. Mabey and G. Salaman, *Strategic Human Resource Management* (London: Blackwell, 1995) and J. Geary, "Pay, Control and Commitment: Linking Appraisal and Reward," *Human Resource Management Journal*, Vol. 2, No. 4 (1992), pp. 36–54 cited in A. Kelly and K. Monks, "View from the Bridge and Life on Deck: Contrasts and Contradictions in Performance-Related Pay," in *Experiencing Human Resource Management*, edited by C. Mabey, C. Skinner, and T. Clark (London: Sage, 1998), pp. 113–28.

32. E. E. Lawler, III and J. R. Hackman, "Impact of Employee Participation in the Development of Incentive Plans: A Field Experiment," *Journal of Applied Psychology*, Vol. 53 (1969), pp. 467–71, and K. C. Schefflen, E. E. Lawler, III and J. R. Hackman "Long Term Impact of Employee Participation in the Development of Pay Incentive Plans: A Field Experiment Revisited," *Journal of Applied Psychology*, Vol. 55 (1971), pp. 182–86, cited in Kelly and Monks in Mabey, et al. (eds) (Note 31).

33. See Note 22, p. 83.

34. S. Ranson and J. Stewart, *Managing for the Public Domain: Enabling the Learning Society* (New York: St. Martin's Press, 1994), p. 263.

35. See Note 22, p. 49.

36. *South China Morning Post*, 20 August 1999.

37. Zajac and Al-Kazemi (Note 23), p. 374.

38. Public Services Division, Government of Singapore (1997) http://www.gov.sg/ps21/case5.html (20 February 1999).

39. D. F. Kettl, "The Global Revolution in Public Management: Driving Themes, Missing Links," *Journal of Policy Analysis and Management*, Vol. 16, No. 3 (1997), p. 454.

40. Ibid.

41. E. M. Berman, *Productivity in Public and Nonprofit Organizations: Strategies and Techniques* (Thousand Oaks, CA.: Sage, 1998). There is an extensive literature on this issue, see for example G. T. Allison, Jr., "Public and Private Management: Are They Fundamentally Alike in All Unimportant Respects?" (1979) in *Current Issues in Public Administration*, edited by F. S. Lane, 3rd ed. (New York: St. Martin's Press, 1986); M. A. Murray, "Comparing Public and Private Management: An Exploratory Essay," *Public Administration Review*, Vol. 35 (July/August 1975), pp. 364–371, H. G. Rainey, *Understanding and Managing Public Organizations*, 2nd ed. (San Francisco: Jossey-Bass,1997); H. G. Rainey, R. W. Backoff, and C. H. Levine "Comparing Public and Private Organizations," *Public Administration Review*, Vol. 36 (1976), pp. 233–44.

42. The "scapegoating" of civil servants in the United States has been identified as a process that began in the 1970s and reached a crescendo in the 1980s. See C. J. Fox and H. T. Miller, *Postmodern Public Administration: Toward Discourse* (Thousand Oaks, CA.: Sage, 1995), p. 5.

43. P. Aucoin, "The Design of Public Organizations of the 21st Century: Why Bureaucracy Will Survive in Public Management," *Canadian Public Administration*, Vol. 40, No. 2 (Summer 1997), pp. 290–306.

44. P. Larson, "Public and Private Values at Odds: Can Private Sector Values Be Transplanted into Public Sector Institutions?" *Public Administration and Development*, No. 17 (1997), pp. 131–139; C. Pollitt and H. Summa, "Trajectories of Reform: Public Management Change in Four Countries," *Public Money and Management*, Vol. 17, No. 1 (1997), pp. 7–18; Zajac and Al-Kazemi (Note 23).

45. Enright, et al. (Note 25); N. Miners, *The Government and Politics of Hong Kong*, 5th edition (Hong Kong: Oxford University Press, 1991).

46. Pollitt and Summa (Note 44).

47. Aucoin (Note 43).

48. Zajac and Al-Kazemi (Note 23), p. 279.

49. Ibid.

50. F. C. Thayer, "The President's Management 'Reforms': Theory X Triumphant," in *Legislating Bureaucratic Change: The Civil Service Reform Act of 1978*, edited by P. W. Ingraham and C. Ban (Albany: State University of New York Press), pp. 29–41.

51. P. C. Light, *The Tides of Reform: Making Government Work, 1945–1995* (New Haven and London: Yale University Press), p. 181.

Selected Bibliography

Adie, R. F. and P. G. Thomas. *Canadian Public Administration: Problematic Perspectives*, 2nd ed. Scarborough: Prentice-Hall, 1987.

Adler, E. and P. Haas. "Conclusion: Epistemic Communities, World Order, and the Creation of a Reflective Research Program." *International Organization,* Vol. 46, No. 1 (1992), pp. 367–90.

Allison, G. T., Jr. "Public and Private Management: Are They Fundamentally Alike in All Unimportant Respects?" In *Current Issues in Public Administration*, edited by F. S. Lane, 3rd ed., pp. 184–200. New York: St. Martin's Press, 1986.

Argyris, C. *Integrating the Individual and the Organisation.* New York: Wiley, 1964.

Ascher, K. *The Politics of Privatisation: Contracting Out Public Services.* London: Macmillan, 1987.

Aucoin, P. "Contraction, Managerialism and Decentralization in Canadian government." *Governance*, Vol. 1, No. 2 (1988), pp. 144–61.

———. "Administrative Reform in Public Management: Paradigms, Principles, Paradoxes and Pendulums." *Governance*, Vol. 3, No. 2 (1990), pp. 115–37.

———. "The Design of Public Organizations for the 21st Century: Why Bureaucracy Will Survive in Public Management." *Canadian Public Administration*, Vol. 4, No. 2 (Summer 1997), pp. 290–306.

Ban, C. "Hiring in the Public Sector: 'Expediency Management' or Structural Reform?" In *Public Personnel Management: Current Concerns, Future Challenges*, 2nd ed., edited by C. Ban and N. M. Riccucci. White Plains, NY: Longman, 1997.

Ban, C. and N. M. Riccucci (eds.) *Public Personnel Management: Current Concerns, Future Challenges*, 2nd ed. White Plains, NY: Longman, 1997.

Barzelay, M. *Breaking Through Bureaucracy: A New Vision for Managing in Government.* Berkeley and Los Angeles: University of California Press, 1992.

Belloubet-Friei, N. and G. Timsit. "Administration Transfigured: A New Administrative Paradigm?" *International Review of Administrative Sciences*, Vol. 59, No. 4 (December 1993), pp. 531–68.

Berman, E. M. *Productivity in Public and Nonprofit Organizations: Strategies and Techniques.* Thousand Oaks, CA.: Sage, 1998.

Birnbaum, P. and G. Wong. "Organizational Structure of Multinational Banks in

Hong Kong from a Culture-Free Perspective." *Administrative Science Quarterly,* Vol. 30 (1985), pp. 262–77.

Bjorkman, J. and C. Altenstetter. "Globalized Concepts and Localized Practice: Convergence and Divergence in National Health Policy Reforms." In *Health Policy Reforms, National Variations and Globalization,* edited by C. Altenstetter and J. Bjorkman. Basingstoke: Macmillan, 1997.

Blair, T. "Modernising Public Service." A speech to a conference on *Transforming Governments in the 21st Century* at Washington, D.C., 18 January 1999.

Boeker, W. "Strategic Change: The Influence of Managerial Characteristics and Organizational Growth." *Academy of Management Journal,* Vol. 40, No. 1 (February 1997), pp. 152–70.

———. "Executive Migration and Strategic Change: The Effect of Top Manager Movement on Product Market Entry." *Administrative Science Quarterly,* Vol. 42, No. 2 (June 1997), pp. 213–36.

Bogdanor, V. "Can Government Be Run Like a Business?" London: Public Finance Foundation: CIPFA — The Chartered Institute of Public Finance and Accountancy. 1994.

Boston, J. et al. *Reshaping the State — New Zealand's Bureaucratic Revolution.* Auckland: Oxford University Press, 1991.

Brewer, B. "Convergence in Public Sector Management." Paper presented to *The State in the Asia-Pacific* conference. Hong Kong: City University of Hong Kong, 6–7 June 1998.

British Government, *Better Accounting for the Taxpayer's Money* (Cmnd 2929). London: HMSO. July 1995.

Bruce, W. *Problem Employee Management.* New York: Quorum Books, 1990.

Burns, J. "Administrative Reform in a Changing Political Environment: The Case of Hong Kong." *Public Administration and Development,* Vol. 14 (1994), pp. 241–52.

Caiden, G. E. *Administration Reform Comes of Age.* New York: de Gruyter, 1991.

Caldwell, B. J. and J. M. Spinks. *The Self-managing School.* London: Falmer Press, 1998.

Campbell, C. and J. Halligan. *Political Leadership in an Age of Constraint: Bureaucratic Politics Under Hawke and Keating.* Sydney: Allen & Unwin, 1992.

Carroll, B. J. (ed.). *Private Means, Public Ends: Private Business in Social Service Delivery.* New York: Praeger Publisher, 1987.

Carter, N., R. Klein and P. Day. *How Organisations Measure Success: The Use of Performance Indicators in Government.* London and New York: Routledge, 1992.

Casper, D. E. *Privatization Policy: An International Perspective.* Monticello, Illinois: Vance Bibliographies, 1987.

Castles, F. G. "The Dynamics of Policy Change: What Happened to the English-speaking Nations in the 1980s?" *European Journal of Political Research*, Vol. 18 (1990), pp. 491–513.

Castles, F. (ed.). *The Impact of Parties: Politics and Policies in Democratic Capitalist States*. London: Sage, 1982.

Castles, F. and C. Pierson. "A New Convergence? Recent Policy Developments in the United Kingdoms, Australia and New Zealand." *Policy and Politics,* Vol. 24, No. 3 (1996), pp. 233–45.

Cave, M., M. Kogan and R. Smith. *Output and Performance Measurement in Government: The State of the Art*. London: Jessica Kingsley, 1990.

Cerny, P. *Globalization and The Changing Logic of Collective Action*, Working Paper No. 5, Department of Politics, University of York (September, 1994).

———. "The Dynamics of Financial Globalization: Technology, Market Structure and Policy Response." *Policy Sciences,* Vol. 24, No. 4 (1994), pp. 319–42.

———. "Paradoxes of the Competition State: The Dynamics of Political Globalization." *Government and Opposition*, Vol. 32, No. 2 (1997), pp. 251–74.

Chan, A. "Continuity and Change." Speech delivered at the 14th Gordon Arthur Ransome Orathion at the 32nd Singapore-Malaysia Congress of Medicine, August, 1998.

Chan, H. M. and J.Y.H. Leung. "Education." In *Social Policy in Hong Kong,* edited by P. Wilding, A. S. Huque and J. P. W. Tao. Cheltenham: Edward Elgar, 1997.

Chan, M. "The Future of Hong Kong." *Annals of the American Academy of Political and Social Science*, Vol. 547 (1996), pp. 11–23.

Chen, M. *Asian Management Systems*. London: ITP, 1995.

Cheung, A.B.L. "The Civil Service." In *The Other Hong Kong Report 1990*, edited by R. Y. C. Wong and J.Y.S. Cheng. Hong Kong: The Chinese University Press, 1990.

———. "The Civil Service." In *The Other Hong Kong Report 1991*, edited by Y. W. Sung and M. K. Lee. Hong Kong: The Chinese University Press, 1991.

———. "Public Sector Reform in Hong Kong: Perspectives and Problems." *The Asian Journal of Public Administration*, Vol. 14, No. 2 (December 1992), pp. 115–48.

———. *The Politics of Administrative Reforms in Hong Kong: Corporatization of Public Services during the 1980s*. Unpublished Ph.D. thesis, London School of Economics, 1995.

———. "The Civil Service in Transition." In *The Other Hong Kong Report 1995*, edited by S.Y.L. Cheung and S.M.H. Sze. Hong Kong: The Chinese University Press, 1995.

———. "Performance Pledges — Power to the Consumer or a Quagmire in Public

Service Legitimation?" *International Journal of Public Administration,* Vol. 19, No. 2 (February 1996), pp. 233–60.

———. "Efficiency as the Rhetoric: Public-Sector Reform in Hong Kong Explained." *International Review of Administrative Sciences,* Vol. 62, No. 1 (March 1996), pp. 31–47.

———. "Civil Service Reform in Shenzhen: Expectations and Problems." In *Economic and Social Development in the Pearl River Delta,* edited by S. MacPherson and J.Y.S. Cheng. Aldershot: Edward Elgar, 1996, pp. 76–106.

———. "Rebureaucratization of Politics in Hong Kong: Prospects after 1997." *Asian Survey,* Vol. 37, No. 9 (1997), pp. 720–37.

———. "Understanding Public-sector Reforms: Global Trends and Diverse Agendas." *International Review of Administrative Science,* Vol. 63 (1997), pp. 435–57.

———. "The Civil Service in Transition." In *The Other Hong Kong Report 1996,* edited by M. K. Nyaw and S. M. Li. Hong Kong: The Chinese University Press, 1997.

Chow, K. W. "Hong Kong Public Administration under Stress: The Significance and Implications of Management Paradoxes." *International Journal of Public Administration,* Vol. 15, No. 9 (1992), pp. 1633–63.

Chun, A. "Discourses of Identity in the Changing Spaces of Public Culture in Taiwan, Hong Kong and Singapore." *Theory, Culture and Society,* Vol. 13, No. 1 (1996), pp. 51–75.

Civil Service Bureau, *Civil Service into the 21st Century — Civil Service Reform.* Hong Kong: Printer Department, 8 March 1999.

Clark, C. and S. Chan. "MNCs and Developmentalism: Domestic Structure as an explanation for East Asian Dynamism." In *Bringing Transnational Relations Back In,* edited by T. Risse-Kappen. Cambridge: Cambridge University Press, 1995.

Clegg, S. W. "Radical Revisions: Power, Discipline and Organizations." *Organizational Studies,* Vol. 10, No. 1 (1989), pp. 97–115.

Common, R. *Global Impacts on Public Administration in Hong Kong.* City University of Hong Kong, Department of Public and Social Administration, Occasional Paper Series, No. 1, 1998.

Cousins, M. "The Quality of Public Services: Clarifying Conceptual Issues." *Administration,* Vol. 44, No. 4 (Winter 1996–97), pp. 83–92.

DeGolyer, M. E. "The Civil Service." In *The Other Hong Kong Report 1998,* edited by L.C.H. Chow and Y. K. Fan. Hong Kong: The Chinese University Press, 1999.

Democratic Party, *What Price Efficiency? A Review of Hong Kong Trading Funds* [in Chinese]. Hong Kong, October 1996.

Derlien, H. U. "Historical Legacy and Recent Developments of the German Higher

Civil Service." *International Review of Administrative Sciences*, Vol. 57, No 3 (September 1991), pp. 385–401.

———. "Administration Research in Europe — Rather Comparable Than Comparative." *Governance*, Vol. 5, No. 3 (July 1992), pp. 279–311.

DiMaggio, P. and W. Powell. (eds.). *The New Institutionalism in Organizational Analysis*. Chicago and London: University of Chicago Press, 1991.

Dong, L. S. "The Establishment of the Chinese Civil Service System: A Delayed Political Reform Programme." In *Administrative Reform in the People's Republic of China since 1978*, Working Papers Series 1. Leiden, The Netherlands (1994), pp. 43–61.

Downs, G. W. and P. D. Larkey. *The Search for Government Efficiency*. Philadelphia: Temple University Press, 1986.

Dunleavy, P. "Explaining the Privatization Boom: Public Choice versus Radical Approaches." *Public Administration*, Vol. 64, No 1 (Spring 1986), pp. 13–34.

———. *Democracy, Bureaucracy and Public Choice — Economic Explanations in Political Science*. Harvester: Wheatsheaf, 1991.

———. "The Globalization of Public Services Production: Can Government be 'Best in the World'?" *Public Policy and Administration,* Vol. 9, No. 2 (1994), pp. 36–64.

Dunsire, A. *Administration: The Word and the Science*. London: Martin Robertson, 1973.

Education Department. *School Management Initiative (SMI) Handbook*. Hong Kong: Government Printer, 1996.

———. *Quality School Education,* Education Commission Report No. 7, Hong Kong: Government Printer, 1997.

Education and Manpower Branch. *Transforming Schools into Dynamic and Accountable Professional Learning Communities, School-based Management Consultation Document*, Hong Kong: Printing Department, February 2000.

Education and Manpower Branch and Education Department, *The School Management Initiative*. Hong Kong: Government Printer, 1991.

Efficiency Unit. *Evaluation of Performance Pledges Programme* (leaflet), Hong Kong: Printing Department, August 1998.

———. *Legislative Council Brief: Trading Fund Bill 1992* (EUCR 11/92). Hong Kong, 1992.

———. *Serving the Community*. Hong Kong: Government Printer, 1995.

Efficiency Unit (UK). *Improving Management in Government: The Next Steps*. London: Her Majesty's Stationery Office, 1989.

Enright, M. J., E. E. Scott and D. Dodwell. *The Hong Kong Advantage*. Hong Kong: Oxford University Press, 1997.

Ferlie, E. L., L. F. Ashburner and A. Pettigrew, *The New Public Management in Action*. Oxford: Oxford University Press, 1996.

Ferranti, Deavid de. "Foreword." In *Decentralization of Education, Teacher Management*, edited by Cathy Gaynor, Washington: The World Bank, 1998.

Finance Branch. *Public Sector Reform*. Hong Kong: Government Printer, 1989.

———. *Report on the Review of the Operation of the Trading Fund Scheme*. Hong Kong: Government Printer, 1996.

———, *Review of the Trading Fund Operation: Update as at March 1997*. Hong Kong: Government Printer, 1997.

Flynn, N. and F. Strehl (eds). *Public Sector Management in Europe*. London: Prentice Hall & Harvester Wheatsheaf, 1996.

Flynn, N. *Public Sector Management*, 3rd ed. Hemel Hempstead: Harvester-Wheatsheaf, 1997.

Forrest, R. and A. Murie. *Selling the Welfare State: The Privatisation of Public Housing*. London: Routledge, 1988.

Fox, C. J. and H. T. Miller. *Postmodern Public Administration: Toward Discourse*. Thousand Oaks, CA.: Sage, 1995.

Fox, C. J. and K. A. Shirkey. "Employee Performance Appraisal: The Keystone Made of Clay." In *Public Personnel Management: Current Concerns, Future Challenges*, 2nd ed., edited by C. Ban and N. M. Riccucci. White Plains, N.Y.: Longman, 1997.

Fraser, R. and M. Wilson. *Privatization: The UK Experience and International Trends*. Harlow, Essex: Longman, 1988.

Frederickson, H. G. "Comparing the Reinventing Government Movement with the New Public Administration." *Public Administration Review*, Vol. 56, No. 3 (1996), pp. 263–70.

Fukuyama, F. *The End of History and the Last Man*. London: Hamish Hamilton, 1992.

Geary, J. "Pay, Control and Commitment: Linking Appraisal and Reward." *Human Resource Management Journal*, Vol. 2, No. 4 (1992), pp. 36–54.

Godwin, C. D. "Pilot Study One: The School Education Programme: Redefining the Relationship between Policy Branch and Department." In *Public Sector Reform in Hong Kong*, edited by J.C.Y. Lee and A.B.L. Cheung. Hong Kong: The Chinese University Press, 1995.

Gore, A. *From Red Tape to Results: Creating a Government That Works Better and Costs Less — Report of the National Performance Review*. New York: Plume, 1993.

Government of Canada. *Public Service 2000: The Renewal of the Public Service of Canada*. Ottawa: Supply & Services, 1990.

Greer, P. *Transforming Central Government: The Next Steps Initiative*. Buckingham: Open University Press, 1994.

Halligan, J. "The Art of Reinvention: The United States National Performance

Review." *Australian Journal of Public Administration*, Vol. 53, No. 2 (June 1994), pp. 135–43.

Hanke, S. H. "The Theory of Privatization." In *The Privatization Option: A Strategy to Shrink the Size of Government*, edited by S. M. Butler. Washington, DC: The Heritage Foundation, 1985.

Harris, P. *Hong Kong: A Study in Bureaucracy and Politics*. Hong Kong: Macmillan, 1998.

Harrop, M. (ed.). "Comparison." In *Power and Policy in Liberal Democracies*. Cambridge, Cambridge University Press, 1992.

Hills, J. *Deregulating Telecoms: Competition and Control in the United States, Japan and Britain*. Westport, Connecticut: Quorum Books, 1986.

Hofstede, G. *Culture's Consequences*. Beverly Hills, CA: Sage, 1980.

———. *Cultures and Organizations*. New York: McGraw-Hill 1997.

Holmes, M. "Public Sector Management Reform: Convergence or Divergence?" *Governance*, Vol. 5, No. 4 (October 1992), pp. 472–83.

Holmes, M. and D. Shand. "Management Reforms: Some Practitioners Perspectives on the Past Ten Years." *Governance*, Vol. 8, No. 4 (1995), pp. 551–78.

Hong Kong Government. *Enhanced Productivity Programme, 1999–2000* (leaflet). Hong Kong: Printing Department 1999.

Hood, C. "Beyond the Public Bureaucracy State? Public Administration in the 1990s." Extended text of an inaugural lecture on 16 January 1990. London: London School of Economics.

———. "De-Sir-Humphrey-fying the Westminster Model of Governance." *Governance*, Vol. 3, No. 2 (April 1990), pp. 205–14.

———. "A Public Management for All Seasons?" *Public Administration*, Vol. 69, No. 1 (Spring 1991), pp. 3–19.

———. *Explaining Economic Policy Reversals*. Buckingham: Open University Press, 1994.

———. "Exploring Variations in 1980s Public Management Reform." In H. Bekke, J. L. Perry and T. A. J. Toonen. (eds). *Civil Service Systems in Comparative Perspective*. Bloomington: Indiana University Press, 1996.

———. "Beyond 'Progressivism': A New 'Global Paradigm' in Public Management?" *International Journal of Public Administration*, Vol. 19, No 2 (February 1996), pp. 151–78.

Hood, C. and M. Jackson. *Administrative Argument*. Aldershot: Dartmouth, 1991.

Hood, C. et al. *Regulation Inside Government: Waste-Watchers, Quality Police and Sleaze-Buster*. Oxford: Oxford University Press, 1999.

Hook, B. "British Views of the Legacy of the Colonial Administration of Hong Kong: A Preliminary Assessment." *The China Quarterly*, No. 151 (1997), pp. 553 66.

Housing Authority. *A Review of Private Sector Involvement in Estates Management and Maintenance Services — A Final Report.* Hong Kong: Hong Kong Government Printer, February 1999.

Hughes, O. E. *Public Management and Administration: An Introduction,* 2nd ed. London: Macmillan Press, 1998.

Huque, A. S., G.O.M. Lee and A.B.L. Cheung. *The Civil Service in Hong Kong: Continuity and Change.* Hong Kong: Hong Kong University Press, 1998.

Ingraham, P. "The Reform Agenda for National Civil Service Systems: External Stress and Internal Strains." In *Civil Service Systems in Comparative Perspective,* edited by H. Bekke, J. Perry and Y. Toonen. Bloomington, Ind.: Indiana University Press, 1996.

Islam, I. and A. Chowdhury. *Asia-Pacific Economies: A Survey.* London: Routledge, 1997.

Kelly, A. and K. Monks. "View from the Bridge and Life on Deck: Contrasts and Contradictions in Performance-Related Pay." In *Experiencing Human Resource Management,* edited by C. Mabey, D. Skinner, and T. Clark. London: Sage, 1998.

Kelly, R. M. "An Inclusive Democratic Polity, Representative Bureaucracies, and the New Public Management." *Public Administration Review,* Vol. 58, No. 8 (1998), pp. 201–8.

Kettl, D. F. "Performance and Accountability: The Challenge of Government by Proxy for Public Administration." *American Review of Public Administration,* Vol. 18 (1 March 1988), pp. 9–28.

———. "Public Administration: The State of the Field." In *Political Science: The State of the Discipline,* edited by A. W. Finifter. Washington, DC: American Political Science Association, 1993, pp. 407–28.

———. "The Global Revolution in Public Management: Driving Themes, Missing Links." *Journal of Policy Analysis and Management,* Vol. 16, No. 3 (1997), pp. 446–62.

Kingdon, J. *Agendas, Alternatives and Public Policies.* Boston: Little Brown, 1984.

Kluth, M. and J. Andersen. "The Globalization of European Research and Technology Organizations (RTOs)." In *Beyond Master and Hierarchy: Interactive Governance and Social Complexity,* edited by A. Amin and J. Hausner. Cheltenham: Edward Elgar, 1997.

Lachman, R., A. Nedd and B. Hinings. "Analyzing Cross-National Management and Organizations: A Theoretical Framework." *Management Science,* Vol. 40, No. 1 (1994), pp. 40–55.

Lam, J. "From a Colonial to an Accountable Administration: Hong Kong's Experience." *Asian Affairs,* Vol. 26 (1995), pp. 305–13.

Lan, Z. Y. and D. H. Rosenbloom. "Public Administration in Transition?" (Editorial),

Public Administration Review, Vol. 52, No. 6 (November/December 1992), pp. 535–37.

Lane, J. E. *The Public Sector*. London: Sage, 1993.

———. "Will Public Management Drive Out Public Administration?" *The Asian Journal of Public Administration*, Vol. 16, No. 2 (Dec 1994), pp. 139–51.

Lane, L. M. and J. F. Wolf. *The Human Resource Crisis in the Public Sector: Rebuilding the Capacity to Govern*. New York: Quorum Books, 1990.

Larson, P. "Public and Private Values at Odds: Can Private Sector Values Be Transplanted into Public Sector Institutions?" *Public Administration and Development*, Vol. 17 (1997), pp. 131–39.

Law, F. "Hong Kong: The Challenge of Managing the Government's Human Resources." In *Public Sector Reform: Critical Issues and Perspectives*, edited by I. Scott and I. Thynne (Hong Kong: AJPA, 1994).

Lawler, E. E. and J. R. Hackman. "Impact of Employee Participation in the Development of Incentive Plans: A Field Experiment." *Journal of Applied Psychology*, Vol. 53 (1969), pp. 467–71.

Lawton, A. and A. G. Rose. *Organisation and Management in the Public Sector*. London: Pitman, 1994.

Lee, E.W.Y. "The Political Economy of Public Sector Reform in Hong Kong: The Case of a Colonial-Developmental State." *International Review of Administrative Sciences*, Vol. 64. No. 4 (December 1998), pp. 625–41.

Lee, G. and A. S. Huque. "Hong Kong: Administrative Reform and Recent Public Sector Changes — The Institutionalisation of New Values." *Australian Journal of Public Administration,* Vol. 55, No. 49 (1996), pp. 13–21.

Lee, J.C.Y. "Civil Servants." In *The Other Hong Kong Report 1994*, edited by D. H. McMillen and S. W. Man. Hong Kong: The Chinese University Press, 1994, pp. 39–59.

Lee, J.C.Y. and A.B.L. Cheung (eds). *Public Sector Reform in Hong Kong*. Hong Kong: The Chinese University Press, 1995.

LeHerissier, R. "Implications of Overseas Experiences for Public Sector Reform in Hong Kong: Perspectives and Limitations." In *Public Sector Reform in Hong Kong*, edited by J.C.Y. Lee and A.B.L. Cheung. Hong Kong: The Chinese University Press, 1995.

Letwin, O. *Privatising the World: A Study of International Privatisation in Theory and Practice*. London: Cassell, 1988.

Likert, R. *New Patterns of Management*. New York: McGraw-Hill, 1961.

Light, P. C. *The Tides of Reform: Making Government Work, 1945–1995*. New Haven and London: Yale University Press, 1997.

Liou, K. T. "Privatizing State-owned Enterprises: The Taiwan Experience." *International Review of Administrative Sciences*, Vol. 58, No. 3 (September 1992), pp. 403–19.

Lui, T. T. "Changing Civil Servants' Values." In *The Hong Kong Civil Service and Its Future*, edited by I. Scott and J. P. Burns. Hong Kong: Oxford University Press, 1988.

———. "Efficiency as a Political Concept in Hong Kong Government: Issues and Problems." In *Asian Civil Service Systems: Improving Efficiency and Productivity*, edited by J. Burns. Singapore: Time Academic Press, 1994.

Luke, J. "Managing Interconnectedness for Public Managers." In *Public Management in as Interconnected World*, edited by M. B. Timney and R. Mayer. Westport, CT: Greenwood Press, 1992.

Lynn Jr, L. E. "The New Public Management as an International Phenomenon: A Skeptical View." Paper presented at the Conference on The New Public Management in International Perspective, St Gallen, Switzerland (11–13 July 1996).

Mabey, C. and G. Salaman. *Strategic Human Resource Management*. London: Blackwell, 1995.

March, J. G. and J. P. Olsen. *Rediscovering Institutions: The Organizational Basis of Politics*. New York: Free Press, 1989.

Massey, A. "In Search of the State: Markets, Myths and Paradigms." In *Globalization and Marketization of Government Services*, edited by A. Massey. Basingstoke: Macmillan, 1997.

McGregor, D. *The Human Side of Enterprise*. New York: McGraw-Hill, 1960.

McKinsey & Co. *The Machinery of Government: A New Framework for Expanding Services*. Hong Kong: Hong Kong Government Printer, 1973.

Metcalfe, L. and S. Richards. *Improving Public Management*, 2nd ed. London: Sage Publications Ltd., 1990.

Metcalfe, L. "Public Management: From Imitation to Innovation." In *Modern Governance*, edited by J. Kooiman. London: Sage, 1993.

Micklethwait, J. and A. Wooldridge. *The Witch Doctors*. London: Heinemann, 1996.

Miners, N. *The Government and Politics of Hong Kong*, 5th ed. Hong Kong: Oxford University Press, 1991.

Moe, R. C. "The 'Reinventing Government' Exercise: Misinterpreting the Problem, Misjudging the Consequences." *Public Administration Review*, Vol. 54, No. 2 (March/April 1994), pp. 111–22.

Mueller, H. E. *Bureaucracy, Education and Monopoly: Civil Service Reforms in England and Prussia*. Berkeley: University of California Press, 1984.

Murray, M. A. "Comparing Public and Private Management: An Exploratory Essay." *Public Administration Review*, Vol. 35 (July/August 1975), pp. 364–71.

Nagel, J. "Radically Reinventing Government: Editor's Introduction." *Journal of Policy Analysis and Management,* Vol.16, No. 3 (1997), pp. 349–56.

OECD. *Public Management: OECD Country Profiles*. Paris: Public Management Service (PUMA), OECD, 1993.

———. *Performance Management in Government: Performance Measurement and Results-Oriented Management.* Paris: OECD Public Management Occasional Papers No. 3, 1994.

———. *Senior Civil Service Pay: A Study of Eleven OECD Countries 1980–1991.* Paris: OECD: Public Management Occasional Papers No. 4, 1994.

———. *Public Management Developments Update 1995.* Paris: Public Management Service (PUMA), OECD, 1995.

———. *Governance in Transition: Public Management Reforms in OECD Countries.* Paris: Public Management Service (PUMA), OECD, 1995.

———. "Globalization: What Challenges and Opportunities for Governments?" Paris: Public Management Service (PUMA), OECD, July 1996.

———. *Measuring Public Employment in OECD Countries: Sources, Methods and Results.* Paris: OECD, 1997.

Olsen, J. P. *The Modernisation of Public Administration in the Nordic Countries.* Bergen: University of Bergen, 1987.

Osborne, D. and P. Plastrik. *Banishing Bureaucracy: The Five Strategies for Reinventing Government.* Reading, MA: Addison-Wesley, 1997.

Osborne, D. and T. Gaebler. *Reinventing Government: How the Entrepreneurial Spirit Is Transforming the Public Sector.* New York: Penguin, 1992.

Peters, B. G. "Theory and Methodology in the Study of Comparative Public Administration." In *Comparative Public Management*, edited by R. Baker. Westport, Conn.: Praeger, 1994.

———. "Models of Governance for the 1990s." In *The State of Public Management*, edited by D. F. Kettl and H. Brinton Milward. Johns Hopkins University Press, 1996.

———. *The Future of Governing: Four Emerging Models,* Kansas: University Press of Kansas, 1996.

———. "Policy Transfers Between Governments: The Case of Administrative Reforms." *West European Politics,* Vol. 20, No. 4 (1997), pp. 71–88.

Peters, B. G. and D. J. Savoie. "Civil Service Reform: Misdiagnosing the Patient." *Public Administration Review*, Vol. 54, No. 5 (September/October 1994), pp. 418–25.

Peters, T. J. and R. H. Waterman. *In Search of Excellence.* New York: Harper & Row, 1982.

Pollitt, C. *Managerialism and the Public Services: The Anglo-American Experience.* Basil and Blackwell: Oxford University Press, 1990.

———. *Managerialism and the Public Services: Cuts or Cultural Change in the 1990s?* 2nd ed. Oxford: Basil Blackwell, 1993.

Pollitt, C. "Justification by Works or by Faith: Evaluating the New Public Management." *Evaluation,* Vol. 1, No. 2 (1995), pp. 133–54.

Pollitt, C. and H. Summa. "Trajectories of Reform: Public Management Change in

Four Countries." *Public Money and Management*, Vol. 17, No. 1 (1997). pp. 7–18.

Price, C. "Economic Regulation of Privatized Monopolies." In *Privatization and Regulation: A Review of the Issues*, edited by P. M. Jackson and C. M. Price. London: Longman, 1994.

Rainey, H. G. *Understanding and Managing Public Organizations*, 2nd ed. San Francisco: Jossey-Bass, 1997.

Rainey, H. G., R. W. Backoff and C. H. Levine. "Comparing Public and Private Organizations." *Public Administration Review*, Vol. 36 (1976), pp. 233–44.

Ranson, S. and J. Stewart. *Management for the Public Domain: Enabling the Learning Society*. New York: St. Martin's Press, 1994.

Rhodes, R. "The New Governance Governing without Government." *Political Studies*, Vol. 44, No. 4 (1996), pp. 652–67.

Richards, S. "Changing Patterns of Legitimation in Public Management." *Public Policy and Administration*, Vol. 7, No. 3 (Winter 1992), pp. 15–28.

Richardson, J. J. (ed.). *Privatisation and Deregulation in Canada and Britain*. Aldershot: Dartmouth, Institute for Research on Public Policy, 1990.

Rockman, B. "The Changing Role of the State." In *Taking stock: Assessing Public Sector Reforms*, edited by B. Peters and D. Savoie. Montreal and Kingston: Canadian Centre for Management Development/McGill-Queen's University Press, 1998.

Root, H. *Small Countries, Big Lessons: Governance and the Rise of East Asia*. Hong Kong: Oxford University Press (China), 1996.

Sankey, C. "Public Sector Reform: Past Development and Recent Trends." *Hong Kong Public Administration*, Vol. 2, No. 1 (1993), pp. 71–93.

Savas, E. S. *Privatization: The Key to Better Government*. New Jersey: Chatham House, 1987.

Schefflen, K. C., E. E. Lawler III and J. R. Hackman. "Long Term Impact of Employee Participation in the Development of Pay Incentive Plans: A Field Experiment Revisited." *Journal of Applied Psychology*, Vol. 55 (1971), pp. 182–86.

Schick, A. "Incremental Budgeting in a Decremental Age." *Policy Sciences*, Vol. 16 (1 September 1983), pp. 1–25.

———. "Macro-budgetary Adaptations to Fiscal Stress in Industrialized Democracies." *Public Administration Review*, Vol. 46 (2 March/April 1986), pp. 124–34.

———. "Micro-budgetary Adaptations to Fiscal Stress in Industrialized Democracies." *Public Administration Review*, Vol. 48 (1 January/February 1988), pp. 23–33.

———. "Why Most Developing Counties Should Not Try New Zealand's Reforms. " *The World Bank Research Observer*, Vol. 13, No. 1 (1998), pp. 123–31.

Schiffer, J. R. *Anatomy of a Laissez-faire Government: The Hong Kong Growth Model Reconsidered.* Hong Kong: Centre of Urban Studies and Urban Planning, University of Hong Kong, 1983.

Schwartz, H. "Reinvention and Retrenchment: Lessons from the Application of the New Zealand Model to Alberta, Canada." *Journal of Policy Analysis and Management,* Vol. 16, No. 3 (1997), pp. 405–22.

Scott, I. "Administration in a Small Capitalist State: The Hong Kong Experience." In *Public Administration in Small and Island States,* edited by R. Baker. West Hartford, Conn.: Kumarian Press, 1992.

Scott, I. and J. P. Burns (eds). *The Hong Kong Civil Service: Personnel Policies and Practices.* Hong Kong: Oxford University Press, 1984.

———. *The Hong Kong Civil Service and Its Future.* Hong Kong: Oxford University Press, 1988.

Seeliger, R. "Conceptualizing and Researching Policy Convergence." *Policy Studies Journal,* Vol. 24, No. 2 (1996), pp. 287–306.

Self, P. *Government By the Market? The Politics of Public Choice.* London: Macmillan, 1993.

Strang, D. and J. Meyer. "Institutional Conditions for Diffusion." *Theory and Society,* Vol. 22, No. 4 (1993), pp. 287–511.

Suleiman, E. N. and J. Waterbury. *The Political Economy of Public Sector Reform and Privatization.* Boulder: Westview Press, 1990.

Swann, D. *The Retreat of the State: Deregulation and Privatisation in the UK and US.* New York: Harvester-Wheatsheaf, 1988.

Terry, L. "Administrative Leadership, Neo-Managerialism, and the Public Management Movement." *Public Administration Review,* Vol. 58, No. 3 (1998), pp. 194–200.

Thayer, F. C. "The President's Management 'Reforms': Theory X Triumphant." In *Legislating Bureaucratic Change: The Civil Service Reform Act of 1978,* edited by P. W. Ingraham and C. Ban. Albany: State University of New York Press, 1984, pp. 29–41.

The Harvard Team, *Improving Hong Kong's Healthcare System: Why and For Whom?* Hong Kong: Hong Kong: Printing Department, April 1999.

Toonen, T.A.J. "Analysing Institutional Change and Administrative Transformation: A Comparative View." *Public Administration,* Vol. 71 (Spring/Summer 1993), pp. 151–68.

Torrington, D. and L. Hall. *Human Resource Management,* 4th ed. London: Prentice Hall, 1998.

Vickers, J. and V. Wright, "The Politics of Industrial Privatization in Western Europe: An Overview." *West European Politics,* Vol. 11, No. 4 (April 1988), pp. 1–30.

Walsh K., V. Lowndes, K. Riley and T. Woollam, "Management in the Public Sector:

A Content Analysis of Journals." *Public Administration*, Vol. 74 (Summer 1996), pp. 315–24.

Waltman, J. and D. Studlar (eds). *Political Economy: Public Policies in the United States and Britain*. Jackson, Miss: University Press of Mississippi, 1987.

Wilensky, H. *The Welfare State and Equality*. London: University of California Press, 1975.

Williamson, O. *The Economic Institutions of Capitalism: Forums, Markets Relational Contracting*. New York: The Free Press, 1985.

Wilson, W. "The Study of Administration." Reprinted in *Political Science Quarterly*, No. 56 (December 1887/1941), pp. 481–506.

Wiltshire, K. *Privatisation: The British Experience*. Harlow, Essex: Longman, 1987.

Wong, F. "The Civil Service." In *The Other Hong Kong Report 1997*, edited by J.Y.S. Cheng. Hong Kong: The Chinese University Press, 1997.

Wong, K. C. "Organizing and Managing Schools." In *Schooling in Hong Kong*, edited by G. A. Postiglione and W. O. Lee. Hong Kong: Hong Kong University Press, 1997.

Wright, V. "Reshaping the State: the Implications for Public Administration." *West European Politics*, Vol. 17, No. 3 (1994), pp. 102–37.

Yeatman, A. *Bureaucrats, Technocrats, Femocrats: Essays on the Contemporary Australian State*. Sydney: Allen & Unwin, 1990.

———. "The Reform of Public Management: An Overview." *Australian Journal of Public Administration*, Vol. 53, No. 3 (September 1994), pp. 287–95.

Yue, D. "Dynamic Public Sector Reform." A speech given to the 17th Graduation Ceremony of the MBA Programme jointly offered by Northwest Louisiana University and Shue Yan College (16 January 1999), Hong Kong.

Zajac, G. and A. Al-Kazemi. "Reinventing Government and Redefining Leadership: Implications for Personnel Management in Government." *Public Productivity and Management Review*, Vol. 20, No. 4 (June 1997), pp. 372–83.

Appendices

APPENDIX A

Finance Branch
Public Sector Reform
(March 1989)

CONTENTS

Reproduced by kind permission of the Hong Kong Government.

PREFACE

Over the last few years the Finance Branch of the Government Secretariat has introduced a number of financial management reforms. They include:—

- a medium range forecast which is now our primary tool in planning public expenditure;
- a resource allocation system to help the Administration make rational decisions about the allocation of resources between policy areas, although at present, this is applied only with regard to new resources;
- the staged transfer of financial authority from Finance Branch giving heads of departments more freedom to manage budgets flexibly;
- greater emphasis on "top-down" value for money studies and the establishment of departmental steering groups to supervise these studies;
- and, arising out of these value for money studies, increased emphasis on performance measurement in order to focus attention on objectives and outcomes rather than activities and outputs.

The Governor, in his address opening the 1988/89 session of the Legislative Council, touched on some of these reforms when he stressed the need to provide a framework for public sector management that would "encourage managers to get more from the resources they are consuming."

In recent months Finance Branch has been considering how this "value for money" concept should be taken forward and, in particular, how achievements already realized should be further developed and expanded into a co-ordinated programme of public sector reform. The result is set out in the following pages.

Essentially, we are seeking a change in the attitude and approach to the spending of public money in order to improve efficiency and give a better service to the public. For the most part we are seeking this change by adapting and developing the structures and procedures that already exist. Thus our proposed reforms are evolutionary rather than revolutionary. However, they do require a change in attitude by civil servants if they are to be successful.

There must be commitment and vision, in particular by top management. But this commitment to more effective management must be in support of the main tasks of the civil service. We must not lose sight of the fact that better management is a means to an end, not an end in itself.

We have made considerable progress in recent years in the field of financial management reform. However, much remains to be done and the issues are somewhat wider than just financial management. We have therefore addressed these issues in the wider context of public sector reform — hence the title of the paper.

We believe that if these ideas for change are implemented, they will result not only in a more efficient and effective service but also greater job satisfaction for all civil servants. **Above all, they will lead to a better service for the community.**

The proposals in this paper are those of Finance Branch and, at this stage, they are proposals for discussion, not agreed policy.

We take this opportunity to acknowledge the help of Francis Plowden, Malcolm Green, David Stafford and, in particular Hugh Ashton all of Coopers & Lybrand. They introduced us to some new concepts in public sector reform based on international experience and the results of this can be seen throughout the paper. They helped us to crystallize our thinking and we are grateful to them for the experience and enthusiasm which they brought to this exercise.

FINANCE BRANCH
FEBRUARY 1989

AIMS AND PRINCIPLES

AIMS OF THE REFORM PROGRAMME

This paper proposes a programme of financial management reforms. The aim of the reform programme is to improve the quality of management within the civil service by promoting an increased awareness of what results are actually being achieved by the government and at what cost.

Why is a reform programme needed? The government is faced with many demands on its resources, both in manpower and financial terms. The level of demand is likely to increase significantly over the next decade, particularly in view of the major infrastructure projects that are now being planned. But resources are limited. An increased expansion of services can therefore only be achieved by improving value for money. So, if broadly the same level of services can be delivered for less resource input, it should be possible to take on the extra commitments.

The reform programme will also give coherence to the various initiatives that we have already begun. These initiatives have been mainly concerned with improving the way resources are allocated and with emphasizing Policy Secretaries' responsibilities for financial management. A comprehensive reform programme can now provide a framework within which these, and other initiatives, can be pursued.

Such a reform programme should concentrate on the following **seven basic principles of financial management reform** to achieve the better management practices we are looking for. In brief, there should be:—

- an ongoing review of the existing base of public expenditure;
- proper evaluation of results;
- better definition of responsibilities;
- a match of resource and management responsibilities;
- appropriate organization and management frameworks;
- clearly defined relationships between policy makers and their executive delivery agents;
- more management and less administration.

A fuller explanation of these principles follows.

THE SEVEN BASIC PRINCIPLES OF FINANCIAL MANAGEMENT REFORM

■ **The fist principle is that the whole of public expenditure should be subjected to regular, systematic review.** At present the annual public expenditure planning cycle is concerned principally with examining the new demands for extra resources, rather than the totality of government spending. In other words, attention is given mainly to the margin, leaving the very substantial base of public expenditure to roll forward into the following year. This base should now be subject to critical review in order to reassess spending priorities in the light of changing circumstances.

■ **The second principle is that a proper system of policy and resource management should be introduced in order to evaluate systematically the achievements and costs of all government activities** and to provide better information for decision-taking. There should be a process by which the government's intentions are put into effect, the results evaluated, and the policy reviewed in the light of experience. This process should be subject to proper management control. At present, little effort is made to evaluate results and the costs incurred. This weakens decision-taking as it means that there is seldom adequate information about achievements and costs.

■ **The third principle is that the responsibility for policy, implementation and resources should be clearly defined and delegated.** In any resource management system it is essential that responsibilities are clearly defined — at all levels, whether at the centre, in branches or in executive agencies.

■ **The fourth principle is that managers should be fully aware of, and be accountable for, all expenditure incurred in support of their policy objectives.** At present, managers responsible for achieving results do not have full responsibility for the resources they consume, particularly for support services, such as vehicles, computing, printing, architectural and engineering services and for some staff.

■ **The fifth principle is that the government should provide services through an organization and a management framework that**

is appropriate to the nature of each service. The functions exercised by the government differ quite fundamentally from each other, depending on whether they are a core service like immigration, a support service like printing or a trading service like the airport. The government also finds it useful to place certain services more or less at arm's length from itself in order to involve wider public participation or to allow management a greater degree of freedom than is possible in a conventional department. A further consideration is the extent to which the cost of the service is met from general revenue or from specific charges on the consumer, as in the case of commercial services.

■ **The sixth principle is that those responsible for policy should ensure that effective relationships with executive agencies are established and made to work.** Whatever the type of executive agency, it will always be necessary to establish a proper relationship between those responsible for policy (usually the Policy Secretary) and the agency. This relationship will define the arrangements for setting objectives, allocating responsibilities and resources, planning, specifying delegated authorities and reporting.

■ **The seventh principle concerns people; every effort should be made to encourage civil servants to become better managers.** Generally, managers should be given increased responsibility for taking decisions within defined policies and budgets. They should also be held accountable for achieving results. This should provide a positive incentive to managers to develop their skills. It will also offer greater job satisfaction. But all this calls for a major change of attitude in the civil service.

OUTLINE OF THIS PAPER

With these broad aims and principles in mind, we set out in this paper to explain how these principles of reform should be applied and to propose what should happen next.

This is done in three parts. In **Part I "Getting the Structure Right"** we describe the three main functions of the civil service, overall resource planning, policy management, and policy execution, and the way in which these functions are carried out. Particular attention is placed on the relationship between policy makers and the executive agencies, and the desired characteristics of this relationship are outlined. We also explore the factors that would lead to the most appropriate choice of executive agency.

The government needs assurance that the seven principles are applied throughout government. The mechanism for obtaining that assurance will vary according to the type of executive agency used — but the management principles remain the same and should be applied in all organizational forms. In **Part II "Getting Service Delivery Right"** we focus in turn on four types of executive agency — traditional departments, departments operating through trading funds, corporations and other non-departmental public bodies. We describe when they should be used and highlight the main issues that need to be addressed with respect to their relationship with their Policy Secretaries. Vital elements of this relationship include clearly established responsibilities and objectives, delegated authorities and a process for planning, monitoring, and reporting results and achievements.

In **Part III "Private Sector Participation"** we describe how the resources and expertise of the private sector can best be tapped.

Finally in **"A Way Forward"** we recognize that there is much to do and there are difficult choices to make. Yet the need for reform is beyond doubt. A management orientated civil service will provide an environment in which we shall be able to see the more rapid germination of ideas into plans and the development of plans into tangible achievements.

**PART I: GETTING THE
STRUCTURE RIGHT**

PART I: GETTING THE STRUCTURE RIGHT

The seven principles of reform must be applied in the context of the three main functions of the civil service:—

- – overall resource planning;
- – policy management;
- – policy execution (i.e. service delivery).

The diagram below illustrates how these functions are fulfilled within the government and indicates the role that different institutions have to play.

**The Main Functions
of the Civil Service**

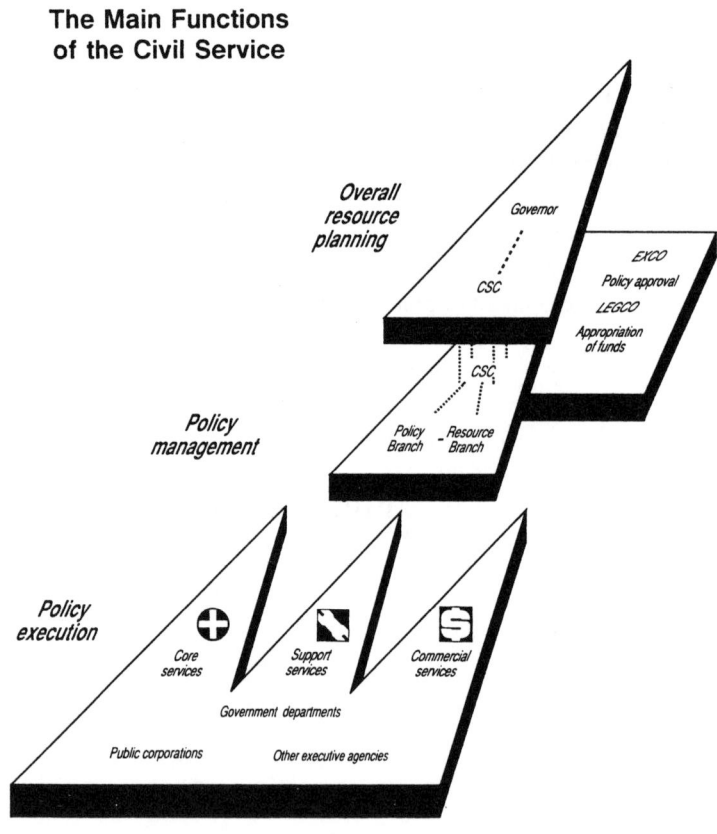

OVERALL RESOURCE PLANNING

Resource allocation decisions are made in the Chief Secretary's Committee.

Traditionally, financial control has been highly centralized. This system is now being changed so that the centre concentrates more on setting the global totals and controlling the overall allocation of resources to Policy Secretaries. Any resources available for new or expanded services are bid for by Policy Secretaries. To date, the debate concerning resource allocation has revolved mainly around the deployment of new resources.

This incremental approach is fundamentally limiting. Attention is focused on new services and activities, and seldom on a re-appraisal of the need for current activities. We suggest that Policy Secretaries should look closely at the deployment of all resources within their areas of responsibility, in particular baseline expenditure i.e. expenditure on current activities, response to demand and the recurrent consequences of capital projects.

POLICY MANAGEMENT

Policy Branches

Policy Secretaries should increasingly become policy managers. As such they will be responsible for:—

- identifying policy issues;
- formulating and reviewing broad policy aims;
- establishing policy objectives;
- deciding on appropriate types of executive agency;
- obtaining resources;
- allocating resources to these executive agencies;
- and, most important, evaluating the results achieved.

To shoulder these responsibilities we suggest that Policy Secretaries should establish and manage a policy and financial framework within which their executive agencies can operate. The diagram p. 255 illustrates the close relationship that should exist between policy branch and executive agency.

The Policy Secretary, in formulating policy aims and defining policy objectives, is influenced on the one hand by social and economic demands and constraints and on the other hand by the ability of the executive agency to deliver. As a result of close dialogue between the Policy Secretary and the executive agency head, the former is able to match policy requirements with the resources available.

The executive agency head is also the provider of information which enables the Policy Secretary to measure progress towards achieving objectives. In this way, the Policy Secretary can be assured that the management principles stated in the preceding section, are being properly applied.

To ensure consistency in policy within the government and give the centre the opportunity to review policy in each area, *we suggest that the Chief Secretary in conjunction with the Financial Secretary should hold annual comprehensive reviews of each policy area by means of a series of bilateral meetings with each Policy Secretary.* These reviews should include broad direction of policy and how this will meet changing needs. Such reviews will support the first principle of reform, ensuring that the whole of public expenditure is reviewed systematically.

These meetings would focus on reviewing:—

- the allocation of resources within the whole of the policy area;
- the achievements (i.e. results) and costs of each main policy programme;
- whether value for money is being achieved, and how this is being demonstrated.

Resource Branches

In addition to policy branches there are two resource branches, Finance Branch and Civil Service Branch. Finance Branch assists the Financial Secretary in managing the financial affairs of the government. In discharging this role the primary functions of the branch should be:—

- the determination of acceptable levels of public expenditure (i.e. the global totals);
- the management of the annual resource allocation exercises;
- ensuring that these resources are used effectively, efficiently and economically.

The emphasis of Finance Branch's activities has changed in recent years. We will delegate more authority to Policy Secretaries and heads of departments as the pace of reform increases. As a first step, policy branches

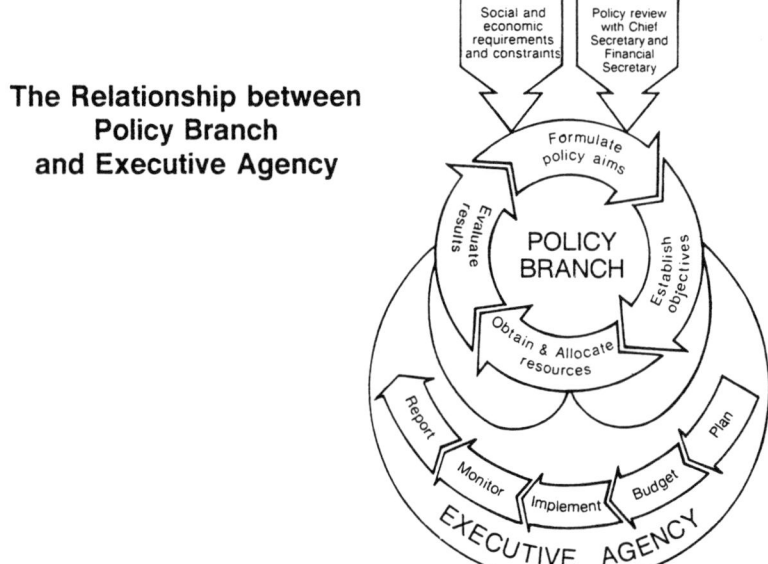

The Relationship between Policy Branch and Executive Agency

should become increasingly involved in resource allocation based on approved operating plans. Some of the resources freed in Finance Branch will be used within the Branch to develop a broader appraisal capability of major new policy initiatives and to provide financial management expertise, particularly in respect of value for money throughout the civil service.

Civil Service Branch has an important management role to play in respect of human resources. In addition it is responsible for:—

- the management of the general grades staff;
- the development and monitoring of service-wide personnel policies.

In its human resource management role, we suggest that Civil Service Branch should also seek to delegate more of its responsibilities to Policy Secretaries and heads of departments in respect of the management of departmental staff and possibly even in respect of certain general grades staff. This will ensure that Policy Secretaries and heads of departments can exercise their new responsibilities with flexibility.

THE RESPONSIBILITIES OF POLICY SECRETARIES AND EXECUTIVE AGENCY HEADS

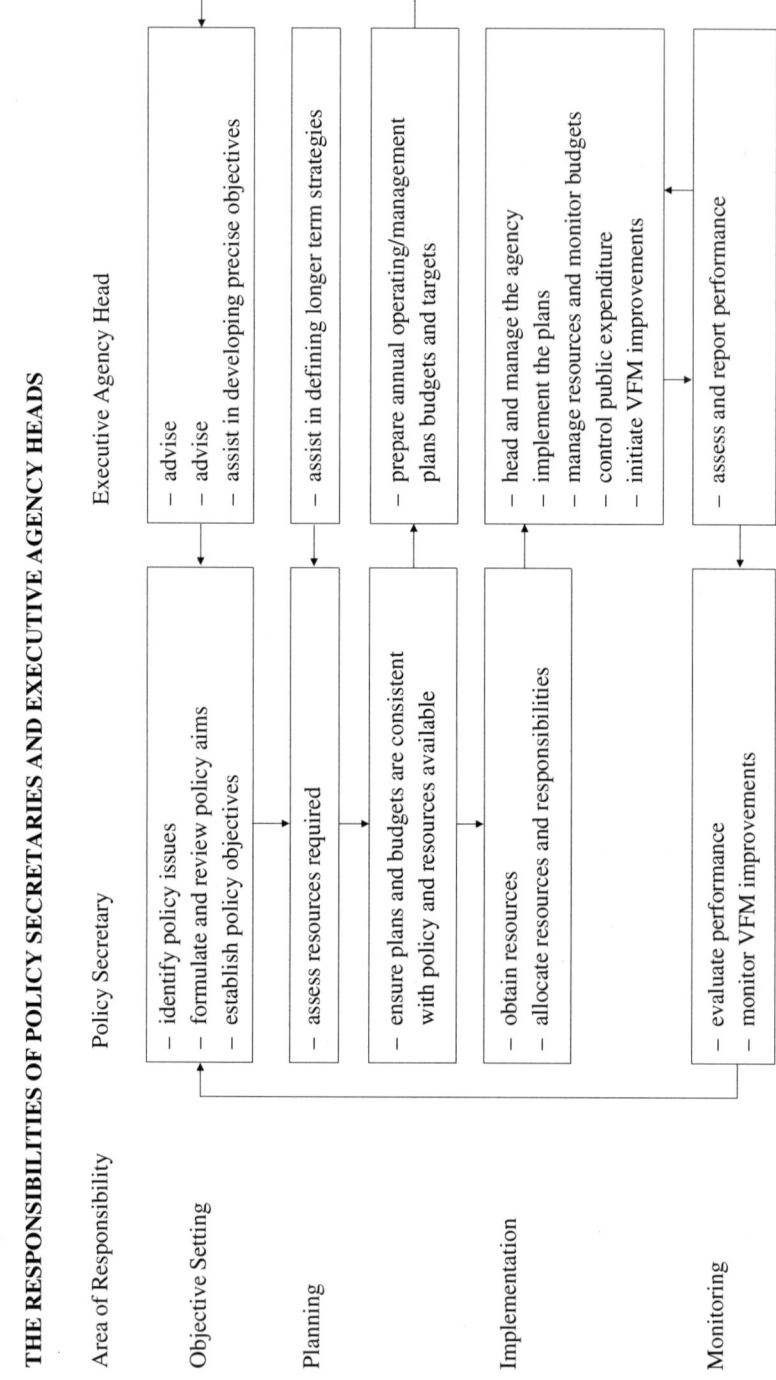

Area of Responsibility

Policy Secretary

Executive Agency Head

Objective Setting

Policy Secretary:
- identify policy issues
- formulate and review policy aims
- establish policy objectives

Executive Agency Head:
- advise
- advise
- assist in developing precise objectives

Planning

Policy Secretary:
- assess resources required
- ensure plans and budgets are consistent with policy and resources available

Executive Agency Head:
- assist in defining longer term strategies
- prepare annual operating/management plans budgets and targets

Implementation

Policy Secretary:
- obtain resources
- allocate resources and responsibilities

Executive Agency Head:
- head and manage the agency
- implement the plans
- manage resources and monitor budgets
- control public expenditure
- initiate VFM improvements

Monitoring

Policy Secretary:
- evaluate performance
- monitor VFM improvements

Executive Agency Head:
- assess and report performance

POLICY EXECUTION

The first two functions, overall resource planning and policy management, absorb a small but crucial part of the government's expenditure. They are necessary to ensure that the third function — policy execution, covering the bulk of the government's resources — is effectively carried out.

The fulfillment of this role depends on the existence of a sound relationship with a clear allocation of responsibilities between branch and executive agency. It will also be greatly helped by choosing the most appropriate executive agencies to deliver the desired services.

The Relationship between Branch and Executive Agency

The interlinked responsibilities for policy formulation and subsequent implementation are shown in the table p. 256. In it we highlight the most important components of this relationship, generally common to all types of executive agency.

It can be seen that final policy **objectives** should be set within the context of an operational plan. The plan in turn should have its own operational targets. This whole **planning** process is resource constrained and there will inevitably need to be some balancing before a match is achieved between the desired policy objectives and the resources available to meet them.

Only after this matching has been successful will resources be obtained by the Policy Secretary and allocated to the executive agency so that policies can be **implemented**.

It is important that the executive agency is able to **monitor** its activities adequately. At a lower level, the agency should measure and monitor whether it has achieved its own operational targets and whether it has done so efficiently and economically. At the higher level, it should measure the outcome of its activities in the context of achieving the agreed policy objectives.

We suggest that Policy Secretaries should take steps to ensure that this relationship is implemented, in particular the assessment of performance against objectives. This will allow secretaries to evaluate the achievements and costs of all government activities and clearly define responsibilities thus supporting the second and third principles of reform. We discuss this is more detail in the box below.

ASSESSMENT OF PERFORMANCE AGAINST OBJECTIVES

The precise approach to performance assessment will be a matter for each executive agency and will vary according to the type of policy area. However, there are some general guidelines which have been developed as part of the UK Government's financial management initiative that can usefully be applied in Hong Kong.

The key to measuring achievement is to be clear on what is being aimed at, and why. Information is therefore required on three aspects:—

- **relevance** — the environment within which the policy is being applied;
- **achievements** — the progress being made towards achieving specific objectives;
- **administrative efficiency** — whether these policy objectives are being achieved cost-effectively.

Relevance

Policies rest on underlying assumptions about circumstances in the community, the government's perception of that environment, and the degree of priority attached to government action being taken to secure changes in that environment. All these underlying assumptions should be monitored as changing conditions may reduce the need for the policy, alter its relative priority, or require policy changes to be made. Executive agencies, therefore, should constantly collect and monitor information about the policy environment and check whether the policy aims are still relevant.

Achievements

Objectives need to be defined in order to provide clear yardsticks for assessing progress. If possible, objectives should be expressed in quantifiable terms but, if not, should at least be stated in a way that permits their achievement to be observed. The objectives should be defined in terms of three elements:—

- the desired results;
- the timetable for achieving results;
- the cost.

The exact measurement of progress will vary from policy area to policy area. It will be necessary, however, to establish systems to inform managers about results and costs.

This aspect of measuring performance can be very difficult because of the intangible nature of some policy areas. But even with respect to services in such policy areas, it is usually possible to assess by survey whether they are reaching the right people and whether they are effective.

Administrative efficiency

Administrative efficiency is also an important dimension of performance assessment, not least because there is frequently a relationship between administrative efficiency and policy effectiveness, in that a desire to be "over-effective" can lead to disproportionately high administrative costs. Executive agencies need to be aware of this relationship and take an informed view of the most appropriate balance to strike. It may be useful, for example, to gather information about the cost of alternative levels of service delivery.

The cost of performance assessment

It has to be acknowledged that the task of performance assessment will cost money. However, without a proper assessment and evaluation of the results of policy, there is little prospect of achieving better value for money. The best way of providing for this cost is to plan at the outset what is required and to make specific budget provision accordingly.

Choosing the Appropriate Type of Executive Agency

Service delivery can be provided through a variety of public sector executive agencies. There is an important role to be played by the private sector in the delivery of services. We return to this in Part III.

The choice of public sector executive agency will depend on a number of factors, reflected in the table pp. 261–262. The most important of these are:—

- the type of service to be delivered;
- the degree of freedom from government control that is desired;
- the pricing strategy to be applied to the service.

There are, broadly, three **types of service**:

- **Core service** — services such as public order, social, economic, or regulatory carried out by the government as a matter of public policy;
- **Support services** — ancillary services such as printing, vehicles, computing, etc. normally provided only to other government bodies;
- **Commercial services** — services which are provided for the general public, at a charge. Such services are frequently monopolies and traditionally have been provided by the government although this need not necessarily be the case. Examples of such services include the Post Office and the airport.

Within these three groups, the **extent of government control** can vary considerably. The government may wish to keep some services under direct control, whereas in other cases there may be advantages in their being at arm's length. The former include services performed exclusively under the authority of the government, e.g. police and immigration services. The latter would include services which would benefit from wider public participation in their management, require an operational flexibility unobtainable within a civil service structure or require skills not normally found in government. This would apply to most forms of trading activity.

The **pricing strategy** adopted for a particular service will also affect the choice of executive agency. It will depend largely on the government's economic, social and fiscal policies. In general terms there are three strategies:—

- **Free** — free to the consumer, except possibly for a nominal charge to discourage frivolous use;
- **Partial cost recovery** — services which earn revenue but which, for one reason or another, are subsidized;

THE CHOICE OF PUBLIC SECTOR EXECUTIVE AGENCY

Type of services	Policy requirements		Example of service activity	Suggested executive agency	Notes
	Arm's length?	Pricing strategy			
CORE SERVICES ✚	No	Free	Law and order	Traditional department	Appropriate for traditional, often strategic, public services provided at no charge to the consumer.
		Partial or Full	Issuing visas, Vehicle registration	Trading fund	Major areas within departments where partial or full cost recovery is sought through fees and charges. This will normally require a separate management/ accounting identity for which the trading fund approach offers many advantages.
	Yes	Free or Partial	Consumer protection Hospital services	Non-departmental public body (NDPB)	There are many examples where a greater degree of freedom from government is required for purposes of independence (e.g. Consumer Council), flexibility (e.g. Trade Development Council) or to change management processes (e.g. Hospital Authority). These bodies are all different forms of NDPBs.
		Full	Urban renewal	Corporation	Where commercial viability is sought, a corporation is appropriate. The Land Development Corporation is an example which allows commercial joint ventures with the private sector to be set up.

THE CHOICE OF PUBLIC SECTOR EXECUTIVE AGENCY (Con't)

Type of services	Policy requirements		Example of service activity	Suggested executive agency	Notes
	Arm's length?	Pricing strategy			
SUPPORT SERVICES	No	Full	Data processing	Trading fund department	Support services should, where practicable be provided on a full cost recovery basis, so that managers of core services can be fully accountable for the resources they consume. The extent to which support services are given a degree of freedom from the government requires determination in each case.
	Yes	Full	Property services	Corporation	
COMMERCIAL SERVICES	No	Partial or Full	Publications Tunnel operations	Trading fund department	Relatively small pockets of commercial activity that warrant a separate management/accounting identity but may not justify the costs/disruption of moving into a fully arm's length organization.
	Yes	Partial or Full	Public transport	Corporation	Trading services will, by their nature, be revenue earning, and so will normally benefit from a separate accounting and management structure. Whilst overall ownership is retained by the government, the corporation approach facilities access to private sector resources, e.g. the KCRC and MTRC.

- **Full cost recovery** — services in which the consumers, including government departments, are charged prices that reflect the full cost of provision, including the cost of capital.

We have used the table to highlight different combinations of factors which can arise. In each case, we give examples of typical services and activities and indicate the most appropriate form of executive agency.

From this we have identified four broad different types of executive agency:—

- **Traditional departments** — funded in the present way on a cash accounting basis;
- **Trading fund departments** — government departments established on a quasi-commercial basis with revenue accruing to the fund;
- **Public corporations** — wholly owned by government and operating according to commercial principles;
- **Non-departmental public bodies** — bodies with a role in government but operating at arm's length.

We suggest that Policy Secretaries and heads of departments should consider which type of agency best suits their requirements in light of the factors identified: type of service; extent of government control; pricing strategy. This will support the fifth principle of reform.

PART II: GETTING SERVICE DELIVERY RIGHT

PART II: GETTING SERVICE DELIVERY RIGHT

| Traditional Departments | Trading Fund | Public Corporation | NDPBs |

In this part of the paper we focus in turn on these four types of executive agency. We discuss their basic characteristics and outline the circumstances where they can be used. We also describe the mechanisms available to Policy Secretaries to ensure that the basic principles of financial management are being applied in each agency.

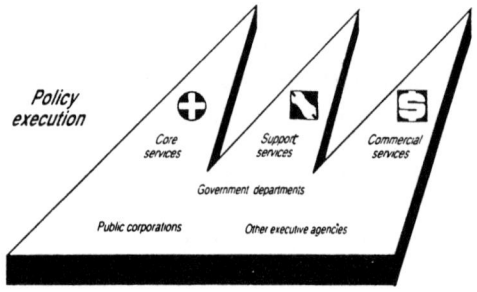

| Traditional Departments |

Their Role

Most of the core responsibilities of the government will continue to be carried out through traditional departments. The activities of these departments will remain controlled through the allocation of funds in vote accounts and, in some cases, by the relevant ordinances and regulations. This is particularly true for the administrative and social functions of government where little, if any, payment towards costs is made by consumers.

Even though the current departmental structures may be appropriate, there is much that can and should be improved in the way objectives are agreed with Policy Secretaries, resources managed and activities planned and implemented within departments. These improvements can be achieved by clarifying and strengthening the existing relationships between departments and policy branches in three areas in particular — planning, delegated authority and reporting.

Planning for Priorities

In respect of planning, the activities of departments as described in their operational plans should clearly set out manpower and financial resource requirements. In the likely event that these resource requirements exceed the resource available, a re-assessment of the policy objectives and the operational plan must take place. Mechanisms are required to ease this potential mismatch, by ensuring that resources are allocated in accordance with identified policy priorities.

The percentage savings option first introduced in 1988 is one such mechanism. Another could be to use a simplified version of priority based budgeting (PBB) as described in the box pp. 266–267. Whatever method is used, the aim must be to effect a concerted attack on baseline expenditure.

Operational plans will take some time to develop because there has to be a compromise between policy objectives and the ability of the department to deliver within its resource constraints. To avoid duplication of effort and problems of later reconciliation, it is vital that the preparation of operational plans should be a fully integrated part of the government's resource allocation and estimates process.

Delegation of Authority

If heads of departments are to be held to account for achieving departmental objectives they need authority over the resources at their disposal (the fourth principle of reform). The traditional approach to civil service management means that much responsibility for the authorization and virement of funds and the appointment, recruitment and promotion of staff is reserved to the two resource branches.

Greater financial authority has been delegated in recent years. This process should be continued.

However, the effective control of staff especially the general grades, remains with Civil Service Branch and it is for consideration whether these arrangements are still appropriate. One possibility, adopted by civil services elsewhere, is for the branch to gradually delegate staff control matters while enhancing its personnel management function.

Financial and staff delegation to a department should also lead to greater delegation of these functions within the department. Line managers responsible for an activity should progressively receive delegated authority to control the resources deployed on the activity. The rate at which this delegation should take place will depend on the degree of confidence that heads of departments have in their line managers to use the authority responsibly.

PRIORITY BASE BUDGETING

Priority Base Budgeting, PBB, is a structured approach to planning and budgeting overhead and service activities. It has been used successfully by many organizations to:—

- effect better allocation of resources;
- improve productivity, and/or reduce costs to achieve greater value for money;
- build commitment within management to the changes required and the performance targets and resource levels to be met.

Limitations of Traditional Budgeting

In traditional budget planning, attention is focused on proposed changes from the previous year's level of spending. Little if any information is provided about performance levels to be achieved, optional levels of service which might be considered, or the savings and other consequences arising from them. As a result the budget review process is often unsatisfactory and may lead as a matter of expediency to arbitrary decision-making.

The PBB Process

PBB has been designed to overcome the most common limitations of traditional budgeting systems. It enables senior management to review more thoroughly the underlying activities and thereby establish tighter control on the use of resources in indirect and service functions.

Under PBB, the managers involved are required to make a radical reassessment of their activities and to document proposals for review by senior management. In doing so, each manager has to:—

- re-establish the purposes of his activities and evaluate alternative means of achieving them;
- define the absolute minimum level (and the lowest cost) at which service could be provided, to satisfy essential requirements only;
- identify successive incremental levels of service and their costs and benefits, to satisfy the more discretionary requirements of the function.

These proposals are discussed with representative users of the service to ensure realism and consistency and to facilitate proposals being ranked in order of priority for funding.

PBB Rating Scales

Ranking is facilitated by rating different levels of service for an activity in accordance with a scale such as:

PBB RATING SCALE

10 Essential to the business — unavoidable corporate or legal requirement
9 Critical — unavoidable without substantial loss or damage
8 Very attractive, important and productive increments of service
7 Important — very hard to see how they could be dropped
6 Significant benefits but could conceivably be dropped
5 Desirable but first to be dropped if funding curtailed

Benchmark

4 Marginal but first to be supported if funding increased
3 Possible but only if much increased funding available
2 Doubtful — not sufficient justification at present
1 Unlikely ever to be funded

Proper Reporting and Evaluation

In addition to vote monitoring systems maintained through the Ledger
Accounting Financial Information System — LAFIS (or manually in
some areas), departments keep statistical information relating to their activities. A number of departments produce annual reports describing the
events of the year but, generally speaking, this is insufficient. As a minimum, departments require information to:—

- understand and control the costs of functions or activities in
  addition to expenditure items i.e. budget and cost centre
  reports;
- calculate unit costs for comparative or charging purposes;
- monitor progress towards achieving policy objectives and operational targets;
- evaluate the effect, efficiency and relevance of policy initiatives.

The first two requirements will be similar in most departments in the
form of some kind of cost centre accounting. Programmes to install costing
systems are underway in several areas. This work will be accelerated across
a broader range of departmental activities.

The information required for monitoring and evaluation will depend on
the types of policies and initiatives on which the department is engaged. It
may be that *ad hoc* surveys are required to monitor the impact of an activity
and to ascertain whether policy objectives are being attained. In some cases,
long term monitoring of trends may be necessary to discern the effects of a
department's activities.

Adequate information systems are prerequisites for improved financial
management. They allow a manager to understand what he is managing and
provide the information from which the performance of the manager can be
judged. Their design and installation should accordingly be given a high
priority, for this will determine the rate at which greater authority can be
delegated to and within departments.

The installation of information systems is a complex process which
should not be underestimated. Some problems associated with developing information systems in the public sector are described in the box
below.

SOME PROBLEMS ASSOCIATED WITH DEVELOPING
INFORMATION SYSTEMS

The information requirements of government organizations are complex and, while some lessons can be learnt from good private sector practice, many of the issues are unique to government. Experience in the UK, and elsewhere has highlighted a number of areas where care should be taken.

Integration

Accounting requirements and those for vote, budget centre and programme purposes should ideally be met from one system. Superimposing decentralized budgetary control requirements on top of existing vote accounting systems can lead to duplication of effort and the consequent waste of resources.

Vote accounts are based on cash, whereas costing for charging purposes (e.g. in a trading fund) may require accruals, depreciation, the cost of capital and other non-cash costs. The systems must be capable of handling cash and non-cash items and reconciling the different bases.

Aggregation

Unlike a private sector organization where many or most of its activities can be expressed in financial terms (e.g. sales, costs, assets) government activities are diverse and cannot be neatly aggregated for presentation to top management. It is therefore sometimes difficult to meaningfully summarize key information.

One consequence of this is a tendency towards the presentation of large volumes of information in a way which is hard to digest.

Interpretation

Performance indicators can be hard to derive and even then may not tell the full story. Care and training are required in their interpretation, particularly in areas of social policy.

Implementation

Information systems can be costly to implement. To minimize the effort involved, it is important that their introduction and development are properly managed, and that lessons are learned from experience elsewhere.

Support to the Department

To take on board the implementation of new systems and the development of appropriate business and planning frameworks, departments will need support. This can take several forms including:—

- additional resources;
- training programmes;
- managerial support.

To undertake further efficiency and value for money exercises, top-down policy reviews, financial appraisals and systems design and implementation, **additional resources** will need to be provided. These resources would be in the form of increased central budgets for procurement and external consultancies, or expanded departmental capability, or increased central support through the provision of management services, data processing and accounting and management information services.

A financial management **training programme** is needed for appropriate staff in financial management techniques and concepts. Although training has already begun, it must be further developed to explain the importance of financial management and its application in policy management and implementation. It will concentrate on the various financial systems and techniques that are already in place, the ideal circumstances where they should be employed and the likely developments, such as technological improvements, that will have an impact on practical applications. It will also appraise developments taking place in the centre and identify the links that need to be established by executive agencies.

Managerial support will be provided by introducing suitably trained and experienced business managers or their equivalent into departments. The box below presents in more detail the role of a business manager. We consider this to be a vital catalyst in accelerating the attitude and management changes fundamental to a reform programme.

Aspects for Consideration

Within the context of the policy branch/executive agency framework discussed earlier, *we suggest that heads of departments should:—*

- *develop operational plans;*
- *improve their management information systems;*
- *identify the support necessary for their departments;*
- *consider, in conjunction with Finance Branch, pilot PBB exercises.*

THE BUSINESS MANAGER

The pre-requisites for effective service delivery include a clear definition of objectives, an operational plan to achieve targets related to these objectives and information systems to monitor the effectiveness and cost of the activities undertaken.

Few departments have these requirements in place. Operationally they are generally well managed but do not have the financial management expertise to respond to the type of initiative proposed in this reform programme. To overcome this we propose the introduction of business managers or their equivalent to major departments to promote and facilitate improvements in these areas.

The duties of the business manager would generally require him to:—

- assist in defining the main objectives of the department and setting out specific operational targets for the department to achieve;
- improve management decision-making by addressing productivity issues and examining alternative methods of service delivery;
- introduce modern technology where appropriate;
- explore new commercial opportunities.

In discharging these duties, the manager would usually report directly to the head of department and work closely with the managers of operational divisions.

It would be up to him to coordinate and mobilize departmental and central resources to generate the required support.

The requirements of individual departments with respect to a business manager would differ significantly but in all cases it will be necessary to ensure that the appointed person has the requisite objectivity, flair and managerial experience.

> **Trading Funds**

What are they?

Trading funds are accounting frameworks established by law for departments providing services on a quasi-commercial basis with the objective of recovering costs. Trading fund departments do not have the same autonomy as a corporation, but have greater financial flexibility than traditional government departments. Their staff, however, remain part of the civil service and subject to its terms and conditions.

Although this concept has been widely applied in the UK it would be an innovation in Hong Kong which has always operated a centralized cash accounts system. We should therefore ensure a full understanding of the issues involved before embarking on any major changes.

How do trading funds differ from the traditional cash accounting/ vote recovery system?

Generally, departments financed by trading funds operate on commercial lines. Major differences between trading funds and vote funding are:

Trading Funds	**Vote Funding**
– On-going basis/continuing year to year	– Annualized
– Accrual basis of accounting	– Cash basis of accounting
– Cash balances retained/ ploughed back	– Cash balances not ploughed back but returned to General Revenue
– Self financing/funding with the need to break-even	– Expenditure limited to budgets. Shortfalls not carried forward.
– Financial performance oriented	– Resource consumption orientated.

When are they used?

Trading funds can be appropriate for activities which are:—

- core services on a partial or full cost recovery basis;
- government support services where a charge can be raised for the services provided;
- commercial services.

For **core services**, trading funds could be established where a large scale operation is able to recover a significant proportion of its costs by charging customers. Financial objectives would be set by Policy Secretaries and address, as necessary, any specific pricing provisions. This could include levies, prices below cost or the basis for arriving at price increases.

With regard to **support services**, the decision to establish a trading fund would be to promote one or more of the following:—

- a more economical use of the service, particularly where no charge has been raised in the past;
- greater efficiency, by exposing the service to competition or to proxy competitive pressures through price comparisons and cost consciousness on the part of the user;
- the reorientation of the service to a customer-led rather than producer-driven organization and culture.

Possible candidate services are printing, accommodation, architectural, electrical and mechanical services, procurement and data processing.

Finally with regard to **commercial services**, the establishment of a formal trading fund could be a transitional step towards corporatization, for example for the Water Supplies Department or the Post Office.

How far should the new trading relationships extend?

At present, departments that require services which are available within the government are generally obliged to use that internal source. Similarly departments supplying support services only do so to other government departments. This situation need not change when a trading fund is set up, but it could.

Since trading funds are intended to operate on a commercial basis, they would charge for their services and user departments would have the choice of using more or less of those services. A real customer/supplier relationship would develop.

Once both parties become familiar with this new relationship, in theory each could turn to the private sector as an extension of its marketplace. The customer departments could seek resources from new suppliers and the service departments could provide services to the private sector if they were competitive.

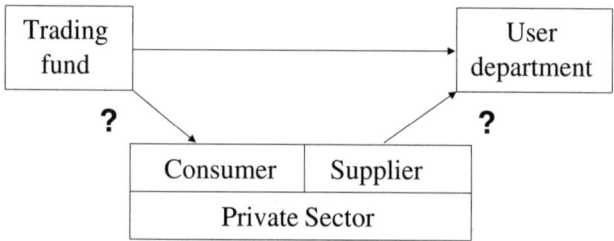

The extent to which these new trading relationships should be allowed to develop will depend on many factors, for instance:—

- the amount of investment in new techniques and equipment required to make the trading fund competitive;
- whether the government is prepared to accept the consequences when the business of a new trading fund grows or contracts in response to its new market position;
- the determination of the government to apply the disciplines of the market place;
- whether the government wishes to retain a capability in a particular service area for strategic reasons.

These issues can only be resolved on a case by case basis.

What needs to be done?

If a decision is taken to introduce the trading fund concept, new legislation would be needed and the planning and financing implications would need to be assessed.

Trading funds operate under specific **legislation** which sets out key elements of the management framework that would prevail, for instance:—

- its broad financial objectives;
- a requirement to agree quality standards, for example, levels of service and safety considerations;
- the form of planning process, and reporting relationships within the government;
- permitted methods of financing and limits on the use and disposal of funds;
- the general responsibilities, accountability and authority of its management.

These would all have to be agreed with Policy Secretaries.

As an integral part of the government machine, trading funds would be subject to the annual **planning processes**. However, the form this participation takes would depend on the role of the fund, how far it is self-financing from charges to other government agencies or the private sector and whether other government agencies are "tied" to it as a sole source of supply.

Whatever the case, the planning process will need to reconcile likely demand from customers with the capacity of the supplying agency operating the fund.

To be effective in this, the agency may need to be given wider **authorities** than those in the rest of the civil service in recognition of the commercial nature of its activities. For example the requirement to meet customer imposed deadlines may only be satisfied through greater flexibility with respect to sanctioning overtime or hiring additional temporary services.

To all intents and purposes trading funds report like any commercial organization. Where **funding** for capital investment or any operating deficit is required, separate provision in the estimates of the "parent" secretary will be required. In addition, customer departments will need to make provision appropriate to their anticipated demand for these services. However, that provision would be an estimate only and not guaranteed to the supplier except possibly during an initial "grace" period. This is another advantage of the trading fund/inter-departmental charging concept in that departments have every incentive to "save" money on support services and perhaps use them for other high priority items.

Some of the main features and financial provisions associated with trading funds are analyzed in more detail in the box below.

Aspects for Consideration

We suggest that the trading fund concept be researched in more detail, and that heads of departments give consideration to areas of activity that would benefit from the approach.

THE MAIN FEATURES OF TRADING FUNDS

Trading funds established to finance the operations of a service-providing department have the following main features:—

- Paid Up Capital — reflecting the government's investment in the organization. This represents the first step towards commercialization;
- Additional Funding — Net working capital requirements are provided by the government. Normally a special central fund is established for this purpose, from which all organizations funded by trading funds draw their working capital;
- Dividends — Returns on government investment are in the form of dividends and are paid from this account;
- Receipts and Payments — All moneys received for the provision of goods and services are paid into this account; and similarly all payments are made from this account;
- Cash Balance/Retained — Trading funds are required at least to break-even taking one year with another. Cash balances are carried forward from one year to the next and retained earnings ploughed back;
- Provisions — Provisions for pensions, gratuity of employees and other similar employee benefits should be made if necessary;
- Statement of Accounts — The annual statement of accounts are subject to independent audit.

> **Public Corporations**

What are they?

A public corporation is a corporate entity established by law. It may be created by transferring the assets of a government department into a company structure. The Kowloon-Canton Railway Corporation (KCRC) was established in this way. Alternatively, a public corporation may be a newly created body such as the Mass Transit Railway Corporation (MTRC).

When are they used?

Public corporations are suitable vehicles for:—

- core government services which need an operational flexibility that cannot be obtained within the civil service, e.g. to form joint ventures with the private sector like the Land Development Corporation (LDC);
- support or commercial services which are best managed outside the civil service because they need the independence, say, to raise external finance, engage staff on alternative terms and conditions of employment, or make explicit that a service does not rely on public subsidy, e.g. the KCRC and MTRC.

Public corporations are more appropriate than trading funds for those activities that are better placed outside the civil service framework for operational, financial, or managerial reasons. There may, however, be other public policy considerations which take precedence over such factors.

One of the most ambitious programmes to create new public corporations was launched in 1987 by the New Zealand government. The results have been dramatic with five out of nine new corporations being turned round from loss making to profitable operations. This is because many activities were overmanned and had surplus capacity or unnecessarily extensive operations.

A number of lessons can be learned from this and other international experience on how the creation of public corporations can increase efficiency and effectiveness:—

- management has greater freedom to identify, and respond rapidly to, new or changing consumer needs;
- a corporation can be organized on business lines and key commercial skills introduced from the private sector (e.g. in marketing);
- fully commercial accounting and management information systems can be put in place;
- greater flexibility can be exercised in the design of remuneration packages including the introduction of performance related pay;
- the corporation can be subjected to the disciplines of private capital markets;
- the creation of an independent public corporation can enable greater and fairer competition to be introduced between the public and private sector.

The Management Framework

The fundamental principle underlying the creation of a public corporation is the transfer of responsibility for day-to-day operational planning and management from government to the corporation. However, the broad direction of corporate policies would need to be agreed between Policy Secretaries and the board of the corporation. The management framework, should therefore be based on this principle, and take account of a number of aspects covering five major areas:—

- the **status** of the corporation: its links with the government, legal forms and regulatory requirements;
- its corporate **strategy**: objectives, areas of business and performance targets;
- the **structure** of the organization: its board, its internal management structure, its financial structure;
- the **system** it needs: for management information, accounting and personnel functions;
- the **style** of its operation: attitude changes and management changes.

Examples of the main issues that should be addressed within these five areas are presented in the form of questions p. 279.

In Hong Kong there are several specific issues relating to public corporations which are of particular importance. These we now discuss.

NEW CORPORATIONS — ISSUES TO ADDRESS

STATUS

Government relations
- who represents government as shareholder?
- what autonomy is the corporation to have?
- what are the corporation's primary objectives to be?
- how will they be determined and monitored?

Legal
- what form of legal entity is to be created?
- what legislation is required?

Public interest
- is the corporation to be subject to an explicit regulatory regime?
- what standards or service and security of supply obligations should be imposed?
- should competition be encouraged in the consumer's interest?

STRATEGY

Business definition and market position
- what types of business is the corporation engaged in?
- what are the market characteristics in each?
- is there a competitive environment?
- if so, is the organization competitive?

Corporate objectives
- does the corporation have a strategic plan?
- what investment and/or diversification programme is required?
- what non-commercial objectives and obligations does the corporation have?
- what standards of service are to be adopted?
- what pricing policy is to be followed?
- what efficiency improvements are to be aimed for?

Performance
- what are the financial targets for the corporation?
- what other performance targets are to be set?
- how is performance to be monitored and by whom?

STRUCTURE

Organization
- what is the corporate structure to be?
- what is the role and composition of the Board to be and how is it to be appointed?
- how is the corporation to be organized internally, by function, by business unit?
- what functions need strengthening?

Financial
- what is the value of the corporation?
- what capital structure is appropriate?

Human Resources
- what management and other human resources are required and how are they to be deployed?
- do we have the right number of managers with the right qualities?
- do we have the right labour skills?

SYSTEMS

Accounting
- are the accounting systems and costing systems in place appropriate for a commercial enterprise?

Management information
- what additional information is required for efficient management?
- are improvements to the information systems required?

Personnel
- are suitable systems in place to support the recruitment, retention, development and motivation of staff the enterprise requires?
- what pay scales and conditions of employment are required to secure, retain and motivate employees of the necessary calibre?

STYLE

Attitudes
- what changes are required in general attitudes towards remuneration, promotion and job security to create the desirable employee culture?
- how are these changes to be achieved?
- how can customer awareness and service attitudes be developed to meet the requirements of a competitive market place?

Management
- what management style is required?
- is there a need to introduce new management?

The Role of the Government

In line with the fundamental principle of delegated responsibility described above, the role of the government and of the corporation must be clearly defined. Lack of clarity permits, and can encourage, inappropriate government intervention.

The government's role should be for Policy Secretaries to agree with each corporation its strategy and objectives, and to monitor performance against the objectives. The corporation's role should be to assume responsibility for managing within the framework of these objectives, and to be accountable to the government for its performance.

At present, there are no formal arrangements within the government for agreeing the strategic issues and framework of objectives within which the corporation should operate. The government has specific powers of direction, but these are intended for use only in extreme circumstances. This shortcoming should be redressed through annual discussions in the context of each corporation's planning process.

The Role of the Board

The role of the board is especially important since the public corporations in Hong Kong have been established with considerable autonomy, and the government's controlling influence over the corporations is largely exercised through its powers of appointment to the board. In the case of the KCRC, for example, the Governor appoints the Chairman and eight non-executive members of the board of whom two are Policy Secretaries.

A shortcoming in these arrangements appears to be that the presence of the Secretaries on the board is relied upon as a channel for conveying the government's views on strategy and objectives. In fact the presence of Secretaries (or their representatives) may well confuse the respective roles of the government and the corporation. In the UK, it is not usual practice to appoint ministerial representatives to the boards of public corporations.

Non-executive members of the board should be appointed for the purpose of contributing a special skill or viewpoint in their personal capacity. The intentions of the corporation in strategic matters should be discussed formally with the appropriate Policy Secretary in a separate forum.

Consequently, it would be preferable to have the two roles fulfilled in different ways. The board of the corporation should establish firm lines of communication with the Policy Secretary. The practice of appointing a government representative to the board should be reviewed.

Agreeing Corporate Strategy

The careful preparation of corporate plans and business plans is a vital ingredient in the efficient and effective management of a public corporation. Such plans provide an appropriate basis for agreeing a clear set of objectives with the corporation's Policy Secretary.

In some countries, particular features of the corporate plan are incorporated in a memorandum of understanding or a "contract" between the government and the corporation. France has developed relatively sophisticated arrangements over a period of twenty years as explained in the box p. 282, but similar practices are being adopted by a growing number of countries around the world such as New Zealand which has introduced a statement of corporate intent.

NEW ZEALAND: STATEMENT OF CORPORATE INTENT

Annual cycle

Board runs the business

Government reviews and Board agrees joint agreement

Statement of corporate intent

- Objectives
- Nature and scope of activities
- Financial and other performance targets
- Non-commercial activities: government compensation
- Dividends and transfers to government
- AOB: board and government

PERFORMANCE CONTRACTS

The concept of performance contracts was first applied in France twenty years ago. A performance contract is a formally signed document, freely negotiated and agreed between government representatives and the management of a public corporation. Its aim is to eliminate the uncertainties and ambiguities in the relations between the government and corporation.

The performance contract will typically include clear specifications of:—

- the corporation's commercial and non-commercial objectives;
- performance standards and indicators for performance measurement;
- the corporation's undertakings to the government, based on its corporate plan;
- the government's undertakings to the corporation;
- the limits of management authority;
- the process for monitoring contract compliance;
- procedures for arbitration and settlement of disputes.

Some performance contracts incorporate management incentive schemes linked to performance targets. Bonuses are awarded for exceeding the targets and sanctions applied for non-performance. Setting appropriate targets is, however, difficult. The choice of a single target may result in too narrow a management focus. The selection of many targets complicates the monitoring and evaluation of performance. A further difficulty arises if the chosen performance measures are significantly affected by factors outside management's control.

The main advantages of performance contracts are that they clarify and define the roles and responsibilities of the government and the corporation, and leave day-to-day management firmly in the hands of the corporation. They can, however, occupy much senior management time during the preparatory and negotiating stages.

Typically, the agreements or contracts cover:—

- commercial and non-commercial objectives, including financial targets and performance aims;
- core and non-core activities and plans for expansion or diversification;
- their policies or plans of concern to the government, such as pricing or safety matters;

- financial flows between the government and the enterprise, such as borrowing or subsidies to be obtained from the government or dividends to be paid to the government;
- the frequency and form of reporting and other arrangements for performance monitoring.

A form of agreement on these lines should be developed for use in Hong Kong. Annual agreements should be introduced for each existing corporation starting with the KCRC and MTRC, and arrangements for such agreements will be included, as appropriate, in the ordinances for new corporations.

Reporting and Monitoring

The main purpose of the reports specified in this annual agreement would be to enable the government to monitor the performance of each corporation against the requirements set out in the ordinance and against the strategy, objectives and targets agreed with the government. The annual monitoring process should be supplemented periodically by more thorough external reviews of specific aspects of the corporation's performance, in order to examine more closely whether the corporation is operating efficiently and in the public interest.

Aspects for consideration

We suggest that Policy Secretaries should seek to:—

- *formalize arrangements for agreeing objectives and accountability. This will involve considering some form of performance contract or statement of corporate intent;*
- *reappraise their own role on the boards of corporations;*
- *conduct, from time to time, external reviews of specific aspects of a corporation's activities.*

Steps taken along these lines would certainly help to clear up some of the misconceptions in the mind of the public and media about the degree of influence which the government is able to exert in specific circumstances.

> **NDPBs**

What are they?

Non-departmental public bodies (NDPBs) are bodies with a role to play for the government in providing a service to the public but operating at arm's length from government. They include, for example, bodies as diverse as the Consumer Council, the Hong Kong Tourist Association and the future Hospital Authority. An NDPB normally has the following characteristics:—

- – it is formally constituted with terms of reference or functions laid down in an ordinance, defined membership, a chairman, and so on;
- – some or all of its members are appointed by the government;
- – the government is answerable for its performance and determines its continued existence.

For the purpose of discussing the role of NDPBs in the context of public sector reform we have not included:—

- – the two municipal councils (although the application of at least some of the reforms discussed in this paper might appropriately apply to these two councils);
- – advisory committees and boards;
- – certain judicial bodies.

We have also excluded public corporations of a trading nature. These are described in the preceding section.

A large number of charitable and other private sector organizations receive subventions from the government for the provision of services. An element of government funding does not, of itself, imply that a body is an NDPB. These organizations are discussed in the next section on the role of the private sector.

The Relationship between the Government and Statutory Bodies

Statutory bodies vary widely in their functions and responsibilities. Their scope of activities and financial and constitutional relationships with the government are set out in their terms of reference and the ordinances under which they are created. Nonetheless, whatever their relationship with the government, it is ultimately the government which is answerable for the activities of that body. It is therefore essential that any major developments in policy should be subject to the approval of the Governor-in-Council and that clear and comprehensive objectives are mutually agreed between the appropriate Policy Secretary and the board of the statutory body.

This can be done through the planning process. All statutory bodies need planning arrangements analogous to and in step with those of the government. As with departments, these plans should formulate objectives in the light of policy guidance in elaboration of their statutory functions. Their operational plans should clearly state the activities that will be undertaken to pursue these objectives and show the allocation of resources accordingly. This plan would then form the basis for reviewing and approving any requested subvention.

For this process to work effectively, it is essential that there is a clear delineation of the roles of the Policy Secretary on the one hand and of the chairman and board of the NDPB on the other. The principles we discussed in relation to corporations are equally applicable here. The distinction between the policy making and implementation roles can be usefully clarified on the appointment of the chairman, by describing his or her terms of reference in the letter of appointment. One aspects, occasionally used in such appointments in the UK, is also to describe the role of the Policy Secretary in the same letter.

It should become part of the annual planning cycle that there is a formal discussion between the secretary and the chairman of the board, which focuses on past achievements and future plans, and provides a clear indication of the detailed role the NDPB is expected to play in the implementation of government policies. It will be the responsibility of the Secretary to satisfy himself that there continues to be a valid role and need for the continued existence of the NDPB.

To serve this purpose, the UK Government in recent years has introduced regular policy reviews of NDPBs. We describe in the box p. 286 the range of issues such a policy review might address in Hong Kong.

Reporting and Monitoring

Once the statutory body's objectives have been agreed within a consistent planning framework, and funds have been allocated, the government should allow them to go about their business independently and without undue interference. It is vital, though, that the government ensures a suitable reporting and monitoring framework is in place so that it can be satisfied that the body is properly discharging its functions.

POLICY REVIEWS

Policy reviews of NDPBs, which were developed in the UK and are now standard practice there, should be undertaken periodically — say every five years — and should be conducted by the policy branch. These reviews are concerned with the basic justification for the body; its functions and policy objectives; its structure; and its relationship with the Policy Secretary.

The review must be fundamental if it is to be of value, and should ask questions such as:—

- what is the body for?
- is the role it performs still appropriate?
- could its functions be more effectively provided by another existing body or by the government itself?
- does the body have adequate arrangements for setting and reviewing corporate objectives annually?
- are any changes desirable in the composition or constitution of the management board?
- should the body be subject to an early financial management survey?

The kinds of information systems required in an NDPB will be determined by the nature of its activities (e.g. those of the Hospital Authority will be very different from those of the Hong Kong Tourist Association).

However, all should follow the principles laid down for departments i.e. the information should allow managers to control and be held to account for the resource they consume in carrying out their responsibilities and to plan and monitor progress against planned achievement.

There is a further reporting requirement. Because NDPBs have been delegated the authority to spend public funds there is a need for them to be able to demonstrate that they have in place arrangements that are likely to lead to good decision making. This is not to say that NDPB decisions should be second-guessed from outside — that would defeat the objectives of setting up the body at arms length. However, there is a need for a mechanism which assures the government that the delegated authorities are being used responsibly and effectively.

To this end, and in addition to monitoring performance against agreed objectives and targets there is a requirement for a periodic external review of NDPB's management arrangements. Such reviews, as described in the box opposite, also serve the purpose of keeping the sponsoring secretary in the picture as to the way in which the NDPB works and some of the problems it faces.

Aspects for Consideration

We suggest that Policy Secretaries:—

- *conduct formal discussions with the chairman of statutory bodies to review performance with future objectives;*
- *consider the introduction of policy reviews and financial management surveys to help achieve the above.*

FINANCIAL MANAGEMENT SURVEYS

The purpose of financial management surveys is to examine the scope for improvements in the way NDPBs plan and control what they do, with a view to improving their performance. They were developed in the UK as part of the Financial Management Initiative within the government and cover all NDPBs. They should be carried out in partnership by policy branches and NDPBs, and at intervals of, say, every three years. Surveys could be undertaken by policy branch staff or by external advisors.

The survey should examine the organization and management processes within an NDPB to ensure that:—

- aims and priorities are clearly defined;
- the arrangements for delegating authority and responsibility between the secretary and the NDPB are clearly specified;
- proper systems exist within the NDPB and between it and the policy branch for planning and managing resources and for assessing the results achieved;
- adequate information flows to and from the NDPB to assist in planning and assessing results, and meeting the secretary's requirements.

The product of a survey should be a plan for action to be taken to strengthen management and secure better value for money.

PART III: PRIVATE SECTOR PARTICIPATION

PART III: PRIVATE SECTOR PARTICIPATION

THE ROLE OF THE PRIVATE SECTOR

The end of the second world war brought with it a dramatic growth in the size and scope of the public sector around the world. This trend did not always carry with it the expected improvements in economic development, and efforts are now being made in many countries to reverse the trend. This is not such an important issue for Hong Kong because the private sector has traditionally played a major role in the provision of public services. For example, utilities like gas, electricity, bus and ferry services are well established private sector operations.

However, Hong Kong should not be complacent as there are many advantages to extending private sector participation. For instance, it helps to reduce the demand for public sector resources and so contain the number of civil servants employed; it makes more flexible use of international expertise and resources and generally brings about increased efficiency and effectiveness in service delivery.

Such participation usually takes one of two forms:—

- divestiture, where the public sector withdraws from providing a service or the ownership of an enterprise is transferred to the private sector;
- contracting out, where the private sector acts as an agent for the government.

In Hong Kong, because the government has tended to restrain the role and functions of the public sector, there are very few areas where it would now wish to withdraw completely from supplying services. On the other hand, there are many areas where contracting out offers advantages, particularly where there are manpower shortages in the public sector, and productivity improvements can be obtained.

It follows that in Hong Kong, we should encourage greater use of the private sector through contracting out. However the possibility of divestiture should not be entirely ruled out.

CONTRACTING OUT

Contracting out is a flexible method of introducing private sector involvement within a contractual framework. Typically, contracting out takes three main forms:—

- – service contracts for specific activities or services, such as cleaning or security;
- – management contracts, typically the granting of a concession to a private sector company to manage a business such as car parks or a dockyard;
- – build-own-operate schemes (BOOs), the granting of a concession to a private sector company or consortium to build, finance and operate a new infrastructure project such as a bridge or tunnel.

These three forms of contracting out represent progressively greater transfer of responsibilities, and risk, from the public to the public sector:—

- – a service contract transfers responsibility for management of the **costs** of service provision;
- – a management contract usually transfers responsibility for managing **costs and revenues**;
- – a BOO scheme transfer responsibility for managing the **costs, revenues and finance**.

Whichever form of contracting out is adopted, care must be exercised in drawing up the contract to safeguard the public interest in terms of price, quality and reliability. A number of steps must be taken to achieve this:—

- – a clear definition of requirements;
- – an invitation to tender, which may be preceded by pre-qualification and shortlisting;
- – contract negotiation which must result in a clear understanding of responsibilities and delegated authorities and establish agreed planning and reporting requirements;
- – contract monitoring, to ensure objectives and performance requirements are being met.

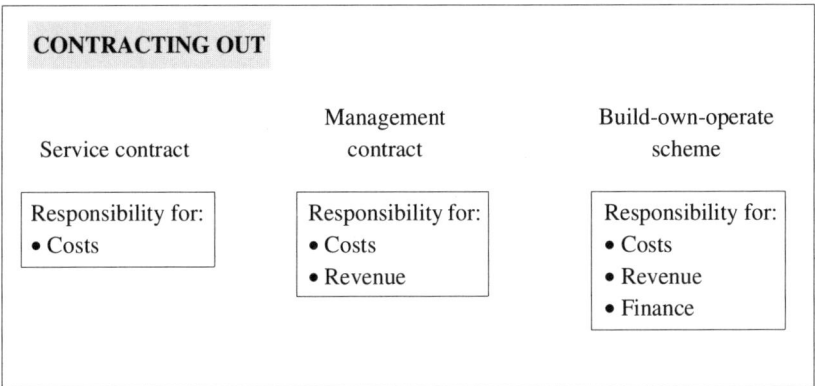

Service Contracts

Service contracts enable the government to take advantage of private sector expertise and resources to provide basic services in return for a negotiated fee. This form of contracting out should be considered where:—

- the service requirements can be easily defined;
- there is adequate private sector expertise and capacity to allow for competitive bidding;
- adequate government control can be maintained to protect the public interest;
- government staff can be redeployed or satisfactory redundancy arrangements can be made;
- there is good reason to believe that the activity would be more efficiently carried out by the private sector.

The government has already entered into many commercial contracts of this type, for services such as cleaning, laundry, grass cutting, security and maintenance.

By means of subventions, the Government also makes use of 'not-for-profit' organizations to provide services in the fields of education, health and social welfare. Bearing in mind that annual public expenditure on subventions in these fields currently amounts to about $10 billion per year, codes of aid should take into account many of the provisions of service contracts as described in the box pp. 292–293.

MAJOR ISSUES IN SERVICE CONTRACTS

Defining the Requirements

The services or activity being contracted out must be precisely defined in the contract, so that the private contractor knows what is required, the public sector obtains what it requires, and the contractor's performance can be monitored. The process of defining requirements can itself bring benefits if it results in modifications to existing practices which meet the user's requirements in a more effective way.

Activities are relatively easy to contract out when:—

- they can be simply defined (e.g. collect refuse once a week);
- demand is reasonably certain (e.g. the number of households requiring refuse collection and the average volume of refuse can be estimated with some precision).

The less well-defined the service, the more complex the contract will be, and the more difficult to negotiate. In such circumstances monitoring performance and assessing whether the quality of service being provided is in accordance with the contract will also pose problems.

Guaranteeing the Service

Effective monitoring is required to ensure that the contractor is complying with the contract. This is sometimes undertaken by the public authority through an inspectorate. If the service is for the direct benefit of individuals, however, monitoring may best be provided through reviews of user complaints. For refuse collection, getting individual households to report shortcomings to the authority may be a more effective way of monitoring performance than inspections by the authority's staff.

To prevent the level or quality of service falling below that specified in the contract, the contract may stipulate payment penalties of some kind. Performance bonds, under which the contractor has to provide a form of financial guarantee to the contracting party when bidding for the contract, are less effective because their cost is often built back into the contract price.

The public authority's ultimate sanction for unsatisfactory performance is to terminate the contract. It may be prudent to include a clause in the contract to allow the public authority, in instances of poor performance or in the event of the contractor's bankruptcy, to take over the capital assets of the contractor to ensure continuity of service.

The Contract Period

The choice of the duration of the contract is a standard problem in all forms of contracting out. It is in the public authority's interests to limit the period in order to retain flexibility and control, and to allow for regular retendering should the need arise. However, the shorter the period, the less attractive the contract will be to potential bidders and the less strong the competition, particularly if expensive capital equipment has to be provided. Professional advice may be needed to make the trade-off between these conflicting interests.

The more capital intensive the work, the longer the contract period needs to be to give the contractor time to recover his fixed costs. Contract periods will typically be for three or more years.

Management Contracts

Management contracts provide a means for introducing private sector management into a revenue-earning business, while ownership of the business is retained by the public sector.

Management contracts should be considered where:—

- private sector skills — such as management, marketing or technology — would increase the efficiency or profitability of a business activity;
- there is no threat to the public interest if management is contracted out to the private sector;
- satisfactory arrangements can be made for any redeployment of stall or redundancies.

The arrangements made to contract out the operation of government car parks (see the box p. 294) is a good example in Hong Kong.

The opportunities for further management contracts are more limited than for service contracts, but could include on-street parking and restaurants in public buildings and recreation areas.

WILSON CAR PARKS

Up to the early 1980s the government built and managed most major car parks in Hong Kong. In 1982, the government decided to contract out to the private sector their management and operation, while retaining ownership.

In early 1983, interested companies were invited to pre-qualify through a notice in the *Government Gazette*. 47 companies expressed interest, of which 26 prequalified and were invited to submit tenders.

The tenders were evaluated in terms of the financial return to government, based on the revenue-sharing formula put forward by the tenders.

In early 1984, Wilson Parking (Hong Kong) Pty. Co. of Australia took over the management of the car parks. The company immediately automated the exit and entry barriers to the car parks and introduced other changes. The car parks are now perceived to be much smarter and more efficiently operated, although it is doubtful that usage has increased as a result of the management contract.

The main benefit for the government has been the saving in staff resources. However it took some time to realize these benefits as the 62 staff who became surplus to requirements had to be absorbed elsewhere within the department.

The financial returns to government are in the form of a share of the revenues. The management company is generally free to fix its own charges subject to minimum occupancy levels being achieved.

New car parks, which have been developed since the early 1980s, have been built by the private sector, often as part of larger commercial developments. Within the near future all car parks in Hong Kong will be operated by the private sector.

Built-Own-Operate (BOO) Schemes

BOO schemes enable the government to transfer responsibility for designing, building, financing, operating and maintaining a major project to a contractor or sponsor in the private sector. Ownership may remain in the private sector throughout the life of the project, or be transferred to the public sector after a specified period or after all debt has been repaid and target equity returns achieved. The latter is termed a build-own-operate-transfer (BOOT) scheme.

For such projects, a special joint venture company is often created, linking the contractor and other interested parties such as the operator and banks. Typically the company is financed by a mixture of equity and debt and the company may be floated to extend capital participation.

BOO schemes should be considered where:—

- the project will generate a revenue stream which will enable the private sector to raise the necessary finance;
- the project is sufficiently free-standing so that the private sector can build and operate the project with minimal demands on the government for staff or other resources;
- the project requires skills or expertise in design, construction or operation which are not readily available in the public sector;
- adequate contingency arrangements can be made to protect the public interest.

The government has used the build-own-operate concept for the Cross Harbour Tunnel, and has, in the past three years, successfully negotiated BOO contracts for two further tunnels, (see the box pp. 296–297) and the Kowloon Bay refuse transfer station.

Potential new build-own-operate projects include:—

- land reclamation with development rights;
- landfill for municipal waste;
- chemical waste treatment plants;
- other environmental improvement schemes;
- infrastructure development packages.

Although finance for a BOO scheme will be raised from the private sector, these schemes should be properly ranked and phased with other public works projects which may not be capable of generating their own revenue. This will ensure that due account is taken of any recurrent expenditure and macro-economic implications of the scheme.

BUILD-OWN-OPERATE TUNNELS

Hong Kong currently has four road tunnels, of which one was built, financed, and is now operated by the private sector, and the other three by the government. The private sector project is the Cross-Harbour Tunnel, completed in the early 1970s. This project was an outstanding commercial success although, at the time the project was initiated, this was uncertain and, as a result, the government acquired 25% of the equity.

Four more tunnels are under construction. The two most commercially attractive are being developed as build-own-operate transfer (BOOT) schemes, the Eastern Harbour Crossing and the Tate's Cairn Tunnel.

Both tunnels are large projects requiring a heavy commitment of resources. Contracting out the tunnels as BOO schemes has relieved the government of the need to find those resources, and will in the future yield substantial benefits from shorter construction periods.

Before seeking bids for the construction of these new tunnels, the government undertook studies to establish their commercial and technical viability and suitable project limits. Within the project limits, all costs were to be borne by the private sector sponsor. Meanwhile, the government agreed to pay for a substantial number of approach roads, outside the project limits.

Interested parties were invited to submit both engineering and financial bids without any pre-qualification. In the case of the **Eastern Harbour Crossing**, the tender document consisted of a single sheet of paper, issued in October 1984. The document requested bids for the construction, operation and financing of a road tunnel between two specific points at the eastern end of the harbour, with a minimum capacity of two lanes in each direction. The bidders were also permitted to add a rail tunnel to their offer if they wished.

The brief for the **Tate's Cairn Tunnel** was more detailed and included a preliminary design for the tunnel. However, the bidders were allowed to submit alternative designs. The brief also included more details of the legislative framework for the project. The use of a tighter brief reduced the bidding and negotiation period by nearly a year.

The government's primary aim for both projects was to obtain the lowest and most stable toll structure for the travelling public. The toll revision clauses have been kept very simple without any guarantees in relation to inflation or other changes in costs. The ordinances for both projects require that the tolls should be "reasonably" but not "excessively" remunerative.

In the case of the Eastern Harbour Crossing, the government gave an undertaking that no passage tax would be charged on the project for five years. For the Tate's Cairn Tunnel project, the government undertook to keep the tolls on the parallel Lion Rock Tunnel equal to those on the newer private tunnel.

The financial return to the government from these private tunnels has been given secondary importance compared with the need to improve the transport network rapidly and efficiently. The financial arrangements are that:—

- the Cross-Harbour Tunnel Company pays a royalty to government of 12.5% of all revenues;
- in the case of the Eastern Harbour Crossing, the government will be given, in place of royalty payments, 5% of the equity on the completion of the project rising to 7.5% of the equity on the completion of the Tate's Cairn Tunnel;
- for the Tate's Cairn Tunnel, the royalty payable will be 2.5% of revenue for the first five years of operation and 5% thereafter, with higher percentages for net operating receipts in excess of those projected.

The concession period for all three projects is 30 years after which ownership will be transferred to the government.

DIVESTITURE

Divestiture generally takes one of three forms:—

- selling all or part of the government's shareholding in existing corporate enterprises;
- withdrawing from providing a service and letting the private sector fill the need;

  –   transferring the ownership of a business and its associated assets to
      the private sector through various forms of sale.

For a variety of reasons the government has a shareholding in a number
of private sector companies. It should keep this portfolio under review
ensuring that it is consistent with relevant policies. The government has
recently reduced its shareholding in the restructured Hong Kong Telecommunications Group.

With the growth of the private sector in size and sophistication over the
past few decades, there may no longer be a need for the government to
provide certain services, either to the public or internally. It may be able to
withdraw from the role of provider of arrange of a service and leave the
users of the service to find alternative outlets in the private sector. Supply
and maintenance of non-specialist vehicles is a possible example.

Finally, the government may wish to transfer the ownership (or at least
a controlling shareholding) of a business to the private sector. This would
generally include the transfer of assets in consideration for a cash payment,
debt or some equity. This is currently proposed for the government abat-
toirs. Various methods of sale are described in the box p. 299.

There are number of issues related to divestiture which include regulation, retaining strategic control, valuation of the business and so on. Since
divestiture is not seen as a priority for the government, we have not
attempted to provide comprehensive coverage of these and other issues that
can arise.

ASPECTS FOR CONSIDERATION

We have discussed a number of areas where there are potential benefits
in involving the private organizations in the supply of services for or on
behalf of the public sector. *We suggest that heads of all executive agencies
should carefully review their activities and identify opportunities for*

tapping these benefits. In the main, contracting out in one form or another will provide the best means of increasing private sector participation, but divestiture should also be considered in the appropriate circumstances.

DIVESTITURE — METHODS OF SALE

Public Flotation

Public flotation is the public offering of shares based on a prospectus. The floated company is listed and its shares are quoted on the stock exchange. Of the various forms of divestiture, public flotation reaches the widest range of private investors and institutions but demands the most preparation and marketing. The government, with the help of professional advisers, has to prepare a prospectus to provide essential information to potential shareholders, and to market the offer vigorously to ensure that it reaches all interested parties.

Private Sale

Private sales are of two kinds:—

- private placements with institutional investors or a group of interested parties;
- trade sales to other private sector companies.

Frequently, part of a public flotation is through **private placements** with institutional investors. Less often, the whole of an offer of shares is placed in this way. A private placement with interested parties may take the form of a sale to a consortium of commercial companies, one of which takes responsibility for managing the enterprise. The outcome is typically some form of joint venture.

A **trade or treaty sale** is a direct sale to a corporate entity. The process may entail a negotiated sale with one potential buyer, or a tender with a number of bidders. The sale is usually based on an information memorandum which is similar in content to, but often less detailed than, a public prospectus. The process is less demanding for the seller than a public flotation because the buying company is able to conduct its own investigation of the acquired business before completing the purchase.

WHERE WE ARE NOW?

We have now completed our survey of the spectrum of public sector activities.

We have stressed the need to look beyond these activities to give a sharper focus to the objectives which are their raison d'être. In doing so we have suggested a number of ways in which procedures and mechanisms to be used in delivering services to the public can be improved.

In particular we have identified a number of different delivery agencies and how these should operate.

We have emphasized the need to allocate responsibilities as between Policy Secretaries and agencies and to establish procedures which enable the former to monitor the activities of the latter.

We have described the necessary interaction in the planning process between achievable objectives and resource constraints. We have suggested how resources can be stretched through constant attacks on the baseline of public expenditure. And we have pointed out how objectives need to be set in the context of the operational plans of various types of executive agency.

And underpinning all this we have emphasized the need for civil servants to become better managers, in particular managers of resources.

We now draw together our thinking on how to achieve these changes in a programme of public sector reform.

A WAY FORWARD

A WAY FORWARD

Next Steps

The next steps must be for the Administration to debate the issues we have raised, to agree on a strategy and to commit itself to the implementation of this strategy.

DEBATE

AGREEMENT

COMMITMENT

ACTION

The views in this paper are intended as a starting point in the debate. Senior civil servants should be encouraged to discuss and debate the issues raised here both informally and formally, the latter in structured sessions.

We have dealt with general principles and board themes. Policy Secretaries and heads of departments will need to consider the extent to which they should be applied in their particular circumstances. We believe that once the concepts have been appreciated and understood, there will be a general consensus and agreement that public sector reform along these lines is worthwhile pursuing.

Commitment from the top is vital if changes are to be successfully implemented. This commitment will demonstrate that the changes are real and that individuals will be increasingly judged on a new set of criteria. There is no shortage of talent, creativity and experience within the civil service; once commitment to public sector reform is given these qualities will be properly harnessed and directed. This, in turn, will lead to much greater job satisfaction within the civil service.

Once expectations of change and reforms have been raised, response must be rapid. There are some aspects which can be introduced service-wide. Other proposals may require more detailed work of pilot projects in specific areas before they can proceed across the service. We have suggested six priority areas for reform in the table pp. 302–303.

SUGGESTED PRIORITY AREAS FOR REFORM

■ Policy Secretaries-Executive Agencies Relationship

A first task should be for Policy Secretaries to identify the current objectives of their executive agencies and to confirm that the most appropriate delivery agencies are being used for carrying out their respective activities.

■ Operational Planning

On a pilot basis, one of each of the three existing types of executive agency should be chosen for the trial development of detailed objectives, operational plans and proper monitoring and reporting arrangements. Where appropriate, some of the more specific proposals described in this report should also be addressed. For instance:

Traditional Departments — some research should be undertaken to see how a process such as Priority Based Budgeting could be used to help departments. Customs and Excise Department may offer opportunities as they are currently investigating changes in their operating procedures.

Corporations — a framework is needed to clarify objectives and relationships for all corporations. In the first instance, it may be appropriate to develop these changes with KCRC or MTRC. The role of government representatives on the boards of all executive bodies should also be reviewed.

NDPBs — some thoughts should be given to introducing techniques such as policy reviews and financial management surveys to improve performance in this area. Perhaps priority should be given to the Provisional Hospital Authority which currently needs to develop its institutional framework and define its relationship to the government.

■ Trading Funds

To develop this fourth type of executive agency, appropriate legislation should be drafted. At least one department should explore on a pilot basis the possibility of using such a fund. This may be appropriate for the Electrical and Mechanical Services Department as it would tie in neatly with the current review of the role of the department and planned costing system development.

■ Private Sector Participation

Heads of executive agencies should be encouraged to appraise the success of those services which are already contracted out to the private sector and also identify any further opportunities for increased private sector participation along the lines outlined in this paper.

■ Support to Departments

Heads of departments should be encouraged to identify the support they require in the way of:—

- computing services;
- accounting services;
- management services;
- business managers.

Initially at least three or four departments should develop longer term strategies for these areas.

■ Training

Service-wide staff training should be expanded to support the increased management role of senior civil servants. Training programmes should also encompass the new techniques of resource management that it is agreed will form part of the public sector reform process.

Follow-Up

Once we have agreed on priorities we will need an action plan setting out the timescale for action, those responsible for achieving desired results and the way in which the whole programmes should be coordinated and guided forward.

APPENDIX B

Trading Fund Ordinance
(May 1993)

CHAPTER 430

(This booklet is published under Section 2(3) of the Laws (Loose-leaf Publication) Ordinance 1990. It is up to date as of 7 May 1993.)

PRINTED AND PUBLISHED BY THE GOVERNMENT PRINTER, HONG KONG

Reproduced by courtesy of the Hong Kong Government.

CHAPTER 430

TRADING FUNDS ORDINANCE

CONTENTS

Section

CHAPTER 430

TRADING FUNDS

An Ordinance to enable certain services of the Government of Hong Kong to be financed under trading funds established by resolution of the Legislative Council on the recommendation of the Financial Secretary and for related matters.

[12 March 1993]

1.   Short title

This Ordinance may be cited as the Trading Funds Ordinance.

2.   Interpretation

(1)   In this Ordinance, unless the context otherwise requires—

"certified statements" (經證明的報表) means the statements of accounts that the Director of Audit has certified that he has examined and audited under section 7(5);

"Finance Committee" (財務委員會) means the Finance Committee of the Legislative Council;

"general manager" (總經理) means the general manager of a trading fund designated under section 6(2);

"government service" (政府服務) means an activity that the Government may undertake and includes the provision of goods or services by a department or public body;

"trading fund" (營運基金) means an accounting entity within the Government (but not having a separate legal existence) established under section 3(1).

(2)   In this Ordinance, a reference to the resolution establishing a trading fund includes a resolution that varies the resolution that establishes the trading fund

3.   Establishment of trading funds

(1)   The Legislative Council may, on the recommendation of the Financial Secretary, by resolution establish a trading fund to manage and account for the operation of a government service for which the Government has the financial objective that the service shall fund itself from the income generated from the government service whether it is a service provided to the Government, to public bodies or to persons other than the Government.

(2)   In considering whether to recommend the establishment of a trading fund for a government service the Financial Secretary is to have regard to the capability of the provider of the government service—

> (*a*)   to provide an efficient and effective operation that meets an appropriate standard of service; and
>
> (*b*)   to have the capacity, within a reasonable time, to meet expenses incurred in the provision of the government service and finance liabilities to be specified in the resolution out of the income of the proposed trading fund.

4.   Assets and liabilities of a trading fund

(1)   The Legislative Council may by resolution appropriate to the trading fund the assets and liabilities on the terms set out in the resolution.

(2)   The net value of the assets appropriated to a trading fund is a government investment shown in the Capital Investment Fund as loan or trading fund capital or partially of one and the balance of the other, on the terms set out in the Legislative Council resolution establishing the trading fund and is to be represented in the accounts of the trading fund as the debt to, or trading fund capital of, the Government.

(3)   Subject to the terms of the resolution establishing a trading fund and any directions of the Financial Secretary given under section 6(5), the general manager may dispose of any asset accounted for under the trading fund.

5.   Income, expenses and liabilities

(1)   Notwithstanding any provision of another Ordinance, the income received for the provision of a government service in respect of which a trading fund is established under section 3 is to be paid into the trading fund.

(2)   The expenses incurred in providing the government service and the financing of liabilities of the trading fund are to be paid out of the trading fund.

(3)   With the approval of the Financial Secretary, the general manager may establish reserves in the accounts of the trading fund and may make transfers into and out of those reserves.

(4)   In this section, "income" (收益) includes a grant from the general revenue.

6. Control and management of a trading fund

(1) The Legislative Council shall prescribe, in the resolution establishing the trading fund, the services to be provided under a trading fund.

(2) The Financial Secretary shall designate a general manager to control and manage a trading fund and who is accountable to the Financial Secretary for the operations of the trading fund.

(3) The general manager is not to vary the services undertaken by a trading fund other than in accordance with the Legislative Council resolution.

(4) Notwithstanding subsection (3), the Financial Secretary may authorize a general manager to undertake additional operations under a trading fund that are incidental to the prescribed services of the trading fund.

(5) The Financial Secretary may issue directions to the general manager for the control and management of a trading fund and the general manager shall comply with the directions.

(6) The general manager shall manage a trading fund with the objectives of—

   (a) providing an efficient and effective operation that meets an appropriate standard of service;

   (b) within a reasonable time, meeting expenses incurred in the provision of the government service and financing liabilities of the trading fund out of the income of the trading fund, taking one year with another; and

   (c) achieving a reasonable return, as determined by the Financial Secretary, on the fixed assets employed.

7. Financial period and accounting requirements

(1) The financial year for a trading fund is from 1 April to 31 March in the following year.

(2) If a trading fund is established after 1 April in any year, the first financial year for the trading fund is from the date it is established until 31 March following.

(3) A general manager shall keep the accounts and records of all transactions of the trading fund in such manner as the Director of Accounting Services may require.

(4) A general manager shall submit statements of the annual accounts of the trading fund prepared in accordance with generally accepted accounting principles and signed by him to the Director of Audit within a reasonable time after the end of each financial year to allow for audit and the tabling of the certified statements and the report of the Director of Audit in accordance with section 8.

(5) The Director of Audit shall examine and audit the statements of the annual accounts of the trading fund and prepare a report on his examination and audit and certify that he has conducted the examination and audit of the statements.

(6) The Director of Audit shall state in the report whether in his opinion the statements—

    (*a*) give a true and fair view of the state of affairs of the trading fund at the end of the financial year;

    (*b*) give a true and fair view of the results of the operations of the trading fund for the financial year then ended; and

    (*c*) have been properly prepared in accordance with the manner provided in subsection (4).

8. Reporting requirements

(1) A general manager shall submit to the Financial Secretary a signed annual report on the operation of the trading fund, the certified statements and the report of the Director of Audit on the certified statements within 14 days of receipt of the certified statements and the report from the Director of Audit.

(2) The Financial Secretary shall table in the Legislative Council not later than 31 October next following the end of each financial year, or such longer period as the Governor may allow—

    (*a*) the signed annual report on the operation of each trading fund; and

    (*b*) the certified statements and the report of the Director of Audit for each trading fund.

9. Investment of funds and borrowings

(1) A general manager may invest trading fund money that is surplus to its immediate requirements in the manner approved by the Financial Secretary.

(2) A general manager may not—

    (*a*) make loans out of the trading fund; or

    (*b*) borrow funds for the trading fund other than—

        (i) from the Capital Investment Fund or the Loan Fund; or

        (ii) by way of temporary overdraft facilities in the manner and up to the limit that the Financial Secretary approves.

10. Surplus funds

(1) If, after having regard to estimated future requirements of the operation of the government service undertaken by a trading fund, the Financial Secretary is satisfied that any surpluses in the nature of distributable

profits disclosed in the certified statements are in excess of the reasonable requirements for the provision of the service including the repayment of loans, the Financial Secretary may direct that the surpluses or a part of the surpluses be transferred into the general revenue.

(2) If fees authorized by an Ordinance are structured so as to recover more than the cost of the provision of a government service, including a reasonable return as set out in section 6(6)(*c*), the Financial Secretary may direct that the whole or part of the fees as determined by the Financial Secretary to be more than the cost of the provision of the service, including a reasonable return as set out in section 6(6)(*c*), shall, after collection, be paid from the trading fund into the general revenue.

11. Application of the Public Finance Ordinance (Cap. 2)

Part I (Preliminary), section 10 (General powers and duties of the Financial Secretary), section 16 (Duties of Director of Accounting Services), section 28 (Guarantees), Part V (Surcharge), section 40 (Power of Governor to give directions), section 40A (Director of Accounting Services may give certain directions, etc. to public officers in receipt of certain moneys) and section 43 (Effect of dissolution of Legislative Council) only of the Public Finance Ordinance (Cap. 2) apply to a trading fund.

12. Closing of trading fund

(1) The Legislative Council may, on the recommendation of the Financial Secretary, resolve to close a trading fund.

(2) The Financial Secretary shall set out the arrangements to be made for the closure of the trading fund in the proposed resolution.

Index

Related Titles from The Chinese University Press

Out of the Shadow of 1997? The 2000 Legislative Council
Elections in Hong Kong
Edited by Kuan Hsin-chi, Lau Siu-kai, Louie Kin-sheun and
Timothy Ka-ying Wong (2002)

New Challenges for Development and Modernization:
Hong Kong and the Asia-Pacific Region in the New Millennium
Edited by Yue-man Yeung (2002)

Entering a New Millennium: Advances in Social Welfare in Hong Kong
Edited by Daniel T. L. Shek (2002)

Hong Kong's Journey to Reunification: Memoirs of Sze-yuen Chung
Sze-yuen Chung (2001)

Social Development and Political Change in Hong Kong
Edited by Lau Siu-kai (2000)

Competition in Hong Kong's Gas Industry
Pun-lee Lam and Sylvia Chan (2000)

Power Transfer and Electoral Politics: the First Legislative Election
in the Hong Kong Special Administrative Region
Edited by Kuan Hsin-chi, Lau Siu-kai, Louie Kin-sheun and
Timothy Ka-ying Wong (1999)